Communist
Political Systems

Alvin Z. Rubinstein, *ed.*

Professor of Political Science
University of Pennsylvania

Communist
Political Systems

PRENTICE-HALL, INC.

Englewood Cliffs, New Jersey

33125

© 1966 by Prentice-Hall, Inc.
Englewood Cliffs, New Jersey

Current printing (last digit):
10   9   8   7   6   5   4   3

Prentice-Hall International, Inc., *London*
Prentice-Hall of Australia, Pty. Ltd., *Sydney*
Prentice-Hall of Canada, Ltd., *Toronto*
Prentice-Hall of India (Private) Ltd., *New Delhi*
Prentice-Hall of Japan, Inc., *Tokyo*

LIBRARY OF CONGRESS CATALOG CARD NUMBER: 66-22331

PRINTED IN THE UNITED STATES OF AMERICA
C-15301

To my parents

Preface

This book is concerned with the internal ordering, operation, and evolution of communist political systems. It rests on the assumption that communist societies are neither monolithic nor uniformly
alike, that they differ in ways that are important to the more than one
billion people who live, love, work, play, and strive for a decent life in
them, and that what happens in these societies will become increasingly
important to the non-communist world in the decades that lie before us.

My purpose in compiling this anthology is to contribute to the development of the study of comparative communist political systems. I hope to
encourage discussion and analysis of the similarities and differences existing among these political systems. The presentation of communism within
a broader political framework may serve to stimulate critical thinking and
meaningful generalizations about why Communist Parties came to power
in the U.S.S.R., China, and Eastern Europe, how they maintain themselves
in power, how they have sought to modernize and restructure society,
wherein they differ, and how they are likely to evolve in the future.

In selecting the essays, I have tried to preserve a balance between communist and non-communist writings. Faced with the practical necessity of
making choices, I have selected analytical material which probes communist realities in Soviet, Chinese, and Eastern European affairs, leaving
the reader to obtain for himself the readily available source material—
national constitutions, documents, and official decrees. Each chapter begins
with an essay which is intended to complement and integrate the readings
and concludes with a selected bibliography.

It is a pleasure to express my deep appreciation for the many constructive criticisms and suggestions made by my colleagues at the University of

Pennsylvania: Dr. Chong-sik Lee, Dr. Herbert S. Levine, Dr. Robert Os-born, Dr. Sidney Ploss, and Dr. Alexander V. Riasanovsky. Working with such comfortable colleagues is a rich and rewarding experience. Grateful acknowledgment is made to all the publishers and authors whose permission to reprint specific material is indicated at the beginning of each reading. I wish also to thank Mrs. Isabel Grossner for her assistance in preparing the final manuscript and the editors and staff of Prentice-Hall, especially Vincent A. D'Arrigo, for their cooperation and counsel. Finally, to my wife, who edited the manuscript and remained a constant source of encouragement, I can only express my deep sense of continued good fortune.

ALVIN Z. RUBINSTEIN

Contents

Chapter Four

*The Party:
The Fulcrum of Power* 104

RULE BY THE PARTY

CHINESE CRITICISMS OF THE C.P.S.U.

DECISION-MAKING

Chapter Five

*Governmental Structures
and Processes*

Chapter Eight

Operational Characteristics and Problems of Communist Economies   258

Chapter Eleven

Whither Communism?   374

Chapter One

The Historical Setting

A nation is shaped by its history. Both the physical determinants—size, location, topography, and resources—and the psychopolitical factors—culture, religion, ethnic composition, and the outlook of the elite—are relevant to an understanding of a nation's development. No particular type of political system is inevitable in the sense that it is predetermined by the ordering of events and ideas. Nonetheless, there is a tendency to explain the outcome of a revolutionary period in terms that are uncomfortably reflective of a deterministic approach to history. Such quasideterminism breeds political myopia. In interpreting the development of political systems, writers are also often influenced by the values, assumptions, and attitudes of their own generation and their own society, and these may not be the ones that predominated in the period being described. Thus the presentation of the past is conditioned by the perception of the present and the hope for the future. Nowhere is this more apparent than in attempts to reconstruct and evaluate the revolutionary events of our own era. We live in an age of supreme irony, an age in which the accumulation of increasingly reliable information seems only to intensify man's confusion.

The contemporary confrontation between Western and communist societies has often been assigned the character of a struggle between good and evil. This has led many to stress the conspiratorial aspects of the successful communist revolutions in Russia in 1917 and in China in 1949. The extension of Soviet hegemony over Eastern Europe after 1945 and the imposition of systems of political rule of the Soviet type, encouraged the West to view communist societies as monolithic. National peculiarities, traditional animosities, and unique cultural patterns were ignored, and communist societies assumed in the minds of Western analysts a mono-

1

lithic character which we now know does not represent political reality. Divergences existed even during the height of Stalinism but were generally not given proper weight because of this preoccupation with superficial institutional similarities and the ubiquitous use of terror in the Soviet empire. Western interpretations of communist political systems reflected the fears engendered by the Cold War and the hostilities arising out of a sense of antithetical values.

The emergence of polycentrism and the airing of the Sino-Soviet dispute have given rise to reevaluations, particularly in the field of international relations, of the once supposedly monolithic character of the world communist movement. Western analysts now recognize the existence of diversity in the *foreign* affairs of the communist world and are reassessing communist motivations, attitudes, and capabilities, but they still neglect the differentiation in *internal* communist politics and practices. This lag is understandable, given the more immediate and visible impact of diversity in communist foreign policies on other nations. But the time has come to reconsider our assumptions concerning the operation and likely evolution of the political systems found in the various communist countries.

The leaders of all communist societies profess their adherence to Marxism-Leninism. Yet not all communist societies exhibit the same degree of centralism or bureaucratism, nor have they used equal measures of force to preserve power, to settle internal rivalries, or to shape a national consensus. One can gain an impression of the persisting uniqueness of each nation by distinguishing the salient features of communism in each country from the prototype of the communist political system that is found in the U.S.S.R.

To account for the institutional and operational differences that mark the communist landscape in the Soviet Union, China, and Eastern Europe, it is necessary to know something of their pre-communist, national roots (Readings 1 and 2). All the countries in which communism came to power were, with the exception of Czechoslovakia, overwhelmingly rural and largely peasant in composition. But despite this shared socio-economic classification, there were deep-rooted and significant differences between, for example, the Russian and Polish peasantry, or the Russian and Yugoslav peasantry. These differences stemmed from the unique cultural and political milieu of each country. In Russia, there were the strength of the central government and the reliance on it and the Czar for all reform and sense of direction, and the survival among the Great Russian peasantry of what might be called a collectivist tradition, i.e., the mir. This contrasted with the Polish and Yugoslav situations. The Polish peasantry is heir to a legacy that exalts individualism, private ownership, and a mistrust of governmental institutions. The Yugoslav peasantry is complex and difficult to categorize. As a country, Yugoslavia is an artificial entity, a post–World War I creation, and wide variations exist among the Serbian, Croatian, and

Slovenian peasants; yet their various traditions and attitudes toward authority differ substantially from those of the Russians. In Serbia, for example, the Zadruga, or extended family group, gave social stability and economic security to the oppressed Serbian peasantry during the 400 years of Turkish rule; it also served as a focus for opposition to the Turks. Such distinctive developments may help explain the elements of uniqueness that appear in the contemporary Soviet, Polish, and Yugoslav political systems.

In Russia and China the social gap between the peasantry and the leadership was greater than in most of Eastern Europe. Serfdom disappeared from Eastern and Central Europe considerably earlier than from Russia, with the result that passivity in politics was more prevalent in Czarist society. Although this political passivity did not preclude the eruption of periodic and bloody peasant revolts, undirected protests which reflected underlying dissatisfaction, it nevertheless led the Russian people to accept changes in leadership unquestioningly, as events ordained by powers beyond their comprehension. This attitude toward leadership changes remains an inherent feature of Soviet political life. In Serbia and Poland, prolonged foreign occupation acted to fuse political and emotional affinities between the national leaders and the people: The clergy, the aristocracy, and the homogeneous population forged a sense of national identity and purpose against the alien occupier.

In Eastern Europe after 1945, Stalin forced Soviet institutions on a recalcitrant but war-weary region. Collectivization sat heavily upon these lands, perhaps because it was an alien imposition, and production and productivity dropped sharply. But in the halcyon days of 1956, the Hungarian and Polish leaders, responsive to the revolutionary impetus of the people they sought to lead, abandoned collectivization and introduced an agricultural institutional framework more consonant with national traditions and temperament. The Yugoslav leadership had acted similarly in the early 1950's. In situations of precarious political stability or unsatisfactory economic performance, East European communist rulers have had recourse to nationalism and national traditions. Indeed, only as advocates of national interests have they been able to function effectively as communists.

Long a subservient satellite which aped Stalinist policies and practices, Romania in the early 1960's claimed for itself domestic prerogatives and limited foreign policy initiatives which had been unthinkable a decade earlier. Internally, Romania remains very much a Stalinist society, but it has become a source of frustration to Moscow. With an astute mixture of cunning and caution, the Romanians have gained a growing measure of control over their own affairs by exploiting Moscow's difficulties with Peking and its desire to retain the support of bloc parties against mounting Chinese claims to leadership of the international communist movement. There have also been modest but undisguised manifestations of Russophobia. Through the ages the Rumanians have known many conquerors, yet have succeeded in preserving their distinctive national ethnocentricity. How this will affect the evolution of communism in Rumania remains to be seen.

Least affected thus far by the post-Stalinist currents of Balkan nationalism has been Bulgaria, a predominantly peasant country which is almost totally collectivized. Under Ottoman rule, Bulgarian revolutionary activity was centered in the rising, but small, commercial and artisan classes; the peasantry was generally inert. Bulgarian nationalists looked to Russia for liberation from the Turks. In the nineteenth century, linguistic and cultural affinities were reinforced by an influx of Russian teachers. Today there are more Russian words in the Bulgarian language than in any of the other related Slavic tongues. This most thoroughly Russified of the East European countries is closely linked to the Soviet Union. Yet dependence is a complex phenomenon. That Bulgarian leaders seem willing administrators of Soviet hegemony is perhaps a reflection of their unpopularity and weakness.

In the U.S.S.R. itself we see clearly the impact of history upon the evolution of a political system. Between the eleventh and thirteenth centuries contrasting approaches to government developed: the monarchic prince; the democratic *Vieche,* or popular assembly, the most important of which sat in Novgorod; and the more-or-less centralized prince in Kiev. Then came the Mongols. For almost three centuries their domination was unchallenged. In this bitter political climate, an indigenous absolutism emerged, yielded to the Mongol yoke, adapted, took root, and survived. The Mongols conquered but did not assimilate; they exacted tribute and obedience but, when all is said and done, they did not supplant the native leaders, thereby permitting a succession of shrewd princes of Muscovy to establish a base from which Moscow eventually drove out the Mongols and unified Russia. Muscovy emerged from nearly three centuries of Mongol domination with the essentials of a political system characterized by absolutism, centralism, social stratification, and a church linked to and dominated by the state. A method of government evolved which rested on unrestrained rule by the few and on coercion. Many of the attributes of this system can be traced to the impact of Byzantium, from which the Russians also received their religion, the idea of empire, an administrative apparatus, and jurisprudence.

During the centuries following the defeat of the Mongols, Russia expanded, consolidated, and developed, by the late eighteenth century, into one of the Great Powers. Astride the hierarchical and pyramidical Czarist society stood the Czar and the nobility; at the base was agrarian Russia, weighted down by serfdom and backwardness. The middle class, which slowly emerged at the beginning of the nineteenth century, was small and ineffectual. An intellectual renaissance in the 1840's and 1850's led to the abolition of serfdom in 1861. But the pace of reform was not rapid enough to forestall the rise of revolutionary movements, mostly socialist, and the increase in peasant restiveness. Successive Czars sought to overcome Russia's economic backwardness and inefficient government. However, the coming of World War I arrested the remarkable economic and industrial advances of the previous three decades and weakened the capacity of an infirm, inefficient, and unpopular regime to resist the tide of revolution.

The Bolsheviks succeeded where other Russian revolutionaries had failed because they were better prepared to exploit the opportunities afforded by the deteriorating conditions in 1917. In adapting to the proscriptions of Czarist rule, they evolved a system of organization and rule (as had, one might speculate, the princes of Muscovy under the Mongols) which was well suited to survival under repression and to a seizure and consolidation of power in a period of crisis. Now, after five decades of development, it seems clear that the absolutism of the Communist Party, the centralization of power, the wedding of quasi-religious symbolism and pageantry to the power and machinery of the state (which became so apparent under Stalin), and the establishment of an official orthodoxy are features of Soviet society that have identifiable roots in the Russian past. Lenin drew on the Russian experience to make a revolution and establish a system that was designed in large measure to overcome the "Russianness" that kept Czarist society backward, inefficient, and stratified; paradoxically, the institutions subsequently established and the style of rule imposed were remarkably Russian in content and form. More than anyone else, Stalin Russified communism.

The Chinese, too, are not untouched by their historical antecedents. Rule by the few, i.e., by the Communist Party, was foreshadowed in the oligarchical rule of the emperor, gentry, and mandarins in Confucian society; the mass mobilization of conscript labor for public projects, e.g., irrigation systems and the Great Wall, has a long tradition in China; and the view of China as the Middle Kingdom, surrounded by barbarian lands, gave to pre-communist Chinese rulers a sense of their intrinsic superiority over all foreigners and foreign political systems, not too dissimilar from the attitudes currently engendered by Marxism-Leninism-Maoism. Communism as a social and political system is still young in China; when its final institutional form is shaped it will assuredly be influenced by China's history, culture, and temperament.

The student of comparative communism is denied the luxury of simplistic and mechanistic formulas for the structure, style, and shape of evolving political systems. Though our focus is on contemporary developments and their implications for the future, we must, in our quest for understanding, retain a sense of the importance of the continuing influence of historical determinants.

Klaus Mehnert

1 THE CHINESE AND THE RUSSIANS

Klaus Mehnert, "The Chinese and the Russians," *Annals of the American Academy of Political and Social Science*, **349** (September, 1963), pp. 2–13. Footnote references have been deleted.

Klaus Mehnert is Professor of Political Science at the Institute of Technology, Aachen, Germany. He has traveled widely in the Soviet Union and China. The editor of the journal Osteuropa, *Dr. Mehnert has written extensively on Soviet and communist bloc affairs. He is the author of* Soviet Man and His World, *and* Peking and Moscow. *This article is an extract from the introductory part of the English edition of* Peking and Moscow, *which was published in 1963 by G. P. Putnam's Sons, New York, and, in an updated pocket-book edition, by the New American Library of World Literature, Inc., New York, in 1964.*

The question of whether one can speak of "the" Chinese, "the" Russians, "the" Soviet people, "the" Americans has been the subject of thorough and often heated discussion. The late Felix M. Keesing, the New Zealand anthropologist, summarized his findings in two theses: first, in the case of each nation, it is possible to prove the existence of a certain national character which distinguishes it from other nations; second, this national character is a variable, not a constant, quantity. In other words: The Chinese differ from the Russians. And the Chinese of today are different from the Chinese of the Confucian era; the Soviet Russian is no longer the muzhik of the days of the czars. Therefore, although national minorities, often with sharply distinguishing characteristics, have long existed both in China and in Russia, we may speak of "the Chinese" and "the Russians," for, in both cases, a politically powerful and culturally outstanding race—in China, the Han (that is, the real Chinese); in Russia, the Great Russians—constituted the vital element which characterized the population as a whole.

Is it correct to say that Chinese or Russian communism is the logical crowning of their history, or is it more accurate to regard it as being in complete contradiction to all that is Chinese or Russian? The thesis of communism as the continuation, the culmination, of the history of these two peoples is propagated not only by Communist leaders, by Stalin, Khrushchev, and Mao, but also—although, of course, with different arguments and different prognoses—by some Western observers, Amaury de Riencourt, for example, when he writes: "The triumph of Marxism in China implies to a very great extent a return to the past," or "Marxism . . . restored China's traditional way of thinking." Riencourt, who is anything but a Communist, has described Chinese communism as "psychologically predetermined." A similarly one-sided view is expressed by an Indian observer: "To substitute the gospel according to Mao for the gospel according to Confucius, conforms to this [that is, traditional Chinese] pattern."

A second thesis, that communism is the complete antithesis of the true nature of China and Russia, is maintained by the Chinese and Russian opponents of communism—Chiang Kai-shek, for instance, and the leaders of the Russian *émigrés*—and many foreigners who, as businessmen and missionaries, became personally acquainted with the China and Russia of the past and who are convinced that the people whom they came to know and respect as human beings are enduring the Communist regime solely because they are compelled to do so by the most brutal terrorism and are yearning for the day when China will re-emerge "as a free united nation" and they can take part in the "triumph of freedom over slavery throughout the world."

Reality corresponds to neither of these two theses; it is more complicated, and thus more interesting, and still leaves the door open to all kinds of possibilities.

The Man

When Aristotle defined man as a *zoon politikon,* a "social animal," he had no idea that in a highly developed culture there already existed a classic example of this concept unlike anything in the Hellenistic world. If the Occidental has always been inclined to give priority to the individual over society, to freedom over bondage, and to pursue individualism to the point of egoism, hedonism, and solipsism, and liberalism to the point of anarchy, the very opposite is true of the Chinese. The Chinese is conditioned by his surroundings, "situation centered," to use the formula of a Chinese sociologist, to an extent almost beyond our Western comprehension, a fact we must accept if we are to understand him.

Chinese ability of adaptation expresses itself with an ingenuity and naturalness that is rather disarming, especially as it is at the same time both rational and wise. The European, with his inhibitions and his preoccupation with principles, is at a loss to find the right word for it; "matter-of-factness" is perhaps the closest. Why get upset about things we can do nothing about anyway! As long as the storm rages over the countryside, the bamboo bends; when calm returns, it rises up again.

Anyone who has lived even for a short time in China is aware of the versatility and adaptability of its people, qualities which enable them to cope with sudden surprises as well as with external pressures which may have been going on for years. It always seemed to me that they positively enjoyed being confronted with the unexpected. For example, our Chinese servants were never happier than when twelve guests turned up for dinner instead of the expected four. They outdid themselves in imagination and inspiration and bustled about, hurrying to the shops across the street, borrowing from the cook of the family downstairs, changing the menu, and stretching whatever food was on hand with the aid of camouflaging sauces.

Ethical rules and taboos apply mainly to behavior toward the family and its members, also toward members of the same sect, but hardly ever to one's "neighbor." Reformers like Mo-tzu, who preached love toward all men, rather than only toward relatives and friends, were not in the long run successful. Mencius, the great restorer of Confucianism, went so far as to assert that a general love for humanity would have an unfavorable effect on filial piety and public justice: to acknowledge neither king nor father was "to be in the state of a beast." Lao-tzu's teaching, the main theme of which was "non-action," was, of course, still less designed to promote humanitarian consciousness.

When directed inwardly, however, as a force not only shaping but penetrating human nature, this attitude is bound to have an anti-impulsive, anti-emotional effect. The imperturbability with which a Chinese can accept his own misfortunes as well as those of others is more than a mask, assumed as the result of generations of caution and training, to hide otherwise uncontrollable passions. He does not demand of life an opportunity to develop his personality, a demand taken for granted by the Western man. As a result, when this opportunity is denied him, he does not suffer, or at least he suffers less. He finds no difficulty in conforming to his environment.

LANGUAGE AND THOUGHT

If we have so far tried to grasp the psyche of the Chinese principally in his relation to his natural environment, we must now mention a powerful historical factor in the formation of his character: his language, both spoken and written.

The Chinese requires thousands of hours—almost his whole life if he is an intellectual or professional—just to become—and remain—proficient in reading and writing. On the one hand, this learning process develops to an astonishing degree his memory, his visual powers of absorption for even minute details, and his aesthetic sense; but, on the other hand, it does not encourage the faculty for logical, analytical thought which has become such a firm tradition in the West since Greek and Roman times. And how indeed should it be exercised, when a sentence is created merely by stringing together a series of undeclined words!

An understanding of the reciprocity between language and thought must be regarded as basic to the modern science of linguistics. Races and cultures have evolved their own immutable forms of linguistic expression, and these in turn exert a formative influence on man: he is "very much at the mercy of the particular language which has become the medium of expression of their society."

I myself have a vivid memory of the Chinese aversion to logic and systematism from the days when I was editing a magazine in Shanghai. The manuscripts of Chinese contributors, at least of those who had not had a Western education, consisted simply of a number of facts or thoughts strung together without logical or causal connection, with not even a conclusion drawn from the sum total. A manuscript concerning, say, modern film-making or some recently published books resembled a catalogue. No attempt was made to arrange the films or books according to subject, significance, or political views of the writer, or any other point of view, or to draw any conclusion or lay down any consistent thesis. Mao Tse-tung once described this Chinese peculiarity as an arrangement of "items in A, B, C, D . . . as if setting up a Chinese drugstore."

Unless he has been Western-trained, the Chinese does not express his opinion by what we would call logical steps but advances it in little thrusts, first from one side, then from the other. His thinking is an "encircling or embracing" process, to quote Lily Abegg. She compares Chinese thinking with arrows which begin by flying around in all directions and only converge on a certain target—the goal or result of the thought—when they sense its nearness. In this process, the Chinese is capable of a degree of concentration which the Occidental, without the Ariadne thread of logical connection, could never attain.

In Hawaii and Shanghai I used to watch my Chinese students writing essays; they sat motionless for a long time beside their Western classmates. These were already busy writing and erasing, but the Chinese would wait till they had completed the composition in their heads and then proceed to write it down at great speed and without further reflection.

CONTRAST OF RUSSIA AND CHINA

If we turn our attention to the Russians, we are immediately struck by the contrast between them and the Chinese on the emotional as well as the rational plane. As long as they were permitted to be themselves, the Russians were conditioned more by emotion than by the mind or the will and were inclined to dream rather than to act, to suffer rather than to resist, to an amiable laziness rather than to systematic effort. When their consciousness was awakened, it was often the best among them who suffered from their inability to emerge from their deep and passionate discussions onto the road of determined action, and they felt they were "superfluous."

This emotional and impulsive temperament of the Russians exemplifies, among all the people of Europe, the strongest contrast to the rational wisdom of the Chinese, at least of the educated Chinese, to his self-control arising out of his continual state of harmony with his environment. More passionately, more fervently than the West, Russia has proclaimed the message of the priority of the soul over the body, the spiritual over the material, of eternal salvation over worldly profit, and, even in our mass age, its great writers have presented the introvert in his most radical form. At the same time, it has provided a vast reserve of wide-eyed, self-immolating idealism, indeed of the utmost fanaticism, for the cultivation of doctrines of salvation and utopias of a very different kind of origin.

It has often been said that Christian dualism, face to face inexorably with the Absolute, has given rise to a new dynamism and has impelled the European spirit to embark on ever new voyages of search and discovery and active reshaping of the world. It was the dialectic principle which led European thought, blossoming to its first full perfection in ancient Greece, later to take its decisive turn toward the idea of constant and inevitable progress. That the first country to be conquered by this idea in its extreme form of Marxism should have been Russia, a country that had experienced neither the strict discipline of the Roman spirit nor the awakening of the Renaissance and of humanism, and that had been affected by the age of enlightenment on the highest social level only, is in my opinion but a further proof of the power of the common European heritage.

In China, as we have seen, these fundamental conditions were lacking: not only the dialectic principle itself, but causal thought in general, the reasoning of strict logic, the reciprocity of analysis and synthesis, of knowledge and its practical application, are all imports from the West and must be systematically acquired if China is to catch up with the West— including the Soviet Union. Meanwhile, those familiar with the industriousness, the endurance, and the patience of the Chinese know better than to pronounce such a thing as impossible; why, by another token, should not China succeed in a task which scarcely a hundred years ago the Japanese people achieved in a few decades?

The Heritage

The Chinese are no more lacking in technical intelligence than the Russians. In many fields, this intelligence led them thousands of years ago to perform feats which would have been unthinkable in the Europe of that time. To Marco Polo, coming from a part of Europe that was particularly advanced for those days, the China of the thirteenth century seemed a highly developed wonderland. But, between Marco Polo's days and our own, nothing much has been added. Generally speaking, things remained as they were until well into the nineteenth century, and we may assume they would have continued to do so had it not been for the stimulus from the West.

The passion for exact weighing, measuring, counting, and experimenting, without which modern natural science could not exist, is typically occidental. The Chinese showed little inclination to do the same. It did not fit into his *Weltanschauung,* into that ancient Chinese conception of the interrelationship of all things in the cosmos—embracing all mankind and its actions—whose harmony was inviolate even to the educated Confucian. When he tried to explore this cosmos, it was only in order to become a part of it, to act in harmony with it, not to rule it, let alone change it. This can be seen from Confucius' cosmic moral code:

> It is through the power of right behavior that heaven and earth work together, that the four seasons harmonize, that the sun and moon shine, that the stars trace their courses, that the rivers flow, that all things flourish, that good and evil are differentiated, that joy and anger find their proper expression, that inferior men obey, that superior men are enlightened, that all things regardless of change are not brought into confusion. If one departs from it, all perishes.

This explains why Chinese philosophy is concerned expressly with problems of daily life; in other words, it is pragmatic. Its interest in metaphysics and in epistemology is slight, and "unfortunately there has been but little development of logic in Chinese philosophy." In essence, then, this philosophy is almost synonymous with ethics. Yet, to call Confucius' teaching utilitarian would be to misunderstand the Master completely. That which benefits not the individual but society is right.

When the occidental—and, in the end, that meant the Christian—observer was confronted with this world of ideas, he was bound to ask, no matter how much he respected its spiritual intensity: Could one speak here of what had long been familiar to him as the most powerful force in his whole existence; was this religion? In Chinese *Weltanschauung,* God and the gods have become dim shadowy forms, and, in their social function, too, they are now almost superfluous. To the Chinese intellectual, they never meant anything; he has no feeling whatsoever for the existential power of religion. The passionate search for a path to God and the world beyond, for redemption and salvation, a search which has never ceased to occupy the finest minds of Russia, in fact of the entire West, is—always allowing for exceptions—unknown to him. As for popular religion, it has no clearly defined limits and no solid structure, other than the Taoist church of the first century A.D., which disintegrated at the beginning of the Tang period. Imperial religious practices were mainly of a ceremonial nature and had little in common with popular religion. The Chinese peasant did not profess to be either a Buddhist or a Taoist; instead, he worshipped gods, spirits, and temples of every imaginable kind and derivation and sought help against demons and the forces of nature wherever he could.

Here we must say something about the renowned tolerance of the Chinese. This is often contrasted with the intolerance practiced in Europe —including Russia, from the schism of the church in 1666 to Stalin's "purges"—and the persecution and branding of dissenters as heretics.

In a work written during the anti-European Boxer rebellion and still showing the effects of the agitation of that time, J. J. M. de Groot has compiled a long list of religious persecutions and religious wars in China. When we examine this more closely, however, we see that the causes of this suppression were mainly political. The ruling class in China restricted its tolerance to such manifestations as did not jeopardize the basic structure of their personal and public life. The accusations which they leveled against their opponents are, therefore, not philosophical in nature but of a social and political kind.

We see, then, that it is not intolerance as such, which exists in Russia as well as in China, that is of interest, but the direction taken by its attacks. In the West it was largely concerned with faith and dogma; in China with state and society.

THE RUSSIAN ANTITHESIS OF CHINA

In its spiritual heritage, old Russia, among all the peoples of Europe, is the antithesis of classical China. The Russian people have been conditioned, permeated, and molded by Christianity more forcefully and more exclusively than any other, except perhaps the Spanish. For almost a thousand years—in 988 it became the state religion—Christianity has been the most powerful spiritual force in Russia, for the peasants until well into the twentieth century, for the upper classes as a whole until the time of Peter the Great and even later for the overwhelming majority of them.

Intellectual life in Russia was until the sixteenth century entirely and until the eighteenth century almost entirely identical with the life of the church and was carried on by men of the church. It was not until the eighteenth century that the influence of the secular West became noticeable. But the great writers—Gogol, Dostoyevsky, Leskov, Tolstoy—to whom not only Russia but the whole world was beginning to listen, remained searchers after God. The formation of a separate intellectual stratum of partially atheistic leanings did not take place until the last two or three generations. The fact that some of its leaders—Chernyshevsky, Dobrolyubov, and the professional revolutionary Stalin, to cite but a few—owed their earliest education to theological seminaries is one of the ironies of history.

Russian thought has been—and still is—of an intensely speculative nature; it ponders ultimate and sublime things, roams infinite spaces—one of the reasons why the Russian loves and extols his own country is its vast size—and only reluctantly finds its way to the shaping of concrete reality. Suffering itself appears as a distinctive virtue. The very words for suffering, endurance, patience, "long-suffering" (*dolgoterpénie*), had for the Russians a sacred ring.

Passionate sectarian movements have dramatically demonstrated the inclination of the Russian nature for extreme and radical upheavals. At times—the most impressive example being Dostoyevsky—these movements took on the proportions of messianic missionary faith embracing the whole human race. In all of them there existed the anticipation of an everlasting kingdom, a kingdom toward which, so they believed, the whole history of mankind was moving.

Thus, the ground was psychologically prepared for the new doctrine of world salvation, albeit only of this world. Idealistic devotion to utopian ideas, the sacrifice of the present in favor of a better future, were as familiar to the Russian as the demand—so puzzling to Westerners—for "partisanship" (*partiynost*). Indeed, as I found often enough in talking even to non-Communist Russians, they were inclined to regard tolerance and willingness for discussion as weakness, or even as a denial of truth.

But the Christian essence of the Russian people contributed a still further element to Lenin's revolution, an element to which it, like the French Revolution, owes a considerable part of its innate strength and vital impetus: the concept of brotherly love.

To what extent have the spiritual heritage and the historically rooted cultures of both races provided a favorable soil for communism? To what extent are they likely to make it endure? Two conclusions present themselves.

First, old Russia owes almost all its cultural impulses to the one among all the great religions of the world which is most concerned with the Hereafter; it was this that gave metaphysical depth to the innate restlessness of the Russian, endowing him with a dynamic impulse toward the Absolute; it was this that shaped the type of man capable of religious devotion and boundless self-sacrifice, without which communism's secular doctrine of salvation cannot exist either.

These psychological conditions could not be produced by the classical culture of China, with its marked preoccupation with this world, with its emphasis on harmony and beauty as the highest of all values. For this reason, it will not be easy for Mao and his followers to maintain the revolutionary impetus of the early days and to renew it from generation to generation. For the first time in Chinese history, communism subordinates the existence of every individual to an absolute goal. Until now, the Chinese were completely indifferent to the fate of others; those who were not Chinese were barbarians. Dostoyevsky's words, "We are all responsible for one another," would have been unthinkable from the lips of a Chinese. Now he is called upon not only to accept the Communist doctrine of salvation himself and to act upon it, but, at the expense of his own sacrifices, to spread it throughout the world.

Second, however, the very nature of the Christian tradition in Russia was bound to be the chief obstacle in the way of communism's final victory. Between the materialistic view, which sees every event as a process either of natural law or of economics, and the belief in an almighty creator and preserver of the world, there can be no reconciliation. Even during the last few years I found people in the Soviet Union who said quite openly to me, a foreigner, that they regarded Stalin as the Antichrist.

In China, however, there has never been a religious force with anything like comparable powers of resistance. Philosophical convictions, even of so ancient a tradition as the Confucian, are no substitute; they exist in outstanding individuals but not in the masses. As for popular religion, this was declining long before the advent of communism; in any case, in its variety and typically Chinese polytheism, it would be incapable of offering any prolonged resistance to the totalitarian ersatz religion.

In short, of the two forces at work in world communism—materialism and messianism—the Chinese respond to materialism, but not to one of an intolerant-messianic type, while the Russians respond to messianism, although not necessarily to one which seeks salvation on the materialistic-utilitarian level.

Society

In any discussion of Red China, the standard question recurs: how could communism triumph in a country in which the family is so strong? The Chinese family system was run on strict hierarchical lines and had the two dominating principles: the older generation always took precedence over the younger—likewise, the older members of each generation had priority over the younger—and the man had priority over the woman. Hence, the younger relative owed obedience to the older one, even when they did not live under the same roof, and the woman owed obedience to the man. But this system also surrounded the life of the individual with human warmth and affection and gave it the outward and inward security which today, in our highly civilized world, shut in by the "walls of loneliness," he often so painfully lacks.

The harshness of the system mainly affected the woman: wedded to a man not of her choosing, often literally bought by his family, living in his family's house as a stranger, separated from her own clan, which was not even allowed to take part in the wedding ceremonies, a servant of her parents-in-law, above all expected to bear sons, virtually without recourse to divorce but at the same time not assured of respect as the sole wife, for the husband, if she gave him no son—and even, if he was a rich man, simply for prestige reasons—was free to take concubines. According to one Chinese sociologist: "The unity of the big family was insured at the expense of the wife."

By far the majority of families, particularly in the country, differed little in size and way of life from those of other peoples at a similar stage of development. Usually they formed a production unit, in farming as well as in handicrafts and trade, and were small, consisting of parents and children, with the grandparents often living with them. Their size has been calculated, after painstaking statistical research, at from four to seven persons, depending on the regions studied.

If, then, certain exaggerated elements have been eliminated from our image of the Chinese family, we must now stress the overwhelming importance—compared to the West—of the larger family unit: the clan (*tsu*). The size of the clans ranged from a few hundred heads to many thousands. Their strength and importance depended on whether their members attained rank and dignity, thus bringing honor and worldly goods to the clan. A rise of this kind was usually followed after a few generations by impoverishment, sometimes decay. There have been many clans, however, which have managed to retain their solidarity, if not their respected position, for hundreds of years. Family and clan embraced a man's life from birth to death and even beyond and were the measure and the core of his existence.

THE ELITE AND THE STATE

Another sociological peculiarity of China was that group which the West has become accustomed to call the "gentry."

As an institution, the gentry was the instrument of the absolutist and centralized state as it was founded following the overthrow of the old feudal system in the third century B.C. The vast expanse of the empire and the multifarious dialects, if not languages, were enough to require an army of officials capable of understanding the language of the capital and of reading orders from headquarters. Who else could be considered for this task but the guardians of the old writings and traditions, the graduates from the schools of the "philosophers," headed by and soon consisting exclusively of Confucians, who had always demanded that the rulers be advised by men of wisdom and noble character? Thus, the mastery of all the principal areas of Chinese culture, and above all of Confucianism, to be demonstrated in state examinations, became the real proof of qualification of the official. This system of examination and selection was developed with great consistency.

Reality, of course, was not quite so democratic. Apart from the members of a few despised occupations, anyone was free to apply for admission to the examinations, but the knowledge required for them demanded years of study, which only a minority could afford. This was where the clan could come to the rescue with stipends: it was always worth while to have an active representative of the clan in the regional or, better still, the central administration. But here, too, the outsiders could not compete with the wealth at the disposal of well-established clans, not to mention the possibilities such clans had of furthering the chances of their own people by having relatives in the examination and selection commissions.

Generally speaking, the strength of the upper classes lay not so much in the exercise of administrative and political functions or in material possessions as in their inner solidarity. They lived on the Confucian heritage which, in spite of many reversals, always renewed itself, and the state examinations were enough to ensure that each successive generation could take possession of it unchanged.

In spite of all the dramatic vicissitudes of its history, this elite has survived two thousand years and, next to the family system, has proved to be the second pillar supporting classical China. Conservative and loyal to its Confucian heritage, as an institution it remained firmly united to the state. The usual danger—present in Russia, too—of a potentially explosive tension between power and intellect was thus largely neutralized, and the creation of an antigovernment or anarchistic intelligentsia was prevented.

After all this, one might wonder that the monarchy could have so easily and almost without resistance been uprooted by Sun Yat-sen and his revolutionaries. But, in the thousands of years of history which it spanned, had it ever been really deeply rooted in the consciousness and emotions of the people? Of course, the peasant needed his "son of heaven" who—even if he was of foreign race—was the mediator between the cosmos and mankind and thus responsible for the weather. But in that very capacity the emperor was too far above him for any human contact, any emotional tie, to develop.

To serve the emperor: that was the duty of the officials. From them was expected loyalty even to an already declining dynasty—and even, although to a lesser degree, at the fall of foreign dynasties. Emperors came and went, dynasties rose and fell, but fields, family, and clan remained. In their self-sufficient life, the peasants felt no need whatever to wax enthusiastic about distant emperors or other heroes.

One must, therefore, in considering the relationship of the Chinese to freedom, distinguish between two things: In his clan, he was not free; there he was bound up in a network of relationships, subject to countless rules and limitations of his freedom of movement and choice. But, in his relationship to the state, he enjoyed a great deal of freedom. Not even in the days of the First Emperor in the third century B.C., and certainly never since that time, have the Chinese people known a government as severe and totalitarian as that of the Communist state.

If any feeling of positive identity with the state was entirely absent, there was also very little nationalist feeling in traditional China. Inwardly, the clan claimed the loyalty of the individual; outwardly, China did not indulge in constant quarrels with other powers of similar strength. After the conquerors had been absorbed, it could quietly go on developing as the Middle Kingdom, which, with its superior power and culture, looked upon other races as barbarians. Its feeling of cultural superiority—which finally reached the stage of belief in a Chinese cultural monopoly—was so strong that, for centuries, the people endured the rule of foreign dynasties without losing their sense of inner security. It was not until the nineteenth century that, as a result of the challenge of the West, the Chinese became nationalistic in our sense of the word. Until that time, we should speak of a cultural rather than of a political nationalism.

So this people achieved unity principally through a common cultural heritage and not least—bridging all variations in dialect and all outside influences of the times—through a common system of writing.

THE DIFFERENT HISTORY OF RUSSIA

Against this background, the Russia of czarist times moves still closer to the rest of Europe, all the more so as recent experience has taught us that Russia's technological backwardness as compared to the West was to be overcome more quickly than expected. While, in China, the clan, legitimized by the state and a powerful moral factor in the people's life, was able to maintain itself until the clash came with the West; in Russia, as far back as the beginning of recorded history, we find it existing as a real power virtually only among the nobility—internal migrations, which took place from early times and far exceeded anything known to the West, may have contributed considerably to the clan's decay. What remained did not differ essentially from the normal European family before the latter began to shrink to the small family of our day.

All the more pronounced was the integration of the Russian with his class, his social environment; on the lowest level, this amounted for hundreds of years to a total integration. As distinct from China, the mass of the peasants was relegated to this lowest level, and, the longer this continued, the more marked it became. In what they were forced to produce in taxes and labor, they formed the broad base of the Muscovite state. The creation of a new service nobility—since Ivan IV and later by Peter the Great and his successors, in particular Catherine II—would have been impossible without the economic maintenance of this service nobility by land and "souls"—that is, without the peasants who worked for it. The difference which originally existed on the great estates between free peasants and serfs gradually disappeared.

This Russian form of serfdom was far harsher than that of Central and Western Europe, and it came very close to slavery; there were no legal restrictions on the exploitation of the human work force. The peasants broke out in bloody revolts which sometimes lasted for years; that of Stenka Razin in the seventeenth century and of Yemelyan Pugachov in the eighteenth are the best known.

The phenomenon of the Chinese gentry is inconceivable either in Russia or the West. The formation of the typically Russian "intelligentsia" could not take place until the encounter with Western culture had advanced on a wide front, and the scarcely less typical figure of the *chinóvnik,* the lower- or middle-class official, belongs to more modern times. Czar Alexis and his son Peter the Great were the first to set up a corps of paid professional officials, in which the sons of the nobility—those, that is, who did not choose a military career—were obliged to serve and which, by way of its higher ranks, also enabled the middle classes to enter the nobility.

The Russian service nobility remained far behind the Chinese gentry in intellectual and professional solidarity and, for this reason, could not oppose the ruler. In addition, however, we must take into account—because Russia, unlike China, was never granted long periods of peace—the continuing preponderance of the military element over the civilian; the system of military discipline strengthened the authority of the czar himself as well. For the masses, and for his devout predecessors on the throne, the power of the czar came from God. This sacred quality was bestowed on the grand dukes by chronicles going back to the twelfth century. What is more important for us, however, is that the church, in proclaiming to the devout that obedience to the czar was a divine duty and manifesting this continually in ceremony and prayer, contributed in large measure, if not decisively, toward making the concept of the "little father" a living reality to the people and, so, to rooting it much more firmly and intimately among the masses than was ever possible with the far-off "son of heaven."

Here, then, we have something, in the upper classes as well as in the masses, which in China has scarcely ever existed: a positive and, in its intensely personal character, extremely effective patriotic feeling for state and nation. Historical events contributed considerably to this patriotism by forcing the Russians to maintain themselves in bitter and fluctuating battles, first against the nomads of the steppes, whose influence was much stronger on Russian evolution than on the Chinese, and later against Turks, Swedes, Poles, and Germans. The fact that these enemies were all of other faiths gave a particular flavor to Russian patriotism.

From these traditions, therefore, the Russian people drew a good portion of their national strength: first in maintaining themselves even under foreign domination, then in long defensive struggles against superior enemies, and later as a driving, dynamic, often aggressive force such as could never result from the cyclical historical thinking of the Chinese. In spite of all the savagery of the struggle for power and all the harshness of oppression, this dynamic force created a community extending from the czar to the serf, and, as a result, the Russian people were far better equipped for their clash with the West than were the Chinese.

Summary

In summing up the results of our comparative observations, we clearly see that the preconditions for the Communist seizure and retention of power differ even more radically in the social and political structure of China and Russia than on the intellectual plane. In both countries, a tradition of freedom is lacking; in both, the individual has become accustomed over the years—thousands of years, even—to find his place in the ranks of a society not of his choosing—but, in its extent and nature, this process differed considerably in the czarist empire and classical China. Not only had the Chinese peasant as an individual remained a free man but even the clan, which so largely circumscribed his life, never held him in almost total servitude, as did the serfdom imposed on the Russian peasant and the tyrannical political power of centuries. Furthermore, the ties of the Chinese peasant were of a completely personal nature and so were not felt to be compulsory to the same extent as the Russian obligations which degraded those subjected to them to the status of slaves.

If, finally, we ask ourselves whether the two nations were prepared to a greater or lesser extent for communism, we find a strangely contradictory picture. On the one hand, to classical China this—or any other—ideology emanating from the West remained, due to the nature and traditions of the people, completely strange; in Russia, in its psychological and sociological structure, one can trace conditions and forces which provide points of contact for this ideology and which it could turn to its own use. Yet, on the other hand, in its struggle with Western ideas, this same China was far more deeply and fatefully convulsed, and hence prepared for drastic changes at all levels, than was ever the case with czarist Russia. The penetration by the West, which the Russian people was in the process of assimilating, brought to the Chinese the end of a world—for thousands of years the only world they could imagine.

C. A. Macartney • A. W. Palmer

2 EASTERN EUROPE BETWEEN THE WORLD WARS: THE ANATOMY OF A REGION IN CRISIS

C. A. Macartney and A. W. Palmer, *Independent Eastern Europe: A History* (New York: St. Martin's Press, Inc.; London: Macmillan & Co., Ltd., 1962), excerpted from pp. 147–50, 153–59, 162, 166–73. Footnote references have been deleted.

C. A. Macartney was a scholar of Trinity College, Cambridge, and since 1936 has been a Fellow of All Souls College, Oxford. From 1951 to 1957 he was Professor of International Relations at the University of Edinburgh. Among his many published works are Hungary and Her Successors (*1937*), *and* The Mediaeval Historians of Hungary (*1953*).

A. W. Palmer was a scholar of Oriel College, Oxford. A specialist in problems of Russian foreign policy and in the history of the South Slav peoples, he is Senior History Master at Highgate School, London.

If the peace settlement marked the end of the old empires of eastern Europe, for the national states which were their successors it was only the very beginning of a beginning. Even those among them to which the settlement brought neither a new international status nor extensive territorial acquisitions—and strictly speaking, only Bulgaria, of them all, was in this position, for Albania could hardly be counted as having properly existed before the settlement, and Hungary's status had been altered by the disappearance of the Monarchy—even they had to adapt themselves radically to the new conditions around them. For the states which were entering on sovereign life for the first time, such as the Baltic states or Czecho-Slovakia, or resuming it after an interval, such as Poland, the proclamation of independence and the assumption of sovereignty within the designated frontiers were simply the assumption of a legal right to carry out a programme, the execution of which must be in the future, and in the case of most of them these programmes entailed drastic transformations not only of their political but also of their social and economic structures.

The political changing of the guard which constituted for them the first step—the replacement of the representatives of the old supernational authorities, or alien nation (or nations), by new administrations, composed of national elements, or at least of elements prepared to carry out the national will—was still insufficient, in most cases, to make the state national in the sense desired by its new masters. Where the alien political control had been prolonged, there had crystallised round it a more or less complete social and economic domination expressed in the ownership of land and of other main sources of wealth, and the new state nations were bound to feel their political power insecure and indeed barren until these positions and sources of economic and social power were in their own hands. Bound up with this was the general problem, very big in the case of states whose frontiers had been generously drawn, of reconciling their own claims to be national states with the existence within their frontiers, often in large numbers, of national minorities.

Where states were not quite new, but had been greatly enlarged, the same problems existed with respect to their newly-acquired territories. Where a state purported to be the national state of more than one people, it had to reach an agreed relationship between its two or more state nations; and where members of the same people, now united in a single state nation, had previously lived under different political dispensations, the differences between them generated by their separate histories had to be ironed out.

Even where there was no alien economic domination to be shaken off, the economic systems of all the states had—to a greater or less degree—to be adapted to the new situation. Links broken by the new political frontiers had to be soldered; where this was impossible, or where one or more of the parties considered it undesirable on political grounds, new sources of supply (or of credit) and new markets had to be found. The extent of this problem may be partially appreciated when it is recalled that before 1918 the Baltic states and Eastern Poland had formed part of a single customs area reaching as far as Vladivostock, and the territory formerly comprising Austria-Hungary, which had also constituted a single customs unit, was now divided between seven economic systems.

Almost all the fourteen states were entering on the new era in a condition of extreme economic distress, which in most of them had contributed to producing a social unrest which was trembling on, or brimming over, the verge of revolution. In its acute form the distress was of course the result of four (in the case of the Balkan states, nearly seven) years of war, during which most of the area had been repeatedly fought over and devastated by vast contending armies, followed and aggravated by the dislocations due to the new frontiers. Factories were in ruins or outworn, stocks exhausted, communications disrupted, the land stripped of live-stock and starved of fertilisers, the population a prey to disease and starvation. But it must be emphasised that these extraordinary tribulations had come on top of a thoroughly unsatisfactory economic and social situation, the *damnosa hereditas* bequeathed to the new Eastern Europe by decades and centuries of its previous history. The outbreak of war had found the area in a state of painful transition, struggling to meet new conditions by means which were inadequate, or at best moved too slowly for their task. The majority of the populations of most of the new states were still engaged in agriculture, and in some areas this was still being carried on by small peasants on a subsistence basis. The standard of living of these peasants had in most places been sinking for decades in consequence of a growth of population which was only partially set-off by improved methods of cultivation, extension of cultivated areas (now almost everywhere reaching its limit), emigration or industrialisation. Commercial farming in Eastern Europe had long been fighting a losing battle on the world markets against the competition of the overseas countries, and the income of the classes engaged in it had been sinking. Such commercial farming had, moreover, usually been carried out by big landowners, and, where this was the case, the growing distress of the landless or near-landless agricultural population had given rise to acute social discontent, even where this was not aggravated by a national difference between landowner and peasant. In industry, the factories were driving out the old local craftsmen, but the factories themselves, with few exceptions, were finding it difficult to meet the competition of Western European or American factories working with more modern methods and backed with larger capital resources. They had done so behind the shelter of tariff walls, and with the help of low wages and bad working conditions which again produced social unrest. Most of the new states would find it difficult to repair the devastation caused by the war, and to remedy the dislocations occasioned by the new frontiers, without foreign help, and even if this were done, there would remain the long-term problem of preventing the increase of the population from further outrunning the accumulation of capital. It was hard to see how this could be effected, ultimately, without foreign help, which, incidentally, would not easily be received for agriculture, where it was perhaps most needed. Foreign capitalists might be tempted to invest in urban real estate, in industries specialising in consumer goods, in mining, lumbering or big public works, but hardly in schemes for agricultural development.

One effect of the conditions sketched above was that the social discontents and antagonisms were more complex than was usual in Western Europe. Revolutionary feeling among the industrial workers was influenced by their hardships and privations, and encouraged by the example of Russia; and economic distress, as well as political revolt against the reactionary character of the old regimes, brought the Socialist and Communist parties considerable numbers of recruits from other classes outside those of the workers. On the other hand, the same fact of their Marxist and international affiliations turned national feeling against them, this repugnance being felt even by some workers.

Another special characteristic of almost the whole area was the increased self-confidence and political purposefulness of the peasants. Agrarian parties had, of course, existed before the war in various countries, but they had seldom been revolutionary; in some places they had actually represented the big land-owners. The war had, however, carried the political education of the East European peasant a long step forward. Shortage of food and raw materials had shown him that his work was still vital to the modern state; enforced travel had enabled him to see cities, or even other farming communities, enjoying a standard of living unknown to him in his village; even his army rations had usually been superior to his accustomed fare. He had had experience of the effectiveness of direct action.

In many of the East European countries there now emerged Peasant Parties in whose programme the demand for land redistribution, where it was present (and it was not always necessary), was only one item. Their final objective was control of the state by the peasant proprietor, and they thus came into sharp conflict, not only with the landed proprietors and the banks, but also with the urban classes as a whole.

This general picture is true of the whole area . . . and of the problems and difficulties which we have mentioned, none was confined to a single one of the fourteen states, and most of them had to be faced by the greater number of them. They were, however, mixed in such varying local proportions that no two states were in quite the same position either as regards the problems which it had to face, or the resources commanded by it for the facing of them. . . .

Poland

With a territory larger than that of Italy and a population, even in 1921, of over 27 millions, and increasing at that with great rapidity, Poland was much the most populous of all the East European states, and territorially the largest of them except Turkey. Alone of them all, at the time, she could reasonably aspire to play Great Power politics, and more than any other she would find it difficult to avoid doing so, even if she wished. Her geographical situation, between Germany and Russia, would have made this inevitable even if her territory had not consisted to a large extent of areas which before 1918 had formed part of those two Powers, both of which, moreover, even if reconciled to the resurrection of a Polish state as such, regarded the frontiers which she had obtained at their expense as unjust and excessive. In addition, two of her three other neighbours—Czecho-Slovakia and Lithuania—were also antagonistic to her; only Roumania had few causes for conflict and an over-riding common interest.

From the outset, the life of Poland was dominated by the difficulties and dangers of her international situation. Foreign political calculations entered into the consideration of every move made, and a very high proportion of the budget was always spent on defence. Poland had, however, many internal problems as well. The most obvious one of these—itself closely connected, in many of its aspects, with her foreign political situation—was her lack of national homogeneity. The Polish census of 1921—the correctness of which was queried even by Polish writers—counted only a little under eighteen millions out of a population of just over twenty-seven millions as Poles; this reckoning as Poles, Masurians, Cassubians and other peoples differentiated by German statisticians. Even this census admitted a figure of nearly four million Ukrainians, over two million Jews, a million White Russians and a million Germans, and a quarter of a million "others," chiefly Czechs and Lithuanians. In 1918 the figure of Germans had certainly been a good half a million higher; the number of Jews was commonly given at at least three million, while some investigators put the Ukrainians at well over five million. . . .

Apart from the measure to which the positions of some of these non-Polish ethnic elements detracted from the completeness of the national structure of the Polish nation, the loyalty of many of them to the Polish state was more than doubtful, and their presence inside it calculated to exacerbate Poland's relations with her neighbours and to provide the latter with reasons or pretexts for attacking her. The very existence of the German minority was bound to stimulate anti-Polish feeling in Germany. The Ukrainians, as we have seen, had been incorporated in Poland only in the face of their own prolonged and bitter resistance, and not only they but even the White Russians might serve the Soviets as a pretext for aggression.

The Poles themselves were not entirely united nationally. A century of history had produced considerable differences of outlook and tradition between the natives of the three Polands, and in 1918 these were finding expression in rather sharp political dissension between the Russian and the Austrian Poles.

Both economically and socially, Poland's position was difficult. Its economy was still mainly agricultural: in 1921 63.9 per cent of the total population, and 72.3 per cent of that gainfully employed, derived its living from agriculture. In Prussian Poland agricultural methods were modern, and here, too, social conditions (as distinct from national) were relatively healthy. It was a country of small or medium sized freehold farms, with a strong co-operative movement. Serfdom had been abolished in 1807. The surplus rural population, where it had not been absorbed in local industry, had moved across Germany into the labour sump of the Ruhr. In Galicia and Russian Poland large estates were the rule. The peasants, emancipated from serfdom only in 1848 in Galicia and in 1864 in Russia, lived in conditions of poverty and degradation, accentuated, especially in Galicia, by a rural overpopulation which had been only partly relieved in the decades before the war by large-scale emigration overseas. . . .

Czecho-Slovakia

Czecho-Slovakia was in many respects the most favourably equipped of all the East European states. She had inherited a high percentage of the industry of the old Monarchy, including 90 per cent of the linen industry, 85 per cent of the silk, hemp, jute and glass industries, and 80 per cent of the cotton industry. There were also big iron-works in Silesia, the all-important Skoda munitions works, sugar-beet factories and, in Slovakia, textile factories, paper mills and valuable forests; it is true that in Eastern Slovakia, and still more in Ruthenia, the exploitation of the local natural resources was still very imperfect. To balance this, Central Bohemia and Moravia, and above all Southern Slovakia, contained rich agricultural land. The banking system, although still partially dependent on Vienna, had partly emancipated itself by 1918. The industry of Bohemia had, indeed, been developed on the assumption that the market of the whole Dual Monarchy would be open to it, and that of Slovakia as part of the planned Hungarian economic unit, so that the new frontiers set the manufacturers difficult problems of marketing. Nevertheless, Czecho-Slovakia had all the makings of a flourishing and well-balanced economy, to which advantages were added that of a population which, at least in Bohemia and Moravia, stood, for Central Europe, on a high educational level, both general and political. In these lands the national-social integration of the population, if it could be taken as a whole, was complete: there was a landed aristocracy, a class of big capitalists, a middle class (both official and unofficial), a working class and a peasantry. In Slovakia, it is true, there was relatively little between the aristocracy and the peasants, for the old Germanic mining and industrial centres of the Zips were far in decay and newer enterprises founded by Hungary under her programme of industrialisation were still only partially developed, while in Ruthenia the great majority of the population were peasants or foresters living under very primitive conditions.

The Czechs themselves were, socially, remarkably homogeneous—a people composed of middle or lower-middle classes, prosperous workers or reasonably comfortable small-holder peasants—a circumstance which enabled them, if not quite to sink their differences, yet not to carry them outside their own closed circle. . . .

Against this, the new state was ethnically the least homogeneous of all the fourteen with which we are concerned. As we have seen, the unity between the Czechs and Slovaks was far from complete, and even taken together these two peoples made up only eight and three-quarters of the thirteen and a half million inhabitants of the Republic. Besides the half-million Ruthenes, who nominally ranked as a sort of near-state nation, there were three and a quarter million Germans (almost one German to every two Czechs in the Historic Lands), something over a million Magyars and a considerable number of Poles and Jews. Of these, the Germans and Magyars were in a stronger position even than the figures would suggest. Little more than a century before the Czechs had been hardly more than a peasant people—with the single exception, indeed, that some of the great landed aristocracy had been of Czech origin and had, out of opposition to German centralism and liberalism, patronised the embryo Czech national movement and later supported its programme. With this exception, the Germans had formed the dominant class, socially, politically and economically, in Bohemia-Moravia. The remarkable Czech national revival of the nineteenth century had enabled the Czechs to break the German monopoly in many fields, and they now formed a powerful minority of Bohemia's skilled labouring class, a considerable professional class and, what was very important for the new state, there was almost a plethora of Czech civil servants, although not normally of the highest grades.

About half the big land-owners were, however, still German, by origin or adoption. Industry and banking were still in the hands of German or germanised Jews, who were also represented in a higher proportion than that of 1:2 in the official, professional and skilled industrial classes. . . .

Czecho-Slovakia's nationality problem was thus enormous in extent and replete with every difficulty. First, the Czechs had to reach agreement with the Slovaks. Even if they did so, they could hardly feel themselves to be truly masters of their state until they had reduced the power-positions of the Germans and Magyars. But this process must embitter the victims of it, whose grievances might easily be taken up by Hungary and—more important—Germany. In any conflict with her neighbours, Czecho-Slovakia would, of course, be at a strategic disadvantage; above all, if Germany and the Austrian Republic should unite, all the borders of Czecho-Slovakia (except for the short stretch of common frontier with Roumania) would be held by potential enemies.

Yugoslavia

The structure of the new Serbo-Croat-Slovene Kingdom was mainly agricultural. At least 77 per cent of the total population was engaged in agriculture, the proportion rising to as high as 90 per cent in the backward areas of Macedonia and Montenegro. In these regions, and in Old Serbia, industry was virtually non-existent. . . . There was a considerable amount of mining in Slovenia and Croatia-Slavonia and, to a lesser extent, in Serbia and Bosnia; for the most part, the mining enterprises produced for export. Industry and mining had been established by foreign capital, and it was rare for managers or skilled workers to be South Slav; the majority were German-Austrian or Hungarian. Even unskilled foreign labour had sometimes been used for work that could not attract the peasant away from his fields; thus, the railway-sleepers on the main Serbian trunk-route had been laid by Italians.

The country was, in general, economically undeveloped and the standard of living, in most parts of it, low. While some of the peasants of Central Serbia and, in particular, the Voivodina, were rich, those of the barren *karstlands* of Dalmatia, Herzegovina and Montenegro existed in a state of almost inconceivable destitution. Serbia had been fighting almost continuously since 1912, and had been cruelly ravaged by war.

While nearly the whole country was thus economically backward, there were relatively few social problems. If there were no capitalists, there was also only a very small industrial proletariat, and not a large rural landless proletariat: the surplus population which had accumulated in the nineteenth century in the congested areas on and near the sea-board had migrated overseas. Large estates existed only in the ex-Hungarian areas of the Voivodina and parts of Croatia, and in Bosnia, the land-owners being in the former case Magyars or Croats (the latter often magyarised), and in Bosnia, Mohammedans of Serbian origin and language, but Islamic faith. In Serbia, Macedonia, Montenegro and the ex-Military Frontier areas of Hungary and Croatia, the land was divided almost exclusively into small peasant free-holdings.

Class considerations had not traditionally played a large part either in the social or the political life of most of the component areas of the new state. In Serbia, Macedonia, Montenegro and the Military Frontier, the ambition of the aspiring peasant's son was to become an army officer, or, the next best thing, a civil servant. . . .

The great problem of the new state was obviously whether it could succeed in reconciling the conflicting ambitions of the component elements of its own nominal state-nation. For the "Yugoslav" feeling which was the theoretical basis of the new state was in fact almost non-existent. The easiest case was that of the million or so Slovenes. Their separate language alone, not to speak of their historical traditions, obviously distinguished them sharply from the other branches of the Southern Slav race, but in their exposed position on the fringe of the German and Italian areas of settlement they would clearly be ready to accept the support and protection of their own kinsfolk, provided this were not accompanied by too much repression and exploitation; and the Serbs could find it in their hearts to pay this price. It was otherwise with the Serbs and Croats. For the vast majority of Serbs, the conception of their nationality was inseparably bound up with their Orthodox religion. The idea that they were nationally identical with the Catholic Croats was to them nonsensical, nor did their political ambitions run in the direction of a federal Serbo-Croat state, but of a Great Serbia. The principle of the unitary state had been and remained fundamental to them, and that state had to be Serbian.

The Croats who genuinely felt themselves one nation with the Serbs were only a handful, and those who genuinely wanted to join Serbia on any other basis than that of complete equality in a very loose federation, almost as few. Moreover, in the eyes of the Croat nationalists, the Croat half of this federation must include all the areas to which Croatia had a historic claim: Croatia-Slavonia, Dalmatia, even Bosnia entire, regardless of the large Serbian elements in parts of these areas. Some Croats also claimed the Sokaz and Bunyevac parts of the Voivodina.

The difficulties of the national problem were accentuated by the fact that the various regions had different economic interests. Croatia had been closely attached to the markets of Hungary, and Slovenia to the markets of Austria. So marked was the division between the two areas of the old Monarchy that there was no direct railway from the Croatian capital, Zagreb, to Vienna. In the areas that had at one time been under Turkish domination, trade still flowed naturally southwards into the Balkans. Railways linking the various provinces of the new state were almost non-existent. A main route joined Ljubljana with Zagreb and Belgrade, but the Adriatic littoral and its hinterland were ill served. No railway connected Croatia with Dalmatia; indeed, the only line running out of Dalmatia at all was one linking Dubrovnik and Sarajevo. In north-eastern Yugoslavia, the Voivodina exported wheat to Hungary and Austria; in the south and west, Montenegro, Herzegovina, Dalmatia and even Slovenia were forced to import wheat, sometimes from overseas.

In this difference of outlook, ambitions and interests, there were abundant seeds of formidable troubles in the future.

Bibliography

CHINA

Chang-tu Hu *et al.*, *China: Its People, Its Society, Its Culture*. New Haven: Human Relations Area Files, Inc., Press, 1960.

Creel, H. G., *Chinese Thought from Confucius to Mao Tse-tung*. Chicago: University of Chicago Press, 1953.

Fairbank, J. K., *The United States and China* (2nd ed.). Cambridge, Mass.: Harvard University Press, 1958.

————, ed., *Chinese Thought and Institutions*. Chicago: University of Chicago Press, 1957.

Fitzgerald, C. P., *Revolution in China*. New York: Frederick A. Praeger, Inc., 1952.

Glubb, O. E., *Twentieth Century China*. New York: Columbia University Press, 1964.

Goodrich, L. C., *A Short History of the Chinese People*. New York: Harper & Row, Publishers, 1959.

Grousset, R., *The Rise and Splendour of the Chinese Empire*. Berkeley, Calif.: University of California Press, 1953.

Latourette, K. S., *The Chinese, Their History and Culture* (4th ed.). New York: The Macmillan Company, 1964.

Levenson, J. R., *Confucian China and Its Modern Fate*. Berkeley, Calif.: University of California Press, 1958.

EASTERN EUROPE

Barnett, C. R., *Poland: Its People, Its Society, Its Culture*. New York: Grove Press, 1958.

Dvornik, F., *The Slavs in European History and Civilization*. New Brunswick, N.J.: Rutgers University Press, 1962.

Macartney, C. A., and A. W. Palmer, *Independent Eastern Europe: A History*. New York: St. Martin's Press, Inc., 1962.

Miller, W., *The Ottoman Empire and Its Successors*. London: Cambridge University Press, 1936.

Roberts, H. L., *Rumania: Political Problems of an Agrarian State*. New Haven: Yale University Press, 1951.

Seton-Watson, H., *Eastern Europe between the Wars*. London: Cambridge University Press, 1945.

Sharp, S. L., *Poland: White Eagle on a Red Field*. Cambridge, Mass.: Harvard University Press, 1953.

Stavrianos, L. S., *The Balkans since 1453*. New York: Holt, Rinehart & Winston, Inc., 1958.

Vasiliev, A. A., *History of the Byzantine Empire*. Madison, Wisc.: University of Wisconsin Press, 1953.

West, R., *Grey Lamb and Black Falcon*. New York: The Viking Press, Inc., 1941.

Wolff, R. L., *The Balkans in Our Time*. Cambridge, Mass.: Harvard University Press, 1956.

RUSSIA

Black, C. E., ed., *The Transformation of Russian Society*. Cambridge, Mass.: Harvard University Press, 1960.

Blum, J., *Lord and Peasant in Russia: From the Ninth to the Nineteenth Century*. Princeton, N.J.: Princeton University Press, 1961.

Clarkson, J. D., *A History of Russia*. New York: Random House, 1961.

Fischer, G., *Russian Liberalism: From Gentry to Intelligentsia*. Cambridge, Mass.: Harvard University Press, 1958.

Florinsky, M. T., *Russia: A History and an Interpretation.* 2 vols. New York: The Macmillan Company, 1953.

Karpovich, M., *Imperial Russia: 1801–1917.* New York: Holt, Rinehart & Winston, Inc., 1944.

Miller, W., *Russians as People.* New York: E. P. Dutton & Co., Inc., 1961.

Pares, B., *A History of Russia* (5th ed). New York: Alfred A. Knopf, Inc., 1958.

Riasanovsky, N. V., *Russia and the West in the Teaching of the Slavophiles: A Study of Romantic Ideology.* Cambridge, Mass.: Harvard University Press, 1952.

Seton-Watson, H., *The Decline of Imperial Russia: 1855–1914.* New York: Frederick A. Praeger, Inc., 1953.

Simmons, E. J., ed., *Continuity and Change in Russian and Soviet Thought.* Cambridge, Mass.: Harvard University Press, 1955.

Treadgold, D. W., *Lenin and His Rivals: The Struggle for Russia's Future.* New York: Frederick A. Praeger, Inc., 1955.

Vernadsky, G., *Kievan Russia.* New Haven: Yale University Press, 1948.

———, *The Mongols and Russia.* New Haven: Yale University Press, 1953.

Chapter Two

The Advent of
Communist Power

One major result of the two world wars was the emergence of communist regimes in Russia, China, and Eastern Europe. Circumstances were favorable for revolution. Widespread war-weariness, inept leadership, military defeats, economic mismanagement and corruption, and the deterioration of traditional institutions found the masses receptive to new leaders and new ideas. In general, successful communist revolutions were made possible by the existence of three conditions: "a critical weakening of the authority of the incumbent government, the ineffectiveness of alternative political reform movements, and an international balance of power favorable to the communists."[1]

When the Czarist government collapsed without a whimper in February 1917, it was supplanted by a mélange of well-intentioned but ineffectual political groups who could not agree on priorities, goals, or methods. Acceding to the pressure from its Western allies, the Provisional Government unwisely kept Russia in a war that it was by then utterly incapable of waging and which its people did not understand and would not support. The Bolshevik slogan, "bread, peace, and land," struck a responsive chord because it linked the liquidation of an intolerable situation with the promise of a brighter future. The inability of the Kerensky government to act decisively—to take Russia out of the war and introduce needed economic and land reforms—and its failure to cope with challenges to its

---

[1] Cyril E. Black and Thomas P. Thornton, eds., *Communism and Revolution: The Strategic Uses of Political Violence* (Princeton, N.J.: Princeton University Press, 1964), p. 425.

31

ιority created a vacuum which the Bolshevik leadership quickly filled. In China, where Mao Tse-tung had almost two decades to prepare his organization and tactics in the outlying province of Yenan, which lay beyond the effective reach of the Nationalist Chinese (Kuomintang) or the Japanese, the take-over stemmed as much from the corrosion of Chiang Kai-shek's forces as from the vigor of communist actions and appeals. One of the ironies for which history is noted is that Chiang Kai-shek won the war against Japan (1937–1945) but lost the peace. Driven by the Japanese in 1937 and 1938 from the major urban and industrial centers on which Chiang Kai-shek depended for his strength, the Kuomintang proved unable to maintain the country's economic stability or to institute reforms while it was supporting an army and fighting the invading Japanese. To finance the war, it taxed the land heavily and requisitioned produce, relying on the conservative landed gentry and local war lords, whose corruption and callousness bred inflation and alienated the peasantry. After 1945, Chiang Kai-shek delayed essential reforms while he sought a "final solution" to the civil war with the communists. But his armies were war-weary, poorly led, and devoid of a sense of purpose and direction. In the end, the Kuomintang, enfeebled by its own internal corruption, incapable of instituting needed reforms, of forestalling a runaway inflation, or of revitalizing the oppressive bureaucracy, and crippled by the despotism of Chiang Kai-shek's family, was not able to modernize or unify China. And so the Kuomintang was swept aside into the "dust-bin of history."

If "revolutions are the locomotives of history," as Karl Marx once wrote, then Lenin, Trotsky, Mao, and Tito were engineers who brilliantly traversed uncertain grades and gorges. At a time of radical internal disequilibrium, they provided centralized direction and organizational discipline; at a time of foreign intervention and invasion, they appealed to patriotic sentiment and led a national struggle; at a time of disillusionment and discredited values, they perceived the yearning for social justice and economic change and offered secular salvation in the form of socialism. Relevant here is mention of the timeless controversy over the role of the individual in history. In retrospect, there is justification for the assertion that without Lenin there would not have been a Bolshevik revolution in 1917. In April 1917, and again in October, Lenin pressed abruptly for policy reversals with which the small circle of Bolshevik leaders reluctantly agreed to go along. And in so doing they made a revolution. Without doubt the communist revolutions in Russia, China, and Yugoslavia would not have succeeded had their architects not been politically resourceful, bold, ruthless, able men.

An impressive aspect of the Bolshevik experience was the mastery of strategy and organization demonstrated by such leaders as Lenin, Trotsky, and Stalin, notwithstanding their lack of previous experience or training in government or military affairs. They improvised brilliantly, especially

Trotsky, who in little more than three years forged a victorious Red Army of five million out of the chaos and despair of the beaten, demoralized Czarist forces. An impassioned orator, he possessed the rare gift of inspiring men, appealing alternately to their patriotism in the fight against the foreign interventionists and to their hopes for a "brave new world." This fiery spirit was also a man of iron determination. With Lenin's full support, he reinstituted in the army unpopular but necessary discipline, a chain of command, and capital punishment for desertion. At the same time, he established a system of political commissars for indoctrinating the peasant and working-class recruits with Bolshevik ideas, as well as for overseeing the loyalty of former Czarist officers who had, out of conviction or fear, joined the Red Army.

But the political success of the Bolsheviks was also due to the fact that the revolution was, at one and the same time, political and ideological in character, more so than were the revolutions in Yugoslavia and China in the 1940's. At the heart of the ideological revolution was the underlying belief in a new world, which would be democratic, egalitarian, and just. And in the revolutionary upheaval that Russia experienced during "war communism," as the 1917–1921 period is known in Soviet history, it was the Bolsheviks who espoused these goals and provided leadership in their name. The masses and the Bolsheviks coalesced at this fateful moment when it was possible for personality to give shape to history.

Little of this sense of history emerges from a reading of official Soviet accounts of the period (Reading 3). Not only is the role of Trotsky and of Bolsheviks other than Lenin ignored, but there is no feeling for the human drama that was "war communism." Totalitarian systems cannot permit the luxury of full and accurate historical memories.

In contrast to the Bolsheviks, the Chinese leadership had time and opportunity to gain experience in government and administration (Reading 7). From 1935 to 1947, when they controlled only a small part of China, whenever the Chinese communists established themselves in a village, they instituted land reforms, lowered interest rates, rent, taxes, and the cost of food, and governed honestly and efficiently. Their record of reform was never matched by the Kuomintang. Indeed, only three times before in recorded Chinese history had leaders placed the stress on economic reform that Mao did during the Yenan period (1935–1947) and after.[2] Whereas the Kuomintang was fearful of grass-roots enthusiasm, the Chinese Communist Party turned it to advantage, gaining the confidence and support of the peasantry and enlisting the allegiance of the students and intellectuals, something the Kuomintang could never accomplish. Whereas the Kuomintang could not cope with the social turmoil and economic dislocation

---

[2] During the reigns of Emperor Wu Ti (second century B.C.), Emperor Wang Mang (first century A.D.), and Wang An-shih (eleventh century A.D.).

occasioned by decades of disruptive Western influences and debilitating wars, the Chinese communists effectively fused Marxism, nationalism, and a program for modernization, and held out the promise of a strong China (Reading 6).

Of all the East European countries only Yugoslavia emerged from World War II firmly under the control of an indigenous communist movement; elsewhere in the region, communism was brought by the Red Army and installed at Moscow's command (Reading 4). In Yugoslavia, the Partisans led by Tito became the dominant political force because only they effectively muted the social, political, religious, and ethnic divisions of pre-war Yugoslavia and organized a National Liberation Front against the invaders (Reading 5). This appeal to nationalism and the promise of a more democratic government after the war, coupled with Tito's de-emphasis of the Marxist-Leninist persuasion of his movement, attracted the young, the idealistic, and the patriotic. One Western scholar described the situation as follows:

> The Partisans began, as did Mihailovich's Chetniks, as a mostly Serbian movement. But their leader was a Croat, and the core of the movement—the Communists—did not care for nationality for its own sake. By 1943 they were gaining followers all over the territory of Yugoslavia; and everywhere, whether in Slovenia, Macedonia, or among the Moslems of Bosnia, there was a small Communist group to lead and to indoctrinate the nonpolitical adherents who wanted no more than to fight the Germans and their own traitors. The Communists did not look down upon any useful human material.[3]

All communist revolutions were made in the name of the working class by intellectuals who were adept at attracting and leading the masses. The rank-and-file of the movements were workers and peasants, but the Party cadres were drawn largely from the middle-class intelligentsia. Though Marxism postulated revolution by the proletariat, Lenin, Mao, and Tito were successful because they were able, in predominantly peasant societies, to recruit from among the peasantry. A time of social dislocation, armed strife, and deteriorating traditional values provided the necessary setting for revolutions; effective leadership made it a certainty.

---

[3] Adam B. Ulam, *Titoism and the Cominform* (Cambridge, Mass.: Harvard University Press, 1952), p. 30.

3 SOVIET REASONS FOR THE SUCCESS OF THE BOLSHEVIK REVOLUTION

History of the Communist Party of the Soviet Union (Moscow: Foreign Languages Publishing House, 1960), pp. 258–62.

The following selection was taken from the official Communist Party history, prepared in 1960 under the general editorship of B. N. Ponomarov, Corresponding Member of the U.S.S.R. Academy of Sciences.

1. The chief reason for the victory of the October Socialist Revolution was that it was led by the working class of Russia. No other detachment of the international army of labour had gained such tremendous experience in so short an historical period. The proletariat of Russia, led by Lenin, was the first of all the classes in the country to form its own party. The working class led the struggle of the whole people against the autocracy and against the dictatorship of the bourgeoisie. The other sections of the working people had convinced themselves that in the proletariat they had a champion of the interests of the whole people, who were languishing under the yoke of the landlords and bourgeoisie. The proletariat of Russia was the principal motive force of the entire social and political development of the country.

2. The October Revolution was victorious because a social force had been created in Russia—the alliance between the proletariat and the peasantry—that broke the resistance of the moribund classes. In the course of the revolution the Bolsheviks had exposed the traitors to the working-class cause, the opportunists, who had maintained that the proletariat could assume and retain power only where it constituted a majority of the population. The Russian proletariat had secured the full backing of the poor peasantry, which constituted the overwhelming majority of the rural population—as much as 65 per cent. The broad masses of the peasantry had realised from their own experience, and as a result of the extensive work carried out by the Bolshevik Party, that only under the leadership of the proletariat could they secure land, peace, bread and liberty. By winning a majority of the labouring peasantry over to the proletariat, the Bolsheviks won the peasant reserves away from the bourgeoisie.

3. The October Revolution differed from all other revolutions in that the workers created their own organs of power. It was in the very midst of

35

the Russian proletariat that a new form of revolutionary authority had arisen—the Soviets of Workers' Deputies. The Soviets of Workers', Soldiers' and Peasants' Deputies were organs of the alliance of the proletariat and the peasantry, a form of organisation that embodied the alliance of the workers and peasants under the leadership of the workers.

> "Had not the creative effort of the revolutionary classes given rise to the Soviets," wrote Lenin, "the proletarian revolution in Russia would have been a hopeless cause" (*Collected Works,* Vol. 26, p. 80).

4. The October Revolution was victorious because it was confronted with a comparatively weak enemy, the Russian bourgeoisie. The entire course of historical development of Russian capitalism, its backwardness as compared with that of the leading capitalist countries, and its dependence on foreign capital explain the political flabbiness, cowardice and inadequate experience of the Russian bourgeoisie. The compromisers, too—the Socialist-Revolutionaries and Mensheviks—proved powerless to help the Russian bourgeoisie. In a struggle that had gone on for many years, they had been exposed by the Bolsheviks as agents of the bourgeoisie. On the eve of the October Revolution these parties openly deserted to the camp of the counter-revolution, they championed the capitalist system.

5. A decisive circumstance that made the victory of the revolution possible was the fact that the masses of the people were headed by the well-tried, militant and revolutionary Bolshevik Party, a party guided by the advanced theory of the working class, the theory of Marxism-Leninism.

While the revolution was being prepared and carried out, the Party did an enormous amount of work in the theoretical field, and enriched Marxism with new propositions. The resolutions of the April Conference and the Sixth Party Congress, the resolutions and decisions of the Central Committee and, most important of all, the works of Lenin, contain the theoretical substantiation and elaboration of a concrete plan for the development of the bourgeois-democratic revolution into the Socialist revolution.

In its fight against the opportunists the Party worked out and upheld the theory that Socialism could be victorious in Russia. It showed that the development of capitalism in this country had created objective conditions in it for the establishment of Socialism, and that the particular acuteness of the contradictions in Russia had made it the weakest link in the chain of imperialism. Lenin developed the Marxist theory of Socialist revolution, discovered, in a republic of Soviets, a political form for the dictatorship of the proletariat, substantiated that view, and further elaborated Marxist views on armed insurrection, developing them into a full-fledged theory.

The Great October Socialist Revolution is a splendid example of the practical application and implementation of Lenin's theory of Socialist revolution.

The toiling masses had seen all the other parties in power, separately and in various combinations. They had seen the Cadets, who represented the bourgeoisie as a whole; they had experienced the rule of a coalition of Cadets, Socialist-Revolutionaries and Mensheviks; they had tested the Socialist-Revolutionaries and Mensheviks by their deeds, when they were in a majority in the Soviets. In the course of the revolution, all the bourgeois and compromising parties had discredited themselves, had revealed their counter-revolutionary essence. The working people turned away from the parties of compromise with the bourgeoisie and, using their right to recall deputies, proceeded to oust from the Soviets those who had betrayed their confidence, electing in their place Bolsheviks, people who had proved by their deeds that they were the only consistent defenders of the people's interests and genuine fighters for freedom and independence. In this way the Mensheviks and Socialist-Revolutionaries were isolated from the masses. The Bolshevik Party was the only party to lead the revolutionary struggle of the proletariat and the working people, as a whole, and do so undividedly.

The Bolshevik Party succeeded in uniting all the diverse revolutionary movements and in directing them towards a single goal, that of overthrowing imperialism. The Party merged into a single revolutionary torrent the movement of the whole people for peace, the peasants' fight for the land and against landlord oppression, the struggle of Russia's oppressed nations against national oppression, and the fight of the proletariat, the leading force in society, for Socialism. Under the leadership of the Bolshevik Party, the workers and poor peasants overthrew the government of the bourgeoisie and established Soviet power.

Such were the chief reasons of a domestic character that ensured the victory of the revolution.

Among the reasons of an international character that ensured the success of the Great October Socialist Revolution was the fact that the revolution began during the imperialist world war. Neither the Anglo-French nor the German bloc was able to give direct armed assistance to the Russian bourgeoisie. They helped it materially and by organising plots, but were unable to provide it with any considerable armed forces. The Russian bourgeoisie, left face to face with the Russian proletariat at the head of all the working people, could not withstand the onslaught of the masses.

The support of the international proletariat was also of enormous significance to the revolution. Under the influence of the October Revolution, the revolutionary mass movement grew stronger in all capitalist countries. The action of the international proletariat tied the hands of the imperialists and thereby facilitated the triumphal march of the Great October Revolution through the country.

Defining the international significance of the Great October Socialist Revolution, Lenin wrote that it manifested itself in two forms: in its influence on the revolutionary movement in other countries, and in the inevitability of a repetition of the basic features of the Russian revolution on an international scale.

All the cardinal questions of the Great October Socialist Revolution are of international importance, in the broad sense of the word. Under the direct influence of the October Revolution, the exploited people throughout the world, languishing under the yoke of imperialism, were moved to action. A number of revolutions—in Germany, Austria-Hungary and several other countries—together with revolutionary mass actions of the workers in Europe and America, shook the capitalist world to its foundations. The enslaved peoples of the colonial countries awoke to action. The Russian revolution began the uniting of the revolutionary actions of the workers and the national liberation struggle into a single force, capable of overthrowing imperialism.

The October Revolution was the clearest manifestation of the sharpening of the general crisis of capitalism. The Russian revolution broke the chain of imperialism and cleared the way for the establishment of a new, Socialist society. It put an end to the undivided rule of imperialism. The banner of Socialism was raised over one-sixth of the globe. The world was split into two camps: the camp of moribund capitalism and the camp of rising Socialism. The October Revolution ushered in a new era in the history of mankind, the era of the abolition of all forms of exploitation, the era of the victory of Communism.

Hugh Seton-Watson

4 THE SEIZURE OF POWER

Hugh Seton-Watson, *The East European Revolution* (New York: Frederick A. Praeger, Inc., 1956), excerpted from pp. 167–71.

Hugh Seton-Watson, who is Professor of History at the University of London, has written a number of books on Soviet and Communist affairs, including The Decline of Imperial Russia, From Lenin to Khrushchev, *and* Neither War Nor Peace.

The regime which has arisen, with local variations, throughout the zone of Soviet domination in Eastern Europe has become known as "Popular Democracy." Though this tautological phrase is an abuse of language, it is a convenient label, and will be used in the rest of this book. Apologists of the regime, both in Eastern Europe and in the West, especially those Western fellow-travellers whose task is to persuade their compatriots that the regime is an improved version of western socialism, and even derives from the liberal tradition, insist on the originality of "Popular Democracy," and the differences between it and the regime prevailing in the U.S.S.R. But every now and then an East European communist of unimpeachable authority lets the cat out of the bag. In his speech to the 5th Congress of the Bulgarian Communist Party, delivered on 25 December 1948, George Dimitrov, former General Secretary of the Comintern and Premier of Bulgaria, 1946–49, declared: "The Soviet regime and the Popular Democratic regime are two forms of one and the same system of government, based on the union between the town and agricultural workers. Both are based on the dictatorship of the proletariat. Soviet experience is the only and the best pattern for the building of socialism in our country as well as in other countries of Popular Democracy." And Matthias Rákosi, leader of the Hungarian communists, a Comintern veteran of no less authority than Dimitrov, and one of the few men living who can claim to have been a member of a communist government as early as 1919, recently described "Popular Democracy" in the party paper *Szabad Nép* as "dictatorship of the proletariat without the Soviet form." Soviets, Rákosi argued, were a form of government arising out of civil war, but the East European states had been spared civil war because the Soviet army, advancing through their territory, had not only defeated the German army but had shattered the old political structure, and disarmed the old ruling classes, of Eastern Europe. Thus Rákosi admitted, what fellow-travellers in the West have taken such pains to deny, that the 1949 version of "proletarian dictatorship" was imposed ready-made by the Red Army.

Rákosi's statement is in fact an over-simplification. . . . [We] must point out that two countries in Eastern Europe—Yugoslavia and Albania—were not spared a civil war, and that a third, Poland, experienced a kind of perverted foreign-imported civil war. Rákosi's explanation of the origin of the new versions of "proletarian dictatorship" is therefore only applicable to four countries—Rumania, Hungary, Bulgaria and Czechoslovakia. But the words of Dimitrov are applicable to all the regimes which have arisen from the political struggles in Eastern Europe since the end of the war.

In Yugoslavia and Albania, as we have seen, the Axis invaders destroyed the old political structure, and could fill the gap only by their incompetent and unpopular quislings. The communists then fought not only a national war against the invaders and quislings, but also a civil war against the patriotic section of the conservative forces—Mihailović, the Balli Kombetar and the Zogists. They came out of the double war with a more or less "monolithic" regime. Communist domination of the "anti-fascist fronts" in both countries had been secured during the fighting. Temporary acceptance by Tito of some liberal exiles from the West made no real change, while Enver Hoxha did not even have to make this formal concession. The political battle had been won.

The course of events in Poland in some ways resembled that in Yugoslavia. The German invaders smashed the old political structure, and showed special savagery to the educated class. But the educated class and the conservative forces were strongly represented, together with the workers and peasants, in the Home Army. The resistance movement in Poland fought only a national war, not a civil war. But when the Red Army entered Poland it fought a double war, for it considered not only the Germans but also the Polish resistance movements as its enemies. The Soviet leaders knew how deep an impression the Katyn case had made. They knew how hostile to them was the Polish army in the West, with its fine war record, and consequent high prestige both in Poland and among the Allies. They created still further bitterness by their failure to save insurgent Warsaw. Having chosen their policy, they took pains to use willing Poles to achieve their aims. The Polish civil war was imported from Russia, and its communist belligerent was created in Russia. The Red Army, the Polish divisions in its ranks, and the Polish security forces of the Lublin Committee together disarmed and hounded down the Home Army. The destruction of the old social and political regime, which was achieved in Yugoslavia and Albania partly by the Germans and partly by a genuine civil war, was achieved in Poland partly by the Germans and partly by the Red Army.

The result was not quite the same. In both Yugoslavia and Poland, democratic exiles returned from the West as a result of pressure by the Western Powers. But whereas in Yugoslavia they had no chance of organising themselves into a force, in Poland they were for a time successful. Mikołajczyk regrouped his great party, and for two years fought a bitter rearguard action. The reasons for the difference are that the Polish Peasant Party was a far more popular and living organisation than were the old democratic parties in Yugoslavia; that the Yugoslav partisan movement was a genuine popular movement, while the Lublin Committee was bogus; and that the Yugoslav communists had built up an efficient police apparatus of their own, while the Polish communists had to rely at first on the Russian military and police machines.

In the other four countries there had been no civil war. German persecution had caused heavy losses to the Czech intelligentsia, but the Czech middle class—both business and professional—was far too strong and numerous to be destroyed. In Slovakia, Hungary, Rumania and Bulgaria the social structure was little different in 1945 from what it had been in 1939. In all four countries therefore the post-war period began with coalition governments, and sovietisation was only achieved by three stages.

The first stage was the genuine coalition. Several political parties, differing in social basis, ideology and long-term programme, and possessing each its own party organisation, combined on a common short-term programme, which nominally included a purge of fascists, fairly radical social reforms, political freedom and a foreign policy friendly to both the U.S.S.R. and the Western Powers. Real freedom of speech and meeting existed, and there was little political censorship except on one subject—the U.S.S.R. Not only might Soviet policy not be criticised, but it was hardly possible to write anything about any aspect of Russia which did not coincide with the official Soviet line. But this seemed a small price to pay. Apart from this, a wide variety of opinions, representing various political views and social categories, could be freely expressed. Nevertheless, already during the first stage the communists seized control of most of the "levers of power"—in particular the security police, the army general staff and the publicity machine. The first stage lasted only a short time in Rumania and Bulgaria. The forced resignation of Dr. G. M. Dimitrov from the secretaryship of the Agrarian Union in January 1945 was the decisive moment in Bulgaria. The practical breakdown of the first stage became clear when the Agrarian and Social Democrat Parties were "captured" by communist nominees in May, and was formally completed by the resignation of Petkov and his colleagues in August. In Rumania the change came suddenly in March 1945, when Vyshinski forced King Michael to give power to Groza's "National Democratic Front" government. Hungary passed more slowly out of the first stage. The decisive crisis was the arrest by the Soviet authorities of Béla Kovács in February 1947, and the transition was completed when Nagy was replaced as Premier by Dinnyes four months later. Czechoslovakia remained in the first stage up to Gottwald's "February (police-) revolution" of 1948.

The second stage may be described as the bogus coalition. The governments still contain non-communist parties, but these are represented by men chosen no longer by the party membership but by the communists. The essential feature of this stage is that the peasant parties, and any bourgeois parties who may have been tolerated at the beginning, are driven into opposition. In this stage opposition is still tolerated, but becomes increasingly difficult. Opposition newspapers may be published, but their distribution becomes dangerous in the capital and almost impossible outside it. Censorship is exercised not only by the government but also by the communist-controlled printers' trade unions, which "indignantly refuse to print reactionary calumnies against the people's authorities." Opposition meetings are broken up by lorryloads of communist toughs, while the police "objectively" take no action against aggressors or aggressed. In Poland this stage existed from the "liberation" onwards, though it was only formally established in the summer of 1946 when Mikołajczyk formally left the government of which he had been no more than a formal member.

It came to an end in the autumn of 1947. In Bulgaria and Rumania it lasted from the spring of 1945 to the autumn of 1947. The introduction into the Groza government of one representative each of the two main opposition parties, as a result of the Moscow conference of December 1945, made no difference, as these men were not consulted by their cabinet "colleagues" and wielded no power. In Hungary the second stage lasted for about a year (spring 1947 to spring 1948), and was not finally liquidated until the arrest of Cardinal Mindszenthy and dissolution of Baránkovics' Catholic Party at the end of 1948. Czechoslovakia in 1948 leaped almost directly from the first to the third stage, for after the "February (police-) revolution" no opposition was tolerated.

The third stage is the "monolithic" regime. There is a single communist-managed "front," with one hierarchy, one centralised discipline and one organisation. An importat feature of this stage is the enforced fusion of the well-purged social democrats with the communists in a United Workers' Party. This is of course more important in the three Central European countries, where social democracy has a strong tradition, than in the four southeastern countries, where it has not. In Rumania and Bulgaria the social democrats played a minor but not insignificant part between "liberation" and absorption: in Yugoslavia and Albania they did not appear at all. In the third stage all open opposition is suppressed, and its leaders either escape abroad or are arrested as "spies of the Western imperialists" and either executed or sentenced to long prison terms. This third stage was established in Yugoslavia and Albania already in 1945: in the other countries its preparation was pushed rapidly ahead after the foundation of the Cominform, and it was completed by the end of 1948.

Moša Pijade

5 ON REASONS FOR THE YUGOSLAV VICTORY

Moša Pijade, *"O tridesetogodišnjici Kommunističke partije Jugo-slavije"* ("On the Thirtieth Anniversary of the Communist Party of Yugoslavia"), *Materijali za ideološki odgoj članova Narodnog fronta* (Zagreb, 1949), Vol. II, excerpted from pp. 118–123.

A long-time communist and confidante of Tito, Moša Pijade was, until his death in 1957, regarded as the leading theoretician of the Yugoslav Communist Party.

In April 1941, the Communist Party of Yugoslavia, and only it, was able to unite all the peoples of Yugoslavia and lead them in an armed liberation struggle. The Communist Party of Yugoslavia did that in a way that was not done by any other Communist Party in the European countries which were brought under the Fascist yoke. Its merit was more than just the fact that it was, in a very short time after the occupation of the country [by the Germans], able to develop a general national armed uprising of the kind that could not be found in the other countries of occupied Europe even at the end of the war.

Much more important are the other facts which sharply distinguish the accomplishment of the Communist Party of Yugoslavia from that which was achieved by other Communist Parties, even those which succeeded in developing to a fair degree the fight of the people against the invaders. In saying this, we are aware of the fact that conditions were not equally favorable everywhere. We are not stating those facts because of some self-praise but in order to record the historical truth. Here are some of the facts that nobody can erase from history.

1. Although the national struggle was placed on the broadest basis, encompassing all democratic and patriotic elements, the Communist Party was powerful enough and capable of ensuring for itself from the very beginning the undivided and undisputed leadership of the national struggle.

2. The Communist Party of Yugoslavia from the very beginning clearly foresaw the need to destroy the old state apparatus in order to ensure the success of the national struggle. No other Communist Party of occupied Europe had the power to do this.

3. After the first experiences of the armed struggle, the Party already perceived the necessity to organize the Partisan units into larger companies, which would be capable of larger movements and maneuvers and which would be the basis for the development of a new, national army. This necessity was not understood by any other Communist Party of occupied Europe. Some even contended that we were on the wrong track for refusing to limit the fight to partisan guerrilla activities.

4. At an early stage the Communist Party of Yugoslavia (CPY) understood the necessity of giving a solid basis to the new people's army and to ensuring its revolutionary character by creating special proletarian units. . . .

5. The formation of the regular army, starting just with proletarian units, meant the separation of the partisan companies from their villages and their districts in order to make large-scale operations possible. It also meant overcoming the local character of the struggle and ensuring a solid, united centralized leadership. . . .

6. The organization of people's liberation committees as the organs of the new, people's government, as well as the organization of the regular people's army, served to link the people's liberation war with the socialist revolution. It meant that the Marxian line of connecting the fight for national liberation with the fight for the aims of the working class had to be followed. And this was accomplished during the war only by the CPY.

7. The CPY maintained that the very facts of the enemy's occupation of the country and of the participation of the Soviet Union in the war presented conditions which obliged any Communist Party to organize a general national armed struggle against the Fascist invaders. The leadership of the Communist Party of Bulgaria, for example, could not be convinced of this view. . . .

8. An important characteristic feature of our military actions stemmed from our view that the primary aim was to destroy the enemy's forces and that it was only of secondary importance to defend the liberated territory. The workers had to be drawn out of the towns and moved into the army, and cities were taken by military action and the government was organized in large areas. Contrary to this, some Communist Parties, which developed otherwise considerable guerrilla activity, maintained that the fight should be limited to guerrilla action, that no large units should be formed, nor transformed into a regular army. They also maintained that towns should not be taken over and that workers should not be taken out of the towns and settlements but that they should remain where they were to take up arms "when the time comes." This attitude meant a complete separation of the national liberation struggle from the fight for democracy and the delay of the fight for democracy until after the war. Nations which were led in such a way during the war paid dearly for those mistakes.[1]

9. It was only with such a correct Marxian approach that it was already

possible in November 1943, in the middle of the war, to constitute Yugo-slavia as a new federal people's state and to emerge from the war with a developed state, socialist in character and in the direction of its develop-ment, and national-democratic in form. This form of socialist state, based on rule by people's committees, was a glorious deed of our Party and showed its capacity to apply independently the science of Marxism and Leninism to the specific conditions of the given historical situation. . . .

10. After the above-mentioned facts, there is no need to emphasize again the great importance that the correct solution of the national problem played in the victory of our people.

11. From the very beginning the CPY understood the importance of a wide participation by the peasant masses in the uprising and in the national liberation struggle, as well as in the building of the army and the govern-ment. For this reason it developed the powerful alliance of workers and peasants as the basis for a general national movement. It gave to this movement the form of the National Front, a solid, all-encompassing political organization in which the CPY was, from the beginning, the leading force, while the coalition elements were always subordinated to the unity of the masses and never played a decisive role.

---

[1] Pijade's allusion here is to Moscow's imposition of Soviet hegemony over Eastern Europe and its use of indigenous but subservient Moscow-trained communists rather than national communists who had stayed behind and fought the Germans.—Ed.

Liu Shao-chi

6   THE TRIUMPH OF MARXISM-LENINISM IN CHINA

Liu Shao-chi, "The Triumph of Marxism-Leninism in China," *World Marxist Review: Problems of Peace and Socialism,* II, No. 10 (October, 1959), excerpted from pp. 15–17.

Liu Shao-chi is, after Mao Tse-tung, recognized as the leading man in the Chinese communist hierarchy. Long regarded as a leading theoretician and spokesman of the Chinese Communist Party, Liu Shao-chi is chairman of the People's Republic of China and a member of the Politburo. He is the nominal head of the government. His 1939 work, How to be a Good Communist, *was reissued several years ago.*

This analysis of the reasons for the success of the Chinese revolution was written on the occasion of the tenth anniversary of the establishment of the communist regime in China and published in the World Marxist Review, *the unofficial but authoritative journal of the Moscow-oriented wing of the international communist movement.*

The victories won by the Chinese people over the past ten years constitute a triumph for Marxism-Leninism; they have been won under the leadership of the Communist Party thanks to the general line of the Party in the democratic and socialist revolutions and in socialist construction.

During the democratic revolution Mao Tse-tung repeatedly enunciated the following idea:

> . . . the revolutionary movement led by the Communist Party is, on the whole, a single movement encompassing both the democratic and the socialist revolution. . . . Only by appreciating the difference between these revolutions and the link connecting them is it possible to provide correct leadership for the revolution in China.

Our Right-wing opportunists, like the Mensheviks of Russia, erected a Chinese wall between the democratic revolution and the socialist revolution; they failed to see the interconnection between the two revolutions. On the one hand they did not see the perspective of the democratic revolution evolving into a socialist revolution, while on the other the "Left"-wing opportunists, like the Trotskyists in Russia, did not see the difference between the two revolutions and tried to implement the socialist tasks at the stage of the democratic revolution to the end. . . . These two deviations caused much harm to the Chinese revolution. As opposed to "Left"-wing and Right-wing opportunism, the correct course in leadership as represented by Mao Tse-tung provided, on the one hand, for implementing the Marxist-Leninist theory of the two stages of the revolution, for distinguishing between the tasks of the democratic and socialist stages, and on the other, for implementing the Marxist-Leninist theory of permanent revolution, for co-ordinating the two stages of the revolution, for preparing the conditions that would make possible the immediate transition to the socialist stage after the triumph of the democratic revolution.

The leadership of the proletariat in the democratic revolution, ensured through its Communist Party, was the key to the complete victory of the democratic revolution and its development into the socialist revolution. No bourgeois party could have offered a consistently anti-imperialist and anti-feudal program or could have carried out the democratic revolution to the end. At the democratic stage the general line of the Party was to rally under the leadership of the proletariat, on the basis of the worker-peasant alliance, all the progressive forces and to wage a consistent struggle against imperialism, feudalism and bureaucratic capital. Mao Tse-tung formulated this line in the following words: "A revolution of the popular masses under proletarian leadership, a revolution spearheaded against imperialism, feudalism and bureaucratic capital."

China was a vast backward country with an 80 per cent rural population of which 70 per cent were poor peasants and farm laborers. The peasant question was, therefore, the central issue in the democratic revolution. The reactionary power in the old China was notorious for its brutality, the revolutionaries were subjected to wholesale arrests and physical destruction. And so at the democratic stage of the revolution the Communist Party retreated deep into the rural areas and for twenty-two years headed the armed struggle for capturing the cities. The Party implemented the "mass line," it relied on the political consciousness and the organized strength of the peasantry, it rallied the peasants to save themselves, to expropriate the landlords, to take the land and keep it, it did not pursue the bourgeois policy of "bestowing" land on the peasants. (The "mass line" was carried out also after the proclamation of the People's Republic when the agrarian reform was implemented.) This enabled the Party to create in the rural areas a reliable revolutionary base, to build up an army and strongpoints, to raise the level of revolutionary activity and discipline of the masses of poor peasants to that of the proletariat; it was from their midst that the Party received the manpower reserves and materials needed for the People's Liberation Army. From its bases the Communist Party waged a revolutionary war. In these areas it implemented a land reform and carried out economic and cultural development. In fact, this was a long rehearsal in preparation for the nationwide victory. During the rehearsal the masses were educated, the army was steeled, revolutionary forces were accumulated, cadres were trained and the Party leadership gained rich experience.

In view of the fact that a close worker-peasant alliance had already been forged we were in a position to solve the question of a united front with the national bourgeoisie. In our country we distinguished two sections of the bourgeoisie. The first—the bureaucratic or the comprador bourgeoisie— was an instrument of imperialism, a supporter and ally of the feudal lords and a bitter enemy of the revolution. It was imperative to wage a decisive struggle against it. And the second—the national bourgeoisie, which was oppressed by the imperialists, the feudal lords and bureaucratic bourgeoisie. This section stood for independent development. Under these conditions its participation in the revolution or its neutrality were possible. However, this bourgeoisie was weak and dual in character, it was both revolutionary and reactionary. It constantly vacillated and occupied an intermediate position. This fact necessitated, on the one hand, an alliance with it on definite terms and joint struggle against imperialism, feudalism and bureaucratic capital, and on the other, combating its conciliatory tendencies. In pursuing this policy we built up the forces of the revolution, won over the intermediate sections, isolated the reactionaries and firmly maintained the proletarian leadership around which the masses were rallied.

At the democratic stage both the Right-wing opportunists (who denied the link between the democratic and socialist revolutions), and the "Left"-wing opportunists (who confused the two revolutions) failed to comprehend the importance of the peasant question and for this reason could not find a correct solution to the problem of the bourgeoisie. The Rightists pursued a line of surrender to the bourgeoisie, maintaining that the democratic revolution served mainly the aims of the bourgeoisie. They did not rely on the worker-peasant alliance but sought to establish a united front with the bourgeoisie, to enter into an alliance with it, refusing to combat it. Thus they discarded the principle of proletarian leadership. When the bourgeoisie betrayed the revolution, the revolution suffered defeat and the cause of the working class and the masses suffered grave injury. This meant that when the conditions for the revolution were ripe and it was necessary to take every advantage of them in the decisive battle, the Rightists hesitated to press for victory and even stood in the way of achieving it. The "Leftists" did not wish to enter into an alliance with the small and national bourgeoisie. Moreover, they were wrong when they held that the main blow should be struck at the intermediate forces, when they denied the need and the possibility of rallying or neutralizing the various intermediate forces. As far as the national bourgeoisie was concerned, they fought against it, they did not enter into alliance with it, and, what is more, did not wish to utilize the contradictions among the enemies or to concentrate the forces for a blow against the main enemy. The result was that they, too, renounced the principle of proletarian leadership, while the working class had to fight single-handed and the revolution was defeated. Both the "Leftists" and the Rightists had one thing in common: they ignored the revolutionary demands and the fighting spirit of the peasantry; they did not believe that we could hold out in the rural areas by creating bases there, that by isolating the towns we could finally capture them. That is why, under certain circumstances, the two deviation trends could be substituted one for the other. Take Wang Ming, for instance. During the Second Civil War he represented the third "Leftist" deviation, and in the war against the Japanese invaders he was the most outstanding Right opportunist.

The Marxist-Leninists headed by Mao Tse-tung steeled the Party in the struggle against both "Left" and Right opportunism, and thanks to this the revolution began to develop along a correct course, gaining one victory after another.

The people's revolution emerged victorious under the leadership of the Communist Party, overthrew the reactionary Kuomintang and smashed its oppressive bureaucratic and military machine. The People's Republic, proclaimed in 1949, is in effect the dictatorship of the proletariat. In this way the transition from the democratic to the socialist revolution was effected. In the fundamental question of the revolution, namely that of power, the founding of the People's Republic marked the completion of the democratic revolution and the beginning of the socialist revolution. The proletariat, in addition to fulfilling its leading role in the democratic revolution, firmly established its hegemony in the sphere of state power with the result that when the task of building socialism arose the question of winning power was no longer on the agenda. This was due to the fact that in the course of the democratic revolution the Party never lost sight of the ultimate goal—the socialist revolution—that in the course of the long revolutionary struggle it made every effort to consolidate the leadership of the proletariat.

Robert Vincent Daniels

7 THE CHINESE REVOLUTION IN RUSSIAN PERSPECTIVE

Robert Vincent Daniels, "The Chinese Revolution in Russian Perspective," *World Politics*, XIII, No. 2 (January, 1961), excerpted from pp. 210–220. Footnote references have been deleted.

Robert Vincent Daniels is Professor of History at the University of Vermont. Among his many published works on the Soviet Union and world communism are The Conscience of the Revolution: Communist Opposition in Soviet Russia; The Nature of Communism; *and* A Documentary History of Communism.

The comparative study of revolutions has suffered from the tendency of historians either to force differing events into the same mold, or to label them unique and abandon attempts at comparison. Naturally, no two revolutions are exactly alike; to expect this would be absurd, but it is equally absurd to hold that they can have nothing in common. The situations of political breakdown and social chaos characteristic of the great revolutions clearly belong to a distinctive category in historical study. Patterns can be discerned in the study of revolutions which either explain events or call attention to deviant events which require special explanation. China no less than any other country can be approached from this standpoint.

The basic pattern of revolution can be stated roughly as follows: development of a revolutionary situation because of social changes and frustrations; collapse of the old, ineffectively repressive regime under the impact of military defeat or an administrative and financial impasse; moderate reform efforts giving way to radical revolutionary experiments and violent social conflict; a "Thermidorean reaction" in which revolutionary emotion subsides; emergence of a dictatorial authority which restores order and curbs the excesses of the revolution. Restoration of the old regime may then occur, but the Russian experience shows that this is not inevitable; nor is the overthrow of the extremist party, if its leaders can adapt themselves to the realities of the post-revolutionary situation as Lenin did in 1921. In any event, the most utopian extremists are suppressed by whatever more practical revolutionaries are in power. Civil war may occur at any stage of the process (in England, after the moderate revolution; in Russia, after the extremists took power). International conflict is likely, thanks to the fears which the ideas and events of the revolution stir up, but the severe instances (France, Germany) are associated with the post-revolutionary dictatorships.

Revolutions of the type considered here may be regarded as a characteristic phenomenon of a certain historical epoch. In every case they represent a transition from a tradition-bound, monarchical political structure—authoritarian in its psychology, but not particularly efficient or centralized—to a rational and centralized state. Revolution seems to be closely associated with the basic transition from an essentially agrarian society to a commercialized or industrial society. Every major Western country has experienced this revolutionary transformation in whole or in part. The liberal states are those with the revolutionary experience farthest back in their histories, while the belated revolutions in central and eastern Europe, occurring under the new conditions of actual or incipient industrialism, have given us the modern phenomenon of totalitarianism.

At its beginning in 1911, when the monarchy collapsed in the face of a military uprising organized by Sun Yat-sen's followers, the Chinese revolution was reasonably similar to its Western counterparts. Events in China then took a completely different turn: the imperial minister Yuan Shi-kai compromised with the revolutionaries, had himself elected President, and ruled as a military dictator until his death in 1916. Then the country fell into the chaos of contending provincial war-lords. So far, the revolution had not brought any substantial change in government or society, but had only succeeded in shattering such central authority as the country possessed. In terms of the progress of the revolution, China from 1911 to the 1920's was comparable to Russia between 1905 and 1917, while the shift of power from the center to the provinces was a distinctive, familiar, and (as it turned out) crucial Chinese development.

In the early 1920's the revolutionaries began to recover. Under Sun's leadership, the Nationalist Party—the Kuomintang—which he had founded in 1912, established itself as the regional authority in Canton and Kwangtung Province (at first shakily, but firmly from 1923 on). Thus the revolutionary movement scored its first real success in the role of a provincial war-lord, virtually immune from interference by Peking. It is difficult to classify this Kuomintang regime as moderate or extremist in the revolutionary scheme; perhaps it can be regarded as intermediate between the more moderate revolutionaries of 1911 and the more extreme tendency represented by the Communists.

During the Canton period of the Kuomintang, certain important developments took place. Close co-operation was established with Soviet Russia and the newly formed Chinese Communist Party; with Communist help the Kuomintang was reorganized along Leninist lines of party discipline and one-party government. At the same time, the military element exemplified by Chiang Kai-shek assumed increasing importance within the movement. Between 1926 and 1928, simultaneous with his victorious "northern expedition," which gave him possession of the central government, Chiang took over control of the Kuomintang. Upon Chiang's defeat of the Communists and the "Left Kuomintang" in 1927, the revolution may be regarded as passing from the phase of quasi-extremism to that of post-revolutionary dictatorship (albeit an inefficient one). Chinese national unity (with some regional exceptions) was thus re-established in 1928 by a movement that had passed the peak of its revolutionary elan.

Meanwhile the remnants of the Nationalists' extremist allies, the Communists, had in turn established themselves as a local war-lord authority, first in the mountains of southeastern Kiangsi Province, and then (after the "Long March" of 1934–1935) in northern Shensi. Like the Kuomintang, the regional Communist authority was in the first instance a military organization, though unlike their rivals the Communists undertook a moderate program of land reform to strengthen their social base among the peasantry. The party lost its old urban base altogether, and became in essence a peasant-based revolutionary movement led by members of the educated class. In Russian terms, the Chinese Communists after the early 1930's were much more comparable to the peasant-oriented Populists of the late nineteenth century than to the Marxists. This basic transformation of the Communist movement was the work of Mao Tse-tung, who thereby made himself the undisputed leader of the movement in China.

. . .

The differences between the situations in which the Russian and the Chinese Communists came to power are immense. The Russians did so near the beginning of the revolutionary process; the Chinese, at the end. The Russian Communists underwent a profound evolution in the course of their first two decades of power, while the Chinese have not shown any fundamental change at all since 1949, either in personnel or in policies or in methods. To parallel the Russians, the Chinese Communists would have had to seize power in 1927–1928, when the party was hotheaded and the country was in a true revolutionary situation. The inference is that no important internal changes are to be expected in the post-revolutionary dictatorship of Chinese communism.

Thanks to their twenty years of regional power, the Chinese Communist leaders who set up the People's Republic in 1949 were not fresh, utopian revolutionaries like their Russian counterparts, but seasoned politicians. The development of a dogmatic totalitarian regime did not lie before them, but had already been accomplished. There was no wrestling with the problems of an old governmental administration newly seized; the existing Communist apparatus was simply imposed upon the country as a whole.

Also different from the Russian experience was the fact that the Chinese Communist regime did not develop in isolation. It was a branch of the international Communist movement already established in Russia. This does not mean that every step in the development of Chinese communism was dictated by Moscow, whatever the official Communist pretense may be. It seems clear that Mao's transformation of the Chinese Communist movement after 1928—from a proletarian class struggle to an essential non-class, rural-based, military revolution—came about in opposition to Soviet expectations. Nevertheless, the Chinese Communists were convinced and dedicated Marxist-Leninists who never ceased to believe in their own orthodoxy and to respect the Soviet example. The fact that Soviet ideology and the Soviet allegiance were self-imposed does not mean that they were any less firmly planted in the Chinese Communist movement.

During the period of regional rural power from 1928 to 1949, the Chinese Communist movement underwent a decisive evolution, as indicated already, it was tempered and steeled; out of utopian protest, stable post-revolutionary dictatorship was forged. Programs like land reform and the class struggle against the landlords, for example, which were matters of revolutionary zeal in the Kiangsi Soviet Republic in the early 1930's, became political devices, to be carefully curtailed or ruthlessly pressed as the situation of the moment dictated. The result was the impression which prevailed in the 1940's that the movement was primarily one of "agrarian reform." The outside world failed to understand how the Chinese Communists could handle the peasants so judiciously, and at the same time effectively apply the Leninist-Stalinist precepts of party organization, dispense with the working class, and retain their Marxist-Leninist philosophy, however irrational this might seem under Chinese conditions.

The psychological change in the Chinese Communists from zealots to tacticians seems closely analogous to the evolution that the Russians underwent between the Communist victory in 1917 and Stalin's attainment of complete personal power in 1929. For both countries this was the phase in which Lenin's principles of a centralized, disciplined, completely unified party and unqualified enforcement of its authority and doctrine were fully realized.

The Stalinizing of the Chinese Communist Party was closely associated with the rise of Mao. To what extent Mao was deliberately imitating Stalin, or to what degree the change was inherent in a party of the Leninist type, is not clear, but the actual development of the Chinese Communist Party ran closely parallel to the Russian, with comparatively little time lag. Mao's rise to the headship of the party and his consolidation of personal control over it between 1928 and 1937 may be compared to Stalin's career in the 1920's. Each rose on the basis of his control over the most effective Communist organization in the particular circumstances—Stalin as boss of the Communist Party apparatus, and Mao as the political leader of the Communists' peasant army. Like Stalin, Mao had to overcome Left and Right opposition: he defeated the leftist, proletarian line of Li Li-san and Wang Ming in the period 1931–1934, and in 1937 he destroyed the right-wing deviation of Chang Kuo-tao, who inclined to non-revolutionary co-operation with the Kuomintang.

With his organizational power secure, Mao then proceeded, as Stalin had done, to impose intense doctrinal discipline on the party, mobilize intellectual work in the direct service of the party, eliminate all expression of individual opinion, and establish unquestionable ideological justification for the party's acts. This appears to be the significance of the "thought-reform" movement of 1942–1944, comparable to and probably modeled on Stalin's imposition of such controls after 1929. As with Stalin, Mao's Marxism-Leninism became a dogmatic reference point for the ideological justification of whatever acts or policies the party found expedient.

In his tactics Mao differed sharply from Stalin. None of his party opponents were physically liquidated; most were allowed to retain some minor post in the movement, though there could be no question of expressing dissenting opinions in public. Subsequently the Chinese Communist Party distinguished itself by its ability to recruit allies of all sorts, ranging from American-educated intellectuals to provincial war-lords, and to bring them under Communist discipline through various careful combinations of concessions and pressure. This might be termed the political analogue of guerrilla warfare—no frontal attack, but infiltration, attrition, and winning over as many of the enemy as possible. The tactical difference between Stalin and Mao probably stems from a number of factors—a vast personality difference, the difficult circumstances which the Chinese Communist movement faced at this stage, and the fact that the Chinese Communists had not yet begun to experience the degeneration into irrationality which is perhaps a natural development in Communist regimes after they come to power. . . .

Together with its organizational and doctrinal development in the 1930's and 1940's, Chinese communism acquired a new social character—organization plus peasants—which brought it into line with the actual circumstances of the rebellious but underdeveloped East. Whereas the workers were an important factor in the Bolshevik victory in Russia in 1917, by no stretch of the imagination can Communist China be regarded as the product of a proletarian revolution. Though the Communists did make headway among the relatively small Chinese urban working class in the 1920's, they lost practically all contact with the cities after Mao's shift to the hinterland. Only two of the forty-four members of the Communist Central Committee of 1945 are known to have proletarian backgrounds. Urban workers did not figure in Chinese communism until the movement was ready to assume rule over the entire mainland in 1948–1949, and then only as a subject group to be mobilized and manipulated. Chinese Communist claims that the party represents working-class leadership of the revolution are a complete sham, sustained in part by classifying rural wage-earners as "proletarians" and by appealing to the allegedly proletarian spirit of the party.

Mao has not only carried out a proletarian revolution without a proletariat; he has waged a class struggle in large part without a struggle of the classes. Apart from inciting the peasants against anyone defined as a landlord—when it was tactically expedient to do so—Chinese communism has not fought anything resembling a class war. It has become instead a movement to discipline and regenerate the nation as a whole. The Chinese Communists have, if anything, underplayed the class factor that was actually involved in their struggle with the Kuomintang; they profess to lead "the people" against "the lackeys of imperialism," whose status is defined not by their social standing but by their political attitude toward the Communist regime. The "national bourgeoisie"—businessmen who accept Communist rule—has been protected and absorbed into the Communist machine rather than combatted as an enemy class. For Chinese communism, class as such has had no real meaning at all; the key test is a mental one—can an individual or group be "remolded" to function within the disciplined totalitarian regime that the Communists have created?

To assert that Communist China has not undergone the Marxist class struggle may seem nonsense at first. The terms must be carefully understood, however, without prejudgment along the lines of the Communists' own official image of themselves. Violence and terror have certainly occurred in China on a wide scale, and it is undeniable that the regime demands an unquestioning profession of faith in the principles of Marxism. But terror does not necessarily mean class struggle, and the profession of a dogma may conceal very different practical attitudes. Detached study of Soviet history reveals that one of the distinctive features of communism is its ideological pretenses—the elaborate development of a rigorously enforced, doctrinal justification of an essentially practical-minded dictatorship. Marxism gives the present-day Communist movement its foci of allegiance and enmity, but very little else. The real nature of the Communist movement must be understood on quite another basis than Marxism and the class struggle. This is particularly true of China.

The equation of revolution and the class struggle is a Communist illusion. It is confuted by an independent appraisal of the Communist revolutions themselves. In Russia, to be sure, the Marxian class struggle was present to a certain degree in the workers' support for the Bolsheviks and the persecution of the upper classes, but class conflict neither defined the basic nature of the movement nor explained its development. The Communist experience demands a thorough review of the general theory of revolution. Revolutions appear to be primarily clashes not between classes, but between opposing systems of social organization and ethics and the loyalties which these or their symbols evoke.

What remains "Communistic" in Chinese communism? A great deal, if one understands the essence of the movement to be not the application of a Marxist program, but the Leninist party, unquestioning devotion to the party and its shibboleths, and an urge to triumph in their name. The Chinese comrades are devout communicants of the Communist faith. Together with this, they observe in the highest degree the principles of the Leninist party and the totalitarian control that these principles both demand and effectuate.

The Chinese Communists differ fundamentally from the Russian Communists in having traversed most of the Russians' post-revolutionary political development before they came to power on a national scale. Their problem was only to extend their stable, doctrinally disciplined, one-party totalitarian rule to the nation at large. For the country as a whole, of course, 1948–1949 did represent a revolutionary situation, and revolutionary enthusiasm and antipathy to the Kuomintang undoubtedly drew large numbers of sympathizers into the Communist camp. These latter-day converts, however, did not give the Communist movement its character, and among the earliest measures of the Communist Party after it assumed central authority were the disciplining and re-education of revolutionary enthusiasts into reliable servants of the post-revolutionary dictatorship. If, for the purpose of comparison, we take 1949 as the equivalent of 1917 in Russia, the Chinese were politically highly precocious, although the economic and cultural development of their country was far behind that of Russia. This is the basic pattern of Chinese communism in relation to Russia at comparable times: politically more advanced, economically more backward.

The Chinese Communists in 1949 had a party machine in which unity, discipline, and monolithic communications were about as firmly established as in Soviet Russia under Stalin. Their mass ideological controls, indoctrination methods, and totalitarian psychology went beyond anything the Russians have ever attained. Their administrative control of the country was rather more effective than anything the Russian Communists enjoyed until 1921. While the Korean War of 1950–1953 was a severe effort for the new Communist regime, it did not involve any such internal chaos or threat to Communist rule as did the Russian Civil War of 1918–1920. The agrarian situation in China of 1949 resembled Russia in 1917, when a sweeping land redistribution was in progress (though in China it was much less spontaneous and more centrally administered than in Russia). However, in the realm of industrial and technical development China was greatly inferior to revolutionary Russia.

Bibliography

CHINA

Barnett, A. D., *China on the Eve of Communist Takeover*. New York: Frederick A. Praeger, Inc., 1963.

Brandt, C., J. K. Fairbank, and B. Schwartz, *A Documentary History of Chinese Communism*. Cambridge, Mass.: Harvard University Press, 1952.

Fitzgerald, C. P., *The Birth of Communist China*. Baltimore: Penguin Books, Inc., 1965.

Isaacs, H. R., *The Tragedy of the Chinese Revolution* (3rd ed.). Stanford, Calif.: Stanford University Press, 1961.

Kan-chih, Ho, *A History of the Modern Chinese Revolution*. Peiping: Foreign Languages Press, 1956. An official version of the revolution.

Johnson, C. A., *Peasant Nationalism and Communist Power*. Stanford, Calif.: Stanford University Press, 1962.

Schwartz, B., *Chinese Communism and the Rise of Mao*. Cambridge, Mass.: Harvard University Press, 1951.

Shao-chuan, L., and N. D. Palmer, *Sun Yat-sen and Communism*. New York: Frederick A. Praeger, Inc., 1961.

Snow, E., *Red Star Over China* (3rd ed.). New York: Random House, 1944.

Tse-tung, C., *The May Fourth Movement: Intellectual Revolution in Modern China*. Cambridge, Mass.: Harvard University Press, 1960.

EASTERN EUROPE

Bishop, R., and E. S. Crayfield, *Russia Astride the Balkans*. New York: Robert M. McBride Co., Inc., 1948.

Burks, R. V., "Eastern Europe," in *Communism and Revolution: The Strategic Uses of Violence*, eds. C. E. Black and T. P. Thornton. Princeton, N.J.: Princeton University Press, 1964.

Ducháček, I., *The Strategy of Communist Infiltration: The Case of Czechoslovakia*. New Haven: Yale Institute of International Studies, 1949.

Helmreich, E. C., ed., *Hungary*. New York: Published for the Mid-European

Studies Center of the Free Europe Committee by Frederick A. Praeger, Inc., 1957.

Korbel, J., *The Communist Subversion of Czechoslovakia: 1938–1948*. Princeton, N.J.: Princeton University Press, 1959.

Nettl, J. P., *The Eastern Zone and Soviet Policy in Germany: 1945–1950*. London: Oxford University Press, 1951.

Ripka, H., *Czechoslovakia Enslaved: The Story of the Communist Coup d'Etat*. New York: The Macmillan Company, 1950.

Rothschild, J., *The Communist Party of Bulgaria: Origins and Development, 1883–1936*. New York: Columbia University Press, 1959.

Seton-Watson, H., *The East European Revolution*. New York: Frederick A. Praeger, Inc., 1951.

Skendi, S., ed., *Albania*. New York: Published for the Mid-European Studies Center of the Free Europe Committee by Frederick A. Praeger, Inc., 1957.

Zinner, P. E., *Communist Strategy and Tactics in Czechoslovakia: 1918–48*. New York: Frederick A. Praeger, Inc., 1963.

U.S.S.R.

Bunyan, J., and H. H. Fisher, eds., *The Bolshevik Revolution: 1917–1918*. Stanford, Calif.: Stanford University Press, 1934.

Carmichael, J., *A Short History of the Russian Revolution*. New York: Basic Books, Inc., 1965.

Carr, E. H., *The Bolshevik Revolution: 1917–1923*. 3 vols. New York: The Macmillan Company, 1951–53.

Chamberlin, W. H., *The Russian Revolution: 1917–1921*. 2 vols. New York: The Macmillan Company, 1935.

Haimson, L. H., *The Russian Marxists and the Origins of Bolshevism*. Cambridge, Mass.: Harvard University Press, 1955.

Kennan, G. F., *Russia Leaves the War*. Princeton, N.J.: Princeton University Press, 1956.

Pipes, R., *The Formation of the Soviet Union: Communism and Nationalism, 1917–1923* (2nd ed.). Cambridge, Mass.: Harvard University Press, 1964.

Reed, J., *Ten Days That Shook the World*. New York: Random House, 1935.

Schapiro, L., *The Origin of the Communist Autocracy*. Cambridge, Mass.: Harvard University Press, 1956.

Sukhanov, N., *The Russian Revolution*. 2 vols. New York: Oxford University Press, Inc., 1955.

Trotsky, L., *History of the Russian Revolution*. 3 vols. New York: Simon and Schuster, Inc., 1932.

Wilson, E., *To the Finland Station*. New York: Doubleday & Company, Inc., 1940.

Wolfe, B., *Three Who Made A Revolution*. New York: The Dial Press, Inc., 1948.

Chapter Three

Ideological Differentiation in the Communist World

All communist elites profess adherence to Marxism-Leninism, a *Weltanschauung* that postulates an integral relationship between ideology and politics, in which the laws governing politics can be perceived when politics is viewed in terms of ideology. They hold that this unity of theory and action provides them with unique instruments "not only to chart a correct path through the labyrinth of social contradictions, but to predict the course events will take, the direction of historical progress and the next stages of social advance."[1] From Lenin's dictum, "Without a revolutionary theory there can be no revolutionary movement" to Mao's call, "shoot the arrow at the target" because "Marxist-Leninist theory bears the same relation to the Chinese revolution as the arrow to the target,"[2] communist leaders have stressed the importance of mastering theory as a precondition for correct prognosis and policy formulation. For them theory is a guide to action.

Yet the growing dissonances within the communist world indicate that when confronting concrete and specific problems the practitioners of Marxism-Leninism often disagree among themselves in their interpretations of political phenomena and desired courses of policy. This suggests that within the Marxist-Leninist conceptual framework there is a considerable gray area, within which subjective evaluations may give rise to

---

[1] O. W. Kuusinen, ed., *Fundamentals of Marxism-Leninism* (Moscow: Foreign Language Publishing House, 1960), p. 17.

[2] Mao Tse-tung, *Rectify the Party's Style in Work* (Peking: Foreign Languages Press, 1955), p. 14.

58

conflicting interpretations and political discord (Reading 12). Voluntarism, which may be defined as "the attribution of primary and decisive importance to the human will as the determinant of social change rather than to objective scientific laws,"[3] thus plays a vital role in the application of the deterministic Marxian model.

As long as the Soviet Union was the only communist country, Moscow remained the undisputed center of international communist authority. Ideological orthodoxy and political direction emanated from the Soviet Communist Party, which operated on the assumption that the defense of the beleaguered and isolated socialist U.S.S.R. was the paramount duty of all communists and was synonymous with the best interests of international communism. Foreign Communist Parties, having no governmental base of their own, acceded to Moscow's *diktat,* often at the sacrifice of their own prospects for attaining power. The ideological antecedents for this relationship evolved out of Stalin's concept, "socialism in one country," which was enunciated in the mid-1920's at the time of the succession struggle with Trotsky for control of the Communist Party of the Soviet Union (CPSU).

At the end of World War II, the Soviet Union was no longer the solitary communist country. A belt of communist states was established in Eastern Europe, as Moscow-trained indigenous communists were installed by the Red Army. Only in Yugoslavia did the Communist Party come to power on its own. Stalin's insistence on unquestioning obeisance to Moscow's political leadership brought him into conflict with the Yugoslavs who, in effect, demanded the right to run their own system. To the surprise of Stalin, who, according to Khrushchev, had irately declared, "I will shake my little finger—and there will be no more Tito. He will fall," excommunication of the heretic did not result either in his overthrow or in the exorcism of the Titoist virus. Rather, it gave rise to "Titoism," which may be described as a fusion of nationalism and communism into an ideology and a movement having a variety of forms and differentiated internal policies, and connoting a measure of domestic autonomy not acceptable to Moscow. But Stalin learned from his searing experience with Tito and avoided direct interference in Chinese domestic politics when Mao came to power in October 1949, even though some Chinese communist policies departed from the Soviet model. For example, Mao called for a prolonged period of conditional domestic acceptance of the bourgeoisie. Writing in 1949, he stated that the "people's democratic dictatorship" in China was based on the alliance of four classes: the working class (proletariat), the peasantry, the urban petty *bourgeoisie,* and the national *bourgeoisie.* Mao said that, under the leadership of the Chinese Communist Party (CCP), this coalition of classes must be maintained because the *bourgeoisie* was

---

[3] R. N. Carew Hunt, *A Guide to Communist Jargon* (New York: The Macmillan Company, 1957), pp. 161–62.

necessary to China's development at this stage of its existence. Mao also departed from the Soviet model in that he revealed a more sanguine attitude toward the problem of reshaping—through indoctrination, education, and ideological remolding—the outlook and behavior of the *bourgeoisie*. And even earlier, Mao had tacitly rejected Soviet ideological orthodoxy as inappropriate to the Chinese situation: In the 1930's, he developed unaided a revolutionary movement based on the peasantry and a strategy of guerrilla warfare that were to give him stature as a military theorist.

The first portents of ideological schism within international communism, however, emerged out of the Soviet-Yugoslav break of 1948. What had started as political and economic differences later developed into a cleavage over ideology, as the Yugoslavs realized that they had to reevaluate their assumptions concerning the Soviet Union, the capitalist world, and the problems of building socialism (Reading 16). Specifically, the Yugoslavs argued that "contemporary socialism is not, and cannot be, pure and homogeneous. . . . Socialist development does not follow a straight line."

> Men build socialism consciously, but in various countries they do so under different conditions: they come into conflict with internal contradictions of varying acuteness, they operate under different influences of spontaneity and of various social and material factors; and, in solving concrete problems, they arrive at different subjective decisions.
>
> The uneven development of socialism and the wide diversity of its paths and forms produce a number of internal contradictions in that development, but at the same time they provide a powerful incentive to its further advance, and to the efforts to achieve increasingly progressive and freer forms of socialist relations. Any attempt at fettering these laws of socialist development cannot but lead to reactionary results.[4]

The Yugoslavs stressed the possibility of a peaceful transition to socialism and denied the inevitability of war between capitalism and socialism, tenets Khrushchev was later to incorporate into the body of Marxist-Leninist ideology.

A major area of difference between Yugoslav and Soviet theoreticians centers on the role of the state and its rate of "withering away." The Yugoslavs argue that a socialist state is one that is withering away. According to Fred Warner Neal, the Yugoslavs see "The tendency of the state, once reconstituted as the dictatorship of the proletariat, not to wither away" as a major contradiction in the socialist process. "This tendency," he continues, "is held to be nurtured by remnants of capitalist elements, and unless it is promptly overcome, the dictatorship of the proletariat, instead of moving toward socialism, degenerates into state capitalism."[5]

---

[4] *The Programme of the League of Yugoslav Communists* (Belgrade: Jugoslavija, 1958), p. 33.

[5] Fred Warner Neal, "Yugoslav Communist Theory," *The American Slavic and East European Review*, XIX, No. 1 (February, 1960), 52.

Failure to initiate the withering-away process results in bureaucratism, which feeds "the tendency to transform the state into an all-embracing force, into a force above society,"[6] and undermines the direct influence of the working people on the policy of state leadership. Bureaucratism, say the Yugoslavs, deforms socialist development and intensifies internal contradictions; it can be forestalled only by ensuring that *control, not just ownership,* of the means of production is turned over to working-class management, i.e., to the Workers' Councils. They mince no words in attacking Soviet bureaucratism and insistence on an ideological monopoly which, they note, is the source of dogmatism.

The Yugoslavs took exception to Stalin's doctrinal formulations of the need to strengthen the state machinery in the period of the building of socialism, maintaining that the state, "or rather its administrative machinery and managerial devices, can in no case be the principal instrument of socialist construction and the solution of the internal contradictions of socialist development." They claim to have developed a more genuinely democratic and socialist society than the Soviets by promoting mass participation in the actual operation and management of the socialized industrial sector of society through the establishment of Workers' Councils. In agriculture, according to Professor Neal:

> [They have] rejected the Leninist doctrine that socialism in the villages was necessary for socialism in the country. Instead, Kardelj devised the concept of what might be called "socialism by osmosis." That is, instead of proceeding with socialism in the villages [i.e., collectivization], the Yugoslavs would let the peasants alone—limiting capitalist influences by imposing a limit on land holdings—and proceed with developing socialism elsewhere through industrialization.[7]

Finally, the Yugoslav leadership, in a pointed attack on Soviet practice, repudiated:

> . . . all pragmatic distortions of Marxist viewpoints on the role of science and art in society and any transformation of science and art into an instrument of short-term political interests . . . [and opposed] "theories" that, in the name of abstract concepts of freedom, actually abolish true freedom of scientific and artistic creation, and in practice subordinate them to reactionary political tendencies.

They also asserted that "The ideological role of the League of Communists should not be the role of a dogmatic arbiter in respect of scientific and artistic trends, schools, and styles."[8] To the Yugoslavs, Soviet pretensions to ideological leadership have foundered on the unappealing, stifling, bureaucratic behavior of the Communist Party of the Soviet Union, which has been overly rigid in its interpretation of doctrine and excessively

6 *The Programme,* p. 125.
7 Neal, *op. cit.,* p. 56.
8 *The Programme,* p. 262.

preoccupied with preserving and extending the monopoly position of the Party.

Chinese criticisms constitute more of a challenge, politically. Mao openly staked his claim to ideological leadership of the international communist movement after the post-1957 deterioration of relations with Moscow. In retrospect it is possible to perceive the roots of ideological schism in Mao's writings of the late 1930's, but it took the conflicting Sino-Soviet approaches to the all-important political problems of how to deal with the West, the underdeveloped countries, and the building of communism to bring them to the surface.

In his essay *On Contradiction,* generally assumed to have been written in 1937, Mao upheld the accepted Marxian law of the unity of opposites as a universal truth: All things are a temporary unity of contradictory aspects; change occurs when, in consequence of the struggle between the two contradictory aspects, one is finally vanquished and transformed, and a new unity is formed. He then elaborated on the theme: There are distinctions "in the character of contradictions"—that is, contradictions may be "antagonistic" or "non-antagonistic." In 1957, applying his interpretation of contradictions to contemporary conditions, he described Chinese society as a mixture of "non-antagonistic contradictions" among the working people and "antagonistic contradictions" between the working people and their class enemies (Reading 13). He asserted that contradictions existed even between the rulers and the ruled in socialist societies, thus contravening Moscow's position that contradictions are found only in capitalist societies. Further, Mao formulated rules on "how to handle correctly contradictions among the people." Asked to comment on Mao's doctrinal innovation in an interview in June 1957, Khrushchev denied that contradictions existed between the Party and the working people in the Soviet Union, but when the text of the interview was reprinted in *Pravda,* both the question and the comment were absent.

In the Chinese contention that contradictions can arise under socialism between the Party and the people lies not only the issue of "correct" interpretation of Marxism-Leninism, but the delineating and handling of ferment, dissatisfaction, and unrest within communist societies. Mao cautions: "Under ordinary circumstances, contradictions among the people are not antagonistic. But if they are not dealt with properly, or if we relax vigilance and lower our guard, antagonism may arise." He later took the Soviet leadership to task for the brutal suppression in Hungary in November 1956, implying that it could have been avoided by the proper application of periodic rectification campaigns.

With the creation of the "people's communes" in 1958, Mao declared that the "transition to communism" could be telescoped via an "uninterrupted revolution" and need not depend on the *a priori* attainment of material abundance. Moscow promptly denounced Peking for pursuing a "reckless" economic policy and ignoring "the objective laws of socialism." Though Peking has mitigated some of the militancy and urgency of the "great leap forward," it persists in the view that the people's commune is the archetypal institution for communist society.

The Chinese have also ridiculed the Soviet thesis, propounded by Khrushchev at the Twenty-second Party Congress and incorporated into the new Party Program (Reading 14), that the concept of the party of the proletariat was now replaced by that of the "party of the people." According to the Chinese, "There is no such thing as a non-class or supra-class political party and there never has been, nor is there such a thing as a 'party of the entire people' that does not represent the interests of a particular class" (Reading 15). To Peking, Moscow has strayed from the path of Marxism-Leninism and has become a purveyor of revisionism.

According to the resolution adopted at the Conference of Communist Parties in Moscow in November 1957, "revisionism is the main danger facing the international Communist movement." But what is revisionism? Evidently, it is the epithet used by a communist to describe the policies of another communist, when he feels that they go beyond the limits of what he is willing to accept as legitimate or creative Marxism. Stalin accused Tito of being a revisionist. Tito, for his part, accused the Soviet leaders of being dogmatists (the obverse term). Mao, who considers himself a creative and genuine Marxist, tars Brezhnev with revisionism and so on and on.

Revisionism in Eastern Europe, however, was politically and sociologically a different phenomenon: It was a revolt by Party intellectuals against the oppressive hand of Soviet and national "Stalinist" rule which led to a critical reevaluation of the assumptions underlying communist doctrine (Reading 17). The peoples of Eastern Europe may very well regard Marxism-Leninism as an alien imposition. That it was brought by the Russians, whom they generally disliked and viewed as representatives of an inferior culture, and that it was disseminated by Moscow-tied proxies, attached to Marxism-Leninism the stigma of foreign imperialism, notwithstanding the nationalist refrain heard from the local communists. Never has there been any ideological Messianism about Eastern European communism, which has been primarily an instrument for wielding power behind the protective shield of Moscow. During the Stalin period, the Soviet variant of the Marxist-Leninist litany was a prerequisite for survival. More recently, Moscow has tolerated Eastern European variations on the Soviet theme, partially because of its acceptance of the doctrine that there are "many roads to socialism" and partially because of its desire to retain the support of the Eastern European Communist Parties *vis-à-vis* Peking. Eastern Europe's Marxism-Leninism is more than anything else a consequence of the proximity of the Soviet Union, with all that this entails politically and economically.

Our focus in this essay has been on the distinctive ways in which Marxism-Leninism has come to be interpreted by different communist elites. In general, communist ideology may be regarded as a systematic body of goals, ideas, and assumptions shared by the elites and affecting their attitudes and behavior. It helps to shape the mode of their response to social, economic, and political phenomena; it conditions their perception of reality, and provides the terminology and the methodological tools for a "scientific" interpretation of history and society's development; and it establishes the categories for dialectically viewing, assessing, and rationalizing political phenomena.

From this definition we see that ideology may serve a number of functions, e.g., it is a way of viewing reality and ordering data (Readings 8 and 9), of rationalizing power and policies (Reading 10), and of setting goals (Reading 11). In relations between Communist Parties, ideology also serves as a vehicle for what Donald S. Zagoria has termed the system of "esoteric communication" within which disputes are debated. This leaves unanswered the general question: How does ideology guide, affect, and circumscribe the range and choice of alternatives being weighed for the solution of concrete domestic problems?

There is no way of knowing the degree to which ideology affects decision making, but we should keep in mind several points. First, since communist leaders say they are Marxist-Leninists, it would be foolish to discount or overlook the importance that their commitment has in conditioning their approach to problems and their choice of policy alternatives. Second, because each elite clearly interprets ideology in the light of its own unique historical experience and because in a deeper sense the conditioning role that ideology plays in influencing behavior depends very much on the personality of individual leaders, it is reasonable to assume that it is only one of many determinants interacting to shape the policies and behavior of an elite. Third, since doctrine is practiced within a confined and controlled milieu, the leadership can act on orthodoxy as it interprets it at any given time. Fourth, ideology is linked inextricably with the monopoly role of the Communist Party: Ideology postulates the historical and leading role of the Party, and the Party sanctifies ideology.

O. W. Kuusinen

8 THE MARXIST-LENINIST WORLD OUTLOOK

O. W. Kuusinen, chief editor, *Fundamentals of Marxism-Leninism* (Moscow: Foreign Languages Publishing House, 1960), excerpted from pp. 16–21.

In order to present an up-to-date and popular interpretation of the essentials of Soviet doctrine, the Central Committee of the Communist Party of the Soviet Union authorized the publication of this analysis of contemporary Marxism-Leninism. Khrushchev was trying to recodify a system of thought that was in confusion in the wake of "de-Stalinization."

Fundamentals of Marxism-Leninism *represents a major effort to relate the ideology to the key concerns of the Soviet leadership. It was also by way of preparation for a new Party Program, which was adopted at the Twenty-second Party Congress in October 1961; it was an answer to the Yugoslav Party Program of 1958, a guideline and warning to the Chinese, and an attempt to reassert Soviet ideological primacy after a long period in which Stalin had downgraded and confused ideology.*

The volume was compiled and edited by leading Soviet theoreticians and Party officials, under the chief editorship of O. W. Kuusinen, a respected old Bolshevik of Finnish birth who died in 1964.

Marxism-Leninism has great merits that distinguish it from all other philosophical systems.

It does not recognise the existence of any supernatural forces or creators. It rests squarely on reality, on the real world in which we live. It liberates mankind, once and for all, from superstition and age-old spiritual bondage. It encourages independent, free and consistent thought.

Marxism-Leninism regards the world such as it actually is, without adding an invented hell or paradise. It proceeds from the fact that all nature, including man himself, consists of matter with its different properties.

And nature, as well as all its individual phenomena, is in constant process of development. The laws of that development have not been ordained by God and do not depend on man's will. They are intrinsic in nature itself and are fully knowable. There are no inherently unknowable things in the world; there are only things which are still unknown, but which will become known through science and practice.

The Marxist-Leninist world outlook stems from science itself and *trusts* science, as long as science is not divorced from reality and practice. It itself develops and becomes richer with the development of science.

Marxism-Leninism teaches that not only the development of nature, but the *development of human society* too, takes place in accordance with objective laws that are independent of man's will.

By revealing the basic laws of social development, Marxism raised history to the level of a genuine science capable of explaining the nature of every social system and the development of society from one social system to another. That was a tremendous victory for scientific thought. . . .

By revealing the laws governing the operation and development of the forces of nature and society, genuine science can always foresee the new. The Marxist science of the laws of social development enables us not only to chart a correct path through the labyrinth of social contradictions, but to predict the course events will take, the direction of historical progress and the next stages of social advance.

Thus, Marxism-Leninism gives us an instrument with which to look into the future and see the outlines of impending historical changes. This "time telescope" has revealed to us the magnificent future of humanity freed from the yoke of capitalism, from the last exploiting system. But when progressive science invites bourgeois scientists (who claim that "nothing can be predicted") to apply the Marxist "time telescope," they simply shut their eyes—they are afraid to look into the future.

But Marxists have no fear of the future. They represent the class to which the future belongs and have no use for illusions, which are shattered the moment they come into contact with the facts, with science.

Headed by Lenin, the Russian Marxists foresaw the socialist revolution in Russia as a task which history had matured. Accordingly, they rallied the working class for decisive struggle against the exploiting system, organised the storming of its bastions and achieved complete victory.

The Marxists-Leninists of the Soviet Union foresaw the possibility of building socialism in their vast country, rallied the working people for the accomplishment of that great task and led them to the victory of socialism.

The Marxists-Leninists of the Soviet Union and other countries foresaw the probability of a second world war being unleashed by fascist Germany. They warned all the nations and predicted Germany's defeat. During the Second World War, it was chiefly the heroic efforts of the Soviet people and its glorious army that routed the forces of the German aggressor and his allies. . . .

Crucial developments in the first half of the century thus provide irrefutable proof that the Communists, armed with the Marxist theory, on the whole, correctly predicted the general course of history. The truth of the Marxist-Leninist conception of history has been fully borne out in practice.

The Marxist-Leninist theory is not a dogma but *a guide to action*. But one has to learn to apply it correctly.

It illumines the path ahead. Without Marxism-Leninism, even progressively-minded people have to grope in the dark, without a genuine and profound understanding of the events taking place around them.

Marxist-Leninist theory provides a scientific basis for revolutionary *policy*. He who bases his policy on subjective desires remains either a futile dreamer or risks being thrust into the background by history. For history does not conform to man's wishes if these are not in accordance with the laws of history. . . .

The Marxist theory, which has grown out of the revolutionary experience and revolutionary thought of all nations, corresponds to the historical mission of the working class as the vanguard and leader of the great movement for emancipation of all the oppressed and exploited. In the proletariat the Marxist world outlook has found its material weapon, just as the proletariat has found in Marxism its spiritual weapon. . . .

The Marxist-Leninist world outlook is a true compass in every sphere of *scientific endeavour,* not only in the social but also in the natural sciences. For is it not true that a correct understanding of the world and its general laws, interrelations and processes greatly helps the natural scientist in his creative research? That understanding is provided by Marxism-Leninism.

It is no accident that their research experiences are now leading many eminent scientists either fully to accept Marxism, or tacitly to adopt some of its elements, in order to gain a more profound knowledge of the secrets of nature and be in a better position to serve the interests of humanity.

The Marxist-Leninist outlook opens up splendid prospects to workers in the *arts and literature*. It directs their creative efforts towards a deeper and richer reflection of reality through artistic media. Without the beneficial influence of a clear, progressive world outlook, the work of contemporary writers and artists is at the best anaemic. In our day, Marxism-Leninism offers the artist a full and clear-cut conception of the world.

Whereas bourgeois literature is more and more succumbing to moods of hopelessness and unrelieved pessimism, the work of progressive writers and poets is imbued with a life-asserting optimism. Their artistic creation is inspired by faith in a brighter future and calls for the building of that future.

Whereas Western bourgeois ideology is caught in a desperate crisis of disbelief in man and the future of civilisation, the Marxist-Leninist world outlook inspires a desire to work for noble social ideals.

Thorough mastery of Marxism-Leninism gives one a profound conviction not only of the correctness of the workers' cause, but of the historical inevitability of the coming triumph of socialism throughout the world. Marxism-Leninism is a source of strength, even to the weak; a source of steadfast political principle. It instils the unshakable ideological conviction that enables one to withstand all trials and ordeals.

V. I. Lenin

9 THREE SOURCES AND THREE COMPONENT PARTS OF MARXISM

V. I. Lenin, *Marx-Engels-Marxism,* 6th English ed. (Moscow: Foreign Languages Publishing House, n.d.), excerpted from pp. 80–85.

V. I. Lenin (1870–1924) was the founder of the Soviet state. As the leader of the Bolshevik Party, he engineered the overthrow of the Provisional Government of Russia on November 7, 1917 and led the new communist state until his death in 1924.

During the long years of exile and underground political activity, Lenin wrote voluminously on the essence and significance of Marxism, as well as on topics relating more directly to the struggle for power. In this essay, written in 1913, Lenin set forth the key elements of Marxism which are especially influential in shaping a Marxist's perception of the world.

The Marxian doctrine is omnipotent because it is true. It is complete and harmonious, and provides men with an integral world conception which is irreconcilable with any form of superstition, reaction, or defence of bourgeois oppression. It is the legitimate successor to the best that was created by mankind in the nineteenth century in the shape of German philosophy, English political economy and French socialism.

On these three sources of Marxism and on its three components parts, we shall briefly dwell.

The philosophy of Marxism is *materialism*. Throughout the modern history of Europe, and especially at the end of the eighteenth century in France, which was the scene of a decisive battle against every kind of medieval rubbish, against feudalism in institutions and ideas, materialism has proved to be the only philosophy that is consistent, true to all the teachings of natural science and hostile to superstition, cant and so forth.

The enemies of democracy therefore exerted all their efforts to "refute," undermine and defame materialism, and advocated various forms of philosophical idealism, which always, in one way or another, amounts to an advocacy or support of religion.

Marx and Engels defended philosophical materialism in the most determined manner and repeatedly explained the profound erroneousness of every deviation from this basis. . . .

But Marx did not stop at the materialism of the eighteenth century: he advanced philosophy. He enriched it with the acquisitions of German classical philosophy, especially of the Hegelian system, which in its turn led to the materialism of Feuerbach. The chief of these acquisitions is *dialectics,* i.e., the doctrine of development in its fullest and deepest form, free of one-sidedness, the doctrine of the relativity of human knowledge, which provides us with a reflection of eternally developing matter. The latest discoveries of natural science—radium, electrons, the transmutation of elements—have remarkably confirmed Marx's dialectical materialism, despite the teachings of the bourgeois philosophers with their "new" reversions to old and rotten idealism.

Deepening and developing philosophical materialism, Marx completed it, extended its knowledge of nature to the knowledge of *human society.* Marx's *historical materialism* was the greatest achievement of scientific thought. The chaos and arbitrariness that had previously reigned in the views on history and politics gave way to a strikingly integral and harmonious scientific theory, which shows how, in consequence of the growth of productive forces, out of one system of social life another and higher system develops—how capitalism, for instance, grows out of feudalism.

Just as man's knowledge reflects nature (i.e., developing matter) which exists independently of him, so man's *social knowledge* (i.e., his various views and doctrines—philosophical, religious, political and so forth) reflects the *economic system* of society. Political institutions are a superstructure on the economic foundation. We see, for example, that the various political forms of the modern European states serve to fortify the rule of the bourgeoisie over the proletariat.

Marx's philosophy is finished philosophical materialism, which has provided mankind, and especially the working class, with powerful instruments of knowledge.

Having recognized that the economic system is the foundation on which the political superstructure is erected, Marx devoted most attention to the study of this economic system. Marx's principal work, *Capital,* is devoted to a study of the economic system of modern, i.e., capitalist, society.

Classical political economy, before Marx, evolved in England, the most developed of the capitalist countries. Adam Smith and David Ricardo, by their investigations of the economic system, laid the foundations of the *labour theory of value.* Marx continued their work. He rigidly proved and consistently developed this theory. He showed that the value of every commodity is determined by the quantity of socially necessary labour time spent on its production.

Where the bourgeois economists saw a relation between things (the exchange of one commodity for another) Marx revealed a *relation between men*. The exchange of commodities expresses the tie between individual producers through the market. *Money* signifies that this tie is becoming closer and closer, inseparably binding the entire economic life of the individual producers into one whole. *Capital* signifies a further development of this tie: man's labour power becomes a commodity. The wage-worker sells his labour power to the owner of the land, factories and instruments of labour. The worker spends one part of the day covering the cost of maintaining himself and his family (wages), while the other part of the day the worker toils without remuneration, creating *surplus value* for the capitalist, the source of profit, the source of the wealth of the capitalist class.

The doctrine of surplus value is the cornerstone of Marx's economic theory.

Capital, created by the labour of the worker, presses on the worker by ruining the small masters and creating an army of unemployed. In industry the victory of large-scale production is at once apparent, but we observe the same phenomenon in agriculture as well; the superiority of large-scale capitalist agriculture increases, the employment of machinery grows, peasant economy falls into the noose of money-capital, it declines and sinks into ruin under the burden of its backward technique. In agriculture, the decline of small-scale production assumes different forms, but the decline itself is an indisputable fact.

By destroying small-scale production, capital leads to an increase in productivity of labour and to the creation of a monopoly position for the associations of big capitalists. Production itself becomes more and more social—hundreds of thousands and millions of workers become bound together in a systematic economic organism—but the product of the collective labour is appropriated by a handful of capitalists. The anarchy of production grows, as do crises, the furious chase after markets and the insecurity of existence of the mass of the population. . . .

When feudalism was overthrown, and *"free"* capitalist society appeared on God's earth, it at once became apparent that this freedom meant a new system of oppression and exploitation of the toilers. Various socialist doctrines immediately began to arise as a reflection of and protest against this oppression. But early socialism was *utopian* socialism. It criticized capitalist society, it condemned and damned it, it dreamed of its destruction, it indulged in fancies of a better order and endeavoured to convince the rich of the immorality of exploitation.

But utopian socialism could not point the real way out. It could not explain the essence of wage slavery under capitalism, nor discover the laws of the latter's development, nor point to the *social force* which is capable of becoming the creator of a new society.

Meanwhile, the stormy revolutions which everywhere in Europe, and especially in France, accompanied the fall of feudalism, of serfdom, more and more clearly revealed the *struggle of classes* as the basis and the driving force of the whole development.

Not a single victory of political freedom over the feudal class was won except against desperate resistance. Not a single capitalist country evolved on a more or less free and democratic basis except by a life and death struggle between the various classes of capitalist society.

The genius of Marx consists in the fact that he was able before anybody else to draw from this and consistently apply the deduction that world history teaches. This deduction is the doctrine of the *class struggle.*

Raymond A. Bauer • Alex Inkeles
Clyde Kluckhohn

10 MYTH AND REALITY
IN SOVIET IDEOLOGY

Raymond A. Bauer, Alex Inkeles, and Clyde Kluckhohn, *How the Soviet System Works* (Cambridge, Mass.: Harvard University Press, 1956), excerpted from pp. 29–35. Footnote references have been deleted. Reprinted by permission of Harvard University Press. Copyright 1956 by the President and Fellows of Harvard College.

Raymond A. Bauer, Professor of Psychology at M.I.T., is author of Nine Soviet Portraits *and other works on the Soviet Union. Alex Inkeles is Professor of Sociology at Harvard University, the author of* Public Opinion in Soviet Russia *and co-author, with Professor Bauer, of* The Soviet Citizen. *Clyde Kluckhohn was, until his death, Professor of Anthropology at Harvard University.*

Basic Soviet doctrine in its most orthodox form is adhered to by only a small group of leaders and doubtless believed in full detail by even a tinier minority. Nevertheless, while there are wide variations in acceptance even within the Party, there is certainly a tendency[1] for individuals, as they rise

---

[1] With some there is undoubtedly also a tendency toward inner disillusionment as they see what really goes on in practice within the system.

in the leadership hierarchy, to conform—in their outward manifestations, at least—more and more completely to Soviet ideology. Apparent receptivity to indoctrination is, in actuality, a factor in promotion. Persons being groomed for advancement in leadership typically undergo at least one year of conditioning in Party schools at each of several stages in their advancement. That this conditioning, in spite of some cynicism, is on the whole remarkably effective is shown by the acts of the Soviet leaders as well as by their words. In the pattern of taking over the satellites, for example, there is a certain formalistic repetitiveness. It is apparent that most Soviet leaders are convinced that you just cannot do even "the correct thing" in the wrong way.

.   .   .

The Soviet propaganda machine does not limit itself—as most other systems of political propaganda have done—to the technique of reiteration, hammering in, and to the suppression of complaints and disturbing information. There must be a positive and developmental side too. It is true that incessant profession of faith is adopted by many as a major path not only to personal security but also to advancement at school, in work, and in every sphere of life. To conform, at least outwardly, is necessary for survival. But the regime wants more than conformity; it wants not so much "belief" (in the sense in which Christians would use that term) as positive identification with the Party as the trustworthy custodian of all fundamental doctrinal questions, an identification normally achieved through actively propagating and executing the Party program and its concrete demands.

There is no subject on which even well-informed Americans show greater misunderstanding than that of Communist ideology. The tendency, in characteristic American fashion, is to make extreme interpretations. Either: "Soviet ideology is an inflexible code, a sort of theology which dictates all plans and policies," or: "Russian Communists no longer believe this stuff. These are just words which are used ritually or for propaganda purposes at home and abroad. They pick the texts they quote to suit the purpose of the moment. They'll say the opposite next week if they feel like it." There are elements of truth in both of these views, but in this instance the full truth does not, as so often, lie somewhere between two extremes. Rather, an adequate statement requires conceptions that are outside the range of ordinary American experience.

It is true that many in the U.S.S.R. are cynical toward the official ideology. Many more are apathetic. It is also true that what remains of the formal ideology is largely what has been found useful, with or without modification, in support of the maintenance and enlargement of power by the regime, at home and abroad. But this does not mean that the *method of thinking* has ceased to influence both the elite and the masses. Seeing the actions of the leaders from the fresh perspective afforded by the descriptions of the system given by the refugees, we are strongly inclined to agree with Leites and others that, despite changes in the formal ideology and in concrete policy goals, there has been a high degree of continuity in Bolshevik behavior, stemming from the persistence of certain "core" ways of thinking and acting, including those we have treated here as operating characteristics.

Moreover, the leadership's use of ideology for cynical manipulation does not mean that the regime does not take ideas as such seriously—quite the contrary. The amount of serious effort that Stalin put into the genetics and linguistics controversies and into his last book was strikingly high. It is as if the President of the United States were to enter into controversies on esoteric matters in *The Quarterly Journal of Economics* and the *International Journal of American Linguistics*.

Ideology plays two roles in the behavior of the Soviet elite: (1) as a system of ideas to which they are committed; (2) as a doctrine to be manipulated by them in the pursuit of practical goals. Some ideological tenets are more "believed" than others, and, of course, there is great variability among individuals. There can be no doubt, however, that the Soviet ruling elite makes persistent attempts to maintain the *appearance* of ideological consistency. Even though policy may change its direction, the orthodoxy of every policy must always be established. The retention of the Marxist slogans "materialism" and "determinism" are a symbolic means of maintaining the legitimacy of contemporary Soviet policies and doctrines. But while in theology the main doctrinal tenets are the most stable elements, in Bolshevik ideology substantive doctrinal tenets are sometimes considered expendable if they conflict with the demands of the immediate action program of the Party. If necessary, the basic statements of Marx, Engels, Lenin, and Stalin are reinterpreted. When such alterations are made, however, argument or citation of appropriate textual quotations, or both, are used to preserve the air of continuity and consistency. The Communist devil is very apt at quoting his scripture to his own purpose.

In the realm of strictly political ideology, the retention of rules and beliefs which have no basis in present-day reality is apparently deliberate. Belief in the myth that practice and theory are one, for example, is thought necessary for the continued existence of the Party. Its basic dogma is that it alone is the custodian of Marxist-Leninist-Stalinist orthodoxy, and to admit departure from that orthodoxy would be to destroy the dogma. Moreover, there is the significant "vanguard theory," according to which the U.S.S.R. is to lead the world into a "better life," and the Party in the Soviet Union is the vanguard of World Communism.

To ask simply, "Are the Communists 'sincere' in their beliefs?" is to ask the wrong question. . . .

The expression of values and political beliefs in a Communist society is not comparable to the expression of such values and beliefs in the West. In the U.S.S.R. such expression plays much more the role which compliance with custom has played in the middle classes of a free society. Soviet citizens generally profess the official "religion" not out of deep conviction but to avoid public disapproval and the legal sanctions against nonconformist behavior, which are much more severe. Beliefs which are expressed for these practical reasons have, of course, persistence and functional significance quite different from those held on the basis of being deeply felt and thought to be "true." In the first place, such pragmatic beliefs are not easily modified by argument or exposure to "truth." The realistic fear of someone who lives within the Soviet system that deviation would weaken his chance of sheer physical survival acts as a kind of insulation and is far more powerful—at least in the short run—than abstract truth. Indeed, literal and complete belief would be an actual danger to the working of the system, for such belief leads to "idealist disillusionment" and disaffection.

Nevertheless, these same doctrines, which at first are held pragmatically, become so habitual that they are almost automatic, however cynically or semicynically they were embraced at first. And so—in spite of cynicism, apathy, and ritualistic lip service—Communist myths are still of genuine importance. We saw this with the *émigré* population. Of our intelligentsia respondents who were born after the Revolution at least 15 per cent made constant use of the Marxian dialectic to explain and to predict; they accepted the inevitability of the class struggle, the assumption that historical laws are external to man, and the opposition of "materialism" and "idealism." Clearly they had learned their lessons all too well, and Marxist doctrine had become part of the unquestioned stuff of their thinking. Yet these were individuals who, if asked the question, "Is Marxism valid as a system?" would reply—in most cases sincerely—"No!" There is a striking parallel here to attitudes toward Soviet institutions. Former Soviet citizens are characterized by their across-the-board rejection of (and hostility to) the Soviet *regime*. Nevertheless, they reveal an acceptance of many of the institutional features of Soviet society. Similarly, these former Soviet citizens indicate, along with their disavowal of "Marxism" and "Communism," a retention of some basic Marxist notions. There is no doubt that a significant number of Soviet intelligentsia perceive nature and society through Marxist spectacles—often without realizing at all that they are wearing these spectacles.

Certainly the Soviet leadership thinks that these myths are important and useful or it would not go to such pains to maintain them. Lower Party leaders who do not operate and talk strictly in terms of the Party charter are disciplined. Acts of the top leadership palpably in violation of the mythology are rationalized, though at the expense of time and money. . . .

Many younger Party members, who did not personally experience the pre-Stalinist days of the Party, are really convinced that myth and "Soviet reality" are largely coterminous. They do not interpret the myths in ways adverse to the regime. Taking the myths as their guide, they exercise right of criticism and self-criticism" to help the Party center disc weaknesses in the work of the lower organizations without creating ei the possibility of undermining authority or the possibility of the organization of opposition. In their hands, Party elections serve as instruments with which the Party center can restrain the lower leaders from abuse of their delegated authority. Although it is true that Party elections are generally "means of registering assent, rather than forums of free choice," Party members have, on occasion, withheld their assent to the election of persons recommended from above. On such occasions, punishment went to the persons rejected in accord with the official mythology, which says that the rejected in this system are unworthy.

The Soviet system lays enormous stress on ideology both as a doctrine and as a practical instrument. The "operating ideology" of the leadership at any given point in time is kept remarkably consistent. The more formal total theoretical system has, in fact, undergone change through time, but much effort is expended to rationalize these changes and preserve the appearance of continuity and consistency. There is good evidence that Communist ideology affects the thinking and the acts of leaders and of other intelligentsia who grow up under the Bolshevik regime.

Allen S. Whiting

11 COMMUNIST THEORY AND THE PROCESS OF MODERNIZATION

Allen S. Whiting, "China" in *Modern Political Systems: Asia,* Robert E. Ward and Roy C. Macridis, eds. (Englewood Cliffs, N.J.: Prentice-Hall, Inc., 1963), pp. 151–53.

Allen S. Whiting received his Ph.D. from Columbia University in 1950. He has taught political science at Northwestern, Michigan State, and Columbia Universities. For a number of years he was a member of the Social Sciences Division of The RAND Corporation, specializing in Chinese Communist foreign policy. Among his published works are Soviet Policies in China, China Crosses the Yalu, *and* Sinkiang: Pawn or Pivot? *Dr. Whiting is at present working for the Department of State.*

The doctrine of Marxism-Leninism-Maoism offers both advantages and disadvantages for achieving the modernization China has been groping for over the past century. Its political appeal, vital to winning mass support for the sacrifices inherent in industrialization based on inadequate resources of capital and technology, won a striking response from the Chinese people down to the economic debacle of 1959–62. The reasons are several. For one thing, the doctrine appears as part of the new world of science, since it claims to have discovered universal laws of human behavior that embody "scientific truth." This identification with the technological revolution is strengthened by the fact that Soviet Russia serves as the font of the new order. Russian sputniks symbolize the triumph of a backward peasant society over the demands of modernization. Whether intellectual or peasant, all Chinese who hope to bring their personal life and their political society abreast of the advanced nations can look to the Russian experience for hope and inspiration in this respect.

But contrary to Western belief, Marxism-Leninism promises more than material, technological gains. It offers spiritual satisfaction when the Communist society is realized and such onerous aspects of government as dictatorial rule and instruments of coercion disappear. Just as the "state will wither away," to be replaced by the "administration of things, not of people," so payment according to work will be replaced by the principle of "from each according to his ability, to each according to his need." These appeals aim at basic desires—utopian, to be sure—which are found in all societies and civilizations, whether the most primitive or the most advanced.

In addition to these domestic spurs to discipline, unity, and obedience which are to be rewarded by material and spiritual benefits at some future time, the ideology posits external threats inherent in "international capitalism and imperialism" which drive the populace toward greater self-sacrifice in support of industrial and military development. This "carrot and stick" combination of promise and threat creates a sense of dedication and urgency that facilitates the consolidation of political power and the direction of that power toward economic mobilization and modernization.

Whether totalitarian means achieve this modernization more rapidly than other political approaches is a subject of continuing debate and one that goes beyond the scope of this essay. It is generally agreed, however, that some controls are needed over consumption, capital accumulation, and investment if a less developed society is to overtake the more advanced industrial countries. China's pronounced shortage of capital for investment as compared with its surplus of labor argues for central direction of manpower, if all resources are to be harnessed for intensive development.

For these reasons, certain aspects of the Communist credo seem well suited to China's needs as defined by the present elite as well as its predecessors. Of course, the goals might be differently arranged. There is no obvious reason why overtaking other countries in the output of iron and steel should have top priority over raising the living standards throughout the country. Yet to a considerable degree, the modernization which Mao Tse-tung has promised to China bears striking resemblance to that offered both by Chiang Kai-shek and Sun Yat-sen.

We shall examine the workings of the CCP later, but it is worth noting at this point that its ideology places a premium on asceticism and self-regeneration. This sense of dedication and sacrifice provides both discipline and drive for the new elite which, in the absence of legal opposition, might easily succumb to the temptations of power and privilege. Indeed, many observers feel that in the Soviet Union, a growing emphasis on consumer goods indicates a "mellowing" of the second-generation Communist elite, toning down its revolutionary fervor. There is even reason to believe that the Chinese Communists share this view of their fellow ally. Against this trend, however, are built-in checks which the ideology explicitly or implicitly offers its followers, such as self-criticism, purges, and ruthless surveillance for "counter-revolutionary activity." These may offset the debilitating force of bureaucracy and keep alive the ends for which the party originally seized power. At least at the working levels, the ideology provides stimulus and cohesion through its clarity of goals, while its injunctions against "back-sliding" seek to assure a consistency of effort in striving toward those goals.

Against this impressive array of assets, we must list some important liabilities. Despite their insistence on adapting Communism to China's "national characteristics," Mao and his colleagues still suffer from the strictures placed on them by ideology and by the reinforcement of these strictures by Soviet practice. Collectivism, for instance, is a Marxist fetish, the economic benefits of which remain in doubt and the economic liabilities of which, at least in agriculture, have been proven through more than forty years of Soviet failure to keep rural productivity growing sufficiently to satisfy industrial and consumer needs. Collective farms may control peasant consumption of foodstuffs and even facilitate the checking of peasant dissidence, but in the crucial realm of output, they still disappoint and bewilder Soviet planners. With China's intensive agriculture, collectivization holds considerably less promise, since the benefits of mechanization—possible only through the merging of small plots into larger holdings—seem impossible to achieve, especially in the wet-rice areas. Yet Peking pushed collectivization to the extreme in its first decade of power, seemingly blind to the economic setbacks experienced by Soviet agriculture.

Another shortcoming attributable to the impact of ideology is the inhibition, if not the prohibition, against criticism from lower ranks against decisions taken by top levels of the Communist Party. The emphasis on discipline and centralized decision-making, coupled with injunctions against factionalism and threats from outside conspiratorial elements, tends to mute necessary and vital complaints from below. Thus the failures which result from the incorrect transfer of institutions from Soviet to Chinese conditions, or from miscalculations by Mao's leadership, may be checked only when their disruptive consequences have done serious, if not irreparable, harm. Mao's criteria for distinguishing "right words from wrong" make "the leadership of the Communist Party" the final arbiter of any dissenting views. We find no public criticism of Mao, Liu, or their immediate colleagues, nor do we know of any private attacks upon them which have been successfully mounted within the CCP. If Soviet precedent serves as an example, such criticism occurs only during a struggle for power. Even at lower levels, persons who attack their superiors often appear to do so only upon instruction from above, as part of a planned program of criticism and correction, not as individual fault-finders acting on their own initiative.

This inhibition on criticism, combined with the imitation of certain Soviet practices, makes rigid what otherwise might be an extremely flexible and adaptable ideology. The point must not be exaggerated, of course. We shall see how Peking has been able to adjust its policies in response to adverse or unanticipated consequences. At the same time, Communism seems to place certain sectors of the society under tremendous pressures, to the point where any effort to reduce pressures—by a "decompression" process—is a difficult and hazardous task. Three such sectors evident in China, as throughout the Soviet bloc, are the intelligentsia, the national minorities, and the peasantry. Sometimes, as in Tibet, this effort at decompression is too little or too late, and revolt occurs. More often, especially amongst the peasants, the threatened explosion is signalled by the murder of Communist Party members and the burning of government granaries. This can alert Peking, which then may attempt, through a combination of repression and decompression, to provide temporary, if not permanent, relief.

In the last analysis, this problem of disruptive tension and its easement may prove to be the most critical one inherent in the Communist credo. Certainly it offsets many of Communism's advantages in achieving modernization. Against the long background of pre-Communist history, the People's Republic of China is still in its infancy after a dozen short years. Its future cannot be predicted with certainty. But the evidence to date suggests that the Communist ideology has basic strengths and weaknesses that are relevant in assessing the foundation of political power for the Chinese Communist Party.

Edvard Kardelj

12 IDEOLOGY AS A LIVING FORCE

Edvard Kardelj, *Socialism and War: A Survey of Chinese Criticism of the Policy of Coexistence* (Belgrade: Publishing House of Jugoslavija, 1960), excerpted from pp. 16–17.

Edvard Kardelj, a leading ideologist of the Yugoslav Communist Party, was elected Chairman of the Federal Assembly, a post tantamount to Premier, in June 1963. Kardelj has been one of Tito's closest confidantes since the mid-1930's.

I do not intend to argue about whose "Marxism" is better or "more correct," the "Yugoslav" or the "Chinese," or any other Marxism. Like every science Marxism is accessible to all, but the extent to which anyone has applied that science in practice is not dependent solely on his desire to be a Marxist. For this reason we do not reproach the Chinese critics for the fact that their Marxism merely serves to conceal their policy—which happens to be just what they reproach us with. But at the same time it is not our view that anybody's policy or any sort of policy can be justified and monopolistically imposed as the "sole Marxist" policy, for a subjectivist self-justification of that sort, even if sincere, never has more than a relative value.

As is frequently emphasised, Marxism is not a dogma but a guide to action. Consequently *to appraise anybody's work what is decisive is not the extent to which he has found fitting quotations to justify definite actions or his personal view of the Marxist guide, but what the actual social-historical effect of that work is.* Only that effect shows whether anyone has made good or bad use of the guide.

Besides, today so many and such diverse social factors speak in the name of Marxism that it is obviously senseless for anyone to pretend to be the only "true" protagonist of "true" Marxism. Marxism has furnished a series of scientific discoveries in the field of social development and together with these has evolved an epoch-making scientific method for the analysis of social contradictions, that is to say, for a more deliberate steering of social developments than had ever been possible in the past. In this way Marxism has influenced, and indeed continues to influence, the whole "range" of social consciousness, from people who deny it in general to those who say they are the only "true" Marxists. Why, even bourgeois

79

political economy in our time has taken what is genuinely new and scientific in it on the whole from Marxism, however much it may deny this. It is precisely in this wide range of the influences it has exercised and still exercises on social development in our day that the epoch-making significance of Marxism as a science resides.

Thus, although Marxism is an indispensable weapon for any conscious and progressive socialist action, nevertheless, on the other hand, the mere formal acceptance of Marxism, or some aspects of Marxism, does not automatically make anyone either the most progressive or an infallible social force. In socialist conditions too men's minds and their actions are the resultant of the interlocking of extremely varied factors and processes: material development, mental reactions, individual characteristics, traditions, manifold contradictions and oppositions, mentalities formed by tradition, and so forth. Marxism has not made nor can it make people immune to the influence of all these factors, nor has it endowed any of them with an "absolute" mentality independent of material processes. Like every ideology and all scientific knowledge, Marxism is a factor of social developments, but not their inner law. Therefore, Chinese policy is not what it is because it is based on Marxism, but because it is the reflection of a specific complex of objective and subjective factors in present-day Chinese society, as this has developed, or might have developed after the revolution. In that development the Marxist ideological orientation is only one of the major—and progressive—factors, but not the only one.

Mao Tse-tung

13 ON THE CORRECT HANDLING OF CONTRADICTIONS IN SOCIALIST SOCIETY

Mao Tse-tung, *On the Correct Handling of Contradictions among the People* (Peking: Foreign Languages Press, 1960), excerpted from pp. 7–26.

Mao Tse-tung, now in his seventies, is the head of the Chinese Communist Party. The son of a rich peasant, he joined the Party in 1921 and has been its head since 1934.

In early 1956, Mao adopted a policy designed to attract greater support from the non-communist intellectuals and technicians upon whom Chinese industrial-

ization and modernization depended. The "let a hundred flowers blossom, let a hundred schools of thought contend" policy invited public comment and criticism of nonpolitical aspects of Chinese Communist internal policy. But the "de-Stalinization" speech of Khrushchev in February 1956 and the revolts in Hungary and Poland in October came as a shock to Mao, particularly since the public criticism in China itself was becoming increasingly political and anti-regime. Disturbed by the growing intensity of student and intellectual unrest, Mao delivered this speech in February 1957 in order to curb the so-called rightists and to set the limits of public criticism. His speech set forth his analysis of the domestic situation.

Led by the working class and the Communist Party, and united as one, our six hundred million people are engaged in the great work of building socialism. Unification of the country, unity of the people and unity among our various nationalities—these are the basic guarantees for the sure triumph of our cause. However, this does not mean that there are no longer any contradictions in our society. It would be naïve to imagine that there are no more contradictions. To do so would be to fly in the face of objective reality. We are confronted by two types of social contradictions—contradictions between ourselves and the enemy and contradictions among the people. These two types of contradictions are totally different in nature.

If we are to have a correct understanding of these two different types of contradictions, we must, first of all, make clear what is meant by "the people" and what is meant by "the enemy."

The term "the people" has different meanings in different countries, and in different historical periods in each country.

. . .

At this stage of building socialism, all classes, strata and social groups which approve, support and work for the cause of socialist construction belong to the category of the people, while those social forces and groups which resist the socialist revolution, and are hostile to and try to wreck socialist construction, are enemies of the people.

The contradictions between ourselves and our enemies are antagonistic ones. Within the ranks of the people, contradictions among the working people are non-antagonistic, while those between the exploiters and the exploited classes have, apart from their antagonistic aspect, a non-antagonistic aspect. Contradictions among the people have always existed. . . . Our people's government is a government that truly represents the interests of the people and serves the people, yet certain contradictions do exist between the government and the masses. These include contradictions between the interests of the state, collective interests and individual interests; between democracy and centralism; between those in positions of leadership and the led, and contradictions arising from the bureaucratic practices of certain state functionaries in their relations with the masses. All these are contradictions among the people. Generally speaking, underlying the contradictions among the people is the basic identity of the interests of the people.

In our country, the contradiction between the working class and the national bourgeoisie is a contradiction among the people. The class struggle waged between the two is, by and large, a class struggle within the ranks of the people. This is because of the dual character of the national bourgeoisie in our country. In the years of the bourgeois-democratic revolution, there was a revolutionary side to their character; there was also a tendency to compromise with the enemy, this was the other side. In the period of the socialist revolution, exploitation of the working class to make profits is one side, while support of the Constitution and willingness to accept socialist transformation is the other. The national bourgeoisie differs from the imperialists, the landlords and the bureaucrat-capitalists. The contradiction between exploiter and exploited, which exists between the national bourgeoisie and the working class, is an antagonistic one. But, in the concrete conditions existing in China, such an antagonistic contradiction, if properly handled, can be transformed into a non-antagonistic one and resolved in a peaceful way. But if it is not properly handled, if, say, we do not follow a policy of uniting, criticizing and educating the national bourgeoisie, or if the national bourgeoisie does not accept this policy, then the contradiction between the working class and the national bourgeoisie can turn into an antagonistic contradiction as between ourselves and the enemy.

Since the contradictions between ourselves and the enemy and those among the people differ in nature, they must be solved in different ways. To put it briefly, the former is a matter of drawing a line between us and our enemies, while the latter is a matter of distinguishing between right and wrong. It is, of course, true that drawing a line between ourselves and our enemies is also a question of distinguishing between right and wrong. For example, the question as to who is right, we or the reactionaries at home and abroad—that is, the imperialists, the feudalists and bureaucrat-capitalists—is also a question of distinguishing between right and wrong, but it is different in nature from questions of right and wrong among the people.

Ours is a people's democratic dictatorship, led by the working class and based on the worker-peasant alliance. What is this dictatorship for? Its first function is to suppress the reactionary classes and elements and those exploiters in the country who range themselves against the socialist revolution, to suppress all those who try to wreck our socialist construction; that is to say, to solve the contradictions between ourselves and the enemy within the country. . . .

The second function of this dictatorship is to protect our country from subversive activities and possible aggression by the external enemy. Should that happen, it is the task of this dictatorship to solve the external contradiction between ourselves and the enemy. The aim of this dictatorship is to protect all our people so that they can work in peace and build China into a socialist country with a modern industry, agriculture, science and culture. . . .

· · ·

While we stand for freedom with leadership and democracy under centralized guidance, in no sense do we mean that coercive measures should be taken to settle ideological matters and questions involving the distinction between right and wrong among the people. Any attempt to deal with ideological matters or questions involving right and wrong by administrative orders or coercive measures will not only be ineffective but harmful. We cannot abolish religion by administrative orders; nor can we force people not to believe in it. We cannot compel people to give up idealism, any more than we can force them to believe in Marxism. In settling matters of an ideological nature or controversial issues among the people, we can only use democratic methods, methods of discussion, of criticism, of persuasion and education, not coercive, high-handed methods. . . .

In 1942 we worked out the formula "unity—criticism—unity" to describe this democratic method of resolving contradictions among the people. To elaborate, this means to start off with a desire for unity and resolve contradictions through criticism or struggle so as to achieve a new unity on a new basis. Our experience shows that this is a proper method of resolving contradictions among the people. In 1942 we used this method to resolve contradictions inside the Communist Party, namely, contradictions between the doctrinaires and the rank-and-file membership, between doctrinairism and Marxism. At one time in waging inner-Party struggle, the "left" doctrinaires used the method of "ruthless struggle and merciless blows." This method was wrong. In place of it, in criticizing "left" doctrinairism, we used a new one: to start from a desire for unity, and thrash out questions of right and wrong through criticism or argument, and so achieve a new unity on a new basis. This was the method used in the "rectification campaign" of 1942. . . .

Under ordinary circumstances, contradictions among the people are not antagonistic. But if they are not dealt with properly, or if we relax vigilance and lower our guard, antagonism may arise. In a socialist country, such a development is usually only of a localized and temporary nature. This is because there the exploitation of man by man has been abolished and the interests of the people are basically the same. Such antagonistic actions on a fairly wide scale as took place during the Hungarian events are accounted for by the fact that domestic and foreign counter-revolutionary elements were at work. These actions were also of a temporary, though special, nature. In a case like this, the reactionaries in a socialist country, in league with the imperialists, take advantage of contradictions among the people to foment disunity and dissension and fan the flames of disorder in an attempt to achieve their conspiratorial aims. This lesson of the Hungarian events deserves our attention.

. . .

Marxist philosophy holds that the law of the unity of opposites is a fundamental law of the universe. This law operates everywhere, in the natural world, in human society, and in man's thinking. Opposites in contradiction unite as well as struggle with each other, and thus impel all things to move and change. Contradictions exist everywhere, but as things differ in nature, so do contradictions. In any given phenomenon or thing, the unity of opposites is conditional, temporary and transitory, and hence relative; whereas struggle between opposites is absolute. Lenin gave a very clear exposition of this law. In our country, a growing number of people have come to understand it. For many people, however, acceptance of this law is one thing, and its application in examining and dealing with problems is quite another. Many dare not acknowledge openly that there still exist contradictions among the people, which are the very forces that move our society forward. Many people refuse to admit that contradictions still exist in a socialist society, with the result that when confronted with social contradictions they become timid and helpless. They do not understand that socialist society grows more united and consolidated precisely through the ceaseless process of correctly dealing with and resolving contradictions. For this reason, we need to explain things to our people, our cadres in the first place, to help them understand contradictions in a socialist society and learn how to deal with such contradictions in a correct way.

Contradictions in a socialist society are fundamentally different from contradictions in old societies, such as capitalist society. Contradictions in capitalist society find expression in acute antagonisms and conflicts, in sharp class struggle, which cannot be resolved by the capitalist system itself and can only be resolved by socialist revolution. Contradictions in socialist society are, on the contrary, not antagonistic and can be resolved one after the other by the socialist system itself.

The basic contradictions in socialist society are still those between the relations of production and the productive forces, and between the superstructure and the economic base. These contradictions, however, are fundamentally different in character and have different features from contradictions between the relations of production and the productive forces and between the superstructure and the economic base in the old societies.

14 ON THE FURTHER PROMOTION OF SOCIALIST DEMOCRACY IN THE SOVIET UNION

Programme of the Communist Party of the Soviet Union (Moscow: Foreign Language Publishing House, 1961), excerpted from pp. 91–93, 122–23.

The new Programme of the Communist Party of the Soviet Union, *adopted at the Twenty-second Congress of the CPSU in October 1961, was a blueprint for the attainment of communism. Soviet leaders explained that the ideological changes introduced derived from the Soviet Union's having evolved from a socialist society to a society entering the "lower stages of communism."*

The dictatorship of the proletariat, born of the socialist revolution, played an epoch-making role by ensuring the victory of socialism in the U.S.S.R. In the course of socialist construction, however, it underwent changes. After the exploiting classes had been abolished, the function of suppressing their resistance ceased to exist. The chief functions of the socialist state—organisation of the economy, culture and education—developed in full measure. The socialist state entered a new period of its development. The state began to grow over into a nation-wide organisation of the working people of socialist society. Proletarian democracy was growing more and more into a socialist democracy of the people as a whole.

The working class is the only class in history that does not aim to perpetuate its power. Having brought about the complete and final victory of socialism—the first phase of communism—and the transition of society to the full-scale construction of communism, the dictatorship of the proletariat has fulfilled its historic mission and has ceased to be indispensable in the U.S.S.R. from the point of view of the tasks of internal development. The state, which arose as a state of the dictatorship of the proletariat, has, in the new, contemporary stage, become a state of the entire people, an organ expressing the interests and will of the people as a whole. Since the working class is the foremost and best organised force of Soviet society, it plays a leading role also in the period of the full-scale construction of communism. The working class will have completed its role of leader of society after communism is built and classes disappear.

The Party holds that the dictatorship of the working class will cease to be necessary before the state withers away. The state as an organisation of the entire people will survive until the complete victory of communism. Expressing the will of the people, it must organise the building up of the material and technical basis of communism, and the transformation of socialist relations into communist relations, must exercise control over the measure of work and the measure of consumption, promote the people's welfare, protect the rights and freedoms of Soviet citizens, socialist law and order and socialist property, instil in the people conscious discipline and a communist attitude to labour, guarantee the defence and security of the country, promote fraternal co-operation with the socialist countries, uphold world peace, and maintain normal relations with all countries.

All-round extension and perfection of socialist democracy, active participation of all citizens in the administration of the state, in the management of economic and cultural development, improvement of the government apparatus, and increased control over its activity by the people constitute the main direction in which socialist statehood develops in the period of the building of communism. As socialist democracy develops, the organs of state power will gradually be transformed into organs of public self-government. The Leninist principle of democratic centralism, which ensures the proper combination of centralised leadership with the maximum encouragement of local initiative, the extension of the rights of the Union republics and greater creative activity of the masses, will be promoted. It is essential to strengthen discipline, constantly control the activities of all the sections of the administrative apparatus, check the execution of the decisions and laws of the Soviet state and heighten the responsibility of every official for the strict and timely implementation of these laws. . . .

As a result of the victory of socialism in the U.S.S.R. and the consolidation of the unity of Soviet society, the Communist Party of the working class has become the vanguard of the Soviet people, a Party of the entire people, and extended its guiding influence to all spheres of social life. The Party is the brain, the honour and the conscience of our epoch, of the Soviet people, the people effecting great revolutionary transformations.

15 ON SOCIALIST SOCIETY AND SOVIET "REVISIONISM": A CHINESE CRITIQUE

On Khrushchev's Phoney Communism and Its Historical Lessons for the World (Peking: Foreign Languages Press, 1964), excerpted from pp. 3–40.

This pamphlet, published in Peking, is one of many published during the acrimonious exchanges between the Chinese and Soviet Communist Parties.

The theories of the proletarian revolution and the dictatorship of the proletariat are the quintessence of Marxism-Leninism. The questions of whether revolution should be upheld or opposed and whether the dictatorship of the proletariat should be upheld or opposed have always been the focus of struggle between Marxism-Leninism and all brands of revisionism and are now the focus of struggle between Marxist-Leninists the world over and the revisionist Khrushchev clique.

At the 22nd Congress of the CPSU (1961), the revisionist Khrushchev clique developed their revisionism into a complete system not only by rounding off their anti-revolutionary theories of "peaceful coexistence," "peaceful competition" and "peaceful transition" but also by declaring that the dictatorship of the proletariat is no longer necessary in the Soviet Union and advancing the absurd theories of the "state of the whole people" and "the party of the entire people."

The Programme put forward by the revisionist Khrushchev clique at the 22nd Congress of the CPSU is a programme of phoney communism, a revisionist programme against proletarian revolution and for the abolition of the dictatorship of the proletariat and the proletarian party.

The revisionist Khrushchev clique abolish the dictatorship of the proletariat behind the camouflage of the "state of the whole people," change the proletarian character of the Communist Party of the Soviet Union behind the camouflage of the "party of the entire people" and pave the way for the restoration of capitalism behind that of "full-scale communist construction." . . .

Let us ascertain who is actually far removed from Marxism-Leninism, what Soviet life is actually like and who actually wants the Soviet Union to return to the past.

Socialist Society
and the Dictatorship of the Proletariat

What is the correct conception of socialist society? Do classes and class struggle exist throughout the stage of socialism? Should the dictatorship of the proletariat be maintained and the socialist revolution be carried through to the end? Or should the dictatorship of the proletariat be abolished so as to pave the way for capitalist restoration? These questions must be answered correctly according to the basic theory of Marxism-Leninism and the historical experience of the dictatorship of the proletariat. . . .

The socialist system is incomparably superior to the capitalist system. In socialist society, the dictatorship of the proletariat replaces bourgeois dictatorship and the public ownership of the means of production replaces private ownership. The proletariat, from being an oppressed and exploited class, turns into the ruling class and a fundamental change takes place in the social position of the working people.

.   .   .

However, one cannot but see that socialist society is a society born out of capitalist society and is only the first phase of communist society. It is not yet a fully mature communist society in the economic and other fields. It is inevitably stamped with the birthmarks of capitalist society. When defining socialist society Marx said:

> What we have to deal with here is a communist society, not as it has *developed* on its own foundations, but, on the contrary, just as it *emerges* from capitalist society; which is thus in every respect, economically, morally and intellectually, still stamped with the birthmarks of the old society from whose womb it emerges.

Lenin also pointed out that in socialist society, which is the first phase of communism, "Communism *cannot* as yet be fully ripe economically and entirely free from traditions or traces of capitalism."

In socialist society, the differences between workers and peasants, between town and country, and between manual and mental labourers still remain, bourgeois rights are not yet completely abolished, it is not possible "at once to eliminate the other injustice, which consists in the distribution of articles of consumption 'according to the amount of labour performed' (and not according to needs)," and therefore differences in wealth still exist. The disappearance of these differences, phenomena and bourgeois rights can only be gradual and long drawn-out. . . .

Marxism-Leninism and the practice of the Soviet Union, China and other socialist countries all teach us that socialist society covers a very, very long historical stage. Throughout this stage, the class struggle between the bourgeoisie and the proletariat goes on and the question of "who will win" between the roads of capitalism and socialism remains, as does the danger of the restoration of capitalism.

. . .

In socialist society, the overthrown bourgeoisie and other reactionary classes remain strong for quite a long time, and indeed in certain respects are quite powerful. They have a thousand and one links with the international bourgeoisie. They are not reconciled to their defeat and stubbornly continue to engage in trials of strength with the proletariat. They conduct open and hidden struggles against the proletariat in every field. Constantly parading such signboards as support for socialism, the Soviet system, the Communist Party and Marxism-Leninism, they work to undermine socialism and restore capitalism. Politically, they persist for a long time as a force antagonistic to the proletariat and constantly attempt to overthrow the dictatorship of the proletariat. They sneak into the government organs, public organizations, economic departments and cultural and educational institutions so as to resist or usurp the leadership of the proletariat. Economically, they employ every means to damage socialist ownership by the whole people and socialist collective ownership and to develop the forces of capitalism. In the ideological, cultural and educational fields, they counterpose the bourgeois world outlook to the proletarian world outlook and try to corrupt the proletariat and other working people with bourgeois ideology.

. . .

The class struggle in socialist society is inevitably reflected in the Communist Party. The bourgeoisie and international imperialism both understand that in order to make a socialist country degenerate into a capitalist country, it is first necessary to make the Communist Party degenerate into a revisionist party. The old and new bourgeois elements, the old and new rich peasants and the degenerate elements of all sorts constitute the social basis of revisionism, and they use every possible means to find agents within the Communist Party. The existence of bourgeois influence is the internal source of revisionism and surrender to imperialist pressure the external source. Throughout the stage of socialism, there is inevitable struggle between Marxism-Leninism and various kinds of opportunism—mainly revisionism—in the Communist Parties of socialist countries. The characteristic of this revisionism is that, denying the existence of classes and class struggle, it sides with the bourgeoisie in attacking the proletariat and turns the dictatorship of the proletariat into the dictatorship of the bourgeoisie.

. . .

In his celebrated work *On the Correct Handling of Contradictions among the People* and in other works, Comrade Mao Tse-tung, basing himself on the fundamental principles of Marxism-Leninism and the historical experience of the dictatorship of the proletariat gives a comprehensive and systematic analysis of classes and class struggle in socialist society, and creatively develops the Marxist-Leninist theory of the dictatorship of the proletariat.

Comrade Mao Tse-tung examines the objective laws of socialist society from the viewpoint of materialist dialectics. He points out that the universal law of the unity and struggle of opposites operating both in the natural world and in human society is applicable to socialist society, too. In socialist society, class contradictions still remain and class struggle does not die out after the socialist transformation of the ownership of the means of production. The struggle between the two roads of socialism and capitalism runs through the entire stage of socialism. To ensure the success of socialist construction and to prevent the restoration of capitalism, it is necessary to carry the socialist revolution through to the end on the political, economic, ideological and cultural fronts. The complete victory of socialism cannot be brought about in one or two generations; to resolve this question thoroughly requires five to ten generations or even longer.

Comrade Mao Tse-tung stresses the fact that two types of social contradictions exist in socialist society, namely, contradictions among the people and contradictions between ourselves and the enemy, and that the former are very numerous. Only by distinguishing between the two types of contradictions, which are different in nature, and by adopting different measures to handle them correctly is it possible to unite the people, who constitute more than 90 per cent of the population, defeat their enemies, who constitute only a few per cent, and consolidate the dictatorship of the proletariat.

The dictatorship of the proletariat is the basic guarantee for the consolidation and development of socialism, for the victory of the proletariat over the bourgeoisie and of socialism in the struggle between the two roads.

Only by emancipating all mankind can the proletariat ultimately emancipate itself. The historical task of the dictatorship of the proletariat has two aspects, one internal and the other international. The internal task consists mainly of completely abolishing all the exploiting classes, developing socialist economy to the maximum, enhancing the communist consciousness of the masses, abolishing the differences between ownership by the whole people and collective ownership, between workers and peasants, between town and country and between mental and manual labourers, eliminating any possibility of the re-emergence of classes and the restoration of capitalism and providing conditions for the realization of a communist society with its principle, "from each according to his ability, to each according to his needs." The international task consists mainly of preventing attacks by international imperialism (including armed intervention and disintegration by peaceful means) and of giving support to the world revolution until the people of all countries finally abolish imperialism, capitalism and the system of exploitation. Before the fulfillment of both tasks and before the advent of a full communist society, the dictatorship of the proletariat is absolutely necessary.

Judging from the actual situation today, the tasks of the dictatorship of the proletariat are still far from accomplished in any of the socialist countries. In all socialist countries without exception, there are classes and class struggle, the struggle between the socialist and the capitalist roads, the question of carrying the socialist revolution through to the end and the question of preventing the restoration of capitalism. . . . Therefore it is necessary for all the socialist countries to uphold the dictatorship of the proletariat.

In these circumstances, the abolition of the dictatorship of the proletariat by the revisionist Khrushchev clique is nothing but the betrayal of socialism and communism.

Antagonistic Classes and Class Struggle Exist in the Soviet Union

In announcing the abolition of the dictatorship of the proletariat in the Soviet Union, the revisionist Khrushchev clique base themselves mainly on the argument that antagonistic classes have been eliminated and that class struggle no longer exists.

But what is the actual situation in the Soviet Union? Are there really no antagonistic classes and no class struggle there?

Following the victory of the Great October Socialist Revolution, the dictatorship of the proletariat was established in the Soviet Union, capitalist private ownership was destroyed and socialist ownership by the whole people and socialist collective ownership were established through the nationalization of industry and the collectivization of agriculture, and great achievements in socialist construction were scored during several decades. All this constituted an indelible victory of tremendous historic significance won by the Communist Party of the Soviet Union and the Soviet people under the leadership of Lenin and Stalin.

However, the old bourgeoisie and other exploiting classes which had been overthrown in the Soviet Union were not eradicated and survived after industry was nationalized and agriculture collectivized. The political and ideological influence of the bourgeoisie remained. Spontaneous capitalist tendencies continued to exist both in the city and in the countryside. New bourgeois elements and kulaks were still incessantly generated.

Throughout the long intervening period, the class struggle between the proletariat and the bourgeoisie and the struggle between the socialist and capitalist roads have continued in the political, economic, and ideological spheres.

As the Soviet Union was the first, and at the time the only, country to build socialism and had no foreign experience to go by, and as Stalin departed from Marxist-Leninist dialectics in his understanding of the laws of class struggle in socialist society, he prematurely declared after agriculture was basically collectivized that there were "no longer antagonistic classes" in the Soviet Union and that it was "free of class conflicts," one-sidedly stressed the internal homogeneity of socialist society and overlooked its contradictions, failed to rely upon the working class and the masses in the struggle against the forces of capitalism and regarded the possibility of the restoration of capitalism as associated only with armed attack by international imperialism. This was wrong both in theory and in practice. Nevertheless, Stalin remained a great Marxist-Leninist. As long as he led the Soviet Party and state, he held fast to the dictatorship of the proletariat and the socialist course, pursued a Marxist-Leninist line and ensured the Soviet Union's victorious advance along the road of socialism.

Ever since Khrushchev seized the leadership of the Soviet Party and state, he has pushed through a whole series of revisionist policies which have greatly hastened the growth of the forces of capitalism and again sharpened the class struggle between the proletariat and the bourgeoisie and the struggle between the roads of socialism and capitalism in the Soviet Union.

Scanning the reports in Soviet newspapers over the last few years, one finds numerous examples demonstrating not only the presence of many elements of the old exploiting classes in Soviet society, but also the generation of new bourgeois elements on a large scale and the acceleration of class polarization.

Let us first look at the activities of the various bourgeois elements in the Soviet enterprises owned by the whole people. Leading functionaries of some state-owned factories and their gangs abuse their positions and amass large fortunes by using the equipment and materials of the factories to set up "underground workshops" for private production, selling the products illicitly and dividing the spoils. Here are some examples. In a Leningrad plant producing military items, the leading functionaries placed their own men in "all key posts" and "turned the state enterprise into a private one." They illicitly engaged in the production of non-military goods and from the sale of fountain pens alone embezzled 1,200,000 old roubles in three years. . . . The manager of a furniture factory in Kharkov set up an "illegal knitwear workshop" and carried on secret operations inside the factory. This man "had several wives, several cars, several houses, 176 neckties, about a hundred shirts and dozens of suits." He was also a big gambler at the horse-races.

Such people do not operate all by themselves. They invariably work hand in glove with functionaries in the state departments in charge of supplies and in the commercial and other departments. They have their own men in the police and judicial departments who protect them and act as their agents. Even high-ranking officials in the state organs support and shield them.

. . .

Obviously all these people belong to a class that is antagonistic to the proletariat—they belong to the bourgeoisie. Their activities against socialism are definitely class struggle with the bourgeoisie attacking the proletariat. Now let us look at the activities of various kulak elements on the collective farms. Some leading collective-farm functionaries and their gangs steal and speculate at will, freely squander public money and fleece the collective farmers. Here are some examples. The chairman of a collective farm in Uzebkistan "held the whole village in terror." All the important posts on this farm "were occupied by his in-laws and other relatives and friends." He squandered "over 132,000 roubles of the collective farm for his personal needs!" He had a car, two motorcycles and three wives, each with a "house of her own." . . . The chairman of a collective farm in the Ukraine made over 50,000 roubles at its expense by forging purchase certificates and cash-account orders in collusion with its woman accountant, who had been praised for keeping "model accounts" and whose deeds had been displayed at the Moscow Exhibition of Achievements of the National Economy. . . .

These examples show that collective farms under the control of such functionaries virtually become their private property. Such men turn socialist collective economic enterprises into economic enterprises of new kulaks. There are often people in their superior organizations who protect them. Their relationship to the collective farmers has likewise become that of oppressors to oppressed, of exploiters to exploited. . . .

Obviously, they all belong to a class that is antagonistic to the proletariat and the labouring farmers, belong to the kulak or rural bourgeois class. Their antisocialist activities are precisely class struggle with the bourgeoisie attacking the proletariat and the labouring farmers.

. . .

These data suffice to show that the unbridled activities of the bourgeoisie against the proletariat are widespread in the Soviet Union, in the city as well as the countryside, in industry as well as agriculture, in the sphere of production as well as the sphere of circulation, all the way from the economic departments to Party and government organizations, and from the grass-roots to the higher leading bodies. These anti-socialist activities are nothing if not the sharp class struggle of the bourgeoisie against the proletariat.

It is not strange that attacks on socialism should be made in a socialist country by old and new bourgeois elements. There is nothing terrifying about this so long as the leadership of the Party and state remains a Marxist-Leninist one. But in the Soviet Union today, the gravity of the situation lies in the fact that the revisionist clique have usurped the leadership of the Soviet Party and state and that a privileged stratum has emerged in Soviet society.

16 YUGOSLAV IDEOLOGICAL INNOVATIONS

Excerpts from *The Programme of the League of Yugoslav Communists* (Belgrade: Yugoslavia, 1958).

The Programme of the League of Yugoslav Communists, *adopted by the VII Congress of the League in April 1958, enunciated many of the ideological deviations which have been a source of continuing friction between Belgrade, on the one hand, and Moscow and Peking, on the other.*

Some Experiences of Socialist Development in the Soviet Union and Other Socialist Countries

In the period between the world wars, the Soviet Union was the first and only country in which socialist forces had come to power and in which socialist relations were being developed. . . .

Under these circumstances overall social development in the Soviet Union had no alternative but to put all its efforts into the construction of the material basis required by the new society, and moreover it had to carry this out with its own resources. . . .

In this situation, the needs of social development demanded that the leading forces in society, the Communist Party and the Soviet State, play a pre-eminent organizational role, first in the sphere of economic life and then over the whole field of social life. This led to a great concentration of power in the machinery of State.

Manifestations of bureaucratic-statist tendencies, however, errors and distortions in the development of the political system of the State, and parallel with this, a more acute and convulsive phase permeated with contradictions typical of the period of transition from capitalism to socialism, began to be associated with this concentration of power in the machinery of State.

In the long run, this course of activity not only resulted in the enhancement of the power of the State, but also led more and more to the rule of one man. This was the soil that gave birth to the "cult of personality," along with attempts to justify it theoretically and ideologically. . . . [Stalin,] for both objective and subjective reasons, did not fight the bureaucratic-statist tendencies engendered by the great concentration of power in the machinery of State and by the merging of the Party and State machinery and unilateral centralism. Moreover, he himself became their political and ideological protagonist.

It was along these lines that a pragmatic revision of some of the fundamental scientific postulates of Marxism and Leninism was carried out—first in the sphere of the theory of State and Party, and then also in the sphere of philosophy, political economy, and the social sciences generally. The Marxist-Leninist theory of the dictatorship of the proletariat as a political system of power in a State which is withering away, and as an instrument of working class struggle in the process of the abolition of the economic foundations of capitalism and the creation of political and material conditions for the free development of new socialist relations, was gradually replaced by Stalin's theory of a State which does not wither away and which must strengthen itself in all fields of social life, a State whose machinery is given too great a role in the construction of socialism and the solution of the internal contradictions of the transition period, a role which sooner or later must lead to stagnation in the development of social and economic factors.

Phenomena of this type after the Second World War also began to make their appearance on the international scene, i.e., in certain elements of Soviet foreign policy and in relations between socialist countries. This was particularly evident in Stalin's action against socialist Yugoslavia, which the 20th Congress of the Communist Party of the Soviet Union unanimously condemned as an action contrary to the real interest of socialism . . .

All these and other negative phenomena and errors—particularly as some of them were transferred to and repeated in certain other socialist countries—inflicted harm both on international socialism and on socialist construction in the Soviet Union. . . .

The Development of Socialist Thought. On Dogmatism and Revisionism

. . . [U]nder the influence of various social factors, Marxist thought in the course of the past few decades has failed to keep in step with the advance of contemporary society, and its subsequent development has not always proceeded consistently from the basic scientific postulates and results of Marxism—these very postulates being frequently subjected to a pragmatic revision. As a result of this, many contemporary social problems have not been fully explained from a scientific Marxist point of view, nor have the laws and contradictions of the period of transition from capitalism to socialism been sufficiently illuminated; thus there are many gaps in the interpretation of contemporary social phenomena. Further development in socialism categorically demands proper treatment of the laws and contradictions of the period of transition from capitalism to socialism, and the liberation of scientific socialist thought from the pragmatic pressure of those social factors which retard its progress. . . .

Primarily, there are two social factors and, consequently, two ideological trends in the workers' movement, which have acted as a brake on socialist theoretical thought, and led to a revision of certain of the basic scientific postulates of Marxism-Leninism.

The first is the phenomenon of bureaucracy and statism. Closely related to this phenomenon is the tendency towards ideological monopoly, as well as the attempt to transform Marxist thought—which can retain its vitality and revolutionary character only by being continually developed on the basis of practice and experience—into a static collection of rigid dogmas and abstract truths, adjusted to meet certain temporary needs. Therein lies the source of contemporary dogmatism and the attempts to carry out specific statist-pragmatic revisions of the determined scientific postulates of Marxism-Leninism. And it is this very dogmatism which, while carrying out a profound anti-scientific revision of Marxism and Leninism, proclaims as revisionism any genuine effort towards the real furtherance of Marxist thought in contemporary social conditions.

That the development of Marxist thought had lagged behind the development of events was also due to the fact that Stalin had, within the orbit of the communist movement, authoritatively and incontrovertibly, for several decades, passed judgment on all contemporary social processes. Some of Stalin's appraisals have proved to be correct, but a number of his theoretical conceptions have been refuted in practice. In his theoretical analysis Stalin made deviations from the materialist dialectical method towards subjectivism and metaphysics. Irrespective of the character of certain of his theories, however, it is clear that such an ideological monopoly was bound to exert an influence in favour of the dogmatization of Marxism and Leninism. . . .

The second factor which had a negative effect on the development of socialist thought was the influence of bourgeois ideologies, opportunism and reformism, declassé anarchism, and so forth. These influences gave rise to attempts to revise the basic scientific postulates of socialism, that is to say, of Marxism and Leninism, along the lines of bourgeois-liberalism and reformism. Revisionism of this type, in fact, is the ideological expression of the abandonment of socialist positions, and it reveals a propensity to reestablish one or another form of bourgeois society. It attacks the revolutionary ideological foundations of the workers' movement, and, under the cloak of pseudo-liberal phrases, sacrifices the interests of the working class and socialism to the interests of reactionary social forces. . . .

Bilateral and Multilateral Cooperation

The Yugoslav Communists do not make an issue of the forms of cooperation between Communist Parties, or between Communist Parties and other socialist and progressive movements, but they do make an issue of the substance of this cooperation. They are in favour of both bilateral and multilateral cooperation, on condition that it is always based on full equality, that neither side imposes its own views on the other, and that there is no interference in the internal relations of the parties involved. Furthermore, this cooperation must be in the interests of peace, socialism, and social progress generally. The League of Yugoslav Communists considers that both bilateral and multilateral forms of cooperation are essential elements in establishing the unity of the activities of the socialist forces and of the progressive efforts of mankind. If, however, the Yugoslav Communists under present conditions attribute significance primarily to various forms of bilateral cooperation, this is because of the above mentioned objective conditions of contemporary socialist development, and because the earlier forms of multilateral cooperation between the workers' parties produced, in addition to their positive aspects (when such forms corresponded to a definite historical period), also negative phenomena which inflicted considerable harm on the struggle for socialism and peace, and which the workers' movement must eradicate if it does not wish the democratic principles of socialist internationalism to be tarnished once again.

Ideological Monopoly

Most notable among these phenomena are tendencies towards ideological monopoly. Tendencies towards ideological monopoly have always been an obstacle to the development of socialist thought, and a source of dogmatism and opportunist-revisionist reaction. And such tendencies brought in their wake rivalry for an unconditional leading role in the workers' movement; and this had many negative consequences at a time when there was not a single working class party in power. Tendencies towards ideological monopoly can inflict even greater damage once working class parties have come to power. The task of the workers' movement

—and especially of the Communists of the larger, more powerful socialist countries, with greater responsibilities—is to fight, both in theory and in practice, for relations of equality. In so doing they should start from the principle that the validity and progressive nature of a given ideology, or of given forms of socialist development, depend exclusively on the vital capacity and verifiability of that ideology in practice, and not on the approval of one or another international body. Any aspect of ideological monopoly which hampered free socialist development in socialist countries would act as a brake on the development of international socialism generally. For this reason the League of Yugoslav Communists considers that those forms of international cooperation which unite, on the widest possible basis, efforts to solve common problems of the struggle for peace, of the struggle for socialism and socialist development, are specially appropriate at the present time.

In the interests of further socialist development, free socialist democratic relations between the parties of the socialist countries are essential. In the struggle for the victory of socialism, it may happen that the working class of one or another country is, for a certain period of time, the standard-bearer of that struggle, or its vanguard, or it may possess greater material power; but that does not entitle it to a monopoly position in the workers' movement, least of all to monopoly in the sphere of ideology. Past experience has shown, and is making even clearer today, that cooperation in the workers' movement is possible only between equals.

Also characteristic of contemporary development is the advent to power of a number of Communist Parties. As a result of this, the question of relations between Communist Parties appears in yet another historically new aspect.

The leaders of the Communist Parties which are in power are not responsible for their work to their membership only, but to the entire nation as well. This fact must find adequate expression in the character of their mutual relations. In their mutual relations Communist Parties in power cannot pass resolutions which are the competence of the elective body, elected by all the citizens. The Communist Parties have often failed to take this into account, thus restricting the significance and role of those representative bodies.

To proclaim the path and form of socialist development in any single country as being the only correct path and form, is nothing but a dogma which obstructs the process of the socialist transformation of the world. The general aims of socialism are common to all, but the rate and forms of the progress of society towards these aims are and must be different, in accordance with the concrete conditions of different countries and different parts of the world. The freedom of internal socialist development and the absence of any attempt to impose specific forms on others, non-interference in the internal life and internal development of other movements, and free and equal exchange of experiences and socialist theoretical thought, should be the fundamental principle in mutual relations between socialist countries and socialist movements. . . .

Socialist Democracy as a Direct Democracy

The League of Yugoslav Communists is also of the opinion that the proclamation of absolute monopoly by the Communist Party of political power as a universal and "perpetual" principle of the dictatorship of the proletariat and of socialist development is an untenable dogma.

In the heat of revolutionary struggle for power and its consolidation, the leading role of the Communist Party in the workers' movement may temporarily assume the character of a maximum of concentration of power in the hands of the party for the purpose of establishing the new regime and creating the basic political conditions for socialist development. But the power of the party cannot be a substitute for all the initiative of the masses and all the varied social development through which the creativeness of the new society finds expression. It is for this reason that continuing the work of democratizing the revolutionary system of government and per-suading the leading socialist forces to rely directly on the activity of the masses are regarded as among the foremost tasks after the victory of the revolution. In Yugoslavia this process has developed in the form of mobilizing the masses—with their various ideological and political views, but united in the common ideal of socialism—through the People's Front and the Socialist Alliance of the Working People of Yugoslavia. In other countries this may find expression in other forms, such as alliances and coalitions with other socialist and progressive movements, with peasant parties and the like.

What is most important in all this is the fact that the working class cannot become master of its own fate, and consequently the main driving force of social progress, unless it secures direct control over management of production and distribution. In this function, no regime of state control over the private owner, no state machinery or state manager, can be substituted for the working class. The further development of the existing forms of democracy towards forms which are an organic component of new socialist economic relations is an indispensable condition and integral part of socialist progress.

Hence, the Communists are not faced with the alternative of a multi-party or a one-party system. Both alternatives may be valid during a particular period in socialist development in different countries. They are faced with the problem of deciding what new forms of democracy should be brought into being by socialist development; what new forms are required by social relations based on social ownership over the means of production? When referring to the multi- or one-party systems as initial forms of socialist democracy, one should not lose sight of the fact that socialist democracy does not exclude, but rather presupposes a variety and versatility of concrete forms of democracy in different countries, and in a single country, during various phases of socialist development.

William E. Griffith

17 REVISIONISM IN EASTERN EUROPE

"What Happened to Revisionism?" *Problems of Communism*, IX, No. 2 (March-April, 1960), excerpted from pp. 2–3. Footnote references have been deleted.

William E. Griffith is Director of the International Communism Project at the M.I.T. Center for International Studies, Professor of Soviet Diplomacy at the Fletcher School of Law and Diplomacy, Tufts University, and Lecturer in Political Science, M.I.T. He is the author of Albania and the Sino-Soviet Rift, The Sino-Soviet Rift, *and other works.*

As it emerged in Eastern Europe after the advent of the post-Stalin political "thaw," revisionism was essentially an effort by party intellectuals to bring about the correction of certain recognized evils in Communist society through a critical reevaluation and reinterpretation of party dogma. It sought to revitalize Marxism-Leninism by restoring to it some of Marxism's earlier qualities of idealism, notably its emphasis on humanistic values, genuine internationalism, and advancement of the general welfare of mankind.

Revisionism derived its initial impetus from growing intellectual disillusionment—especially among the younger intellectuals, many of whom had supported Stalinism—with the practical consequences of Stalinist rule: the complete suppression of individual liberties and cultural freedom of expression, widespread economic suffering, and the reign of police terror. The first manifestations in 1955 were largely confined to protests against rigid party controls over cultural activity, but following Khrushchev's revelation of Stalin's crimes at the 20th CPSU Congress, the revolt rapidly spread into the areas of politics, economics, and party ideology. Refusing to accept the Soviet explanation of Stalin's crimes as merely the result of "the cult of personality," the revisionists saw the deeper causes of Stalinist misrule in defects inherent in the Communist system itself, and this in turn led them to challenge the validity of certain basic principles first of Stalinist, then of Leninist, and finally—in some cases—even Marxist dogma. While it embraced varying shades and degrees of opinion, revisionist thinking on the main points at issue may be briefly summarized as follows:

1. In regard to the position of the Soviet Union and CPSU vis-à-vis other Communist states and parties, the revisionists generally rejected the Stalinist interpretation of "proletarian internationalism" which required the complete subordination of the orbit regimes to "the leading role of the Soviet Union." Instead, they insisted that intra-bloc relations be based on genuine national and party equality. It was this revisionist principle which the Soviet Union opposed most inflexibly, and which—in the extreme form it took in Hungary—led to Soviet armed intervention. Revisionism also stressed the principle of "separate roads to socialism," which had already received official Soviet recognition in the June 1955 Khrushchev-Tito joint declaration and again in Khrushchev's official 20th Congress report.

2. In the crucial area of political doctrine, the revisionists strongly opposed the narrow Leninist-Stalinist concept of "the dictatorship of the proletariat" on the ground that it meant, in effect, absolute party dictatorship and inevitably led to "bureaucratism" and "state capitalism." To forestall a recurrence of these dangers, they urged the establishment of a dual system of institutional safeguards against over-concentration of power: on the one hand, genuine democratization of the inner-party structure, procedures, and rules of discipline; and, on the other, external checks upon the party's power in the form of a more independent and authoritative role for parliament and—in the more radical forms of revisionism—the institution of a limited multi-party system which would allow the independent political existence of other parties generally subscribing to socialist principles. Some extreme revisionists advocated the decidedly un-Leninist concept of the party's role as primarily that of political educator of the masses.

3. In the economic sphere, revisionism placed major emphasis on ending the rigid application of certain policies which, under Stalin, had acquired the force of economic doctrine: principally, forced collectivization of agriculture, the priority development of heavy industry at the expense of consumer needs, extreme centralization of economic authority, and severely exploitative labor practices. Instead, the revisionists stood for a gradualist approach to collectivization, greater emphasis on the production and distribution of consumer goods, economic decentralization, reduced capital investment programs, more rational and balanced planning, restoration of a free market in some sectors of the economy, lower production norms for workers, profit-sharing, and—above all—greater "economic democracy" through workers' councils functioning as organs of

factory self-government. Some of the more radical revisionists, however, went so far as to challenge fundamental Marxist theories regarding the evolution of capitalism (pauperization of the working class, etc.) and the ultimate necessity of its overthrow by proletarian revolution. Arguing that modern technology and industrial organization have tended to transform capitalist relations of production, they foresaw a progressive emancipation of the working class under capitalism and a gradual rapprochement between the capitalist and socialist systems of production and social organization, obviating the necessity of violent revolution.

4. Finally, in the intellectual and cultural sphere, revisionism stood for the complete sweeping away of Stalinist restrictions upon freedom of thought and expression, including restrictions upon the freedom to criticize and re-evaluate party ideology in the light of objective historical truth. It also called for a return to Marxist "humanism" and adherence to absolute standards of morality as an indispensable basis for preventing a recurrence of the flagrant abuses of power and mass crimes of the Stalinist era.

Bibliography

Berdyaev, N., *The Origins of Russian Communism*. New York: Charles Scribner's Sons, 1937.

Carew-Hunt, R. N., *The Theory and Practice of Communism*. London: Geoffrey Bles, Ltd., 1950.

Cohen, A. A., *The Communism of Mao Tse-tung*. Chicago: University of Chicago Press, 1964.

Daniels, R. V., ed., *A Documentary History of Communism*. New York: Random House, 1960.

Drachkovitch, M. M., *Marxism in the Modern World*. Stanford, Calif.: Stanford University Press, 1965.

Labedz, L., ed., *Revisionism: Essays on the History of Marxist Ideas*. New York: Frederick A. Praeger, Inc., 1962.

Lapenna, I., *State and Law: Soviet and Yugoslav Theory*. New Haven: Yale University Press, 1964.

Leites, N., *A Study of Bolshevism*. New York: Free Press of Glencoe, Inc., 1953.

Marcuse, H., *Soviet Marxism: A Critical Analysis*. New York: Columbia University Press, 1958.

Mendel, A. P., ed., *Essential Works of Marxism*. New York: Bantam Books, Inc., 1961.

Meyer, A., *Leninism*. Cambridge, Mass.: Harvard University Press, 1957.

———, *Marxism: The Unity of Theory and Practice*. Cambridge, Mass.: Harvard University Press, 1954.

Mills, C. W., ed., *The Marxists*. New York: Dell Publishing Co., Inc., 1962.

Moore, B., Jr., *Soviet Politics: The Dilemma of Power.* Cambridge, Mass.: Harvard University Press, 1950.

Schram, S. R., *The Political Thought of Mao Tse-tung.* New York: Frederick A. Praeger, Inc., 1963.

Schwartz, B., *Chinese Communism and the Rise of Mao.* Cambridge, Mass.: Harvard University Press, 1952.

Wetter, G. A., *Dialectical Materialism.* New York: Frederick A. Praeger, Inc., 1958. Translated from the German.

Wolfe, B. D., *Marxism: One Hundred Years in the Life of a Doctrine.* New York: The Dial Press, Inc., 1965.

Chapter Four

The Party:
The Fulcrum of Power

Lenin's greatest contribution to the establishment and preservation of communist power was the centralized revolutionary Party. Guided by the most "scientific" theory and staffed by cadres of professionals, this disciplined, hierarchical, politically tempered elite constituted itself the vanguard of the working class. Moving beyond Marx's general belief in the historical inevitability of the proletarian triumph, Lenin fashioned the instrument for its realization. But the Party machine really came of age during the Stalin era. Stalin perfected the organizational weapon and emerged from the succession struggle of the 1920's both as champion and master of the *apparatchiki,* or professional Party organization men. He realized the potential of the Party and shaped it to establish undisputed control over society. Stalin gave the Party its contemporary form and pervasive functions (Reading 18).

Is one-man rule a requisite feature of all communist systems? Or are they evolving as oligarchies? For almost a generation, ultimate authority in the Soviet Union rested with Stalin, as it does today in China with Mao and in Yugoslavia with Tito. This has led many Western observers to conclude that one-man rule is inevitable, even necessary, in a communist system. They cite Trotsky's prescient denunciation, in 1904, long before he joined the Bolsheviks, of the Leninist conception of the Party: "In Lenin's scheme, the Party takes the place of the working class; the Party organization displaces the Party; the Central Committee displaces the Party organization; and finally the dictator displaces the Central Committee." On the other hand, there are those who argue that such a view of Soviet (and communist) politics is too mechanistic, too undifferentiated, and too nonpolitical. They posit instead the existence of an oligarchy, composed of minor oligarchs standing at the head of competing subgroups which are engaged in a continual struggle over power and policy (Reading 22). The oligarchy may at any given time be small—5, 50, or 150—but it nonetheless involves the interplay of rival factions which may form temporary alliances on particular policies. The leader, who may be regarded as first among almost-equals, can carry the day through a reliance on prestige, persuasion, and adept juggling of arch-rivals within the oligarchy rather than through a reliance on physical terror. He will survive all struggles for power as long as he can retain the support of a majority of the oligarchy because, in the perceptive words of Boris Nicolaevsky:

> This struggle for power need by no means at each moment be a struggle for the overthrow of the government or removal of the Central Committee first secretary. Such "maximalist" goals always are fixed at the end of a long road of development which is marked by heightening animosities. On this road there are always many intermediary phases, when the contending groups set "limited objectives" . . .[1]

Such a situation appears to characterize the political strife in post-Stalin U.S.S.R. Western specialists have discerned that in China, too, where Mao's primacy is presumably unassailable, there are disagreements at the highest levels of the Party. For example, some important individuals in the power structure of the Chinese Communist Party "would have preferred to moderate the ideological dispute with the Soviet Union" and to have taken a less intractable stand,[2] and agreement on the "great leap forward" was less than unanimous, "some comrades" clinging to such outmoded ideas as "keeping to the right is better than keeping to the left."[3]

The administrative organization of Communist Parties is remarkably similar. Pyramidal and centralist, the Parties have at their base a vast network of primary Party organizations or cells—approximately three hundred thousand in the U.S.S.R. and more than a million in China—and at their apogee a Presidium or Politburo, which retains overriding authority (Reading 21). In addition, there is a Party Secretariat which operates "under the direction" of the Presidium, supervising and coordinating the execution of policy on a daily basis through the Party central organs, bureaus, and committees. The powers of the Party First Secretary, or his equivalent, are frequently misunderstood. The position of First Secretary is the all-important key to political power not because of any monopoly over senior-level appointments (Stalin's Politburo made them, according to

---

[1] Quoted by Sidney Ploss, *Conflict and Decision-making in Soviet Russia* (Princeton, N.J.: Princeton University Press, 1965), pp. 284–85.
[2] "Reflections on the Unity of the Chinese Communist Leadership," *Current Scene*, II, No. 26 (January 1, 1964), 3.
[3] *Ibid.,* p. 4.

Soviet literature, and Khrushchev certainly did not control the professional advancement of all top Party and government bosses), but because it assures a major channel of information and communication to the Presidium and a means of close, continuing contact with lower and upper-level personnel. Control of the flow of communications is a powerful weapon in struggles for power. Through a system of multiple and indirect elections, and through selective membership and carefully reviewed promotions, Party leaders insulate themselves against any sudden disenfranchising grass-roots revolts. Changes in leadership are wrought at the top, and the effects filter downward in the Party pyramid.

All Communist Parties are guided by the organizational principle of democratic centralism, which the Rules of the Communist Party of China interpret as "centralism on the basis of democracy and democracy under centralized guidance." The Party encourages "inner-Party democracy" and "lively contact between the higher and lower Party organizations." But at the same time it emphasizes that democratic centralism "demands that every Party organization should strictly abide by the principle of collective leadership coupled with individual responsibility and that every Party member and Party organization should be subject to Party supervision from above and from below."[4] Shortcomings in the Party are acknowledged to exist, but are considered remediable, being the result of "subjectivist" failings (Readings 23 and 24); they are not regarded as inherent, as the inevitable flaws of a monopolistic power apparatus in which protracted dissent is viewed as "treason."

There are two alternative channels for issuing directives—Party and governmental—but the driving force behind both is the Party. The relation of government to the Party is quite simple and direct: The government's duty is to carry out Party policy. At each level, Party activists check on the governmental apparatus to ensure proper implementation of policy. The government serves as the legitimizing constitutional structure through which Party directives are enacted. In the Soviet Union, the highest authority in the Communist Party is theoretically the All-Union Congress; in China, the National Party Congress. In both cases they consist of delegates from regional Party organs. Between sessions the Party Congresses vest their power in a Central Committee which in turn elects a Presidium in the U.S.S.R., or a Politburo in China, and a Secretariat. In practice this power relationship is reversed; the real core of power is in the Presidium and Secretariat. Governmental authority is placed in the Supreme Soviet in the U.S.S.R. and in the National People's Congress in China, each of which in reality has little power. Elected for four years, the government deputies meet infrequently, and then only to ratify decisions or proposals which have already been decided on by the Party.

---

[4] *The Constitution of the Communist Party of China* (Peking: Foreign Languages Press, 1956), p. 14.

In communist dictatorships, the similarities in the Party and government structures are striking. Theoretically, both the Party Congress and the supreme governmental body are the highest authority in the Party and government, respectively. Both are actually the least authoritative; both vest their supposed powers in smaller bodies which are the actual wielders of power. Another similarity lies in the nature of the leadership. As a rule, the most important members of the Party hold the important government posts. This network of interlocking directorates assures the Party control of the governmental hierarchy. There have been some notable exceptions, the result of special circumstances: Stalin did not hold any formal government position between 1930 and 1941; and Mao Tse-tung resigned as Chairman of the People's Republic of China, the equivalent of President, on December 17, 1958, retaining only his Party posts.

That the Party is *the* power pyramid is evident from even a cursory examination of the situation in communist countries. There is, for example, the experience of Brezhnev, who was made President in 1960 and elevated to the Secretariat in June 1963. When he was groomed for the succession by Khrushchev, Brezhnev resigned as President of the Soviet Union and devoted full time to his activities in the all-important Party Secretariat. The post of President is not a key to power, but a combination of duties in the Party Presidium and Secretariat is a sure indication of an individual's rising importance. In Poland, Wladyslaw Gomulka, the First Secretary of the Polish United Workers (Communist) Party, does not hold a top government post, yet he is the acknowledged leader. He announces major decisions and determines Poland's policies toward foreign countries. When a new President had to be elected because of the sudden death of the incumbent in August 1964, it was Gomulka who proposed Edward Ochab's name, thereby making unanimous approval by the rubber-stamp Sejm (Parliament) a foregone conclusion. In Hungary, in the wake of the abortive 1956 revolution, Janos Kadar was installed by Moscow as the First Secretary of the Hungarian Socialist Workers (Communist) Party because the function of steering political business rested in the Secretariat. As Moscow's proxy, Kadar has set the line for reform and innovation. Clearly, for the ambitious, the aim is advancement within the Party, not the governmental, hierarchy.

A continual struggle over functions, funds, and prestige is waged within the Party power structure and between the Party apparatus and the other institutional centers, i.e., the military establishment, economic bureaucracy, and secret police. The intra-Party rivalries have heretofore been the most important. Stalin and Khrushchev both rose to the top of the political pyramid by packing, then dominating, the executive organs of the Party: the Central Committee, Presidium, and Secretariat. But there were differences. A secure Party base sufficed for Stalin to establish his rule because there were not in 1929 any rival centers of power. The Party was, as in Lenin's day, the unchallenged repository of power. However, the key to

Stalin's subsequent despotism lay in his ability to utilize terror to diminish the Party's stature and to transform it into a compliant instrument which was dwarfed, controlled, and manipulated like any other bureaucratic institution of Soviet society. Stalin also cultivated among his lieutenants, who headed the various loci of power, feuds which only he could settle. On the other hand, for Khrushchev, control of the Party was only one stage of the power struggle, which required also the emasculation of the secret police and the neutralizing of the bureaucracy and the military. In contrast to Stalin, Khrushchev restored the Party, and particularly the Party's executive bodies, to the politically preeminent role that they had played under Lenin. But in his last years in power, Khrushchev insisted upon burdening the Party with additional responsibilities for the direct operation of the economy, a factor that was instrumental in his deposal; indeed, it may have been *the* most important catalyst behind the palace coup.

Over the decades, there have been significantly different concepts concerning the role of the Party—from the "general direction" of Stalin to the "technical functionalism" of Khrushchev and back to the generalist position of Stalin (Reading 19). The post-Khrushchev Soviet leadership has reasserted the primacy of the political function of the Party, reversing the trend, under Khrushchev, to more direct involvement in the managerial and administrative aspects of the country's economic life. One of the first decisions made by Brezhnev and Kosygin was to merge (in November 1964) the industrial and rural territorial party organizations, which had been separated two years earlier by Khrushchev. Deploring [Khrushchev's] "addiction to half-baked reorganizations," *Pravda* observed that "Where the scientific approach is replaced by subjectivism, by an infatuation with schemes for the sake of schemes, and by arbitrary and hasty decisions, failures are inevitable and errors cannot be avoided." To the Chinese these differences over the role of the Party are insignificant since they see the post-Stalin CPSU as having been undermined and corrupted by "bourgeois" attitudes and behavior (Reading 20).

The Party is once again the dominant institution of Soviet life. But there is this important difference between the U.S.S.R. of Lenin and that of today: Under Lenin, the Party formulated its policies and imposed them as it deemed appropriate without having to weigh the views of the technical intelligentsia, most of whose representatives did not hold Party membership; today, the Party must consider the information and reactions that assuredly come from the various interest groups which have developed within the Party as a consequence of the nation's industrialization and modernization, and of the liberalized policy of admission to the Party. The Party organs are the ultimate arena within which policy alternatives are selected, but the "generalist" Party leaders dare not ignore the views and pressures of such technicians as the military and the industrial managers. Indeed, protagonists within the Party organs have their allies (and rivals) in all the main institutional centers of political authority.

The Party oligarchy is therefore not monolithic, nor is it manipulated at the whim of one man. Instead, it is composed of ever-adjusting coalitions which derive important measures of support from the senior members of the technological elite who, we may assume, are consulted and accommodated on policies affecting their particular bailiwicks. A leader neglects at his own peril to conciliate the technical specialists. Thus, the dissatisfaction of segments of the military and industrial establishment over Khrushchev's penchant for tampering with economic priorities may have induced them to support the coalition that deposed the First Secretary. The more economically developed the society, the more differentiated are the interest groups, and the more the political elite have to be responsive to the views of the technically competent.

In less-developed China, by way of contrast, the only significant opposition to Party policies, with the exception of the 1954 Kao Kang affair, appears to have come from segments of the military.[5] In 1958, for example, disagreements arose within the military and between military and Party men over military objections to Mao's old thesis that "weapons are an important factor in war but not the decisive one; it is man and not material that is decisive." The Party rebuked the professional military men for questioning the wisdom of diverting human and physical resources of the armed forces "away from military preparedness and into economic construction and political study,"[6] and purged a number of senior officers.

The Chinese oligarchy is very likely smaller than its Soviet counterpart, as a result of the different ages of their revolutions and the different stages of their economic development. Ultimate power in China resides with Mao and the handful of trusted, time-tested Party veterans of Yenan days: Liu Shao-ch'i, Teng Hsiao-ping, Chou En-lai, Lin Piao, Tung Pi-wu, Lo Jui-ching, and Peng Chen. The leadership circle probably does not extend beyond the membership of the Central Committee, which, it may be noted, is only about half the size of its Soviet counterpart, a statistic suggesting that the Soviet oligarchy is more broadly based and reflective of more interest groups; this acquires added cogency when one considers that the Chinese Communist Party has almost twice the eleven million membership of the Communist Party of the Soviet Union.

The recruitment and circulation of political leaders is an essential function in any society. By whom and by what process are the leaders

---

[5] Kao Kang, a member of the Standing Committee of the Politburo, a Vice-Premier and a member of the Central Committee, was accused of trying to establish his personal hegemony in northeast China and "instigate Party members in the army to support his conspiracy against the Central Committee of the Party." According to the Chinese Communist Party, after he was warned to desist from his "anti-party" activities, "Kao Kang not only did not admit his guilt to the Party, but committed suicide as an ultimate expression of his betrayal of the Party." [Quoted material from John Wilson Lewis, *Major Doctrines of Communist China* (New York: W. W. Norton & Company, Inc., 1964) p. 37.]

[6] *Current Scene, op. cit.,* p. 4.

chosen in communist societies? How is the succession determined in the absence of orderly constitutional procedures? Communist societies are young and have experienced few transfers of power. China and Yugoslavia have yet to face a succession crisis; the stability and longevity of their leaders is an extraordinary phenomenon, rare among revolutionary movements. Our data are limited primarily to the Soviet experience (Reading 25). The Soviet Union has surmounted three succession crises—Lenin, Stalin, and Khrushchev—but always after a period of political struggle, a selecting-out of the major contestants for power. The number of electors has been small and not responsible to mass constituencies.

The deposal of Khrushchev was sudden, dramatic, and complete. He was deposed when he was no longer able to command the loyalty of the very men whom he had elevated to positions of authority. The removal, once accomplished, was given an official imprimatur in accordance with Party and governmental constitutional procedures. The initial explanation given to the Soviet people was that:

> The plenary meeting of the CPSU central committee granted N. S. Khrushchev's request that he be relieved of his duties as First Secretary of the CPSU central committee, member of the presidium of the CPSU central committee and Chairman of the USSR Council of Ministers in view of his advanced age and the deterioration of his health.

Within a matter of days, however, Khrushchev was tacitly denounced for "harebrained" policies and excessive concentration of personal power. It is clear, from the suddenness of the deposal and the secrecy which surrounded its planning and excution, that Khrushchev did not step down from office; he was pushed out. The "election" of October 14, 1964, brought to power a new leadership, which has no fixed term of office within which to prove its mettle and which must ever be on guard against a repetition of the very act that led it to the pinnacle.

In the spring of 1965, there were two leadership crises in Eastern Europe: one because of death, the other because of an abortive coup. In late March, the Rumanian communist leader, Georghiu-Dej, died and was replaced by his heir-apparent, Nicolae Ceausescu. A few weeks later, in Bulgaria, a group of Army officers and Party officials attempted unsuccessfully to unseat the Moscow-dominated Party leadership headed by Todor Zhivkov. Here, as in the Soviet Union, the elevation and retention of political leaders was the result of a round of Party cabals, the workings of which remain shrouded in the secrecy and isolation that characterize all communist leadership circles. Although we do not know how the "elections" or transfers of power are conducted, we do know that each "election" has differed somewhat from the previous one and has affected, and in turn been affected by, the evolving political system.

Joseph Stalin

18 THE ROLE
OF THE COMMUNIST PARTY
IN SOVIET POLITICAL LIFE

Joseph Stalin, *Problems of Leninism* (Moscow: Foreign Languages Publishing House, 1953), excerpted from pp. 97–99, 100, 102–118.

Joseph Vissarionovich Djugashvili, better known to history as Joseph Stalin, was born in 1879 and died in 1953. An early adherent of the underground revolutionary Marxist movement, he rose rapidly in the Bolshevik Party (renamed the Communist Party in 1918) and emerged as an important member of the Politburo during the period of "war communism" (1917–1921). He was appointed General-Secretary of the Communist Party in April 1922, and extended his control over the Party within a few years after the death of V. I. Lenin in January 1924. From 1929 to 1953, Stalin ruled the Soviet Union. Though denigrated since the Twentieth Congress of 1956 for his arbitrariness and tyranny, Stalin's conception of the Communist Party remains an accepted feature of the Soviet political system.

There is a necessity for a new party, a militant party, a revolutionary party, one bold enough to lead the proletarians in the struggle for power, sufficiently experienced to find its bearings amidst the complex conditions of a revolutionary situation, and sufficiently flexible to steer clear of all submerged rocks in the path to its goal.

Without such a party it is useless even to think of overthrowing imperialism and achieving the dictatorship of the proletariat.

This new party is the party of Leninism.

What are the specific features of this new party?

THE PARTY AS THE VANGUARD OF THE WORKING CLASS

The Party must be, first of all, the *vanguard* of the working class. The Party must absorb all the best elements of the working class, their experience, their revolutionary spirit, their selfless devotion to the cause of the proletariat. But in order that it may really be the vanguard, the Party must be armed with revolutionary theory, with a knowledge of the laws of

111

the movement, with a knowledge of the laws of revolution. Without this it will be incapable of directing the struggle of the proletariat, of leading the proletariat. The Party cannot be a real party if it limits itself to registering what the masses of the working class feel and think, if it drags at the tail of the spontaneous movement, if it is unable to overcome the inertness and the political indifference of the spontaneous movement, if it is unable to rise above the momentary interests of the proletariat, if it is unable to elevate the masses to the understanding of the class interests of the proletariat. The Party must stand at the head of the working class; it must see farther than the working class; it must lead the proletariat, and not follow in the tail of the spontaneous movement.

.   .   .

No army at war can dispense with an experienced General Staff if it does not want to be doomed to certain defeat. Is it not clear that the proletariat can still less dispense with such a General Staff if it does not want to give itself up to be devoured by its moral enemies? But where is this General Staff? Only the revolutionary party of the proletariat can serve as this General Staff. The working class without a revolutionary party is an army without a General Staff.

The Party is the General Staff of the proletariat.

But the Party cannot be only a *vanguard* detachment. It must at the same time be a detachment of the *class,* part of the class, closely bound up with it by all the fibres of its being. The distinction between the vanguard and the main body of the working class, between Party members and non-Party people, cannot disappear until classes disappear; it will exist as long as the ranks of the proletariat continue to be replenished with newcomers from other classes, as long as the working class as a whole is not in a position to rise to the level of the vanguard.

.   .   .

THE PARTY AS THE HIGHEST FORM
OF CLASS ORGANIZATION OF THE PROLETARIAT

The Party is the organized detachment of the working class. But the Party is not the only organization of the working class. The proletariat has also a number of other organizations, without which it cannot properly wage the struggle against capital: trade unions, cooperative societies, factory organizations, parliamentary groups, non-Party women's associations, the press, cultural and educational organizations, youth leagues, revolutionary fighting organizations (in times of open revolutionary action), Soviets of deputies as the form of state organization (if the proletariat is in power), etc. The overwhelming majority of these organizations are non-Party, and only some of them adhere directly to the Party, or represent its off-shoots. All these organizations, under certain conditions, are absolutely necessary for the working class, for without them it would be impossible to consolidate the class positions of the proletariat in the diverse spheres of struggle; for without them it would be impossible to steel the proletariat as the force whose mission it is to replace the bourgeois order by the socialist order. But how can single leadership be exercised with such an abundance of organizations? What guarantee is there that this multiplicity of organizations will not lead to divergency in leadership? It might be argued that each of these organizations carries on its work in its own special field, and that therefore these organizations cannot hinder one another. This, of course, is true. But it is also true that all these organizations should work in one direction for they serve *one* class, the class of the proletarians. The question then arises: who is to determine the line, the general direction, along which the work of all these organizations is to be conducted? Where is that central organization which is not only able, because it has the necessary experience, to work out such a general line, but, in addition, is in a position, because it has sufficient prestige, to induce all these organizations to carry out this line, so as to attain unity of leadership and to preclude the possibility of working at cross purposes?

This organization is the Party of the proletariat.

The Party possesses all the necessary qualifications for this because, in the first place, it is the rallying centre of the finest elements in the working class, who have direct connections with the non-Party organizations of the proletariat and very frequently lead them; because, secondly, the Party, as the rallying centre of the finest members of the working class, is the best school for training leaders of the working class, capable of directing every form of organization of their class; because, thirdly, the Party, as the best school for training leaders of the working class, is, by reason of its experience and prestige, the only organization capable of centralizing the leadership of the struggle of the proletariat, thus transforming each and every non-Party organization of the working class into an auxiliary body and transmission belt linking the Party with the class.

The Party is the highest form of class organization of the proletariat.

. . .

THE PARTY AS THE INSTRUMENT
OF THE DICTATORSHIP OF THE PROLETARIAT

The Party is the highest form of organization of the proletariat. The Party is the principal guiding force within the class of the proletarians and among the organizations of that class. But it does not by any means follow from this that the Party can be regarded as an end in itself, as a self-sufficient force. The Party is not only the highest form of class association of the proletarians; it is at the same time an *instrument* in the hands of the proletariat *for* achieving the dictatorship when that has not yet been achieved and *for* consolidating and expanding the dictatorship when it has already been achieved. . . . The proletariat needs the Party first of all as its General Staff, which it must have for the successful seizure of power. It need hardly be proved that without a Party capable of rallying around itself the mass organizations of the proletariat, and of centralizing the leadership of the entire movement during the progress of the struggle, the proletariat in Russia could never have established its revolutionary dictatorship.

. . .

THE PARTY AS THE EMBODIMENT OF UNITY OF WILL, INCOMPATIBLE WITH THE EXISTENCE OF FACTIONS

The achievement and maintenance of the dictatorship of the proletariat is impossible without a party which is strong by reason of its solidarity and iron discipline. But iron discipline in the Party is inconceivable without unity of will, without complete and absolute unity of action on the part of all members of the Party. This does not mean, of course, that the possibility of contests of opinion within the Party is thereby precluded. On the contrary, iron discipline does not preclude but presupposes criticism and contest of opinion within the Party. Least of all does it mean that discipline must be "blind." On the contrary, iron discipline does not preclude but presupposes conscious and voluntary submission, for only conscious discipline can be truly iron discipline. But after a contest of opinion has been closed, after criticism has been exhausted and a decision has been arrived at, unity of will and unity of action of all Party members are the necessary conditions without which neither Party unity nor iron discipline in the Party is conceivable.

. . .

[From] this it follows that the existence of factions is incompatible either with the Party's unity or with its iron discipline. It need hardly be proved that the existence of factions leads to the existence of a number of centres, and the existence of a number of centres connotes the absence of one common centre in the Party, the breaking up of the unity of will, the weakening and disintegration of the dictatorship. . . . [The] parties of the Communist International, whose activities are conditioned by the task of achieving and consolidating the dictatorship of the proletariat, cannot afford to be "liberal" or to permit freedom of factions.

The Party represents unity of will, which precludes all factionalism and division of authority in the Party. Hence Lenin's warning about the "danger of factionalism from the point of view of Party unity and of effecting the unity of will of the vanguard of the proletariat as the fundamental condition for the success of the dictatorship of the proletariat," which is embodied in the special resolution of the Tenth Congress of our Party, "On Party Unity." Hence Lenin's demand for the "complete elimination of all factionalism" and the "immediate dissolution of all groups, without exception, that had been formed on the basis of various platforms," on pain of unconditional and immediate expulsion from the Party.

19 THREE CONTRASTING SOVIET VIEWS OF THE ROLE OF THE PARTY

Debate over the role that the Party should play has long been a crucial item in intra-Party discussions. This Reading consists of three selections which demonstrate the differences between Stalin and Khrushchev, and between Khrushchev and his successors—general direction vs. technical functionalism.

Joseph Stalin

STYLE IN WORK

Joseph Stalin, "Style in Work," from "The Foundations of Leninism" in *Problems of Leninism* (Moscow: Foreign Languages Publishing House, 1953), pp. 110–12.

This excerpt is from a speech Stalin delivered in 1924.

I am not referring to literary style. What I have in mind is style in work, that specific and peculiar feature in the practice of Leninism which creates the special type of Leninist worker. Leninism is a school of theory and practice which trains a special type of Party and state worker, creates a special Leninist style in work.

What are the characteristic features of this style? What are its peculiarities?

It has two specific features:

a. the Russian revolutionary sweep and
b. American efficiency.

The style of Leninism is a combination of these two specific features in Party and state work.

The Russian revolutionary sweep is an antidote to inertness, routine, conservatism, mental stagnation and slavish submission to ancestral traditions. The Russian revolutionary sweep is the life-giving force which stimulates thought, impels things forward, breaks the past and opens up perspectives. Without it no progress is possible.

But Russian revolutionary sweep has every chance of degenerating in practice into empty "revolutionary" Manilovism[1] if it is not combined with American efficiency in work. Examples of this degeneration are only too numerous. Who does not know the disease of "revolutionary" improvisation and "revolutionary" plan concocting, which springs from the belief in the power of decrees to arrange everything and reform everything? A Russian writer, I. Ehrenburg, in his story *The Percomman (The Perfect Communist Man)*, has portrayed the type of a "Bolshevik" afflicted with this disease, who set himself the task of finding a formula for the ideally perfect man and . . . became "submerged" in this "work." Some gross exaggerations are spun into this story, but it certainly gives a correct likeness of the disease. But no one, I think, has so ruthlessly and bitterly ridiculed those afflicted with this disease as Lenin has done. Lenin stigmatized this morbid belief in improvisation and in concocting decrees as "communist vanity."

> "Communist vanity," says Lenin, "is characteristic of a man who, while still a member of the Communist Party, not having yet been combed out of it, imagines that he can solve all his problems by issuing communist decrees." (See Vol. XXVII, pp. 50–51.)

Lenin usually contrasted hollow "revolutionary" phrasemongering with plain everyday work, thus emphasizing that "revolutionary" improvisation is repugnant to the spirit and the letter of true Leninism.

> "Fewer pompous phrases, more plain, *everyday* work," says Lenin.
> "Less political fireworks and more attention to the simplest but vital facts of communist construction. . . ." (See Vol. XXIV, pp. 343, 335).

American efficiency, on the other hand, is an antidote to "revolutionary" Manilovism and fantastic improvisation. American efficiency is that indomitable force which neither knows nor recognizes obstacles; which with its businesslike perseverance brushes aside all obstacles; which continues at a task once started until it is finished, even if it is a minor task; and without which serious constructive work is inconceivable.

---

[1] Manilov was a landowner in Gogol's novel, *Dead Souls,* who was given to daydreaming and impractical scheming.—Ed.

But American efficiency has every chance of degenerating into narrow and unprincipled commercialism if it is not combined with the Russian revolutionary sweep. Who has not heard of that disease of narrow practicality and unprincipled commercialism which has not infrequently caused certain "Bolsheviks" to degenerate and to abandon the cause of the revolution? We find a reflection of this peculiar disease in a story by B. Pilnyak, entitled *The Barren Year,* which depicts types of Russian "Bolsheviks" of strong will and practical determination who "function" very "energetically," but without vision, without knowing "what it is all about," and who, therefore, stray from the path of revolutionary work. No one has been more incisive in his ridicule of this disease of narrow commercialism than Lenin. He branded it as "narrow-minded practicality" and "brainless commercialism." He usually contrasted it with vital revolutionary work and the necessity of having a revolutionary perspective in all our daily activities, thus emphasizing that this unprincipled commercialism is as repugnant to true Leninism as "revolutionary" improvisation.

The combination of the Russian revolutionary sweep with American efficiency is the essence of Leninism in Party and state work.

This combination alone produces the finished type of Leninist worker, the style of Leninism in work.

Nikita S. Khrushchev

THE PARTY
AND TECHNICAL FUNCTIONALISM

Nikita S. Khrushchev, *Current Digest of the Soviet Press,* XI, No. 27 (August 5, 1959), 7. Published weekly at Columbia University. Copyright 1959. By permission.

This comment by Khrushchev was made on June 29, 1959, at a plenum of the Central Committee.

Our Party work will be successful if it is firmly linked with life, is specific and is purposeful. Our Party work rests on the revolutionary theory of Marxism-Leninism which lights the way ahead. But, comrades, we must clearly realize that now, when the power of the state is in the hands of the working class, when the Party directs the entire work of communist construction, material production must be expanded in every way so that this theory will be firmly established in the people's minds and our state strengthened. Therefore the question of production organization is a major part of our entire ideological work at the present stage. (*Applause.*)

Comrades, when Marx was creating his theory and when Lenin was extending it, the working class had not yet had any experience in socialist construction. There was no socialist state in Marx's time. The revolutionaries then had to devote themselves to studying theory and organizing the masses for a revolution, for taking power and for creating real possibilities for building a new life on the basis of the revolutionary theory. Guided by Marxism-Leninism, the working class of our country, headed by the Communist Party, has carried out a socialist revolution. For nearly 42 years the peoples of our country have been building socialism successfully. We have ascended to the skies, having created the first artificial satellites and an artificial planet. In order to secure complete victory we must develop our production in every way, provide more material benefits for the people who are building socialism and communism. (*Stormy applause.*)

It is inadmissible to belittle the role of our theoreticians, but, comrades, it is likewise in no way admissible to belittle others who are forging socialism and communism. They are accomplishing a great task!

One comrade here sent me a note saying: Comrade Khrushchev, all the speakers talk about industry and no one says anything about Party work. My dear comrade, if at the factory where you conduct Party work a defective article is produced while you are giving a lecture on the establishment of communism in our country (*stir in the hall*), wouldn't it be more useful if you organized the people for scientific, better-quality work? This is precisely what Party work is, when everyone does his job, when everyone knows his trade, produces good parts and assembles good machines. What you propose is to give primacy to delivering lectures about how people will think 100 years after the triumph of communism. True, that is a wonderful lecture, and don't you think that I am against good lectures, but we can wait with such reports and lectures for 50 or 80 years or so. (*Laughter, applause.*) But if we turn out defective machines and poor quality articles, we shall not get very far.

V. Stepanov

OPPOSITION TO
"NARROW PRACTICALITY"
IN PARTY WORK

V. Stepanov, "Higher Ideals and Day-to-Day Concerns of the Party," *Pravda* (May 17, 1965), translated in *Current Digest of the Soviet Press,* XVII, No. 20 (June 9, 1965), excerpted from pp. 21–22. Published weekly at Columbia University. Copyright 1965. By permission.

V. Stepanov is a Party functionary at the Institute of Marxism-Leninism in Moscow.

In individual cases in recent years deviations from the Leninist style have been permitted in the practice of Party and state work and in the management of the economy and public life: Certain decisions were made without taking into account the actual possibilities for carrying them out, and important steps were taken under the influence of one or another impression without serious scientific grounding. This kind of haste in deciding questions, putting the cart before the horse and the desire to pass off wishful thinking as achievements are characteristics thoroughly alien to the Leninist style of work.

At its plenary sessions in October and November, 1964, and March, 1965, the Party Central Committee sharply condemned these methods and this style of work, characterizing them as subjectivism and voluntarism, which have nothing in common with Leninism. . . .

Subjectivism is a poor aid in matters of administration; it is usually a substitute for scientific leadership. For those leaders who ignore science, the experience of others and the advice of comrades and who rely in all things solely on their own imagination, things turn out precisely as Lenin said of them:

> The car gets out of control. It is as if a person were sitting at the wheel driving it, but the car does not go where it is steered . . . it does not travel quite in the way, and very frequently not at all in the way, that the person sitting at the wheel of this car imagines.

Subjectivism and the "strong-willed" method deriving from it of deciding important questions of principle are accompanied as a rule by an attitude of disdain for theory, for science. The Soviet people are building a communist society. But it is not yet built and is therefore in considerable part still in the sphere of theory, not reality. Therefore, the theoretical elaboration of all the principles of communism, the paths that lead to it and the means by which it is created constitute one of the most important tasks of the Party and of our social sciences.

In recent years one could frequently come across one-sided, at times even primitive, ideas and opinions about communism as a society whose purpose is merely to satisfy material requirements, and simply interpreted requirements at that. The satisfaction of people's requirements is one of the fundamental principles of communism, but the matter does not come down to this alone. Communism is being built to ensure the *complete* well-being and the free development of *all* people. In order to achieve this, it is essential to resolve both in theory and practice such socio-economic, political and ideological problems as the growth of material production, the development of the forms of property and labor, the complete overcoming of class distinctions, the drawing together of the nations, the improvement of socialist social relations, the comprehensive development of people's capabilities and the molding of people's world outlook.

The Party Program states that communism affirms the high ideals that are common to all mankind, ideals for which a struggle has been in progress for centuries: peace, labor, freedom, equality, brotherhood and the happiness of all peoples. Therefore, to sum up the main purpose of communism merely as satisfaction of "the requirements of the stomach," as narrow practicality that is blind to the broad horizons of the future and the higher ideals would be profoundly incorrect. In various periods of the development of Marxist-Leninist literature, similar ideas about communism, which have nothing in common with Marxist, scientific communism, have been unmasked. . . .

The decisions of the March plenary session of the C.P.S.U. Central Committee are now being studied in the country, and the work of carrying them out is under way. The Central Committee plenary session was a major political event in the life of the Party and the country. Its decisions not only ensure the necessary conditions for the development of agriculture but also take a new stride toward the decisive restoration of the Leninist style in Party and state work. . . .

The task now consists not only of carrying out the decisions of the C.P.S.U. Central Committee plenary session—this goes without saying— but also of fully imbuing the work of all our Party committees and Party organizations with the style, spirit and atmosphere of the Central Committee plenary session. For this it is necessary to completely eradicate the residue of the discredited methods that had previously taken root in Party work. . . .

At one time the incorrect opinion held sway that the only task worthy of the attention of Party organizations was economic management and that Party work as such did not exist outside of this. The management of the economy is one of the necessary functions of Party organizations, but it does not exhaust *all* the aspects of Party work. A one-sided understanding of the role of Party organizations led to the neglect of intra-Party political work. Having adopted such a viewpoint, the Party committees as a rule stood above the economic organizations, supplanted them or became their appendages, relinquishing their own role as political agencies of leadership, and did a poor job of dealing with the economy. This gave rise to turmoil and parallelism.

Even at Party meetings it was mainly economic questions, in the narrow production-technical sense, that were discussed. This is necessary at times, but the main thing—people, their feelings and thoughts and their world outlook—cannot be forgotten. The Party meeting is a school for the ideological and political molding of the Communist as a Party fighter. Here he speaks his views frankly on all the questions of life and receives a correct, Party elucidation of these questions. Public opinion, which plays a major role in our life, is created and channeled through the meetings of Communists. Party organizations are called upon to teach people to see beyond all the petty details of day-to-day, specific matters to the broad horizons of communist construction taken as a whole.

20 THE NEW CLASS IN THE SOVIET UNION: A CHINESE VIEW

On Khrushchev's Phoney Communism and Its Historical Lessons for the World, by the editorial departments of *Jenmin Jibao* (*People's Daily*) and *Hongqi* (*Red Flag*) (Peking: Foreign Languages Press, 1964), excerpted from pp. 36–47.

This is an excerpt from a pamphlet published in Peking during the acrimonious exchanges that took place between the Chinese and Soviet Communist Parties after 1961.

The privileged stratum in contemporary Soviet society is composed of degenerate elements from among the leading cadres of Party and government organizations, enterprises and farms as well as bourgeois intellectuals; it stands in opposition to the workers, the peasants and the overwhelming majority of the intellectuals and cadres of the Soviet Union.

. . .

The Communist Party of the Soviet Union headed by Stalin adhered to the dictatorship of the proletariat and the road of socialism and waged a staunch struggle against the forces of capitalism. Stalin's struggles against the Trotskyites, Zinovievites and Bukharinites were in essence a reflection within the Party of the class struggle between the proletariat and the bourgeoisie and of the struggle between the two roads of socialism and capitalism. Victory in these struggles smashed the vain plot of the bourgeoisie to restore capitalism in the Soviet Union.

It cannot be denied that before Stalin's death high salaries were already being paid to certain groups and that some cadres had already degenerated and become bourgeois elements. The Central Committee of the CPSU pointed out in its report to the 19th Party Congress in October 1952 that degeneration and corruption had appeared in certain Party organizations. The leaders of these organizations had turned them into small communities composed exclusively of their own people, "setting their group interests higher than the interests of the Party and the state.". . .

Since Khrushchev usurped the leadership of the Soviet Party and state, there has been a fundamental change in the state of the class struggle in the Soviet Union. Khrushchev has carried out a series of revisionist policies serving the interests of the bourgeoisie and rapidly swelling the forces of capitalism in the Soviet Union.

On the pretext of "combating the personality cult," Khrushchev has defamed the dictatorship of the proletariat and the socialist system and thus in fact paved the way for the restoration of capitalism in the Soviet Union. In completely negating Stalin, he has in fact negated Marxism-Leninism which was upheld by Stalin and opened the floodgates for the revisionist deluge.

Khrushchev has substituted "material incentive" for the socialist principle, "from each according to his ability, to each according to his work." He has widened, and not narrowed, the gap between the incomes of a small minority and those of the workers, peasants, and ordinary intellectuals. He has supported the degenerates in leading positions, encouraging them to become even more unscrupulous in abusing their powers and to appropriate the fruits of labour of the Soviet people. Thus he has accelerated the polarization of classes in Soviet society.

Khrushchev sabotages the socialist planned economy, applies the capitalist principle of profit, develops capitalist free competition and undermines socialist ownership by the whole people. Khrushchev attacks the system of socialist agricultural planning, describing it as "bureaucratic" and "unnecessary." Eager to learn from the big proprietors of American farms, he is encouraging capitalist management, fostering a kulak economy and undermining the socialist collective economy.

.   .   .

The line Khrushchev pursues is a revisionist line through and through. Guided by this line, not only have the old bourgeois elements run wild but new bourgeois elements have appeared in large numbers among the leading cadres of the Soviet Party and government, the chiefs of state enterprises and collective farms, and the higher intellectuals in the fields of culture, art, science, and technology.

In the Soviet Union at present, not only have the new bourgeois elements increased in number as never before, but their social status has fundamentally changed. Before Khrushchev came to power, they did not occupy the ruling position in Soviet society. Their activities were restricted in many ways and they were subject to attack. But since Khrushchev took over, usurping the leadership of the Party and the state step by step, the new bourgeois elements have gradually risen to the ruling position in the Party and government and in the economic, cultural and other departments, and formed a privileged stratum in Soviet society.

This privileged stratum is the principal component of the bourgeoisie in the Soviet Union today and the main social basis of the revisionist Khrushchev clique. The revisionist Khrushchev clique are political representatives of the Soviet bourgeoisie, and particularly of its privileged stratum.

.   .   .

The members of this privileged stratum appropriate the fruits of the Soviet people's labour and pocket incomes that are dozens or even a hundred times those of the average Soviet worker and peasant. They not only secure high incomes in the form of high salaries, high awards, high royalties and a great variety of personal subsidies, but also use their privileged position to appropriate public property by graft and bribery. Completely divorced from the working people of the Soviet Union, they live the parasitical and decadent life of the bourgeoisie.

The members of this privileged stratum have become utterly degenerate ideologically, have completely departed from the revolutionary traditions of the Bolshevik Party and discarded the lofty ideals of the Soviet working class. They are opposed to Marxism-Leninism and socialism. They betray the revolution and forbid others to make revolution. Their sole concern is to consolidate their economic position and political rule. All their activities resolve around the private interests of their own privileged stratum.

Having usurped the leadership of the Soviet Party and state, the Khrushchev clique are turning the Marxist-Leninist Communist Party of the Soviet Union with its glorious revolutionary history into a revisionist party; they are turning the Soviet state under the dictatorship of the proletariat into a state under the dictatorship of the revisionist Khrushchev clique; and, step by step, they are turning socialist ownership by the whole people and socialist collective ownership into ownership by the privileged stratum.

People have seen how in Yugoslavia, although the Tito clique still displays the banner of "socialism," a bureaucrat bourgeoisie opposed to the Yugoslav people has gradually come into being since the Tito clique took the road of revisionism, transforming the Yugoslav state from a dictatorship of the proletariat into the dictatorship of the bureaucrat bourgeoisie and its socialist public economy into state capitalism. Now people see the Khrushchev clique taking the road already travelled by the Tito clique. Khrushchev looks to Belgrade as his Mecca, saying again and again that he will learn from the Tito clique's experience and declaring that he and the Tito clique "belong to one and the same idea and are guided by the same theory." This is not at all surprising.

As a result of Khrushchev's revisionism, the first socialist country in the world built by the great Soviet people with their blood and sweat is now facing an unprecedented danger of capitalist restoration.

The Khrushchev clique are spreading the tale that "there are no longer antagonistic classes and class struggle in the Soviet Union" in order to cover up the facts about their own ruthless class struggle against the Soviet people.

The Soviet privileged stratum represented by the revisionist Khrushchev clique constitutes only a few per cent of the Soviet population. Among the Soviet cadres its numbers are also small. It stands diametrically opposed to the Soviet people, who constitute more than 90 percent of the total population, and to the great majority of the Soviet cadres and Communists. The contradiction between the Soviet people and this privileged stratum is now the principal contradiction inside the Soviet Union, and it is an irreconcilable and antagonistic class contradiction.

21 NATIONAL POLICY MACHINERY IN COMMUNIST CHINA

"National Policy Machinery in Communist China," Study of the Senate Committee on Government Operations, Subcommittee on National Policy Machinery, 86th Congress, 1st session, 1959. (Washington, D.C.: Government Printing Office, 1959), excerpted from pp. 4–9, 12–13.

Policy in China, as in the Soviet Union, is made in the decision-making centers of the Party. The organizational structures of the two Parties are remarkably similar, as are the functions of the various organs.

The Supremacy of the Party

Basic to an understanding of the present-day organization for policy-making and execution in Communist China is an appreciation of the all-powerful position of the Chinese Communist Party.[1] . . . whose position —explicitly defined in the country's constitution as "the vanguard of the Chinese working class"—juridically entitles them to lead the worker-peasant alliance, the theoretical basis of the Chinese People's Republic.

As further insurance that it will continue to dominate the country's policymaking apparatus, the party makes use of two other principles. The first involves the organic structure of the Chinese People's Republic; no provision is made for a balance of power between legislative, executive, and judicial organs of government to check undue concentration of authority. Rather, authority is merged in a system of overlapping and interlocking organs, which makes effective control from the center possible.

The other principle, that of "democratic centralism," requires that "the minority shall obey the majority, lower organizations shall obey high organizations, and organizations shall uniformly obey the control organization." This principle is illustrated, for example, during party conferences. Whenever a party unit convenes, there is present a representative of the next higher organ who is expected to tell the conference what it ought to achieve. This is very often done when he addresses the conference at its opening session. He may then sit through all other sessions and even take part in the deliberations. Occasionally he may be called on to explain the

---

[1] At the end of 1964, it numbered approximately 18 million members.

wishes or policies of the higher party organs. Finally, he is expected to sum up in a concluding address the outcome of the conference and his comments. The Chinese Communists call these "conclusions," and they cover practically all of the major decisions the conference is supposed to reach. When the conference is over, the representative has to report back to his own organ on the proceedings of the conference, adding his own observations and recommendations. In other words, this representative serves as a party whip for the conference, whose duty it is to see that the party line is strictly observed.

As the central nervous system of the entire body politic, providing direction and purpose, and coordinating many diverse activities, the party accomplishes its task by placing a host of members throughout the government. These individuals serve as catalytic agents, imparting momentum, guiding and goading the government bureaucracy.

The party is thus the activating and directing force, but Communist theoreticians stress that it must remain organizationally distinct from government agencies, to which is delegated the actual work of administration. Ordinarily, the presence of party members in governmental organizations assures the implementation of policy at all levels without formal orders to the agencies concerned. The system requires a party apparatus roughly parallel, in its organizational hierarchy, to the governmental apparatus. The duplication extends to local areas.

The party constitution makes a point of delineating the policy-formulation role of the central and local units.

> All questions of a national character or questions that require a uniform decision for the whole country shall be handled by the central party organizations so as to contribute to the centralism and unity of the party. All questions of a local character . . . shall be handled by the local party organizations. . . .

Despite this apparent separation of power, control remains ultimately at the party center, for it is constitutionally stipulated that "decisions taken by lower organizations must not run counter to those made by higher organizations." And, of course, the power to decide whether the decisions are in conflict resides in the "higher organizations."

The Party Congress

The present constitution of the Chinese Communist Party ordains that the National Party Congress is "the highest leading body of the party." As such, its constitutional functions include the duty to "hear and examine" reports of central party organs, to determine the party's mass line and policy, to revise the party constitution, and to elect the Central

Committee. It is nominally, but not really, the principal policymaking organ.

The party constitution provides that the convocation of a congress may be postponed indefinitely by the Central Committee elected in the previous session. In other words, the congress does not meet until the party leaders have formulated the party line for the congress to approve. The fact that no National Party Congress was convened from 1945 to 1956 illustrates how readily the Chinest Communist Party found force and direction for policy formulation in other quarters. The National Party Congress is in fact a rubberstamp organization convened as a sop to party "democracy."

The position of the National Party Congress is well illustrated by the 1956 meeting. Delegates, elected at lower levels, totaled slightly over 1,000 when assembled in Peiping. Such a large-scale convocation is in itself evidence of ineffectiveness; fruitful debate and positive policymaking can scarcely be carried out in such a meeting.

The size of that congress dictated the election of a presidium to coordinate and direct activities. It is in the composition of this body that a picture of effective control by an elite, higher echelon of party members begins to emerge. The 63-man Presidium of the Eighth National Party Congress contained all the full members of the Central Committee, save 4 of minor importance. This Presidium then elected a Standing Committee, which was identical with the membership of the powerful Central Political Bureau, or Politburo, the group at the heart of Chinese Communist policy formulation. . . .

When it came time to pass on the composition of a new Central Committee, the power of the higher party echelon again appeared. Through a complex series of straw votes the elections were carefully rigged so that, with one exception, all the old Central Committee membership was reelected and ranked in proper order of precedence.

Thus, the congress itself did not formulate policy; it merely listened to explanations of previously formulated policy and gave its stamp of approval. To any serious observer it was clear that major Chinese Communist policy originated at a level no lower than the party Central Committee.

The Central Committee

Like the National Party Congress, the Central Committee is equipped with a constitutional basis for major policy formulation and execution. Its task is defined as one of directing the entire work of the party, representing it in relations with other parties and organizations, setting up and directing new party organs, and supervising and allocating party cadres.

While the constitution provides that the Central Committee shall meet in plenary session at least twice a year, it suffers a legal limitation on this prerogative, as does the National Party Congress, since it is called into session at the convenience of the Politburo. Furthermore, just as the Central Committee acts for the National Party Congress when that body is not in session, so the Politburo exercises the powers and functions of the Central Committee when it is not convened.

The fact that only seven plenary sessions were held between 1945 and 1956, and 4 years elapsed between the third plenum in 1950 and the fourth in 1954, illustrates the limited role of the Central Committee in policy formulation. Moreover, meetings from 1945 to 1956 occurred only in connection with the inauguration of new policy lines. At these meetings the policy to be decided upon was served up ready made. For example, the plenum of October 1955 decided on the rapid collectivization of agriculture, admitting its action was "based on the speech of Comrade Mao Tsetung at the meeting of provincial secretaries." In actual fact, accelerated collectivization was well underway before the October "decision" of the Central Committee.

In line with the post-1956 emphasis on a greater display of democratic forms in party affairs, the Central Committee has since met at least twice a year. However, the short sessions and the enlarged size of the body, which reached 192 members in 1958, suggest that as a deliberative group the Central Committee may be a trifle unwieldy to be useful in direct policy formulation. It is possible, however, that an issue on which the topmost party leaders were seriously divided could be referred to the Central Committee for decision.

While the Central Committee as an organization has been relatively unimportant in the formulation of broad national policy, many of its members are responsible for policy execution at a lower level of party and government. The present membership of the Central Committee is drawn in roughly equal proportions from four major groups: central party organizations, provincial party organizations, central and provincial government organizations, and the armed forces. By approving party policy as elaborated to them while in session, the members of the Central Committee are better equipped to implement it at their own official level.

The exact relationship of the Central Committee to government, mass organizations, and the armed forces is spelled out explicitly in the party's 1956 constitution. The Central Committee is charged with guiding "the work of the central state organs and people's organizations of a national character through leading party members' groups within them." This task is partly accomplished by the election of four smaller executive agencies, composed of Central Committee members, who exercise daily supervision over party affairs. One of these, the Central Control Commission, has no policymaking function. The remaining three—the Central Political Bureau, the Standing Committee of the Central Political Bureau, and the Central Secretariat—are examined below. They constitute the central core of the policy-formulation and policy-implementation machinery in Communist China.

The Central Political Bureau

The Central Political Bureau (Politburo) is authorized by the party constitution to exercise the powers and functions of the Central Committee when that body is not in session. This is a sweeping grant of power to the top of the party hierarchy. As of August 1959, the Politburo consisted of 26 men, all long and faithful party members. Twenty were full (voting) members, and six (nonvoting) alternates. A variety of background and talent was represented, providing the competence for decisions cutting across many fields.

The position of Mao Tse-tung as Chairman of the party is of paramount importance and has been singled out for discussion below. . . .

The Politburo is very important as a discussion group and perhaps also as a voting body with respect to major policy decisions. It seems highly probable that a definitive stand by Mao on any major issue prevails, since there is little evidence that the members will not vote with the Chairman on those questions where his position is known. In the absence of a definitive personal stand, however, Mao probably is responsive to counsel from different groups in the Politburo. The strongest apparent group, of "party-machine" leaders, is headed by Liu Shao-chi. The group is so called because its members are linked by long and close association in key party posts, as distinguished from those who have made their mark primarily as government administrators or army leaders. Should conditions be right (e.g., in the selection of a successor after Mao's death), the various groups in the Politburo might struggle for power.

Once policy has been formulated, its execution is readily promoted through the interlocking system of concurrent key posts held by many Politburo members in the government. Politburo Vice Chairman Liu is concurrently chairman of the government and thus the formal head of state. Chou En-lai, third-ranking Politburo member, is Premier, while 16 other members serve concurrently as Vice Premiers.

The Standing Committee of the Politburo

Before 1956, a Politburo Standing Committee was not provided for in the party constitution. In its place there was a Secretariat which attended "to the daily work of the Central Committee, according to the decisions of the Politburo." Composed of the five ranking Politburo members, this Secretariat became an inner cabinet, lending a final degree of centrality and exclusiveness to party policymaking and execution.

In the party constitution of 1956, this locus of real power was formally identified as a Standing Committee, practically identical in membership with the pre-1956 Secretariat. Presumably it acts on the many occasions when Mao does not choose to convene the full Politburo, and its decisions have the force of full Politburo decisions. The leadership, however, apparently considers meetings of the entire Politburo desirable to consider and sanction major policy shifts. For example, the Chinese party line which took issue with the Soviet criticism of Stalin was announced after an April 1956 meeting of the Politburo.

With few exceptions, the same handful of men have remained at the top of the old Secretariat or on the Standing Committee since 1949. A high degree of consistent force and direction has thereby been supplied. The small size of the body and the continuity of membership probably facilitates policy decisions without intricate formal machinery for reaching consensus. A conversation between members would in effect constitute a meeting. Personality factors are of extreme importance at this level, in particular the traits and methods of Mao Tse-tung.

THE SPECIAL POSITION OF MAO TSE-TUNG

At the present time Mao is unquestionably the supreme authority in Communist China. Within the confines of Marxist philosophy he has exercised considerable imagination and originality in applying principles to indigenous Chinese conditions. The personal factors which brought Mao to the top and allowed him to maintain his position include great self-confidence, ability to evoke strong loyalties from subordinate party members and the military, and an ability to maintain a balance of power among competing individuals and factions. Recognition that Mao is the ultimate arbiter minimizes serious factional disputes.

While consolidating his control in earlier years, Mao did resort to the liquidation of rivals. More recently the Chairman has treated opposition more magnanimously, preferring as a rule (not always) to reindoctrinate and thus rehabilitate opponents, or, as he puts it, "treat the disease and save the patient." As a result, the Chinese Communist Party has attained a degree of unity and stability at its higher levels which is unequaled by other major Communist parties.

Mao's reputation as national leader was slowly acquired. By the mid-1930's he had outdistanced most of his major rivals for party leadership, although he was still to consolidate his leading position. In the 1940's he followed the world Communist tactic of the "united front" and thus appeared as the sponsor of resistance against Japan. Chinese Communist guerrilla operations during the war added to his reputation. Later, especially following the death of Stalin, his writings on doctrine have been hailed as significant "enrichments" or "additions" to Marxist theory.

Mao feels that his all-important position in policy formulation requires freedom from the administrative and ceremonial tasks that beset the top men of many countries. Currently, he holds no position in government and allows himself almost full time for the observation and reflective thinking he regards as the essential prerequisite to sound policy formulation. In recent years he has apparently made very little attempt to intervene in matters of detail and has, in the main, left the execution of programs to his trusted subordinates.

. . .

THE PARTY SECRETARIAT

The Secretariat created by the 1956 constitution operates "under the direction" of the Politburo and its Standing Committee in attending to "the daily work of the Central Committee." Supervision and coordination of policy, rather than formulation, appears its primary responsibility. The political stature of its membership suggests that the Secretariat's powers exceed the mere monitoring and reporting of measures to implement party policy; it can and does enforce its decisions on party personnel responsible for carrying out policy directives. The Secretariat is directed by Teng Hsiao-ping who, as Secretary General of the party, has overall responsibility for translating Politburo directives into action and for supervising the subordinate departments. Teng is the only top leader concurrently a member of the three most important central organs—Politburo, Standing Committee, and Secretariat. The second through fifth ranking secretaries are also full members of the Politburo.

CENTRAL ORGANS OF THE PARTY

At least nine central organs function under the Secretariat. From the party standpoint, the Organization Department is probably the most important. In the past it was entrusted with many aspects of party personnel administration, including recruitment, training, promotion, allocation of cadres, and maintenance of personnel records. With regard to the party's top personnel, it has almost certainly given up some of its functions to the higher level Secretariat; but it probably is still very important in party personnel matters anywhere below the top level.

The Propaganda Department is responsible for supervising and directing a part of the training—principally indoctrination—of party members through the organization of programs, schools and the like. In the main, however, it acts as the nerve center for a large system of propaganda and thought-control activities carried out at lower party levels and in the government apparatus. Its activities extend to the whole range of literary and educational work.

The Social Affairs Department remains one of the most shadowy of the central organizations. It is believed to exercise the function of investigating the loyalty and security of party members, and it probably directs some intelligence, counterintelligence, and public security work. This department exercises close control over the governmental Ministry of Public Security and keeps its separate social affairs or security units in operation throughout the government and the armed forces. Army loyalty is a concern of the General Political Department, empowered by the party constitution with taking "charge of the ideological and organizational work of the party in the army."

The United Front Department is concerned with the puppet political parties that exist in China's democratic facade, important non-Communist figures, national minority groups, and overseas Chinese. The department and its local branches are responsible for maintaining liaison with these individuals and groups and enlisting their cooperation and support.

The tasks of the Rural Work Department and the Industrial Work Department are parallel. Rural conditions are investigated by the former, and party policy in the field of agriculture is implemented by it. The Industrial Work Department seems responsible for activities in industrial enterprises, and branches of it may exist for heavy, light, and local industry.

The Finance and Trade Department has apparently been newly raised to departmental status. Finance and trade committees existed on the provincial level for some years, and the establishment of a department was probably necessitated by the increasingly complex problems in these fields. The department's main concern would be with party committees which supervise governmental activities in finance, trade, taxation, banking, and food distribution.

Also relatively new is the Communications Work Department, organized in 1956. This organ replaced the party's older political departments in the ministries of railways, communications, and posts and telecommunications.

There is also a Liaison Department for contacts with other Communist parties. Peiping does not identify this department publicly.

Under the party constitution, departmental organs are authorized at the local as well as the provincial level of party hierarchy. For example, the central committee of a province has departments responsible to it which are roughly parallel to the organs considered above, and serve to implement party policy at the provincial level.

In addition to the party's central departments, various party committees operate under the guidance of the Secretariat. Whereas the departments are standing bodies, the committees appear to be convened irregularly to enunciate policy. For example, the Women's Work Committee periodically states party policy in the realm of women's activities.

Branches of the party reach into every government office. The party groups work in two ways: first by stating party policy in the office; and second by sending reports to higher party organizations which can give any necessary instructions to the higher level government office. Such a system must inevitably result in complex and difficult relations between higher and lower governmental offices. This in turn must involve the Communist regime in an even sterner struggle against rank growth in the bureaucracy than is the case in states where the party is not so closely identified with government. However, it does promote continuing vigilance to ensure that executive decisions are consistent with party-formulated policy.

Sidney Ploss

22 CONFLICT AND DECISION-MAKING IN SOVIET RUSSIA: THE POLITICS OF AGRICULTURAL POLICY

Sidney Ploss, *Conflict and Decision-Making in Soviet Russia: A Case Study of Agricultural Policy, 1953–1963* (Princeton, N.J.: Princeton University Press, 1965), pp. 278–87. Footnote references have been deleted. Reprinted by permission of Princeton University Press. Copyright 1965 by Princeton University Press.

Sidney Ploss is currently Assistant Professor of Political Science and member of the Foreign Policy Research Institute at the University of Pennsylvania.

Struggle for power has never been merely a raucous pastime in the Kremlin. It has always been a fundamental factor motivating the behavior of Soviet leaders in dealings with outsiders and one another. This has been no less true of the formation of policy in the post-Stalin period. The heads of succeeding regimes could not master anything like the plenitude of power which Stalin accumulated during the timespan of fifteen years and under hypertense conditions, internally and abroad. Malenkov, and Khrushchev after him, had to seek to achieve their major goals through resort to persuasion and intrigue within a structure of diffused power. At the same time, other leaders had both the right to express personal dissent and, most important, the capability to marshal support for opposing viewpoints. The general effect of this systematized competition for personal prestige and sovereignty of ideas was the creation willy-nilly of "checks and balances" in the mechanics of government. This in turn led to dilatory and half-hearted solution of pressing national problems that required the kind of prompt and bold action urged by more forward-looking elements in the leadership, chiefly Khrushchev.

Issues and Attitudes

The internal political disputes of the last decade originated in whirlpools of vendetta, patronage, opportunism, and rival convictions. The personal antagonisms of Khrushchev and Beriya dated back to the war years, those between Khrushchev and Malenkov were recurrent in the postwar period, and Kozlov and Suslov in all probability deeply resented Khrushchev's organizational insult to them in 1957–1960. The ties of some leaders with the directors of certain bureaucratic departments evidently were too close for them to resist distress calls to block unsettling changes in departmental routine. (The relationships of Malenkov—agricultural planning—Benediktov's ministry, and of Kozlov—investment planning procedures—V. N. Novikov's state committee, are suggestive here.) The lure of temporary advantage may be inferred to have figured in the insurrections of Malenkov's economic deputies in 1954–1955, Matskevich in 1959–1960, and Podgornyy in 1963.

The typical leader of stature, however, did not appear to be a mere "careerist" or political weathercock, but someone of definite attitude who strove for the adoption of mutually reinforcing decisions. The patterns of oratory and career movement in the upper stratum tended to confirm Mikoyan's characterization of the 1956–1957 struggle in the party Presidium: "These differences with the conservative-dogmatic group were not over particular organizational or isolated political questions. No. They concerned the determination of the entire policy of the party in the new stage of historical development, its general line." The same might be said of the arguments between the Khrushchev and Kozlov-Suslov groups in 1958–1963.

Hardly by chance did the competing groups devote so much attention to manipulation of the Stalin symbol. Their basic divergencies of outlook concerned Stalin's method of government. In economics, the neo-Stalinists were uninterested in short-term improvement of the welfare of the broadest circles of the population. In administration, they favored curtailment of local autonomy and reliance on authoritarian centralism. The neo-Stalinists' low estimate of the moral cohesiveness of the nation, masked by their stress on inner unity in regard to "contradictions," made them wary of badly needed measures to decentralize the topheavy bureaucracy and provide broad scope for a display of initiative on the periphery. Austerity and regimentation for the multitude; material and order-giving privileges for the metropolitan elite—such were the nostalgic values of conservative politicians from Malenkov and Molotov in the 1950's to Kozlov and Suslov in the 1960's. Small wonder that Mao Tse-tung as well as Stalin cropped up as a hero of the conservatives in the 1961 struggle over the draft party Program.

The alternative course of conciliation found its partisans in older leaders like Khrushchev and Mikoyan and younger ones like Polyanskiy. They persistently championed the underdog causes of higher priority for agriculture, meaningful labor rewards for the largest number of citizens, and the shifting of administrative gravity to local levels. This reform party emphasized the cohesion of the regime, but argumentatively and with simultaneous focus on inner "contradictions" like the production-consumption dilemma. It also made strenuous efforts to debunk the Stalin myth. The distinguishing features of the reformists' propaganda and the nature of their proposals betrayed an awareness of serious flaws in the basic arrangements of national life The reformists' definition of underlying problems may in time overshadow the magnitude of their setbacks in party forums.

Some of the main determinants of attitude among those who exercised influence in the system of closed politics were professional interest, age, and regional affiliation. Besides priding himself on being a *narodnik,* or peasant socialist, Khrushchev asserted his "weakness for agriculture" and happily recalled his contacts with farmers on his days off. These statements cannot be dismissed as sheer demagoguery. A self-made agronomist who retained a farm technician as a personal secretary, Khrushchev consistently utilized institutional prerogatives to advance agricultural questions to a high position on the political agenda. Moreover, his frank diagnoses of conditions on the land were accompanied by specific recommendations heedful of the state's commitments and potential. Again, it was scarcely a coincidence that the rivals of Khrushchev were trained in fields not merely remote from the interests of agriculture, but antithetic to them. Malenkov and Kozlov were educated as industrial engineers and henceforth were intimate with business executives whose sprawling empires were founded on the expropriation of rural wealth. Like other industrial trainees of the Stalin era, Malenkov and Kozlov assumedly were prone to regimentation and might be expected on that basis alone to have favored tighter control of farming—as indeed the case appears to have been. The "generalist" type of leader like Molotov and Suslov, whether out of conviction or to justify his position of authority, acted as the guardian of a corpus of doctrine which ruthlessly legitimated the total supremacy of cities over villages. The reorganization of the party along production rather than territorial lines, which Khrushchev sponsored in 1962, was fashioned to undercut the authority of these technically inexperienced bosses.

Khrushchev's spokesmen maintained that a rejuvenating current amongst office-holders of the party bureaucracy was one of the most salutary effects of the 1962 reorganization. Of course, no absolute statements regarding the age factor can be made in searching for the roots of conflicting orientations in the elite. Reformers and conservatives existed at all points on the age scale. But, generally speaking, the men who embarked on apparatus careers in the late 1920's and early 1930's leaned toward bland acceptance of the established order. They in particular were tagged for replacement in the periodic "efficiency" and "integrity" campaigns which Khrushchev's innovator group launched for ulterior, political reasons. In short, the alleged power of Communist doctrine to unify the generations proved more illusory than real. This may have especially important consequences for the Soviet future.

Regional diversity also had its impact on behavior in the hierarchy. The Great Russian-Ukrainian dichotomy made itself felt in the conflicts over the kolkhoz federation in 1959 and the role of district party committees in 1962. Northerners by and large abided by their heritage of centralized administration, while southerners individualistically favored the dispersal of authority in their own bailiwicks. The sectional jealousies help to explain the otherwise scholastic arguments over Ukrainian party history which raged in 1960–1962, paralleling the shifting fortunes of Khrushchev's "Ukrainian" protégés Brezhnev, Kirichenko, and Kirilenko. Indeed, Khrushchev appears to have made references at that time to Stalin's hostility toward the Ukrainian bureaucracy with a view to denigrating the anti-Ukrainian cabals of the Great Russian traditionalists Kozlov and Suslov.

Legislative Procedure

The sham parliament which the Soviet leaders maintain in the form of the U.S.S.R. Supreme Soviet has deservedly received little attention from Western students of Soviet affairs. But without carefully reading the Soviet press and under the enthrallment of deterministic theories about "totalitarianism," some of these students have constructed a no less ingenuous model of legislative procedure in Soviet Russia. It is an essentially apolitical model of dispassionate staff studies, cool discussion in the top leadership, and finally of autocratic whim. As indicated, however, by the 1947 incident over the projected waterworks at Kakhovka, factionalism basically influenced the course of decision-making even in the Stalin period. Once intuition is discarded and hard research undertaken, a notable regularity is observable in the sequence of major events attending changes of policy in

Soviet economy and administration. This regularity in the post-Stalin period enables one to detect a genuinely oligarchic procedure for policy-making, and its most outstanding feature is conflict.

While the proposal for change was still in embryonic form, organizational maneuver commenced. A bureaucratic department might have to be overhauled for the purpose of instilling the proper bias in its staff work. The allegiance of a local party caucus might have to be secured. Always, opinion leaders of the bureaucratic elite had to be told to utilize the press and conference hall to shape the appropriate consensus. These opinion leaders included party and government operatives, economic experts, the editors of newspapers and magazines, "theorists" in party and academic work, and literati. A substantial body of empiricist, doctrinaire, and opportunist talent resided in opinion-shaping circles and was at the disposal of feuding groups at the highest level. Next, the proposal, and perhaps a counterproposal, were submitted to the party Presidium or Central Committee. Deliberation occurred at expanded meetings of the Presidium, with as many as 90 persons involved. The proposal might be adopted by a majority vote of Presidium members or be tabled for additional study. The cycle was usually terminated with the rise and fall of underlings of patronage chiefs in the top leadership.

The Chief Executive

The record indicates that in 1959–1963 Khrushchev aspired to major reform of domestic policy and was effectively opposed. How then could he stay on as party first secretary and premier? This question must arise in view of the death-struggle image of Soviet politics which was created by the collapse of the Malenkov regime in just less than two years and the showdown in the party Presidium which occurred about two years after that. It brings to mind the wise teaching of Boris Nicolaevsky about the Fabian quality of post-Stalin strife in the Kremlin:

> This struggle for power need by no means at each moment be a struggle for the overthrow of the government or removal of the Central Committee first secretary. Such "maximalist" goals always are fixed at the end of a long road of development which is marked by heightening animosities. On this road there are always many intermediary phases, when the contending groups set "limited objectives. . . ."

Nonetheless, since the crisis of 1957 there appear to have been times when Khrushchev was in danger of enforced retirement. He seems to have responded by turning into controversies the ultimate issues of "collective leadership" and "peaceful coexistence." Khrushchev strongly hinted to the few thousand constituents of the top leadership that his rivals were disposed toward courses of action which would jeopardize the principle of group rule and world tranquillity. The elite's paramount desire for normality and the inquisitorial backgrounds of Khrushchev's main adversaries, Kozlov and Suslov, would have sufficed to dampen any ardor for impeachment proceedings similar to those of 1957. If all this seems reminiscent of Stalin's tactic of playing on bureaucratic fears of Trotsky's militaristic reputation in the power struggles of the 1920's, it can only be said that the issues, attitudes, and gambits in Soviet politics are notably predictable. It is only the capricious resolution of individual conflicts which eludes accurate prophecy, but usefully reminds us that we are dealing here with the classic instance of a government of men.

The ability to make controversies of issues is in itself an instrument of power and Khrushchev on occasion has skillfully wielded it. He repeatedly attempted to transfer discussion from the smaller to the larger party organ, where the influence of rivals might not count for as much. However, the independent behavior of Central Committee members was so flagrant that Khrushchev's play often miscarried. There is reason to believe the claim that Malenkov was boastful of his successes over Khrushchev in the closed meetings held at Central Committee plenums after the death of Stalin.[1] The latter-day standard-bearers of conservatism, Kozlov and Suslov, presumably formed majorities of their own in the debates on administrative and investment policy at the December 1959 and March 1962 Central Committee sessions, respectively. The evidence of such free-wheeling conduct of Committee members tends to refute the notion that the party first secretary controls the appointment of key personnel. Along with the fact that the Malenkovite Ponomarenko was intrusted with implementing Khrushchev's policy of land expansion in Kazakhstan, it indicates that such appointments are negotiated among equals in the party Presidium. Viewed in perspective, the foremost consequence of Khruschev's frequent resort to the Central Committee as a political tool was that it enabled him to stabilize his interim regime. It was at once the source of his executive longevity and of the muddled nature of internal policies which, however unfairly, will often be associated with his name.

Over the long run, expanding the arena of conflict by familiarizing the public with the nature of some policy differences may have been Khrushchev's most important contribution to the betterment of his countrymen. It was a step toward developing a kind of public opinion which in time may

---

[1] The following passage in the speech of Furtseva to the 22nd party Congress relates to a meeting of the party Presidium held shortly before the crisis of June 1957. Khrushchev asked for the rehabilitation of generals shot in 1937 and accused Malenkov and Molotov of implication in the crimes: "Malenkov even said to Nikita Sergeyevich: Are you frightening us with a plenum? The plenum is like our own home; we shall go and tell all to the plenum." (*XXII S"yezd KPSS*, I, 396. This is not in the original version of Furtseva's speech, in *Pravda*, October 22, 1961.)

alter the thinking of the ruling class at large. (Encouraging public opinion polls and fostering in the party Program of the idea of popular referendums on internal and foreign policy questions were rudimentary moves in the same direction.) It was one of the more hopeful signs that eventually the Soviet regime may forsake its conspiratorial demeanor and act in a fully responsible manner toward its own people and those in the rest of the world.

23 ON OVERCOMING THE PERSONALITY CULT AND ITS CONSEQUENCES

On Overcoming the Personality Cult and Its Consequences, Decision of the Central Committee of the C.P.S.U. (Moscow: June 30, 1956), excerpted from pp. 6–21.

On February 24 and 25, 1956, Nikita S. Khrushchev, then the First Secretary of the C.P.S.U., delivered a special report to a closed and secret session of its 20th Congress. This report, which has never been published in the Soviet Union, indicted Stalin for 20 years of terror and tyranny. It denounced Stalin for the murder of hundreds of thousands of Party members during the purges of the 1930's, for his incompetence as a war leader, and for his betrayal of Leninism. Khrushchev's secret speech provided the impetus for far-ranging political, economic, social, and educational reforms. De-Stalinization has wrought changes in the character and atmposphere of Soviet society; it has not yet run its full course, and many questions crucial to an understanding of the Soviet system of rule remain unanswered but ever-present.

On June 30, 1956, the Central Committee of the C.P.S.U. issued a decree On Overcoming the Personality Cult and Its Consequences *that not only publicly acknowledged all that Khrushchev had told at the secret session, but also raised many of the questions concerning the nature of the Soviet system of government that have continuing relevance for the student of communist political systems.*

How could the Stalin personality cult, with all its adverse effects, arise and spread under the Soviet socialist system?

In examining this question it is important to bear in mind both the objective, concrete historical conditions in which socialism was built in the

U.S.S.R., and certain subjective factors arising from the personality of Stalin. . . .

For over a quarter of a century the Soviet Union was the only country paving mankind's path to socialism. It was like a besieged fortress surrounded on all sides by capitalism. After the failure of the fourteen-nation intervention in 1918–20, its enemies in East and West continued to prepare new "crusades" against the U.S.S.R. They sent large numbers of spies and saboteurs into the Soviet Union, seeking to undermine the world's first socialist state by every possible means. The menace of fresh imperialist aggression against the U.S.S.R. became especially pronounced after the fascists came to power in Germany in 1933. . . .

The intrigues of international reaction were all the more dangerous because, within the country, a prolonged and fierce class struggle was in progress to resolve the question "who will win?" Lenin's death was followed by an increase in the activity of hostile trends within the Party— the Trotskyites, Right opportunists, bourgeois nationalists—who repudiated Lenin's theory that socialism could triumph in one country. In practice, their attitude would have led to the restoration of capitalism in the U.S.S.R. The Party launched a relentless struggle against these enemies of Leninism. . . .

This complex international and internal situation required iron discipline, constantly growing vigilance, the strictest centralization of leadership, which was bound to have an unfavourable effect on the development of certain democratic forms. Our country, locked in bitter struggle against the entire world of imperialism, was constrained to introduce some restrictions of democracy, justified by the logic of our people's struggle for socialism in conditions of capitalist encirclement. But even at that time, the Party and people regarded these restrictions as temporary, to be repealed as the Soviet state became stronger and the democratic and socialist forces throughout the world developed. Our people consciously accepted these temporary sacrifices, knowing that every passing day brought continued progress for the Soviet social system. . . .

As General Secretary of the Central Committee of the Party, a post which he held for a long time, Stalin, together with other leaders of the Party, fought vigorously to implement Lenin's behests. He was devoted to Marxism-Leninism, and as a theoretician and skillful organizer he headed the Party's struggle against the Trotskyites, Right opportunists and bourgeois-nationalists, against the intrigues of the capitalist encirclement. In this political and ideological struggle Stalin acquired much authority and popularity. But all our impressive victories came to be wrongly associated with his name. The successes won by the Communist Party and the country, and the praise lavished on his person, turned Stalin's head. It was in this atmosphere that the Stalin personality cult gradually developed.

Its development was to a very great degree facilitated by certain personal characteristics of Stalin, whose undesirable nature was pointed out by Lenin. Towards the end of 1922, Lenin addressed a letter to the forthcoming Party Congress, in which he wrote:

"Comrade Stalin, having become General Secretary, has concentrated in his hands boundless power, and I am not sure that he will always be able to employ that power with sufficient caution." In a supplement to this letter, written in the early days of January 1923, Lenin reverted to this question of certain undesirable personal characteristics of Stalin which are impermissible in a leader.

"Stalin is too rude," Lenin wrote, "and this defect, while quite tolerable in our midst and in intercourse between us Communists, becomes intolerable in a person holding the post of General Secretary. For that reason, I suggest that the comrades think of some method of removing Stalin from that post and appointing another person who in all other aspects differs from Comrade Stalin in possessing only one advantage—that of being more tolerant, more loyal, more polite and considerate to comrades, less capricious, etc."

At the Thirteenth Party Congress, held soon after Lenin's death, his letters were made known to the delegations. They were discussed, and it was found advisable to allow Stalin to remain General Secretary, on the understanding, however, that he would heed this criticism of Lenin's and draw all the necessary conclusions therefrom.

Remaining as General Secretary of the Central Committee, Stalin did heed Lenin's critical remarks in the period immediately after Lenin's death. But subsequently, grossly overestimating his own services, Stalin began to believe he was infallible. Certain restrictions upon inner-Party and Soviet democracy, inevitable during bitter struggle against the class enemy and its agents, and during the war against the nazi invader, were gradually transformed by Stalin into regular features of government and Party life, in outright violation of Lenin's principles of leadership. Central Committee Plenary Sessions and Party Congresses were convened irregularly, and subsequently none were held for many years. Stalin in fact came to be above criticism.

Stalin's erroneous formulation that the class struggle would become more and more acute as the Soviet Union advanced to socialism did great damage to the building of socialism and the development of democracy within the Party and in the country. This formulation, correct only for definite stages of the transition period when the issue "who will win?" was being decided, when the laying of the foundations of socialism was accompanied by bitter class struggle, was pushed to the forefront in 1937—at a time when socialism had already triumphed in our country and when the exploiting classes and their economic base had been abolished. In practice, this erroneous theoretical formulation served as the basis for the grossest violations of socialist legality and mass repressions.

It was in these circumstances that the state security agencies acquired a special status. Great confidence was placed in them, for they had rendered undoubted services to the people and country in defending the gains of the revolution. For a long period, the state security agencies justified this confidence, and their special status did not entail any danger. But things changed when Party and government control over the security agencies was gradually replaced by the personal control of Stalin, and the normal administration of justice not infrequently replaced by his personal decisions. The situation was further aggravated when the state security system came to be headed by the criminal gang of Beria, that agent of international imperialism. There were grave infractions of Soviet legality, and mass repressions. As a result of enemy intrigue, many honest Communists and non-Party Soviet citizens were slandered and suffered innocently.

· · ·

It is generally known that during the war, Central Committee members and distinguished Soviet military leaders assumed control over certain fields of activity at the front and in the rear, took independent actions on organizational, political, economic and military matters, and, in conjunction with local Party and governmental organizations, ensured the victory of the Soviet people. The negative consequences of the personality cult made themselves strongly felt again after that victory.

Immediately after Stalin's death, the Leninist nucleus of the Central Committee began resolutely to combat the personality cult and its serious consequences.

The question may arise: why did not these people openly oppose Stalin and remove him from the leadership? That could not be done in the conditions then prevailing. Indisputably, the facts show that Stalin was responsible for many unlawful actions, particularly during the concluding period of his life. But it should not be forgotten that the Soviet people knew Stalin as a man who always defended the U.S.S.R. against the intrigues of its enemies and as a man who fought for the socialist cause. In this struggle he at times resorted to unworthy methods and violated the Leninist principles and standards of Party life. Herein lay the tragedy of Stalin. But at the same time, all this made it difficult to combat the illegalities then being committed, for the successes in the building of socialism and the strengthening of the U.S.S.R. were, in this atmosphere of the personality cult, credited to Stalin.

In these circumstances, any opposition to Stalin would not have been understood by the people; it was not at all a matter of lack of personal courage. Clearly, anyone who opposed Stalin would not, in this situation, have had the support of the people. More, such opposition would under the circumstances have been regarded as opposition to the building of socialism, as an extremely dangerous attempt to undermine the unity of the Party and the country, surrounded as it was by capitalist states. . . .

The personality cult undoubtedly did grave damage to the cause of the Communist Party and to Soviet society. But it would be a gross error to infer from the existence of the personality cult in the past that the social system of the U.S.S.R. has changed somehow, or that the personality cult stemmed from the very nature of Soviet society. Both inferences are asolutely wrong, for they do not accord with realities, they run counter to the facts.

Despite all the evil which the Stalin personality cult caused the Party and people, it could not and did not alter the nature of our social system. No personality cult could change the nature of a socialist state, which is founded on public ownership of the means of production, the alliance of the working class and peasantry, and friendship of the peoples, though this cult did cause serious damage to the development of socialist democracy and to the creative initiative of the millions.

The belief that any individual, even of Stalin's magnitude, can change our social and political system is deeply contrary to the facts, to Marxism, to the truth, represents a lapse into idealism. That view would ascribe to individuals such extraordinary and superhuman powers as ability to change the structure of a society, and moreover of a society in which millions of working people are the decisive force. . . .

The personality cult, as we know, resulted in certain serious mistakes in the management of various branches of Party and governmental work, both in home and foreign affairs. Mention might be made, in particular, of Stalin's serious mistakes in directing agriculture, in organizing the country's preparedness to repel the fascist invader, and of the gross arbitrary actions which led to the conflict with Yugoslavia after the war. . . .

Our enemies allege that the Stalin personality cult was due not to particular historical conditions, which have now receded into the past, but to the Soviet system itself, to what they consider to be its lack of democracy, etc. These slanderous assertions are refuted by the whole history of the Soviet state.

János Kádár

24 CHALLENGE AND CRISIS IN THE HUNGARIAN COMMUNIST PARTY

János Kádár, *Socialist Construction in Hungary* (Budapest: Kossuth Printing House, 1962), excerpted from pp. 107–14.

János Kádár (b. 1912) is the First Secretary of the Central Committee of the Hungarian Socialist Workers' (Communist Party) and Prime Minister of the Hungarian People's Republic. He was brought to power by Moscow, after the Soviet Government suppressed the Hungarian revolution of 1956. Since 1957, Mr. Kádár has succeeded in reestablishing effective Communist Party control over the country and in keeping Hungary in the Soviet bloc.

In this speech, which was delivered before the Budapest Party Executive Committee on August 23, 1957, he set forth in relatively unambiguous fashion the communist explanation for the revolt of 1956 and outlined Party policies designed to forestall another such outbreak. His analysis of the underlying dissatisfaction with, and shortcomings of, Communist Party policies has relevance for an understanding of the problems faced by other Communist Party oligarchies in Eastern Europe.

The internal class enemy and the imperialists have scored success on three issues in this country—and by this they have managed to extend their influence to certain categories of the working people. Their influence has been exceedingly strong among intellectuals, not inconsiderable among workers, and it was felt in some degree also among the peasants.

1. The first of these issues is nationalism. It was in the matter of nationalism that the counter-revolution scored its greatest success because, above all, this idea is very deeply rooted in the minds of the people, and because it is linked with the specific trends of Hungarian history. Wherever nationalism gets the upper hand, class outlook goes down the drain.

In such cases, it goes without saying, communist principles are undermined. Therefore, in our educational and propaganda activities we shall have to devote a good deal of attention to nationalism, and treat it with circumspection.

If you study the history of Hungary you may realize that there have been some doctrines we ought to have combated long ago, but have failed to do so. Progressive national heritage is one of the matters we have failed to

144

treat in the proper way. Why is this important? I'll tell you why. To take one example, here is the legacy of Sándor Petőfi and the young revolutionaries of 1848. To us, that legacy is a precious national heritage, but it is no longer progressive. If we study the views held by Petőfi and the youth of 1848, we find that those views, absolutely progressive at that time, have in some degree become reactionary under our present conditions. This problem has to be studied as a matter of principle.

· · ·

2. The demagogic, rabble-rousing demand of human rights, of democratic freedoms, is the second issue on which our enemies have scored great successes. They want freedom for all, freedom for everybody to be able to preach whatever he pleases, and so forth. At the first hearing, this demand appeals to everyone. What harm could come from everybody being free to speak his mind? We have not answered this question as yet; yet the answer will have to be given, and the implications of this demand must be laid bare. The democratic character of our system should be contrasted with that of western capitalism.

3. Social welfare demagogy is the third issue on which they have been successful and which we have to continue to combat. Let us examine this issue, too.

The living standard rose considerably during the past year, and it has now ceased to be the chief concern of the workers—at least of the decent majority—to demand more. What they feel concerned about today is that we may whittle away some of their gains, for, as they say, they only got those benefits because we were "scared into granting them." This problem deserves our serious attention.

· · ·

We must talk about the housing problem, too. Housing conditions in this country are bad—no question of it. In this connection, however, let me point out but one phenomenon. At a local council meeting the question arose whether there was today a single worker who would not undertake, without a moment's hesitation, to pay the rent of a three-room flat. By contrast, housing conditions in old Hungary were such that people lived under conditions worse than today's, and tens of thousands were living without a roof over their heads for years on end, while thousands of flats remained untenanted simply because workers did not have enough money to pay rent. Now, why not talk about that for once?

As for the readjustment of wages and salaries, it should be pointed out that this was in fact begun in 1956, and not merely after the counter-revolution. We have been straining our resources to the extreme limit, and the present level can be maintained—provided, of course, earnings are backed by actual labour, by production! These questions must be made our point of departure, or we shall not be able to get ahead in our work. It is on the questions of nationalism, the democratic character of our system, and the rising living standard that we have to defend our point of view. There is no reason for us to fight shy of any of these issues, for it is we who are in the right.

Thus, nationalism, democracy, and socialist construction are now the three decisive issues, they will be the ones to claim our close attention for a long time to come. We shall have to work out arguments concerning these matters. In our hands we have the living matter of life itself and if we do not work out our arguments now, we never will.

The other group of problems concerns the establishment of relations with the masses, problems that were also discussed at the Party Conference. It is impossible to carry on fruitful propaganda activity among the masses, or establish good relations with them, unless the political barriers that obstruct our progress are removed. This is a problem that has to be solved within the party and it comprises the need to overcome self-complacency and to get rid of the bureaucratic spirit. Symptoms of these diseases became apparent at lower party levels early this year and had gone far by the beginning of last May. We have been combating these diseases but have not conquered them as yet.

1. The coercive spirit is the chief obstacle impeding the further progress of political education among the masses. Now I don't want to be misunderstood! I am not suggesting that there is no need to remove some people from their posts or to lock them up. But we have the proper authorities to take care of that, so do not let party organizations concern themselves with it. The primary responsibility of the party organizations is to win over the masses. And the spirit of coercion has to be exorcised from the party.

2. The question of the relationship between party members and non-party people. The Party Conference thesis that, by and large, draws the most fire from the body of party opinion is the one which permits non-party people to occupy leading posts. Difficult though it may be, communists will have to accept the principle that, in the eyes of the law, party members have not an iota more right than do non-party people. We must fight to assert this principle; and if it should be found that some people joined the party because they thought that membership would entail more rights for them, then steps should be taken to discourage such people from party membership. What distinguishes party members from non-party people is quite another thing—it is the fact that members of the party work in a proper and exemplary way. A communist who does good work enjoys such respect and prestige in the party committee or the branch organization that no office whatever could give him that much. All members of the party will have to put up with the fact that they are granted no more civic rights than non-party people. Once they have understood this, they will work efficiently.

3. Failure to create an atmosphere of freedom is the third problem listed among the obstacles in the way of political mass work. At membership meetings for members of the party, and at open party meetings for all those present (I mean of course honest people), an atmosphere must be created in which they may freely speak their minds, make their criticisms and advance suggestions. Failing such an atmosphere, we have no means of knowing what the masses think and in that case are unable to win them over. Our starting point shall always be: What is the attitude of the masses? If we hinder the party from knowing what the masses think, we are nipping the party's work in the bud. If, however, the working people see that at the party meeting they may raise any question of vital importance to them and will get an answer, then they will readily come to the meeting. In this manner the party will build up contact with the masses.

.   .   .

It is time we devoted some attention to theoretical studies and got out our books on Marxism. What, with this mix-up we've been through, we haven't read a book in almost a year. Comrade Lenin, for instance, writing of problems of administration, explains repeatedly that to use force without carrying on political educational work among the masses is—a crime. Now the fault is ours, for if we gave attention to this problem, people would understand us before long.

With regard to the mass organizations. You will have to accept the fact that there are at present—and there will be in the future—two kinds of contact between the party and the masses, namely direct and indirect contact. It is a case of direct contact when, for example, the party announces a meeting, and there, before the assembled masses of people, we give an exposition of our views. Indirect contact means that a great deal—at least half—of the communist propaganda work is relegated to the trade unions, the youth league, the local councils, and the Patriotic People's Front. Thus one half of the work is performed by the party—the direct way—while the other half is taken care of by the mass organizations —the indirect way. The trade unions have a total membership of more than one and a half million. If the communists will do nothing else than bring those one and a half million people closely under their influence, they will have done significant work. You'll have to get used to the idea that indirect means are of high importance, too. Yesterday, we talked with members of the Young Communist League, and problems of this kind were discussed in relation to them. Indirect means should be made use of also in political propaganda work among the masses. The foremost requirement put to the working people should not be that they love the party, but that they love our country, the people's democratic system. This is a moral requirement which can be put to 90 per cent of the population. Once a man has understood this, he has come close to developing respect for the communist party, because this party is the defender of *his* political system. The fields of work in mass organizations acquire extraordinary importance owing to the fact that they enable us to get into close touch with the masses politically. For you cannot demand that the working people accept the communist viewpoint forthwith. There are hundreds of thousands of people who are not communists, and probably will not become communists within a short time; yet for all that, they may be honest people who are loyal to the People's Democracy. As things are today, most party activists have developed a classification of their own in which people who have joined the party are labelled "honest"; while on the other hand, they tend to despise the others—non-party people and former members of the H.W.P.P. who have not re-entered. People who think that way are no enemies of the party, they mean well in their own way, but they must be made to understand that in this way they only harm the party.

Robert Conquest

25 AFTER THE FALL: SOME LESSONS

Robert Conquest, "After the Fall: Some Lessons," *Problems of Communism*, XIV, No. 2 (January-February, 1965), excerpted from pp. 17–22. Footnote references have been deleted.

Robert Conquest is well known as a British poet and an author of books and articles on Soviet affairs. His writings include Power and Policy in the U.S.S.R. *and* Russia After Khrushchev.

The purpose of this brief inquiry . . . is to examine Khrushchev's fall for the lessons it may teach us regarding the general nature of Soviet leadership politics.

If the principals in the latest upheaval had been specifically asked to provide us with a dramatic illustration of how Soviet politics works, they could not have chosen a more auspicious time. For during the past few years a certain air of accord had seemed to emanate from the Soviet political scene, and it had again become possible for those so inclined to dismiss as fantasy interpretations of Soviet events that pointed to discord at a high level.

This view, which does not recognize conflict as the dynamic force activating Soviet political life at its highest reaches—and which may be conveniently called the "non-conflict model" of Soviet politics—had made its appearances in the pages of this journal itself. To be sure, other observers were quick to combat it.

In 1961, this writer stated in his *Power and Policy in the U.S.S.R.:*

> *To assume that harmony now prevails among the Soviet leadership would be to assume that a very extraordinary change had taken place in the system. This is not, perhaps, impossible, but at least one can say the assumption is the most speculative that could be made. It would be uncharitable to name the sources, but I have seen the assumption that stability has been achieved at last and that a collective leadership based on mutual restraint has finally emerged, put forward after the death of Stalin; after the fall of Beria; at the time of the 20th Congress; and at almost every other critical point in recent Soviet history. . . .*

Perhaps a momentary lapse from charity will be conceded, just to provide one recent, if extreme, illustration of a basically erroneous attitude toward Soviet politics. In *Problems of Communism* of May–June 1964, a correspondent (A. Allison) expressed notions which in a general way still affect some students. He held that those who find Soviet political life permeated with conflict rely on "inferential and selective evidence while heavily discounting what appear to be simple and obvious realities." Such "realities" included the public appearance of harmony, or at any rate of political stability, in the highest party councils.

But it is ancient history that public figures are capable of public behavior—indeed of private behavior—which conceals their political aims.

· · ·

. . . Malenkov and Beria were in public—and perhaps in private— notable cronies until the moment of truth; and similarly with Khrushchev and Bulganin. No, to take such superficial observance of the conventional amenities as meaning anything at all in any political society is to mislead oneself.

All this is far indeed from the cold-bloodedness of the Soviet oligarchy and the harshness of the struggle for power which recent events have just revealed in all their true crudity. We recognize the complexity, and the idiosyncrasies, of the polity to which we are accustomed, but we are all too apt to oversimplify our ideas of societies of which our knowledge is more indirect. We are inclined to construct models of strange political systems on too simple a basis, especially when the true facts are not readily available. Our notions about the Soviet polity are distorted by the fact that these events are taking place in the 20th century, among people who wear flannel suits and are called "Minister." If they wore turbans and were known as "Wazir," we would be less inclined to make mistakes about them. And similarly, their "Marxism" is a dialect, however debased, of the political language of the West.

What is more, a faint notion of people discussing scientific propositions still attaches to the political polemics of the Kremlin; this, too, is to some extent delusive. In any society, even the most primitive, policy matters are debated in a more or less rational way, but this in itself does not necessarily mean that the political style resembles that of the advanced democracies. It is quite inappropriate to think of Soviet politics in anything like Western terms, if only because there is no mechanism in the U.S.S.R. for the social forces to express themselves. In advanced countries, society and polity virtually coincide; in the Soviet Union, the political world is limited to a few thousand members of a self-perpetuating elite. Moreover, this elite was originally formed, and has been trained for decades, to force its will upon society as a whole.

In the overthrow of Khrushchev, one of the most striking things of all was the absolute passivity of the Russian masses. Another was the absolute inattention of the leaders to the views of the people; the citizens' right to information, let alone participation, seems to have occurred to no one in the Kremlin. The gulf between this sort of attitude and anything resembling democracy is going to be a major crux as the Soviet Union faces problems which can scarcely be settled without the genuine involvement of the public. In fact, far from democracy being anywhere visible, it became clear from the pronouncements of the new regime that not even rational and consistent oligarchy could be found at the basis of the system. For Khrushchev had, it was now alleged, put through a whole series of hastily prepared and ill-considered schemes, disrupting industry, agriculture, and the party organization itself over the past few years, without the other leaders being able to do anything effective to stop him.

In his *L'Esprit des lois* (Book XI, Chapter 4), Montesquieu wrote: "C'est une expérience éternelle que tout homme qui a du pouvoir est porté à en abuser: il va jusqu'à ce qu'il trouve des limites."[1] In democracies these limits are fairly well defined. In the Soviet Union there is no such specificity, no properly established institutional bar. The ruler goes as far as he can until *ad hoc* opposition is mustered in sufficient strength to stop him.

The *mode* of Khrushchev's dismissal is in itself a great demonstration of the nature of Soviet politics. It was carried through with all the correct Moscovite trappings—almost to the point of caricature: the complete secrecy; the sudden coup; the issuing of a short and almost perfunctorily misleading statement about age and health; the simple cessation of reference to the name of the man who had just been the most powerful in the country; the oblique, but obvious, attacks on his methods; the removal

---

[1] "It is an invariable experience that every man who has power is led to abuse it: he goes on until he finds limits."

from office of his closest adherent (Adzhubei) without comment or announcement until his replacement was mentioned casually a week or so later. . . . In particular, the evident absence of any idea on the part of the new rulers that such procedures might be found odd by anyone (including foreign Communist parties) shows flatly a complete, unself-conscious attachment to the traditionalisms of Soviet politics.

But to return again to Western analysis. The non-conflict model of the Soviet political system is defective on three counts. First, there is no such thing as non-conflict politics. "To govern is to choose," and so there will always be "conservative" and "progressive," "left" and "right" divisions in any political grouping, however narrow its spectrum of ideas. The only exception must be a one-man dictatorship so pure that no subordinate dare venture an opinion at all. Even Stalin's Russia did not reach that position.

Second (and still arguing *a priori*), the Soviet system is especially susceptible to conflict because it is constructed to force ideological solutions upon the recalcitrant crises it must continuously deal with; because it is based on an ideology that is liable to various interpretations and subject to fissiparous trends; and because its leaders have over the years been selected for their ruthlessness, ambition and intrigue. Third (and at last *a posteriori*), evidence showing or suggesting conflict within the system is continually available.

Against all this, there is only one serious consideration. Since Soviet convention demands that all party decisions be the product of monolithic agreement, evidence of dispute at the highest level is not allowed to appear in open form—or at least not at the time of the agreement. Thus, those who take the view that conflict does not occur are free to regard the obliqueness of the evidence as a sign of its nullity.

But there are many circumstances, in many fields, where evidence must be indirect. The logic of the other way of thinking is as follows: "The visible part of the iceberg must constitute the whole of it. It is true that some observers claim to see something below the waterline, but even they admit that the submerged part is only obscurely and temporarily visible, and that it may well be something else really, such as a reflection, or a delusion, or a whale. Then again, they deduce from the movements of the visible portion and the laws of dynamics that there must be something below; but after all, this is mere deduction. In fact, the whole evidence is circumstantial, and I prefer to believe what I can see with my eyes." Such a view is not simply mistaken at a superficial level; it reflects a wholly and basically erroneous notion of the nature of Soviet politics.

In the West . . . there is a lack of knowledge about the different situations in different Socialist countries. . . . Some situations seem difficult to understand. In many cases one has the impression that there are differences of opinion among the leading groups, but one does not know if this is really so, and what the differences are." So wrote Togliatti (if only for public consumption) in the memoir composed shortly before his death—and not long before the overthrow of Khrushchev. His basic conclusion was right; and so were his feelings about the difficulty of following the course of the political struggle in the Soviet Union. Nevertheless, throughout the period he was concerned with, much evidence of disunity at the top was available.

Item: There have been issues in Soviet political life on which it has been impossible to make any decision at all. For example, no official account, true or false, of the 1936–38 trials has been available for eight or nine years.

Item: There have been sudden shifts from one policy to another, associated with the rise or decline in prominence of a particular spokesman. Note, for example, the tough approach to literature in early 1963, associated with Kozlov, and the change of the May 1st, 1963, slogan on Yugoslavia, coincident with his fading-out.

. . .

Item: Discussions have taken place in which different party organizations have taken different lines. For example, at the 22nd Congress, delegates from only half the republics called for the expulsion of the "anti-party" group.

Item: Plans to which the head of the party and government has publicly committed himself, while admitting that "some comrades" opposed him, have been abandoned: *e.g.,* the issue of the fertilizer target for 1970.

Item: Individual party leaders have made remarks which, though couched in terms within the protocol of collective leadership, can best be interpreted as political criticism of another faction. For example, after the reorganization of the party into industrial and agricultural sections, Kozlov commented that this could "not in any circumstances be allowed" to split the urban and rural party organizations—just what it obviously was doing—and we now know that Kozlov was expressing the reservations of many members of the Presidium. Again, at the 22nd Congress, Kosygin declared that the "anti-party" group was not a present danger, and was only being attacked

> to show the party and the people once again what the personality cult leads
> to. . . . We must and will do everything in our power to insure that our
> party and our society have no room for a personality cult in the future
> either. . . .

This writer commented at the time—and surely it was reasonable to do so—that "this was an obvious criticism of the Khrushchev cult."

It is true that this sort of evidence requires delicate handling and considerable confirmation from the context. But it is not to be dismissed out of hand and will be disregarded only by those who have inadequately studied the tone of Soviet pronouncements. To be sure, alternative explanations *can* be found for all types of evidence we have listed, but though it may be fragmentary, inadequate, and sometimes even misleading, it is the only evidence we have, and properly interpreted, it has always led to sounder conclusions than have assumptions of its meaninglessness.

So much, then, for the non-conflict model. But this is not the only relevant issue which has been debated over the last years in these pages as well as in others. For, it may be urged, even a good old-fashioned, non-Platonic, down-to-earth conflict model admits of various interpretations. There is, for instance, nothing in it that would necessarily have prevented one from concluding that Khrushchev is bound to win any conflict. And some such position was widely maintained.

As one of the contributors to this journal who did not hold that view, and as one who is on record as putting forward the possibility that Khrushchev might fall, I should say that the key word is "possibility." There were many good arguments about the strength of Khrushchev's position, and it was perfectly reasonable to give him the odds. It was simply a methodological error to construct a model of Soviet politics in which a possibility was excluded. It turned out that Khrushchev's ouster was precisely the possibility that happened to become a fact, and so the thesis proved self-refuting. But if Khrushchev had won, that would not have proved the inevitability of his victory. The lesson of the recent events is that in dealing with Soviet politics we must never think that a restricted view of the possibilities is prudent, or commonsensical, or respectable, or admirable in any other way. From the vantage point of 1953, the major events of the first post-Stalin decade would have been contrary to "reasonable" anticipation. We should realize once and for all that communism is in a state of continuous crisis, and that it is basically unhistorical to predict for it a smooth and logical evolution. If we do not allow for even quite extravagant possibilities, we are bound to be taken by surprise. Serious consideration of Soviet prospects must deal with every variation that is formally possible.

Meanwhile, we can at least predict further struggle. For it is clear that the frictions of the past few years were not polarized between Khrushchev on the one hand and all the other members of the Presidium on the other. There must have been some support, besides Khrushchev's, for the political acts now most condemned, and there must certainly be some who were less opposed to him than others. In any case, the conspiracy against him would scarcely have waited until it had attained absolute unanimity in the Presidium. Rather, the conspirators struck as soon as their forces were adequate; the alternative would have been appallingly poor security. So there must now be vulnerable men at the top.

But even the allies who mounted the coup, and are now benefiting from it, are united only in their opposition to Khrushchev. In the Soviet past, every group that has risen against a rival has, after victory, quarreled over the disposal of the spoils, as well as on policy grounds. It is hard to see how the present rulers, even if they see the advantages of an agreed share-out, could possibly find a formula adequate to end this old tendency, this law of Soviet politics.

There are all sorts of elements in the current situation—the provocative and anomalous power of the Ukrainian contingent in the leadership, for example—which augur continued struggle. But rather than start, at this stage, on a detailed Kremlinological analysis, it may be worth registering a general point which seems to distinguish this period from earlier ones.

When Shamil, the great leader of Caucasian resistance to the Russians, asked his council who would succeed him, the answer was: "Venerated Imam, your successor will be the man with the sharpest sword." Conditions in the Kremlin are different from those in the *auls* of Daghestan and Chechenia, and it might be suggested that the knife in the back, rather than the scimitar at the breast, is the symbolic weapon more appropriate to Kremlin conditions. In any case, there are certain qualities specially required of a man if he is to become, in any true sense, Khrushchev's successor as the leader of the Soviet Communist Party and the Soviet state.

In the first place, political prestige seems essential. We saw in 1957 that a great concentration of such prestige is not adequate in itself; there must be credibility about a man's assumption to the leading position. And he must also, in the ordinary course of events, have the necessary skill and experience in the required infighting and manipulation of the *apparat*.

Strictly speaking, Khrushchev was the only member of the Presidium who had all these qualities. The immediate future must then involve either a series of attempts to maintain collective leadership—a situation which is automatically unstable in Soviet conditions; *or* the calling-in of fallen leaders with greater prestige; *or* the rather quick development of the necessary leadership qualities by one or another of the present contenders. Meanwhile, we are entitled to regard the period as inherently unstable.

In the post-Stalin succession crisis, a handful of leaders in the Presidium had so much more experience, confidence and prestige than the rank-and-file members of the Central Commitee that none of the latter could have reasonably entertained the possibility of an early rise to the top. But when the leading contenders are a Brezhnev or a Podgorny, there are a score or so, at the very least, of officials who only a few years ago ranked with the men currently at the front, or even above them, and they are unlikely to think of the Brezhnevs as in any way their superiors. The thought must be natural that the way to the top is now open, or might be open, to any ambitious provincial secretary. As Finlay writes of a Byzantine ruler,

he had risen to the highest rank without rendering himself remarkable either for his valor or his ability; the successful career of Romanus therefore excited . . . the ambition of every enterprising officer.

In dealing with the membership of the present Presidium and Secretariat, we should never fail to keep in mind the fact that, over the past six or seven years, membership of these bodies has been precarious, and that they contain a number of men whose advancement over their contemporaries is recent and unlikely to be thought of as part of the established nature of things by either their seniors or their juniors.

Although Khrushchev, with his erratic and changeable policies, has to some degree shaken the old solidarities and certitudes of the party, he has, nevertheless, provided the main element of political stability and continuity in the recent period. For the regime has at least been centered in one man of long experience and political credibility. With his removal, we now see the disintegration, which has long marked the economic and intellectual spheres, reach into the political realm as well. Although it would be going too far to say that this development is irreversible, it yet seems quite probable that the Soviet system has thereby entered a general crisis from which it can only emerge transformed out of all recognition.

Bibliography

CHINA

Bowie, R., and J. K. Fairbank, eds., *Communist China, 1955–1959: Policy Documents with Analysis.* Cambridge, Mass.: Harvard University Press, 1962.

China Quarterly (London). The best periodical dealing with contemporary Chinese problems and developments.

Compton, B., trans., *Mao's China: Party Reform Documents, 1942–1944.* Seattle: University of Washington Press, 1952.

Lewis, J. W., *Leadership in Communist China.* Ithaca, N.Y.: Cornell University Press, 1963.

North, R. C., *Moscow and the Chinese Communists* (2nd ed.). Stanford, Calif.: Stanford University Press, 1964.

Paloczi-Horvath, G., *Mao Tse-tung: Emperor of the Blue Ants.* New York: Doubleday & Company, Inc., 1963.

"Statesmen and Succession," *Journal of International Affairs,* XVIII, No. 1 (1964), 1–11.

Tang, P. S., *Communist China Today* (rev. ed.). 2 vols. Washington, D.C.: Research Institute on the Sino-Soviet Bloc, 1961.

Walker, R. L., *China Under Communism: The First Five Years.* New Haven: Yale University Press, 1955.

EASTERN EUROPE

Brzezinski, Z. K., *The Soviet Bloc: Unity and Conflict.* Cambridge, Mass.: Harvard University Press, 1960.

Dziewanowski, M. K., *The Communist Party of Poland: An Outline of History.* Cambridge, Mass.: Harvard University Press, 1959.

Gadourek, I., *The Political Control of Czechoslovakia.* New York: Frederick A. Praeger, Inc., 1955.

Hoffman, G., and F. W. Neal, *Yugoslavia and the New Communism.* New York: Twentieth Century Fund, 1962.

Ionescu, G., *Communism in Rumania: 1944–1962.* New York: Oxford University Press, Inc., 1964.

Neal, F. W., *Titoism in Action.* Berkeley, Calif.: University of California Press, 1958.

Skilling, H. G., *Communism: National and International.* Toronto: University of Toronto Press, 1964.

Starr, R. F., *Poland, 1944–1962: The Sovietization of a Captive People.* Baton Rouge: Louisiana State University Press, 1962.

Taborsky, E., *Communism in Czechoslovakia: 1948–1960.* Princeton, N.J.: Princeton University Press, 1961.

Vali, F. A., *Rift and Revolt in Hungary: Nationalism vs. Communism.* Cambridge, Mass.: Harvard University Press, 1961.

Zinner, P. E., *Revolution in Hungary.* New York: Columbia University Press, 1962.

————, ed., *National Communism and Popular Revolt in Eastern Europe: A Selection of Documents on Events in Poland and Hungary, February-November 1956.* New York: Columbia University Press, 1956.

U.S.S.R.

Armstrong, J. A., *The Politics of Totalitarianism: The Communist Party of the Soviet Union from 1934 to the Present.* New York: Random House, 1961.

————, *The Soviet Bureaucratic Elite: A Case Study of the Ukrainian Apparatus.* New York: Frederick A. Praeger, Inc., 1959.

Brumberg, A., ed., *Russia Under Khrushchev.* New York: Frederick A. Praeger, Inc., 1962.

Conquest, R., *Power and Policy in the Soviet Union.* New York: St. Martin's Press, Inc., 1961.

Daniels, R. V., *The Conscience of the Revolution.* Cambridge, Mass.: Harvard University Press, 1960.

Deutscher, I., *Stalin: A Political Biography.* New York: Oxford University Press, Inc., 1949.

————, *The Prophet Armed: Trotsky 1879–1921.* New York: Oxford University Press, Inc., 1954.

————, *The Prophet Unarmed: Trotsky 1921–1929*. New York: Oxford University Press, Inc., 1959.

————, *The Prophet Outcast: Trotsky 1929–1940*. New York: Oxford University Press, Inc., 1963.

Fainsod, M., *How Russia Is Ruled* (2nd ed.). Cambridge, Mass.: Harvard University Press, 1963.

Fischer, L., *The Life of Lenin*. New York: Harper & Row, Publishers, 1964.

Leonhard, W., *The Kremlin Since Stalin*. New York: Frederick A. Praeger, Inc., 1962.

Paloczi-Horvath, G., *Khrushchev: The Road to Power*. Boston: Little, Brown & Co., 1960.

Pethybridge, R., *A Key to Soviet Politics: The Crisis of the Anti-Party Group*. New York: Frederick A. Praeger, Inc., 1962.

Pistrak, L., *The Grand Tactician: Khrushchev's Rise to Power*. New York: Frederick A. Praeger, Inc., 1961.

Ploss, S., *Conflict and Decision-Making in Soviet Russia: A Case Study of Agricultural Policy, 1953–1963*. Princeton, N.J.: Princeton University Press, 1965.

Reshetar, J. S., *A Concise History of the Communist Party of the Soviet Union*. New York: Frederick A. Praeger, Inc., 1960.

Rush, M., *Political Succession in the U.S.S.R.* New York: Columbia University Press, 1965.

————, *The Rise of Khrushchev*. Washington, D.C.: Public Affairs Press, 1958.

Schapiro, L., *The Communist Party of the Soviet Union*. New York: Random House, 1960.

Swearer, H. R., ed., *The Politics of Succession in the U.S.S.R.: Materials on Khrushchev's Rise to Leadership*. Boston: Little, Brown & Co., 1964.

Chapter Five

Governmental Structures and Processes

Formal governmental structures in communist countries have several purposes, chief of which is to provide an institutional framework within which the economy is administered. Though basic policy decisions are made by the Party, they are implemented through the government. At the national and regional levels, the Party wields its power through interlocking directorates of top Party and government posts, a system that characterizes the leadership patterns in communist countries (Reading 30); at the local level, it encourages widespread office-holding by non-Party citizens, who carry out necessary governmental and welfare functions. A second function of constitutional structures and processes is to give concrete but circumscribed expression to claims concerning the democratic character of communist society. Communist elites have discovered, as have elites the world over, that constitutions and elections are requisite political trappings in an age of mass persuasion and manipulation. Finally, communist elites have found the constitutional framework of government a suitable arrangement for handling the nationality question (see Chapter Six), which has been a major problem for every communist country except Albania, East Germany, and Poland.

There are a few minor but interesting differences in the constitutional structures and provisions of communist countries. First, whereas the U.S.S.R. and Yugoslavia are federal in form, Communist China, Bulgaria, Czechoslovakia, Hungary, Poland, etc., are unitary states. Second, the Soviet Constitution grants the right of secession to each of its 15 constituent union republics, and is the only communist constitution which contains such a provision. Third, the U.S.S.R. and Yugoslavia have each established a separate chamber in the legislature to provide representation for their respective nationality groups.

Both the Soviet and Chinese constitutions describe the legislative branches of the national government as the highest organs of state power. In reality, neither has any power; they meet infrequently and dispose rapidly of the complex and voluminous business of government, always unanimously approving all decrees, bills, and resolutions which are submitted to them by the Party-dominated executive echelons of government. In the U.S.S.R., the legislative power is theoretically vested in the Supreme Soviet, which is composed of two houses—the Soviet of the Union and the Soviet of Nationalities. Unlike the delegates to the All-Union Congress of the CPSU, the deputies to the Supreme Soviet are elected directly by the people and "may be recalled at any moment by a decision of the majority of the electorate in the respective constituency, if he has failed to justify the trust reposed in him by his constituents, or has behaved in a manner unworthy of the high office of a Deputy." They are considered to embody the "sovereign power" of the working people. In China, the constitution places the highest governmental authority in the unicameral National People's Congress (Reading 26). Its more than 3,000 delegates are elected for a term of four years and are supposed to meet once a year, a provision that has not always been carried out in practice (Reading 27).

In modest contrast to the rubber-stamp legislatures of the U.S.S.R., China, and most East European countries, the legislatures of Poland and Yugoslavia have recently been granted some substantive functions. In Poland, the Sejm (Parliament) is permitting its permanent committees (e.g., Economic Planning, Finances and Budget, Administrative and Judiciary) to assume a limited role in proposing "not only amendments of detail but of principle as well"; they may even recommend "total rejection of measures under consideration."[1] It is also encouraging the committees "to help the government and the communist party in controlling bureaucratic extravagance and waste." But only in Yugoslavia has the Party adopted more flexible, and possibly more meaningful, constitutional forms of Party-government relationships and governmental institutions (Reading 29). This effort has perhaps been possible because Yugoslavia has fewer ties to an inherited and deeply ingrained tradition of authoritarian, centralized control by the State, than do the U.S.S.R. and China. The institution of the Workers' Councils introduced a measure of decentralized decision-making authority that is unique in communist countries (Reading 28). The Yugoslavs contend that it provides genuine "self-government" for the

---

[1] Vincent C. Chrypinski, "Poland's Parliamentary Committees," *East Europe*, XIV, No. 1 (January, 1965), 18.

workers, thereby averting the bureaucratic and non-democratic aspects of the Soviet system.[2]

To enhance efficiency and responsiveness in the administration of their respective economies, communist leaders, particularly in the Soviet Union, have experimented with the shifting of carefully delineated amounts of administrative initiative from the center to the regional and local governmental subdivisions, while retaining undiminished centralized power. Indeed, a distinguishing feature of the Khrushchev era was the frequency of administrative reorganizations (Reading 31).

Ever-reluctant to relinquish close control over managerial personnel and economic administrators, and wishing to ensure efficiency and proper implementation of its directives, the Communist Party of the Soviet Union has always maintained separate supervisory agencies, the most recent of which is the Party-State Control Committee established in 1961 and renamed the Committee of People's Control in late 1965. There are also formal legal controls over administration which are exercised through three channels:[3] (1) the Procuracy, which functions as the Party's watchdog over the Courts and local administrators; (2) the courts; and (3) "the system of state arbitration (*Gosarbitrazh*) for settling disputes between government agencies."[4] These are supplemented by various forms of Party pressure and exhortation.

In addition to utilizing government institutions to administer the economy, the Party uses them to give the masses a sense of participation in representative government. It expends considerable energy on elections, on the process whereby deputies are elected to local, regional, and national legislative and executive bodies. In Western societies elections are designed

---

[2] A noted authority on comparative economic systems has written:

"One basic question must not be omitted: Do the real lines of control of enterprise policy-making on those matters legally within the jurisdiction of a Workers' Council in fact lead back to the *workers per se,* or to the *Communist Party?* Is the entire machinery of Workers' Councils a mere facade to give party control the appearance of decentralized and democratized control of production by workers? This question does not apply to the economic forces directly controlled by the Social Plan, for there the party is clearly in control. However, with respect to those managerial decisions which a supposedly democratically elected Workers' Council theoretically makes by majority vote, is the party in fact pulling the strings behind the scenes and are the Workers' Council members mere puppets? Do party members, even though they may be a minority in a Workers' Council, usually exercise control over decisions by strength of personality, by being most vocal, or by sheer force of the fact that they are known to be party-affiliated? Such questions go to the very heart of the problem of whether what appears unique in the philosophy of Yugoslav communism is practiced or is merely preached for its external effect." William N. Loucks, "Workers' Self-Government in Yugoslav Industry," *World Politics,* XI, No. 1 (October, 1958), 78.

[3] Merle Fainsod, *How Russia Is Ruled,* rev. ed. (Cambridge, Mass.: Harvard University Press, 1963), p. 411. This distinguished study contains a separate chapter on public administration in the Soviet Union.

[4] *Ibid.*

to select the leaders of society; in communist countries they serve other purposes, which must be considered sufficiently important by the rulers to justify the time, effort, and resources expended on them. In the Soviet Union, for example, a total of almost 142 million people voted in the March 1965 government elections —99.93 per cent of the electorate. In the 2,010,540 electoral districts, "deputies were elected to 120 territorial and regional Soviets (councils), 10 area Soviets of national districts, 2,942 districts, 1,789 urban, 39,623 rural and 3,252 local community Soviets."[5] More than two million deputies were elected to these 47,736 Soviets. Great care was taken to have the elections reflect the various socio-economic groups of the country. Thus, the deputies elected from the 15 union republics "included 856,866 women (42.6 per cent of the total), 579,256 workers (28.8 per cent) and 677,082 collective farmers (33.4 per cent), as well as scientists, educationalists, public health workers, public and government leaders, writers, artists, and representatives of other professionals."[6] There was only one candidate for each office. Why, then, did the regime go to all the trouble?

First, the Party views the elections as expressions of mass support for its leadership and policies. Though assured of an overwhelming popular mandate through its control over the entire electoral paraphernalia, it nonetheless desires the reassurance of public endorsement, manufactured though this may be. As one scholar has observed, this endorsement,

> one suspects, is not only to legitimize the leadership in the mass mind and to help identify the people with its policies, but also to reassure the leadership itself of its popularity and infallibility. In this sense elections serve as a plebiscite giving the regime a blank check to run the state.[7]

Second, elections are a form of civic education. They are designed to involve the people in the administration and management of the country's economic and cultural affairs. According to one Election Manifesto of the Central Committee, "The Party has set the aim of having more and more millions of working people in town and country go through the school of administration of the state."[8] Through participation in the election process, particularly at the local level, the Party seeks to encourage vigilance on the part of every citizen and a sense of responsibility for exposing local corruption and inefficiency:

> Constant and effective public control over the implementation of the laws of the Soviet state must be organized and every care must be taken that no one

---

[5] *Soviet News,* No. 5114 (April, 1965), p. 166.

[6] *Ibid.*

[7] Howard R. Swearer, "The Functions of Soviet Local Elections," *Midwest Journal of Political Science,* V, No. 2 (May, 1961), 145.

[8] *Soviet News,* No. 4617 (February 16, 1962), p. 119.

escapes the eye of the people's control. Public control is a reliable weapon in the drive against bureaucracy, red-tape and pilfering of the people's property; it is a school for the communist education of the people.[9]

Third, elections serve as demonstrations of national loyalty and pride. They are festive occasions, holidays on which the people are shepherded to the polls and enabled to show their allegiance to the leadership and to the system.

John N. Hazard, Professor of Government at Columbia University, has written:

> The blending of popular and dictatorial institutions in a fashion that fools the public may be said to be one of the characteristics of the modern totalitarian state. It is here that the totalitarians have been able to improve upon the system of the authoritarians, typified by the Tsars of Russia.[10]

Certainly, the experience of the Soviet Union and the other communist countries with constitutions and democratic forms shows that these are not enough to ensure a democratic society.

---

[9] *Ibid.*

[10] John N. Hazard, *The Soviet System of Government,* 3rd ed. (Chicago: The University of Chicago Press, 1964), p. 204.

26 THE PARTY AND THE GOVERNMENT

Senate Committee on Government Operations, Subcommittee on National Policy Machinery, *National Policy Machinery in Communist China*, 86th Cong., 1st sess., 1959 (Washington, D.C.: Government Printing Office, 1959), excerpted from pp. 14–17.

This study was prepared for the Senate Subcommittee on National Policy machinery.

Insofar as broad national policy is concerned, the government in China is clearly subservient to the party. As the Chinese put it, "In all departments of state, all decisions on important questions are made on the proposal and according to the directives of the party." The correct policy line having been indicated, it becomes the general duty of the government to formulate and execute plans for the implementation of policy. Party committees both inside and outside the various organs of government monitor performance to ensure compliance with policy directives.

The National People's Congress

In theory, ultimate governmental authority resides in a system of people's congresses on the village, county, provincial, and national level. Popular election is constitutionally provided at the village level, while at higher levels delegates are elected by the next lower congress. But the democratic patina is thin, since all candidates are screened by the party prior to election so that only "safe" candidates stand and are elected.

At the apex of the congressional pyramid is a body known as the National People's Congress, defined in the 1954 constitution as "the highest organ of state authority" in Communist China and the "exclusive legislative authority in the country." In practice, the National People's Congress has no real power and acts primarily as a sounding board for Communist policy statements and as a channel for transmitting party policy to the nation. An examination of the congress to date bears this out. Sessions have been short, voting has been characterized by "unanimous decision," and speeches have parroted the party line after it has been explained to the session.

When the National People's Congress is not in session, its Standing Committee acts for it in conjunction with the Chairman of the Chinese People's Republic. Constitutionally the Standing Committee is empowered to interpret laws, issue decrees, ratify treaties, declare war, proclaim martial law, and order mobilization. It appoints or removes, on the Premier's recommendation, vice premiers, ministers, and heads of commissions. On its own initiative it can appoint or remove many other less important state officials. It is also empowered to supervise the State Council and can annul decisions of this body when such contravene the constitution or other laws and decrees. All such powers appear to be formal rather than actual, however; there is no evidence that the Standing Committee has contravened any previous action of the State Council.

The Chairman of the Chinese People's Republic

The formal head of state is the Chairman of the Republic, elected by the National People's Congress. This office is invested by the constitution with broad administrative and appointive powers. These include nomination of the Premier and members of the National Defense Council, together with the right to preside over that body and sessions of the Supreme State Conference. Most of the Chairman's rights are procedural, however, and require the concurrence of the National People's Congress or its Standing Committee. The Chairman has no direct control over the State Council or the ministries which comprise the day-to-day administrative centers of government. The office of Chairman of the Republic in itself, therefore, is unimportant either for the formulation or implementation of policy. The office has been reserved for the highest ranking members of the party, Mao Tse-tung and Liu Shao-chi, and the party attaches great symbolic importance to the post, since its occupant can be cast in the traditional paternal image of the Emperor.

Two bodies are directly responsible to the Chairman of the Republic: the aforementioned National Defense Council, and the Supreme State Conference. The Supreme State Conference is theoretically an advisory body consisting of the ranking personnel of all major agencies of the central government. It is convened whenever necessary by the Chairman, and sessions are usually attended by more than 300 government officials. The Supreme State Conference, as in the case of many of the other organizations described above, appears to provide merely another convenient sounding board for the explanation and publication of policy formulated by the party.

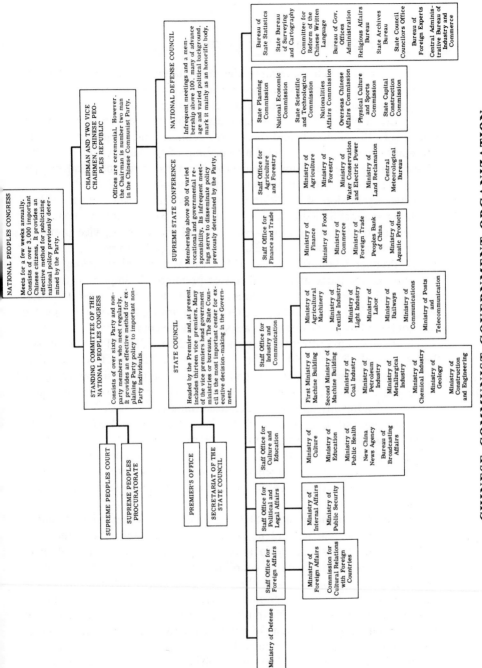

NATIONAL PEOPLES CONGRESS

Meets for a few weeks annually. Consists of over 3,000 important Chinese citizens. It provides an effective method for publicizing national policy previously determined by the Party.

STANDING COMMITTEE OF THE NATIONAL PEOPLES CONGRESS

Consists of over sixty Party and non-party members who meet regularly. It provides an effective method for explaining Party policy to important non-Party individuals.

CHAIRMAN AND TWO VICE CHAIRMEN, CHINESE PEOPLES REPUBLIC

Offices are ceremonial. However, the Chairman is number two man in the Chinese Communist Party.

SUPREME STATE CONFERENCE

Membership above 300 of varied vocational and governmental responsibility. Its infrequent meetings serve to disseminate policy previously determined by the Party.

NATIONAL DEFENSE COUNCIL

Infrequent meetings and a membership above 100, many of advance age and varied political background mark it mainly as an honorific body.

SUPREME PEOPLES COURT

SUPREME PEOPLES PROCURATORATE

STATE COUNCIL

Headed by the Premier and, at present, includes thirteen vice premiers. Many of the vice premiers head government ministries or bureaus. The State Council is the most important center for executive decision-making in the Government.

PREMIER'S OFFICE

SECRETARIAT OF THE STATE COUNCIL

Ministry of Defense

Staff Office for Foreign Affairs

Ministry of Foreign Affairs

Commission for Cultural Relations with Foreign Countries

Staff Office for Political and Legal Affairs

Ministry of Internal Affairs

Ministry of Public Security

Staff Office for Culture and Education

Ministry of Culture

Ministry of Education

Ministry of Public Health

New China News Agency

Bureau of Broadcasting Affairs

Staff Office for Industry and Communication

First Ministry of Machine Building

Second Ministry of Machine Building

Ministry of Coal Industry

Ministry of Petroleum Industry

Ministry of Metallurgical Industry

Ministry of Chemical Industry

Ministry of Geology

Ministry of Construction and Engineering

Ministry of Agricultural Machinery

Ministry of Textile Industry

Ministry of Light Industry

Ministry of Labor

Ministry of Railways

Ministry of Communications

Ministry of Posts and Telecommunication

Staff Office for Finance and Trade

Ministry of Finance

Ministry of Food

Ministry of Commerce

Ministry of Foreign Trade

Peoples Bank of China

Ministry of Aquatic Products

Staff Office for Agriculture and Forestry

Ministry of Agriculture

Ministry of Forestry

Ministry of Water Conservation and Electric Power

Ministry of Land Reclamation

Central Meteorological Bureau

State Planning Commission

National Economic Commission

State Scientific and Technological Commission

Nationalities Affairs Commission

Overseas Chinese Affairs Commission

Physical Culture and Sports Commission

State Capital Construction Commission

Bureau of State Statistics

State Bureau of Surveying and Cartography

Committee for Reform of the Chinese Written Language

Bureau of Gov. Offices Administration

Religious Affairs Bureau

State Archives Bureau

State Council Councilors Office

Bureau of Foreign Experts

Central Administrative Bureau of Industry and Commerce

CHINESE COMMUNIST GOVERNMENT ORGANIZATION

The State Council and the Premier

The State Council supervises the formulation of national plans to implement party directives and makes the necessary high-level decisions for carrying out policy. Envisioned by the constitution as the "highest administrative organ of the State," it is made up of the Premier, 16 vice premiers, and over 30 ministers and heads of commissions, together with the secretary general. The high-level membership of the State Council includes a wide range of occupational backgrounds; thus experience and competence characterize Communist China's top executive personnel.

A plenary session of the State Council is scheduled monthly to include all the above-mentioned officials. There is, however, an informal Standing Committee or "inner cabinet"—composed of the Premier, vice premiers, and the secretary general as available—which appears to meet much more often. Premier Chou En-lai and 12 of the vice premiers belong to the Politburo of the party and the other vice premiers are important Communists. In this inner group, the Premier seems to carry by far the most weight. It is likely that in making executive decisions, the Premier is guided but not bound by the advice of his associates in the council.

The formal administrative purview of the State Council is very broad, including such diverse fields as the development of defense forces, conduct of foreign relations, formulation and execution of the national economic plan, and direction of governmental activity in the fields of culture and education, nationality affairs, and overseas Chinese.

In carrying out its duties, the State Council directs and coordinates the work of 30 ministries, plus a number of commissions and special agencies. The power of the State Council to annul or reject any "inappropriate directives" issued by the agencies for which it is responsible gives it effective control over the entire central administrative structure of government.

To date, the operation of the State Council suggests that it has in fact as well as in theory carried out its constitutional function and is the most important and active agency in government engaged in the execution of national policy. Administrative coordination by the State Council is exercised primarily through six staff offices and secondarily through the personnel in a secretariat and a premier's office. Two of the staff offices are headed by members of the Politburo, and the remainder by members of the Central Committee. The areas of concern for the staff offices are: foreign affairs, internal security and related judicial matters, education and culture, finance and trade, industry and communication, and agriculture and conservation. These staff offices are supervised by central departments of the party Central Committee. Several party leaders in effect supervise themselves, holding concurrently the central department and staff office posts.

Below the staff-office level, an extensive reorganization of the various ministries and commissions, as well as the bureaus and special agencies under the State Council, was commenced in 1957. The reorganization apparently was designed to streamline a governmental apparatus which had become increasingly topheavy and bureaucratic. Superfluous staff has been reduced by reassigning cadres to more "productive" jobs at lower levels. From a high point of 48 ministries and commissions, the number has been reduced to 39. The majority—some 23—are concerned with economic matters, four with social matters, two with political affairs, and one with military affairs. Reorganizations of this sort have been fairly frequent since the regime was established in 1949, as the Communists keep striving for better machinery to carry out the policy lines set by the party.

Hsiang Nai-kuang

27 A POLITICAL PORTRAIT OF THE CHINESE CONGRESS

Hsiang Nai-kuang, "An Analysis of the First Session of the Third National People's Congress of the Peiping Regime," *Chinese Communist Affairs*, II, No. 1 (February, 1965), excerpted from pp. 1–10.

Hsiang Nai-kuang is a political commentator on the Nationalist Chinese island of Taiwan.

The Chinese Communist system of People's Congress, which assumes the parliamentary appearance of a democracy, is in fact a democratic mask of the totalitarian rule. The top organization of the Congress is the National People's Congress, which meets once a year. A standing committee functions for it during adjournment. Peiping's Constitution stipulates that the tenure of the Congress' deputies is four years. The first session of the First National People's Congress, which approved the Constitution, was held in September 1954. The third session of the Second National People's Congress was convened in April 1959. According to the Constitution, the Second Congress should end in 1963. However, it had been a year and eight months overdue before the first session of the Third People's

Congress met from December 20, 1964, to January 4, 1965. The 1961 session was cancelled because of the grave situation on the mainland.

Before the opening of the first session of the third NPC, elections for deputies were conducted between September and November of 1964 in every province, autonomous region, and city. All told, 3,040 were elected, but three of them died before they had the chance to take the seat. The new Congress has 1,814 more deputies than the last one with 1,226 deputies. . . .

Backgrounds of the Deputies

The composition of the third NPC deputies shows two special features. First, except 234 (including 55 deceased), all of the 1,226 deputies of the previous Congress were re-elected. Second, the number of deputies of the third Congress was increased by 1,817, or about 146 per cent. Mass re-election of old deputies indicated that the foundation of the regime had undergone no remarkable change in the past five years. The expansion of membership revealed that politically Peiping had left no stone unturned in broadening the foundation of the regime through elections. The second feature, therefore, is more noteworthy than the first one.

What is the composition of the 1,817 new deputies? According to our analysis, most of them are workers, peasants, scientists, and engineering and technical personnel. Women and minority nationalities also have additional representation.

1. In November 1963, the fourth session of the Second People's Congress approved Peng Chen's "Interpretations of Matters Concerning Numbers of Deputies and Their Elections to the Third People's Congress." The Chinese Communists asserted at the meeting that the membership of the new Congress must be expanded on account of increased activities of socialist construction, the necessity of including distinguished personalities from various fronts, and increasing consolidation of the united front based on the leadership of the workers' class and the alliance between peasants and workers. It was also resolved that one deputy should be elected to represent every 400,000 people in provinces and autonomous regions. As for municipalities and industrial cities with a population of over 300,000, and cities, industrial, mining, and logging centers with less than 300,000 workers and more than 200,000 workers' dependants, one deputy should be elected for every 50,000 people. This resolution showed the predominance of workers in the elections. Many of the so-called progressive producers in various industries were elected to the Congress by the Chinese Communists to show their deference to the tenet of Marxism and Leninism.

2. Peasants, like workers, are heavily represented. Peiping is fervently enforcing the so-called "socialist education" in the countryside and has

declared repeatedly that the class line of relying on the poor, lower and middle peasants must be firmly adhered to. . . .

3. The Chinese Communists have adopted the policy of playing up scientists and engineering and technical personnel in order to strengthen their economic and defense construction. The policy has been especially stressed since Peiping exploded its first nuclear device [October 1964]. There are many scientists and engineers in the new Congress. Among the re-elected deputies, 120 have either scientific or technological background. A number of new deputies are specialized in natural science and engineering. . . .

4. Women deputies in the third Congress number 520, or more than 14 per cent, as compared with the 150, or about 12 per cent, in the second one. The increase indicated that Peiping intended to raise women's political status through the elections. Among the elected were Mao Tse-tung's wife Chiang Ching, alias Lan Pin, Liu Shao-chi's wife Wang Kuang-mei, and Chen Yi's wife Chang Chien.

5. The number of deputies representing ethnic minorities was increased from 150 to 300. The increase seems modest considering the impressive 150 per cent expansion of the Congress' total membership. But it is enough to testify that Peiping has attached much importance to these groups. Fifty-one of them are represented in the third Congress, 10 more than in the preceding one. The newly represented groups are Achang, Pulang, Pumi, Nu, Penglung, Tulung, Tazik, Hsipo, Tartars, and Russians. Forty-one of the 53 deputies elected by the Uighur Autonomous Region belong to ethnic minorities. Their election indicated Peiping's eagerness to win the minority nationalities in Sinkiang in its struggle with the Russians.

. . .

Why Certain Deputies Were Dropped

It is intriguing to follow the ups and downs of important Communist figures in the elections. The study is helpful in tracing the course taken by Peiping. About 180 deputies of the Second Congress failed to be re-elected, not including the 55 deceased. . . . [The exclusion of certain members shows] that Peiping is engaged in the liquidation of the "Peng-Huang anti-Party group," purge of the pro-Russian elements, and punishment of Tibetan leaders.

1. Liquidation of the Peng-Huang anti-Party group. It is beyond doubt that Peng Teh-huai and Huang Ke-cheng were liquidated owing to their opposition to Mao Tse-tung's "Three Red Flags."[1]

---

[1] Peng Teh-huai was a Marshal of the Chinese People's Liberation Army, Minister of Defense, Head of the Military Affairs Committee, and member of the Party's Politburo in 1958. Peng and his followers in the Party and the military establishment

2. Purge of pro-Russian elements—Chang Wen-tien's and Yang Hsien-chen's exclusion from the new Congress is indicative of Peiping's purge of pro-Russian elements. Chang Wen-tien, alias Lo Fu, is a graduate of the Moscow's Sun Yat-sen University. . . . In 1945, he was elected to the Central Committee and the Political Bureau of the Chinese Communist Party. He became Peiping's ambassador to Moscow in 1951 and was transferred to the post of vice foreign minister in November 1954. In the Central Committee, he was downgraded to alternate membership in September 1956. Since he was removed from the post of vice foreign minister following the reorganization of the State Council in 1959, he has never appeared in public. His failure in the elections indicated that he had been purged. The reason could be that he had supported the Russian Communists in the Moscow-Peiping struggle. . . . Yang Hsien-chen had engaged in theoretic work in Moscow for years before he was assigned to Peiping's Marx-Lenin-Stalin College as vice president and promoted to the presidency when it was converted into the Higher Party School in 1956. In September of that year, he was elected alternate member of the Central Committee of CCP. He revisited Moscow when he accompanied Mao Tse-tung there in November 1957. The Russian-educated theoretician got his full membership in the Central Committee in 1958. He was demoted in 1961 to the vice presidency of the Higher Party School, one year after the Moscow-Peiping conflict started. . . . Mao called him a revisionist and subjected him to all-out criticism. His failure in the elections is entirely understandable.

3. Punishment of Tibetan leaders—One thing especially noteworthy is the failure of Panchen and his right-hand men Chan Tung and Chi Chin-mei in the Tibetan elections. Panchen was Peiping's puppet, groomed to replace Dalai. Peiping made him head of the Preparatory Committee for Tibet Autonomous Region to take the place of Dalai before his flight to India. Though a puppet of the Peiping regime, Panchen symbolizes the interest of top Tibetans, religiously, politically, and economically. They used his position and his relations with the Chinese Communists to obstruct Peiping's "reform" programs in Tibet. As a result, the conflict between Peiping and the Tibetans became the conflict between Peiping and Panchen. Panchen was present at the opening ceremony of the seventh session of the Preparatory Committee in last October, but was not seen at

---

were purged in September 1959, in part, for advocating the professionalization of the armed forces in opposition to Mao Tse-tung's view that the masses should be organized as an enormous civilian militia. In 1958, as a concomitant of the Great Leap Forward, Mao instituted a "Make everyone a soldier" campaign. The "Three red flags" are the cornerstones of Mao's program to transform China into an industrialized modernized state: (1) the general line; (2) the Great Leap Forward; and (3) the commune program.—Ed.

the closing meeting. Since the Chinese Communists had shouted the slogan of "fight feudalism" at the meeting and charged that some people had engaged in counter-revolutionary activities under the cloak of religion, it was quite possible the meeting was designed to attack Panchen and his followers. Panchen was removed from the list of NPC deputies representing Tibet but he was allowed to retain his membership in the Fourth National Committee of the Chinese People's Political Consultative Conference, representing minority nationalities, while Chan Tung and Chi Chin-mei were barred from the CPPCC as well as the NPC. This is an indication that Peiping has encountered strong opposition from the Tibetan leaders.

The above are typical figures who have been excluded from the Third National People's Congress as rightists, revisionists, and leading minority nationalities.

Josip Broz Tito

28 ON THE WORKERS' COUNCILS

Josip Broz Tito, *Selected Speeches and Articles:* 1941–1961 (Zagreb: Naprijed, 1963), excerpted from pp. 190–96.

Tito is the father of the Yugoslav revolution, the head of the League of Communists, and the President of Yugoslavia. At the First Congress of Workers' Councils, held in Belgrade in June 1957, Tito spoke on the contributions that the establishment of Workers' Councils had made to Yugoslav society and on the existing shortcomings of the institution.

In a few days time it will be seven years since we passed the Law on the transfer of factories and enterprises to management by the producers, by the workers of our country. This was a major, one can say historic, act in the development of our socialist social system, an act dictated by our social needs at a particular stage, that is to say, the need for democratisation in the economy, the establishment of new, socialist relationships in production, based on the wide participation of workers, not only in the management of production but also in its further development and in distribution. The aim of this act was to make it possible for workers to develop their creative abilities and self-initiative to the maximum, a development which had been held back by centralised management of production.

At that time there was a great deal of scepticism about whether our young working class, during its influx from the country into the towns and factories at the peak of the industrialisation period, would be fit for such a complex task as the management of factories and enterprises. We, however, did not entertain any doubts about our working class when we passed this law. Because even then we were able to see for ourselves its creative potentialities in action. Yes, we were aware that most of our working class were young, but then—so was the great achievement of our revolution, the new Yugoslavia itself. As a heritage from the old underdeveloped Yugoslavia there was a very small number of skilled, competent personnel; and then again the Liberation War, that is to say, the People's Revolution, had claimed from the most skilled ranks of the small working class particularly heavy sacrifices. . . .

Should we then have hesitated and harboured doubts about whether our workers, who had shown such creative skill in production, would be capable of taking over the management of that production? No. We believed that they would master that, although we were aware of the various difficulties and obstacles in the way of the development of social management, something which you here today know best yourselves.

Here you will be talking about these various shortcomings, because they must be pointed out so that they may be overcome as soon as possible, particularly those of a subjective character. There are difficulties and shortcomings of an objective character, but there are also subjective ones, which are more easily eliminated or avoided, because that is something depending on you yourselves. The objective difficulties which were in the way of a more rapid and suitable development of workers self-management must be discussed by those of us who are responsible for the over-all development of socialist construction in this country. For we cannot and must not fail to admit our responsibility for delays in eliminating certain obsolete regulations and devices which slow down the rate of production and, as a result of this, curb the rise in our workers' living standards. In so far as in the immediate past there have been certain difficulties of an objective character, difficulties of a material nature, we are not to blame for them, for it is outside our power to eliminate them. But it does happen that difficulties of an objective character become subjective; and then, we who are in leading positions must do all we can to remove these shortcomings as quickly as possible, because that depends on us, in the leadership. Such is the case, for example, with the wage system, which has been pending a settlement for some time now, and this is something on which a rise in labour productivity very largely depends.

Allow me, comrades, since I am talking about undesirable phenomena occurring here and there in the workers' collectives, to mention the most marked of these, which, if they are not eliminated, might have very bad consequences on the building up of our monolithic socialist community.

First in this category is localism, failure to take account of the interests of the whole community. Such localism shows itself in various forms, and it is incompatible with a proper understanding of socialist relations in our community. It should not be forgotten that our socialist society is an enormous collective in which the interests of the individual must coincide with the interests of the whole community. It is very harmful for the community if, instead of real socialist relationships in factories and undertakings, the principle of the stronger prevails. Disloyal competition, and the setting up of a number of enterprises of the same sort, merely for the sake of competition with already existing enterprises, is exceedingly harmful, because too much investment is absorbed which could be more usefully employed for other purposes. Another harmful practice is when certain enterprises refrain from any co-operation which might result in cheaper production of certain products, and so on. These and similar shortcomings must be eliminated, for it will be to the benefit of the workers themselves and the whole of our community.

. . .

When the apologists of a certain dogmatism of doubtful origin today contest the value of our system of workers self-management, calling it anarchy and such like names, we have not the slightest need to justify theoretically, from the Marxist standpoint, the rightness and outstanding efficiency of our system of workers self-management, because it has proved its value to the full in practice. The results speak for themselves. But at the same time it has shown the vital force and rightness of the Marxist theory of socialising the means of production, in that the producers themselves are managing the means of production, whereby truly democratic and socialist relations in production are established.

It goes without saying that we have no intention of imposing our system on anyone else, as is often alleged against us; but we do have the duty of defending it against those who are blind and deaf to the facts, who refuse to see the real state of affairs in our country. I think that the positive results achieved in practice are the best proof of the soundness of our system. These results are not only seen by the direct participants in production, our workers who are the managers, but they are also seen and felt by the whole population, and indeed they are known far beyond our frontiers.

Neither have we any intention of competing to see whose system is better and more democratic, because that is a matter which the producers can best judge for themselves, the wide masses of workers in every socialist country. Our workers have come to the conclusion that their self-management in factories and enterprises is a great achievement which offers them the best prospects for creating a better life and prosperity for themselves. . . .

The workers' councils should deal not only with the technical problems of production but also with the economic problems both of the enterprise itself and of the market—and with other problems. We are aware that here and there certain people in leading positions in the enterprises deny these rights to the workers' councils; and the workers in turn have given in too easily to such improper treatment of the role of the workers' councils. More energy should be spent in eliminating such improper conceptions.

Alvin Z. Rubinstein

29 YUGOSLAVIA'S OPENING SOCIETY

Alvin Z. Rubinstein, "Yugoslavia's Opening Society," *Current History,* XLVIII, No. 283 (March, 1965), 149–53, 179.

Alvin Z. Rubinstein is Associate Professor of Political Science at the University of Pennsylvania and author of The Foreign Policy of the Soviet Union *and* The Soviets in International Organizations.

A journey through Yugoslavia affords the Western observer a unique opportunity to travel freely in a Communist state. This is the only Communist country where unregulated travel, extensive contacts with citizens from different walks of life, and open discussion of controversial subjects are possible. The contrasting mood and manner of the people in Yugoslavia and in the Soviet Union reflects a fundamental difference in the approach of these two Communist governments to their people, to the development of a Communist society, and to the world at large. Yugoslav society has a tolerance of dissent in art and literature; and there is a freedom to emigrate and to communicate with foreigners which is unknown anywhere in the Soviet bloc.

At present the country is comprised of six republics: Bosnia and Hercegovina, Croatia, Macedonia, Montenegro, Serbia, and Slovenia. By virtue of their size and population, Croatia and Serbia are the most important. Croatia, for centuries a part of the Austro-Hungarian Empire, is Latin in culture, Austro-German in temperament, and Roman Catholic in religion; Serbia, which was long dominated by the Turks, is more Balkan in atmosphere, volatile in temperament, and Greek Orthodox in religion. As recently as the Second World War, the two cultures and nationalities were engaged in bitter, internecine war, and relations among the various nation-alities were poor. One of the impressive achievements of the Tito regime has been the amelioration of these ancient feuds and the implementation of a constructive nationality policy which is the present regime's greatest contribution to the development of a stable and united Yugoslavia.

Despite some economic setbacks and difficulties, Yugoslavia has con-tinued to move in recent years toward a growing measure of decentraliza-tion and liberalization of its economic, social, cultural, and political life. There have been periodic reversals and reimpositions of Party control, but the trend has been toward an ever-broadening sphere of relaxation. Yugo-slavia will continue in the foreseeable future to be a one-party state in which ultimate political authority rests with the League of Yugoslav Communists (LYC), and the goal remains the creation of a Communist society. But beyond this undisputed political condition there remains the need to evaluate the intriguing and important developments that have recently transpired in the institutional and constitutional realms of govern-ment and Party affairs and that signify a further broadening of citizen responsibility and initiative in local affairs, a strengthening of constitutional guarantees for the individual against the state, and a diminution of direct Party controls over the society. Only time can tell how integral a part of the political process these innovations will become; but it may be of interest to examine these changes and speculate on their significance for the evolution of the Yugoslav political system.

The New Constitution

On April 7, 1963, the Yugoslav Federal Assembly (Parliament) adopted the new Constitution of the Socialist Federal Republic of Yugo-slavia. Out of the crucible of more than four years of intra-Party discussion and disagreement emerged one of the longest (257 articles) and most complex constitutions in the world. The provisions reflect the desire of the leaders to continue toward greater decentralization and democratization, though within an institutional framework which safeguards the leading position of the Communist Party and its role as "the fundamental initiator of political activity necessary to protect and to promote the achievements of the Socialist Revolution."

Implicit in the Constitution is a change in the role of the state in a socialist society. The Constitution encourages the expansion of local self-government and the reduction of the functions of the state to a minimal level, consonant with external and internal security and with the regulation of those economic difficulties which arise in a transitional society. The framers sought to strengthen self-government among the working and production organizations, and to introduce effective checks on the power of the Federal Government. Their efforts to make this goal a reality involved a major struggle between the entrenched interests in the Government and Party and those who insisted that these institutions must be adapted more extensively to the changing character of Yugoslav society.

Behind the goals of a more viable, responsive governmental system lay basic dissatisfaction with the shortcomings that had cropped up under the previous Constitution and had interfered with the development of social democracy: the Federal Executive Council (the highest executive body) was too powerful; the Federal Assembly functioned in rubber-stamp fashion and lacked vitality; the bureaucracy had swollen in size and influence and dampened local initiative; the position of the Workers' Councils and the operation of the individual enterprises required stronger constitutional guarantees.

Of particular interest to Westerners are the new institutional changes introduced, the most important being those which restrict the legislative and executive branches, while strengthening the judiciary. The power of the Federal Assembly is to be controlled through diffusion of authority and limitation on terms in office. The Assembly is unusual in that it consists of five Chambers, each with 120 deputies who are elected by indirect suffrage (Articles 166–167). Though all the Chambers are nominally co-equal, the Federal Chamber, or upper house, is most important because it has the responsibility for electing the members of the influential Federal Executive Council; for determining basic policy, pertaining to international relations, national defense, and general internal affairs; and for electing and removing the members of the Constitutional Court. Each of the other Chambers has responsibility for a specific area—economics, education and culture, social welfare and health, and general organizational-political-administrative affairs, including the passing of the federal budget (unlike other Communist countries, Yugoslavia permits the various republics and communes to draw up supplementary budgets and levy local taxes). Members of the Chambers are elected from the functioning institutions of society, such as trade unions, educational institutions, Workers' Councils, and communal assemblies; they will tend therefore, the Yugoslavs reason, to be workers and technocrats, rather than politicians. Under this system of differentiation and specialization, the federal deputy is expected to reflect and represent the direct interests of the group that elected him, thus bringing the operations of the Federal Assembly into closer contact with those of the local units of government.

Another innovation calls for limiting the tenure of office to two four-year terms. Because the Federal Executive Council will be chosen from members of the upper Chamber, its power is expected to diminish with the limited tenure of its members. However, this reduced stature of the Council may be illusory, since the Standing Committees of the Federal Chambers still enjoy much quasi-legislative and executive power. By establishing a system of rotation in office, the regime hopes to stimulate greater public interest and to attract a higher quality of person to government service, particularly from the communes (the basic units of government). Yugoslav jurists believe that the eight-year ceiling on federal office will substantially weaken the attractiveness of politics as a career, thus reducing the likelihood that "careerists" (a derogatory description for those who seek employ in the Government or Party in order to acquire personal power and privilege) will dominate the Government. They acknowledge that this could result in a strengthening of the Party in relation to the Government, but justify this in terms of a need to ensure the Party's preeminent position in a decentralizing society during the transition period to social democracy; an increase in local autonomy and a weakening of the Federal Government's power make unifying and centralizing instruments necessary in the event of a threatening imbalance in the society. The possibility is not admitted that the Party may be seeking deliberately to weaken the Governmental sector not merely out of a desire for greater administrative efficiency, but because it has of late become concerned with the mushrooming power of the technocrats who run the economy. Top Party leaders are largely professional politicians, not managers or administrators; they are proud of the economic and social advances of the decentralized industrial sector, but are disturbed by some of the innovative ideas of the new generation of technocrats, both in the government and in the Party. In this sense, one can discern the outlines of a struggle for dominance within the Communist Party between, on the one hand, the old-line generation of Party leaders who made and stabilized the revoluution and the professionals who staff the Party apparatus, and, on the other hand, the emerging generation of managers, trade union leaders, and intellectuals who have other ideas on how best to extend the benefits of the revolution.

The Succession Problem

One crucial question, rarely raised or discussed, concerns the matter of Tito's successor. During the past decade, Tito has acquired the stature of a benevolent national patriarch, a symbol of national unity who is above the hurly-burly of day-to-day politics. He devotes his time almost exclusively to top-level policy. Much of his time is spent on the island of Brioni, meeting with visiting dignitaries and resolving internal disputes, or traveling abroad. He enjoys wide popularity and his position and person are unassailable. He has no rival. A measure of the general affection and esteem with which Tito is held can be seen in the minimal security precautions taken for him on his travels through the country, a noticeable contrast with the situation a decade ago. All Yugoslavs also know that as long as Tito lives, the complex, traditionally divisive nationality question will remain quiescent, improving slowly but surely, and thereby enhancing Yugoslavia's chances of a future continuation of the present stability and domestic tranquility. But he is seventy-two years old. His successor and, more important, the political wisdom of that successor, remain a very big question mark for the future of Yugoslav society.

The new Constitution contains an important change in the office of the Presidency which, however, is specifically excluded from application to Marshal Tito. The President is elected by the Federal Assembly "for a term of four years and may be re-elected for one further consecutive term" (Article 220). Tito, however, is President for life. Whether the constitutional power of the President, which is considerable, will be diminished as a consequence of limiting his tenure in office appears doubtful, particularly if, as seems likely, he will couple leadership of the Communist Party with Government office. The Vice-Presidency could become an important position, but this will depend on the Vice-President's role in the Party and on how the Constitution is interpreted (Article 223 states that "During absence of the President of the Republic, his powers shall be exercised by the Vice-President of the Republic"). The Constitution does not provide any more explicit information concerning the succession problem. The chairman or "prime minister" of the Federal Executive Council is also invested with important powers and must be regarded as a possible rival for the Presidency.

The President's powers are extensive: he is head of the Government and Commander-in-Chief of the armed forces; he appoints a Prime Minister who presides over the Federal Executive Council; he nominates members of the Constitutional Court of Yugoslavia; and he is empowered to promulgate laws by decree and veto decrees of the Council. When confronted with critical problems, the President may call upon the Council of the Federation, which can be likened in function to the Privy Council in Great Britain. Composed of key members of the Federal Executive Council, of state officers of the republics, and of officials of the social-political and other organizations of public life, the Council of the Federation does not have any legislative or executive powers; it is to discuss and advise. Though the President is not bound by its recommendations, he is likely to be much influenced by its views.

The Constitutional Court

Another major innovation is the establishment of a Constitutional Court. The Court, consisting of a President and ten judges elected for a term of eight years by the Federal Assembly, shall decide any question of constitutionality or legality that has been raised concerning a regulation or law that conflicts with the Constitution of Yugoslavia, the Federal law, the republican constitutions, or republican law.

The Constitutional Court is responsible for protecting the rights of the communes and Workers' Councils against encroachment by the republic or federal governments. It is also charged with upholding individual liberties and acting as a watchdog against arbitrary government actions. Finally, the Court is to keep itself informed of pending legislation and "shall offer to the Federal Assembly its opinions and proposals to pass laws and to undertake other measures to secure constitutionality and legality . . ." (Article 242). Thus, the Court has the authority to raise constitutional issues of its own accord, an initiative not accorded the Courts in other Communist (or Western, for that matter) countries.

Once the Court has determined that a law or statute does not conform to the Constitution, the Federal or Republic Assembly (as appropriate) "shall bring the law into conformity with the Constitution not later than six months from the date of publication of the decision of the Constitutional Court." If the appropriate Assembly fails to act, the law that conflicts with the Constitution "shall cease to be valid." This is the first time that a Communist country has granted to its highest Court the authority to declare acts of the legislature unconstitutional. Furthermore, the Yugoslavs have written into the Constitution not only the right of judicial review, but have apparently provided for a degree of judicial legislating by the Court. Article 250 states:

> If in proceedings on a point of constitutionality and legality the Constitutional Court of Yugoslavia finds that the law or other provision in question is not at variance with the Constitution of Yugoslavia or with federal law, it may for purposes of enforcement of the provision establish the interpretation which conforms to the Constitution or federal law.

There have been many cases in recent decades of Communist countries with Constitutions that are impressively democratic in form but clearly powerless to forestall "gross violations of socialist legality" and the entrenchment of arbitrary, unchecked, despotic one-man rule. No Constitution was more "democratic" in its provisions and safeguards than the one adopted by the Soviet Union in 1936, ironically on the very eve of the worst phase of the bloody purges that wracked Soviet society during the 1936–1938 period. The record of adherence by East European countries to constitutional provisions is also not encouraging and raises doubts about the significance of constitutions under Communist political systems.

In the Yugoslav situation, time alone can tell whether the judges who are elected by the Federal Assembly will be able to function as a judiciary independent of control by the legislative and executive branches of government and, perhaps more important, by the Communist Party. A great deal will depend on the political courage and astuteness of the judges, as well as on the permissible frontiers set by the Party. There is no doubt that the Constitutional Court is a unique institution for a Communist society. To weigh acts of government against the provisions of a written Constitution is alien to classical Communist theory which regards a Constitution as a legal document embodying the existing stage of development, and not as the supreme law of the land.

The Constitution devotes considerable attention to strengthening the Workers' Councils and to furthering the current trend toward decentralization of all governmental institutions; it calls for greater public participation in the conduct of local affairs and implies self-imposed restrictions by the Party upon the use of force or arbitrary action as a means of reinforcing or securing its privileged position. Through continued decentralization, Party leaders hope to promote social democracy; yet, they do not want democratization to erode the Party's guiding role in society. The line between the two is delicate and uncharted.

The Constitution also provides an impressive Bill of Rights: it guarantees, among others, freedom of thought, freedom of religion, and freedom of the press, association, and assemblage, but qualifies all of them by noting that "These freedoms shall not be used by anyone to overthrow the foundations of the socialist democratic order determined by the Constitution, to endanger the peace . . . or the independence of the country, to disseminate national, racial, or religious hatred or intolerance, or to incite to crime, or in any manner that offends public decency." It contains new safeguards against arbitrary arrest and added guarantees for the protection of individual rights "in proceedings before court, administrative and other organs, institutions and organizations."

The Party and the State

The knottiest problem, on which the new Constitution provides no information, centers on the future role of the Communist Party and its relationship to the changed governmental institutions. Can the unifying and central role of the Party in the political life of the country be maintained without either transforming the Constitution into a sham document or else undermining the effectiveness and morale of Party members? Aside from stating in the Preamble that the Communist Party will retain its preeminent political position in Yugoslav society, the Constitution offers no clue as to how efforts to protect and extend the autonomy, initiative, and responsibility of local units of self-government will be reconciled with the persisting and unchallenged tendency of the Party to keep a firm grip on the reins of power.

A revealing barometer of Party intent was the Eighth Congress of the League of Communists which was held in Belgrade in December 1964. The Congress was convened in order to redefine the "guiding" role that the Communist Party is to play under the 1963 Constitution. In essence,

Yugoslav Communist leaders contend that it is possible for the LYC to lead society without governing it.

The complete documentation of the Congress was not available at the time that this article was written; however, it may be of interest to mention the initial impressions of foreign observers. First, Tito retains his unquestioned authority in the Party. He was re-elected Secretary General of the LYC (the other three secretaries are Edvard Kardelj, Aleksandr Ranković, and Veljko Vlahović). Second, the Party remains centralized, hierarchical, elitist. Expectations of a democratization of Party political life, especially with respect to the right of a dissenting minority to carry on its criticism and discussion of Party policy, proved premature. The Congress rejected such proposals of the "liberal" faction which were aired at the sixth plenum of the Party's Central Committee nine months earlier, in March 1964. Instead the leadership emphasized the Leninist character of the Party, with its strictures on criticism and opposition to established Party policy. Third, the Congress called for more active recruitment among young workers and for renewed efforts to combat "bureaucratism" and persisting "local nationalisms." (There are approximately one million members of the LYC, only one-third of whom are workers).

Whither Yugoslavia?

Yugoslavia has been described as a country with one capital, two alphabets, three languages, four religions, five nationalities, and six republics.[1] Its society has an attractive vigor and vitality. The people are straight-forward and friendly to foreigners. They welcome foreign guests in their homes with a warmth and hospitality that make an American feel more at home than in most places in Europe. Yugoslavia is a Communist country, but its Communist Party chooses, in the words of a former American Ambassador, "To let people be people"; it does not want to create a "new Yugoslav man."

In a real sense, the objectives and methods of the regime have been accepted by the country. Such opposition as exists is fragmented, politically inert, unable to agree among itself on any issue having an emotional claim on popular sentiment, and incapable of reversing the direction of postwar social and economic change. During the past decade and a half, Yugoslavia has experienced a startling transformation. From a Stalinist prototype of

---

[1] The capital is Belgrade; the two alphabets are the Cyrillic and the Latin; the three languages are Serbo-Croatian, Slovenian, and Macedonian; the four religions: Moslem, Protestant, Roman Catholic, and Greek Orthodox; the five nationalities: Croatian, Macedonian, Montenegran, Serbian, Slovenian; and the six republics: Bosnia and Hercegovina, Croatia, Macedonia, Montenegro, Serbia, and Slovenia.

"socialism" it has moved toward the establishment of institutions and procedures committed to democratic processes.

There is good reason to believe that the Yugoslav leadership is sincere in its efforts to take another major step along its "road to socialism": a road along which governmental power is diffused throughout the system with the intent to strengthen institutions functioning at the local level. But there is also no doubt that it intends these advances in individual and material well-being to be accomplished within a system that ensures the concentration of ultimate political decision-making authority in the hands of the Communist Party. Can a society function effectively and productively under a decentralizing system which permits ultimate political power to remain highly centralized? Yugoslavia is groping its way toward increasingly non-authoritarian solutions to its complex problems; the operation of the new Constitution will be a measure of its success.

Andrew Gyorgy

30 LEADERSHIP PATTERNS IN EASTERN EUROPE

Andrew Gyorgy, "The Internal Political Order," in *Eastern Europe in the Sixties,* ed. Stephen Fischer-Galati (New York: Frederick A. Praeger, Inc., 1963), pp. 176–80. Footnote references have been deleted.

Andrew Gyorgy is Professor of Government at Boston University. He is the author of Geopolitics, The New German Science, *and* Governments of Danubian Europe, *and has written extensively on Eastern Europe.*

The dialectics of the leadership process have a certain international logic in Soviet politics. The collective-leadership principle emerged as a more or less expected development and as a fairly intelligible socio-economic pattern. Beyond the obvious, pedestrian reason that the Soviet Union insisted on its acceptance and popularization, it also reflected more profound political trends. The assumption of power by a group of men and their shared participation in the top-level decision-making process was, first of all, a repudiation of Stalinist one-man rule, a useful governmental and

Party technique of promising "better things" for the future in the form of a much-desired relaxation along political and economic lines.

Collective leadership also responded elastically to demands for both *external* and *internal* relaxations of tension. As a result of the intriguing Belgrade reconciliation between Tito and Khrushchev, other bloc members began to soften their adamantly belligerent foreign policies toward Yugoslavia, and in the ensuing period of *rapprochement* at least one major area of tension tended to disappear. In internal matters, the adoption of the "Malenkov line" brought gradual relief to the East European consumer, so shabbily treated in the Stalin era. Here the new collective-leadership elite could formally assume the responsibility and get credit for assorted improvements in the standard of living and on the economic home front. Furthermore, at least the first half of this period witnessed a veritable thaw in cultural, artistic, and intellectual life, with a significant lowering of the previously air-tight Iron Curtain barriers toward the West. The voices of writers, poets, and literary figures—so long silent under the black oppression of Stalinism—began to be heard again and were promptly reinforced by the multiple philosophical and political debates carried on by a re-alerted and more relaxed urban white-collar intelligentsia.

Last, but certainly not least, the very human "search for a scapegoat" complex had to be brought into play. The temporary disappearance (or even better—the official removal with censure) of the one-man leader figure successfully pinned the blame for the terrible mistakes of the immediate past on a single, and thus most obvious, culprit. Denunciation of the "cult of personality" from Moscow automatically demanded a chain reaction of similar denunciations on the local scene. De-Stalinization finally reached the political summit in the satellite countries—the Chervenkovs and Rákosis had to go, or at least fade away, for a period of years. The slogan of the day was that somebody would have to pay for the crimes of Stalin. Except for Walter Ulbricht, apparently irreplaceable as the military satrap and omnipotent *Gauleiter* of East Germany, the crises of top personnel affected every East European state. Even Gheorghiu-Dej, ruthless boss of the Rumanian Workers' (Communist) Party, had to relinquish his post of First Secretary in 1954 and join a new Secretariat as one of its four ruling Party members.[1]

The implementation of collective leadership in the satellites resulted in a job-splitting process on the highest levels: One leader, usually the "boss," retained the position of first secretary (formerly secretary general) of the Party, while another, generally the No. 2 man, became Prime Minister on the government side. Around them clustered a small group of about five to

---

[1] It must be noted, however, that Gheorghiu-Dej still retained the position of Prime Minister and eventually switched again, resigning as Premier and taking back the post of First Secretary. [Gheorghiu-Dej died in March 1965, and was succeeded by Nicolae Ceausescu.—Ed.]

eight colleagues, who were then identified as the "collective" leaders of *both* Party and government. In some satellites the team was incorporated into an all-powerful politburo, while in others it appeared to the outside world as a cabinet of ministers with the inner group of the "collective" holding the more important cabinet portfolios. Thus, while the formal power structure seemed to be of a dual character, fairly evenly split between Party and government, it was essentially monolithic in shielding a strong Party leader behind the relatively thin facade of the new "collective."

It is clear in retrospect that this neither-single-nor-group type of leadership, with its variegated and fluctuating pattern of "now you see me, now you don't," soon became a source of political instability and ideological uncertainty on the satellite scene. The Soviet Union's East European empire was geared to solid and *truly single* leadership, which apparently could not be delegated to and diffused among the members of a group enjoying a rather dubious state of co-equality. After a few months of sharing political power and the public spotlight, these elite groups were unable to reach clear-cut, forceful decisions, and the whole governmental process slowed down to a hesitant pace. An atmosphere of watchful waiting pervaded the satellite scene, with all members of the "collective" anxiously eyeing the Kremlin for further instructions either in a liberalizing direction or toward a general retightening.

The eventual *coup de grâce* was delivered by the Polish and Hungarian revolts of 1956. Although the collective-leadership era did not come to a sudden stop, it was significantly complicated by the impact of these two great popular explosions and, by 1958 at the latest, was forced to give way to an already familiar leadership pattern: that of the one-man rule. The tense and fundamentally unsatisfactory conditions in post-revolutionary Poland and Hungary forced the hand of the local elites and of the Soviet Party leadership into reintroducing the political "cult of personality" on the highest levels of government and Party. In the hope that this would be a somewhat different pattern, marked by a distinctly non-Stalinist flavor, the satellite countries fell in step with this round of developments.

After the Soviet signal had been given in March, 1958, the end of leadership duality in Eastern Europe came swiftly. In the final stage of consolidating his power, First Secretary Khrushchev accepted the resignation of Marshal Bulganin as Chairman of the Council of Ministers and assumed the office himself. This event denoted the terminal point of the already moribund collective-leadership principle both at home and abroad. The dialectic process of twentieth-century Communism again asserted itself with a major qualitative shift toward the more authoritarian and highly centralized form of single leadership.

In its technical aspects, this latest phase did not alter the job-splitting process described above. *Formally,* the duality of power, in terms of different leaders holding the positions of first secretary and prime minister, has been maintained everywhere except in Hungary.[2] Invariably, however, true political authority rested with the first secretary, the Party boss. The ceremonially maintained, but substantively near-meaningless position of prime minister, more commonly known as chairman of the council of ministers, remained in the hands of such superannuated permanent figureheads as Otto Grotewohl in East Germany, Jozef Cyrankiewicz in Poland, and Ion Gheorghe Maurer in Rumania. The first two are ex-Socialists and have never been quite forgiven by their arch-Communist colleagues. Most chairmen of councils have been "kicked upstairs," as it were, and have held their tenuous positions primarily as a reward for past services rendered to the dominant Workers' (Communist) Party. The Bulgarian pattern has presented a slight variation in that the chairmen of councils have been shifted around, appointed, and demoted in fairly rapid succession, while the first secretaryship has for the past several years been firmly anchored in the hands of party chief Todor Zhivkov.

While job-splitting has prevailed on the prime minister–first secretary level, the absolute monopoly of one-man rule has been quietly strengthened in another direction. In at least three of the satellite countries, recently introduced constitutional reforms have led to the consolidation of the chief-of-state powers in the hands of the Party boss. Thus Antonin Novotný, the No. 1 Czechoslovak Communist of today, has been able to add the country's Presidency to his office of First Secretary of the Party upon the death of his predecessor in 1957. Thus Walter Ulbricht and Gheorghe Gheorghiu-Dej also have been "elected" presidents of their respective state councils, merging the highest Party and government offices in their hands and becoming both *real* and *titular* heads of their states. The designation of the same political figure as head of state as well as head of Party has run counter to the generally Soviet-imposed fashion in the bloc. Observers have noted with interest that the replacement of a Soviet-style presidium by this new state council has made at least the East German and Rumanian governmental structures resemble more closely the system of Yugoslavia than that of the Soviet Union. In the former, Tito has also occupied the Presidency of a seventeen-member State Council on the government side, while presiding as unchallenged boss over the Yugoslav Communist Party.

These reform developments have had a twofold political significance. In

---

[2] Since the upheavals of October–November, 1956, Hungary's pattern has vacillated. After the revolution János Kádár emerged as both First Secretary of the Party and Prime Minister. Two years later, he stepped down from the Premiership in favor of a long-time Communist and self-styled "specialist in revolutions," Ferenc Muennich. However, in a major shake-up of his regime, Kádár dropped Muennich in September, 1961, and replaced him as Prime Minister while still retaining the Party leadership. . . .

each of the four countries, they tended to increase the prestige and status of the top Party *apparatchik* and also accomplished a closer identification of the executive powers of the government apparatus with the politburos and central committees of the respective Communist parties. To this extent there is today an emphatically monolithic aspect to political power in Czechoslovakia, East Germany, Rumania, and—of course—Yugoslavia that is not to be found in the other East and Southeast European countries as yet.

Howard R. Swearer

31 DECENTRALIZATION IN RECENT SOVIET ADMINISTRATIVE PRACTICE

Howard R. Swearer, "Decentralization in Recent Soviet Administrative Practice," *Slavic Review*, XXI, No. 3 (September, 1962), excerpted from pp. 456–70. Footnote references have been deleted.

Howard R. Swearer is Associate Professor of Political Science at the University of California, Los Angeles, and author of The Politics of Succession in the U.S.S.R.

The Soviet Union, as an administrative state par excellence, is a Parkinsonian nightmare. Although the leadership is armed with broad powers and unhampered by formal restraints in its control of the bureaucracy, it is nevertheless hard pressed to keep the huge administrative structures of the Soviet system efficient and responsive to central direction. The success or failure of a regime depends in large measure on how effectively it can get its policies translated into action by the bureaucracy.

Most schematic descriptions of the Soviet system by Western commentators, especially those written in the early 1950's, emphasized the division of the state into several highly centralized, vertically structured, and functionally specialized administrations—party, police, armed forces, and the economic bureaucracy. Within these broad categories there was frequently even further vertical-functional fractionization. For example, within the industrial bureaucracy there were various specialized ministries and a separation between planners and managers. In the party, one could discern differences of interests and functions among at least the regular territorial party hierarchy, Stalin's personal secretariat headed by Poskrebyshev, and the party Control Committee. Stalin was depicted as standing above these various hierarchies, balancing them and playing one off against another. The significant divisions and the possible points of friction within the total bureaucracy were thus seen to be primarily between these vertical structures. This organizational model produced a number of useful hypotheses about the distribution and exercise of political power in the Soviet Union.

It may now prove equally useful to postulate a model of Soviet administration that depicts the major divisions in the Soviet bureaucracy as horizontal or territorial—rather than functional—and the major tensions as between the territorial-administrative layers (all union, republic, oblast, city, and raion) of the hierarchical state pyramid. According to official doctrine there is no fundamental problem of central-local relations, because by definition national and local interests coincide in a socialist state. Any frictions are seen as temporary aberrations caused by individual idiosyncrasies, organizational mistakes, or improper ideological training.

This paper will argue, on the contrary, that conflicts of interest between central and regional functionaries present a major and growing problem in the Soviet Union, and that a consideration of central-local relations may help to clarify the administrative modifications of the Khrushchev era. These modifications have been (1) a carefully controlled bureaucratic decentralization, (2) concomitant moves to reinforce territorial-administrative units as the basis of administration, and (3) an increase in the authority and responsibility of the party apparatus for supervising the revamped governmental structure. As we shall see, these administrative renovations have been the product both of substantive problems connected with managing a maturing and ever more complex society, and the leadership struggle from which Khrushchev emerged the apparent victor in 1958.

Problems of Decentralization

Since the mid-1950's the Soviet leadership has endeavored to readjust administrative relationships to permit greater flexibility and resourcefulness to lower administrative echelons, while retaining central control and attempting to make it even more effective. This cautious decentralization of management has been prompted not by popular demand but by the leadership's belief that some redistribution of functions within the unitary Soviet state was required for continued rapid economic growth and the development of capable lower cadres. The almost unbelievable centralization of decision-making during the later Stalin period made some devolution of managerial authority mandatory if the administration was not to choke in red tape. In addition, by removing from Moscow the squabbling centralized industrial ministries and by pushing to lower levels some of the day-by-day management of the economy, the leadership sought to attain a better perspective on administrative problems and thus exercise more effective leadership.

What is the nature and extent of the devolution of administrative authority? To provide a definitive answer would require an analysis of the entire range of state functions, but several observations and examples may help to indicate the trend.

First, there has been no intention of making lower administrative echelons in any way independent. . . . Bureaucratic decentralization does not mean the creation of autonomous or semiautonomous administrative units on, say, even the Yugoslav model.

It appears that most of the administrative discretion that has been transferred to lower levels, has come to rest in the republics, oblasts, and major cities such as Moscow and Leningrad. In 1957 the operative management of the bulk of industry was centered in the regional economic councils (sovnarkhozy), which, with some exceptions, are located at the level of the oblast and smaller republics. Republics have been granted greater discretion, within the gross income and expenditure limits of their budgets, to establish the budgets of subordinate soviets; they issue statutes on local soviets and mass organizations; and they form and abolish local soviets except at the oblast level. Some additional authority for decision-making has found its way to still lower levels. Local administrators have been encouraged, with mixed results, to play a greater role in planning production, especially in agriculture. Within the framework of all-union laws on educational reform, the industrial reorganization, the abolition of the MTS, and so forth, officials at the republic and lower levels have been allowed to take some account of local conditions when executing these programs. Local authorities, with central guidance, have also experimented with pruning and restructuring the local bureaucracy.

Local officials have been urged, indeed warned, to assume more responsibility and to show more initiative in the execution of central plans. . . . Moreover, a number of devices have been built into the administrative system to stimulate local officials to greater efforts in fulfilling state plans. For example, a sizable part of the budgetary income of a local soviet derives from deductions from national taxes. Since these deductions are fixed on a percentage and not on an absolute ruble basis, it behooves local officials to see that all economic enterprises in their areas (not merely those under their direct jurisdiction) operate at full throttle and that national revenues are rigorously collected.

Yet another innovation has been the freer and fuller discussion at all administrative levels of national problems and projects of reform. Although much of this debate is stimulated from the top and controlled within the framework laid down by central authorities, such drastic changes as the abolition of the MTS and the educational reform of 1958 were preceded by months of discussion among officials at all levels, even though much of this discussion did not reach the press. The rights of factory managers, the relation between the sovnarkhozy and Gosplan, projects for alterations in the kolkhoz system, such as the establishment of kolkhoz unions and the transformation of kolkhozy into sovkhozy, have also been topics for serious discussion throughout the bureaucracy. Khrushchev has attempted to tap opinions at all levels on a number of thorny problems, and has tried also to give local officials a sense of vicarious participation in decision-making. The limits of discussion have been widened by largely withdrawing these issues, at least temporarily, from the realm of ideology and casting them in a nonpolitical, technical framework. Nevertheless, the problems are real and have important implications for the whole system. Final decisions on major reforms are made in the Central Committee Presidium, but they are now made on the basis of a better knowledge of local attitudes, and frequently after local authorities have experimented with various alternatives.

Bureaucratic decentralization has met with only partial success. As will presently be discussed, the leadership has backtracked to some extent because of difficulties encountered in the revamped administration. And despite the determined drive to push responsibility for policy execution down the administrative ladder, it tenaciously creeps upward again—partly because of the overlapping jurisdictions within the local bureaucracy. This arrangement was designed to provide inconclusiveness of authority, so that significant disputes in the localities would be called to the attention of higher authorities. Moreover, since party and governmental authorities at each territorial level are ultimately responsible for all happenings within their geographic area, they often feel compelled to intervene at lower levels. The lower the officials are in the hierarchy of soviets, the more they are restricted from dealing independently with local affairs; at the bottom level, most decisions of the rural soviet executive committee conclude with: "Ask the raion executive committee to affirm the present decision." Under these conditions published laws and instructions about decentralization are not always a reliable guide to administrative practice. Complaints in the press make it clear that higher administrators frequently behave in an arbitrary manner toward their subordinates. For example, an oblast soviet executive committee may decree that the surplus revenues of a particular raion be used elsewhere in the oblast, even though the raion is legally entitled to spend the funds.

Emphasis on a Territorial
From of Organization

An important feature of the decentralization program has been a shift to a territorial, instead of an industrial-branch or functional, form of organization. Instead of decentralizing the administration within the framework of many partly autonomous and functionally specialized vertical ministries, administrative authority over a wide variety of activities was consolidated in the hands of territorially-based party secretaries and officials of soviet executive committees in republics, cities, oblasts, and raions. Since efforts had been made between 1955 and 1957 to decentralize within the ministerial system by transforming a number of all-union ministries into union-republic and republic ministries, the reorganization of industrial management in the late spring of 1957 marked a drastic break with past organizational principles. The great bulk of Moscow-based, industrially specialized ministries were abolished, and industrial management of most industry was placed in the hands of over a hundred industrially nonspecialized sovnarkhozy. A sovnarkhoz manages, with some exceptions, all the most important industrial activities within its geographical boundaries. In addition "local industry" (e.g., handicrafts, small brick factories, bakeries, etc.) has been placed more firmly under the control of the executive committees of local soviets in oblasts, cities, and raions. Specialized republic industrial ministries, which used to administer directly many of the locally significant economic enterprises, have been either abolished or consolidated and now intervene less directly in the daily management of local industry.

In the nonindustrial realm, also, local departments (e.g., public education and public health) have been made more responsible to local soviet executive committees than to their respective ministries for day-to-day management. . . .

This is not to say that all industrial-branch and functional elements in the party and governmental bureaucracies have been abolished. They continue to exist in the departments of the Central Committee Secretariat, in Gosplan, in the Ministry of Finance, in the regional party and governmental structures, and elsewhere. But these industrial-branch and functional elements are now more fully incorporated into a territorial pattern of organization.

Administrative Consolidation

Intimately connected with the emphasis on territorial administration has been a massive drive to consolidate the bureaucracy. Consolidation has taken several forms, including sweeping mergers of specialized staffs and departments at all administrative levels and of local soviets themselves. For example, in conjunction with the 1957 industrial reorganization, republic ministries, administrations, trusts, combines, and enterprises under both sovnarkhozy and local soviets were amalgamated with a vengeance.

. . .

Central Controls

How has the leadership sought to maintain control over these consolidated and strengthened lower territorial administrations, which now have more authority in local affairs? How has it tackled the dilemma of permitting, indeed encouraging, local initiative and, at the same time, ensuring local response to Moscow's dictates?

Moscow has, in part, sought to make the bureaucracy responsive to its will through several key centralized control mechanisms, such as the Ministry of Finance, Gosplan, the Procuracy, the Commission of State Control, and, of course, the party, which cut across the prevailing territorial organizations. With the exception of the party—whose role will be discussed presently—these are planning, co-ordinating, and inspecting agencies, which in theory are to provide central direction but are not to subvert lower territorial administrations. In practice this division of functions is less well defined.

As might be expected, Gosplan and the Ministry of Finance, as the two main agencies of central direction over the economy, frequently encroach upon the prerogatives of territorial administrations. It is with good reason that as the movement toward decentralized territorial administration gathered momentum, criticism directed at Gosplan and the Ministry of Finance by local officials grew in vehemence. . . .

The almost frenzied campaign to whip up "public control" is also, in part, a device to check the lower bureaucracy. The mushrooming of so-called nonstaff instructors and inspectors attached to territorial party committees and executive committees of local soviets; Central Committee decrees ordering increased attention by party cadres to workers' complaints and suggestions; the growth and activation of standing committees of local soviets and a myriad of other mass organizations; and other aspects of the comprehensive drive to stimulate popular participation are designed, in part, to enlist the aid of the masses in keeping tabs on the local bureaucracy. Through "criticism from below" the leadership can obtain information about events in the provinces that local bosses might prefer to have hushed up. . . .

Still another technique to inhibit a divergence in outlook between central and local functionaries, whether party or government, has been to ensure representation of the regional point of view in central policy-making bodies. Since mid-1957 regional functionaries on the Central Committee Presidium (including candidate members) have never constituted less than 30 per cent of the total membership. Many officials with administrative experience in the provinces, who consequently are intimately familiar with the problems and skulduggery of lower functionaries, have been assigned to positions in Moscow. Conferences in Moscow and provincial centers for administrators and specialists in various fields provide an opportunity for central authorities personally to survey difficulties in applying national policies and to castigate and cajole local functionaries for distorting these policies.

It is the party apparatus, however, which Khrushchev has charged with primary responsibility for ensuring centralized direction of society. Heavy burdens and responsibility have been placed on the approximately 250,000 party *apparatchiki* to integrate local actions with national policies. Because of the administrative decentralization and emphasis upon a territorial form of administrative organization, party secretaries in republics, oblasts, cities, and raions have had both more latitude to supervise the state administration within their bailiwicks and greater responsibility to protect national interests, as defined by the leadership, from localist deviations. Territorial party secretaries were thrown directly into administrative command of the economy: in agriculture in late 1953 at the raion level, and in industry in mid-1957 at the oblast and republic level.

It should be noted that strengthening the party apparatus was connected with Khrushchev's bid for power. Between 1953 and 1957 he asserted party primacy successively over the police, agriculture, industry, and the military. Thus, although administrative decentralization on the basis of a territorial form of organization was at least in part a response to the very real malaise in the top-heavy and self-strangulating bureaucracy, it was also directly related to the leadership power struggle. An increase in the authority and responsibility of the entire professional party apparatus from top to bottom bolstered the power position of the party's First Secretary, Nikita Khrushchev.[1]

Current Trends

Since 1958 there have been some reversals in the initial thrust of the post-Stalin administrative reorganization and substantial efforts to revamp and increase the effectiveness of the central control system. As indicated below, there are signs of a renewed trend toward centralization in the state apparatus and new emphases in the party's role, including its partial withdrawal from direct administrative work.

---

[1] Khrushchev was deposed on October 15, 1964—Ed.

A partial explanation for these current trends lies undoubtedly in the ubiquitous struggle for power and influence among personalities and blocs. Perhaps Khrushchev has had to make concessions to groups in the governmental bureaucracy to maintain his political equilibrium; or he may have deliberately buttressed the position of these groups to balance the power of other cliques. After Khrushchev had defeated the "anti-party" group and assumed the Premiership in early 1958, his personal fortunes may no longer have been so tightly bound to the party, and he thus had greater freedom of maneuver to handle substantive problems that developed in the bureaucracy after his initial reforms. Leaving Kremlinology aside, however, one can detect bureaucratic difficulties which provide substantial justification for more recent organizational modifications.

As one could anticipate, the major problems in administration after 1957 were in maintaining effective central guidance of the strengthened territorial administrative commands. If the major difficulties of the Stalin bureaucracy were the excessive centralism and "parochialism" of the various vertical, semi-autonomous ministries, which jealously guarded their far-flung empires and co-operated only hesitatingly, then the shortcoming of the Khrushchev administration has been "localism." Localism is an imprecise term covering a wide variety of sins, but generally connotes an erroneous and harmful administrative perspective that places local before national interests. It may entail laxity in delivering products to another economic region; the diversion of investment funds from items of national importance to those of local significance; attempts to make a locality as self-sufficient as possible, even though self-sufficiency may be economically wasteful; or machinations of all kinds—including outright fraud—to mislead central authorities about the true state of affairs in an area.

Localism became particularly dangerous because it began to infect the party apparatus on which Khrushchev had relied as the principal lever of central control. The strains placed on the lower reaches of the party apparatus threatened to undermine party discipline and militancy. Lower party functionaries all too often began to identify their interests with local affairs and became involved in "family groups" with other local officials. In industry, charges of localism leveled against industrial managers and sovnarkhoz officials were, on occasion, also extended to regional party secretaries who were charged with keeping them under surveillance. . . . In sum, the lower echelons of the party apparatus began to crack under the heavy burdens placed on them in connection with the administrative decentralization.

As a result, the party's role is being redefined. The organizational position of the party apparatus is being shifted so that it may supervise the governmental bureaucracy without finding itself committed to too much routine administration. Greater emphasis in party work is now placed on mobilizing mass organizations through party groups within them to perform minor functions transferred to them from the state and to check on the local bureaucracy. The official line, as stated at the 22nd Party Congress and in the new party program and statutes, emphasizes that party control of the governmental administration at lower levels should be more indirect through the primary party organizations located in administrative agencies. The party functionary is to pay more attention to propaganda and agitational activities and ideological indoctrination. A vigorous debureaucratization campaign was begun some time ago to trim party staffs and red tape. By these means, the leadership hopes to make the party a more reliable lever of central guidance. It should be noted, however, that these nostrums are not easy to apply; as long as the party secretary in each territorial administration is ultimately responsible for all events in his area, he will find it difficult to avoid becoming enmeshed in daily administrative chores nominally assigned to other bureaucrats. . . .

Bureaucracy in Flux

This article has attempted to examine and put into perspective several salient features of bureaucratic organization and operation since the death of Stalin. One final point, though obvious, needs to be made. Although Khrushchev seems to display, as one of his Presidium opponents put it in 1957, a special "organizational itch," constant flux appears to be a part of the pathology of the Soviet bureaucracy. In addition to the continuous minor shake-ups, there are periodic large-scale upheavals in the bureaucracy based on one ruling principle or another. These momentary panaceas —whether the functional, industrial-branch, or territorial principle of organization; centralized or decentralized management; or collegial versus one-man administration—may remedy the bureaucratic ills of the moment. However, as the bureaucracy oscillates between various organizational alternatives, one is impressed by the seemingly institutionalized instability of the bureaucratic structure.

The constant tinkering with the bureaucracy is no doubt partly produced by the exigencies of controlling and co-ordinating a rapidly industrializing and increasingly more complex society, but it also yields desirable results. Connections based on family ties or friendship, which reduce the effectiveness of central command and communications channels, are broken; new blood and ideas are brought into administrative ranks. There is also an ideological factor. Since the discrepancy between the official ideology and reality is often great, but the ideology is sacrosanct and is only slowly modified over long periods, it is necessary to lay the blame on reality, that is, on individuals' mistakes or organizational shortcomings. Marxism-Leninism is steeped in the nineteenth-century rationalist belief that man can scientifically order society. Hence, the response to failures in administration is apt to be bold and sweeping reorganization of the bureaucracy.

Bibliography

U.S.S.R.

Berman, H. J., *Justice in the U.S.S.R.* (2nd ed.). Cambridge, Mass.: Harvard University Press, 1963.

Carson, G. B., *Electoral Practices in the U.S.S.R.* New York: Frederick A. Praeger, Inc., 1955.

Conquest, R., *Russia After Khrushchev.* New York: Frederick A. Praeger, Inc., 1965.

Fainsod, M., *How Russia Is Ruled* (2nd ed.). Cambridge, Mass.: Harvard University Press, 1963.

Gsovski, V., and K. Grzybowski, eds., *Government, Law, and Courts in the Soviet Union and Eastern Europe.* 2 vols. New York: Frederick A. Praeger, Inc., 1960.

Guins, G. C., *Soviet Law and Soviet Society.* The Hague: Martinus Nijhoff, 1954.

Hazard, J. N., *The Soviet System of Government* (3rd ed.). Chicago: University of Chicago Press, 1964.

Meyer, A. G., *The Soviet Political System.* New York: Random House, 1965.

Scott, D. J. R., *Russian Political Institutions.* New York: Holt, Rinehart & Winston, Inc., 1957.

Shachtman, M., *The Bureaucratic Revolution: The Rise of the Stalinist State.* New York: The Ronald Press, 1962.

Towster, J., *Political Power in the U.S.S.R.: 1917–1947.* New York: Oxford University Press, Inc., 1948.

CHINA

Ch'ien Tuan-sheng, *The Government and Politics of China* (2nd. ed.). Cambridge, Mass.: Harvard University Press, 1961.

Gluckstein, Y., *Mao's China: Economic and Political Survey.* London: George Allen & Unwin, 1957.

Kessing, D. B., *Use of Top-Level Personnel by the Chinese Communist Government: 1949–1953.* Cambridge, Mass.: Massachusetts Institute of Technology Press, 1954.

Rudolph, P., *North Korea's Political and Economic Structure.* New York: Institute of Pacific Relations, 1959.

Senate Committee on Government Operations, Subcommittee on National Policy Machinery, *National Policy Machinery in Communist China,* 86th Cong., 1st sess., 1959. Washington, D.C.: Government Printing Office, 1959.

Thomas, S. B., *Government and Administration in Communist China.* New York: Institute of Pacific Relations, 1953.

Union Research Institute, *Communist China, 1949–1959.* Hong Kong: Kowloon, 1961.

EASTERN EUROPE

Brzezinski, Z. K., *The Soviet Bloc.* Cambridge, Mass.: Harvard University Press, 1960.

Floyd, D., *Rumania: Russia's Dissident Ally.* New York: Frederick A. Praeger, Inc., 1965.

Freidin, S., *The Forgotten People.* New York: Charles Scribner's Sons, 1962.

Gibney, F., *The Frozen Revolution: Poland, A Study in Communist Decay.* New York: Farrar, Straus & Giroux, Inc., 1959.

Laqueur, W., and L. Labedz, eds., *Polycentrism: The New Factor in International Communism.* New York: Frederick A. Praeger, Inc., 1962.

Neal, F. W., *Titoism in Action: The Reforms in Yugoslavia After 1948.* Berkeley, Calif.: University of California Press, 1958.

Oakes, J. B., *The Edge of Freedom.* New York: Harper & Row, Publishers, 1961.

Roberts, H. L., ed., "The Satellites in Eastern Europe," *The Annals of the American Academy of Political and Social Science,* CCCXVII (May, 1958).

Rozmaryn, S., *The Seym and People's Councils in Poland.* Warsaw: Polonia Publishing House, 1958.

Stehle, H., *The Independent Satellite: Society and Politics in Poland since 1945.* New York: Frederick A. Praeger, Inc., 1965.

Stern, C., *Ulbricht: A Political Biography.* New York: Frederick A. Praeger, Inc., 1965.

Chapter Six

The Nationality Problem:
A Case Study
of Govermental Policy

The treatment a regime accords its national minorities is one important indication of its political character. Historically, national minorities have been convenient scapegoats, a target for fear and failure. They are also regarded as "security risks" by contemporary totalitarian rulers, who have made a fetish of conformity, a crime of dissent. In societies in which totalitarian elites demand total commitment to official ideology, values, and institutions, in which the line between disagreement and treason has been narrowed nearly to the vanishing point, cultural, ethnic, and religious diversity is presumed to contain the seeds of political opposition. Thus, the pressure to conform, to adapt, to discard traditions and ties that derive from sources other than those officially sanctioned by communist society is ever-present. Every communist country, with the exception of Albania, East Germany, and Poland, has a serious nationality problem. Each regime's approach has differed, and each has had its successes and failures.

The Soviet Union has the most extensive nationality problem, the most complex demographic mosaic of distinguishable races, nationalities, and tribes, speaking more than a hundred different languages and practicing a variety of religions. In Czarist Russia, as more and more non-Russian speaking, non-Slavic areas were incorporated into the empire, the dominating concept guiding official policy toward the myriad national minorities was, "One Czar, one religion, one language." All ethnic groups other than those of Great Russian derivation were considered *inorodtsi* (aliens by origin). Russification was not, however, pushed with unremitting and unvaried determination; its implementation fluctuated throughout the nineteenth and early twentieth centuries. Often, under a policy of divide and rule, ethnic animosities were encouraged. At the time of the Bolshevik revolution, Russia was seething with nationality discord.

To their credit, the Bolsheviks realized very early the importance of the nationality problem, both to their victorious emergence from "war communism" and to their subsequent shaping of the Soviet state along federal lines. By 1922, a clear plan had evolved. The larger nationality groups, situated along the periphery of the Soviet land mass, were constituted as union-republics, with the legal right to secede. Politically, however, this option is meaningless, since the Communist Party, which heads the proletariat of these union-republics, assumes that no proletarian group would ever want to exercise it. Nevertheless, cultural autonomy was advanced, especially in education, local government, the performing arts, and the publication of newspapers and books in minority languages. Cultural autonomy means the right of a nationality to use its own language (in schools in the non-Russian areas, the Russian language is taught as the first foreign language), to retain many cultural traditions, and to have as local officials nationals of the region. Until 1917, these rights were virtually unknown to the minority peoples. The Soviet leaders, because of their belief in economic determinism, assumed that the less advanced development of the non-Russian peoples was rooted in economic backwardness, and that with the elimination of economic exploitation from society, ethnic and nationality animosities would also disappear.

During the period between the two constitutions (1924–1936), the development of national minority groups was seriously hindered by the survival of Great Russian chauvinism and by the understandable distrust on the part of peoples who had been persecuted for so long. There was also discrimination by *non*-Russian republics against the other national minorities residing within their boundaries, e.g., Georgian chauvinism was directed against the Armenians, Ossets, Adjarians, and other minorities living in the Georgian Republic. Indeed, so disruptive and threatening had the various difficulties become that Stalin, in a speech delivered at the Sixteenth Congress of the Party on June 27, 1930, sharply denounced the growing manifestations of Great Russian chauvinism and local nationalism. He maintained that the encouragement of national cultures was consonant with Marxist concepts: A national culture under the Dictatorship of the Proletariat is "a culture *socialist* in content and national in form, the aim of which is to educate the masses in the spirit of internationalism and to consolidate the Dictatorship of the Proletariat."[1] There

---

[1] Joseph Stalin, *Marxism and the National and Colonial Question* (London: Lawrence and Wishart, 1947), p. 260.

is nothing strange, he said, in the favoring of national cultures, for their expansion and maturation must be permitted "in order to create the conditions necessary for their fusion into a single, common culture with a single, common language."[2]

Several sections were included in the 1936 constitution specifically to guarantee representation to the national minorities. Article 17 reaffirms the right of each union-republic to secede; Article 35 establishes the Soviet of Nationalities as one of the two Chambers of the federal legislature (the Supreme Soviet) and ensures that all the national groups organized in territorial areas of their own will be represented; and Article 121 recognizes the primacy of language in the life of the minority peoples and permits the language of the dominant nationality group in any given region to be used in all official matters. Earlier, in the 1920's, Soviet leaders had actually created written languages for several national groups that had none previously.

While the goal of communist leaders is a common communist culture, they acknowledge that "the obliteration of national distinctions, and especially of language distinctions, is a considerably longer process than the obliteration of class distinctions" (Reading 32). In the meantime, the Party remains committed to the continued improvement of the cultural and economic conditions of non-Russian nationality groups. But this commitment ironically serves to reinforce ethnocentric propensities among the nationalities, who resist cultural absorption into a "common communist culture" which by its very nature would be preponderantly Great Russian and Slavic in character.

The Soviet record has been a mixed one (Reading 33). Many of the gains of the 1920's and 1930's were offset by the genocide practiced during World War II against nationality groups who were deemed "security risks," *inter alia,* the Volga Germans (who had lived in the Crimea and lower Volga region since the sixteenth century), the Crimean Tatars, the Kalmyks, and the Ossetians. Their subsequent rehabilitation under Khrushchev, who laid the blame on Stalin's xenophobia, contrasts markedly with the Soviet government's increasingly arbitrary and discriminatory treatment of the Jews, and with the related phenomenon of anti-Semitism.

Soviet Jews are classified as a nationality but are denied the constitutional rights of one. On the internal passport which every Soviet citizen is required to carry, Jews must identify their nationality as "Jewish" (*Yevrei*) just as other nationalities identify themselves as Russians, Uzbeks, or Armenians. Consequently, although the Jew may be a Russian, Uzbek, Armenian, Lithuanian, Georgian, or Ukrainian, he must list himself instead as "Jewish," a procedure that effectively bars his assimilation into Soviet life. His identity papers thus become a badge of discrimination. Since 1948, when a wave of anti-Semitism surged through the Soviet world, in

---

[2] *Ibid.,* p. 261.

part the aftermath of the enthusiasm publicly shown by Soviet Jewry for the establishment of the State of Israel, Soviet Jews have been deprived of their cultural rights. They have suffered denial of the ecclesiastical concessions granted to other religious groups, and have no theatre and no schools. The few postwar publications in their own language date only from 1960. Inhabiting no discrete geographical area where they are in a majority or even a significant minority (the Birobijan experiment of the 1930's, designed to resettle Jews in the Mongolian hinterlands, was a complete failure), they are denied the rights of other nationality groups and, at the same time, they are prevented by their nationality classification from being assimilated.

In 1964, the Soviet Government rehabilitated the Volga Germans. Its accompanying reconstitution of German cultural institutions and nationality rights invites comparison with the mounting hostility manifested toward the Jews. The two nationality groups have a number of things in common:

> Soviet Germans, who numbered 1,619,655 according to the 1959 census, constitute a much smaller group than the Jews [approximately 3,000,000]. Both are geographically dispersed and lack their own national territory in the U.S.S.R. The Germans, like the Jews, have national and family ties with a country outside the Soviet Union. The Germans were deprived of their traditional cultural rights in 1941, after the Nazi invasion; the Jews were deprived of theirs in 1948, after the establishment of the State of Israel. Both minorities have experienced the ambiguous treatment traditionally accorded to "alien" elements.[3]

Three crucial variables help explain the different treatment being accorded the Jews by the Soviet Government. First, in addition to their status as a nationality, the Jews are also a religious group with strong emotional attachments outside the Soviet Union and communism. Moscow's antagonism toward Judaism (and Zionism) inheres in its suspicion of any movement capable of effecting a symbiosis of internationalism and religious appeal which competes with the universality of Marxist-Leninist ideology. Second, anti-Semitism and anti-Zionism have become useful adjuncts of Soviet diplomatic relations with Arab countries. Finally, anti-Semitism in the Soviet Union is not a new phenomenon; it existed in Czarist times and is still deeply rooted in Soviet society. Anti-Semitism in the Soviet press is interwoven with anti-Western, anti-American, anti-Israeli, and anti-imperialist themes. Jews are never attacked openly as Jews but are linked, domestically, with the "rootless cosmopolitans" and "bourgeois-nationalists" and, internationally, with Zionists and the "warmongers of Wall Street." Yet there is an irony in the frequency with which

---

[3] *Jews in Eastern Europe,* III, No. 2 (May, 1965), 7.

history reveals how the calculations of self-styled molders of society are thwarted by the unforeseen. It may well come to pass that the discriminatory classification of *Yevrei* will serve, through this period of trial and proscription, as the bond which links Soviet Jews to their Jewish traditions, just as Moscow's raising of the social and economic levels of national minorities may strengthen their determination and capacity to resist absorption into a common communist culture.

The trend in Soviet society is toward the cultivation of an overriding *Soviet* nationalism. Though the various ethnic groups are permitted to retain their linguistic and cultural identities, their history and traditions are being blended into an all-encompassing Soviet patriotism—the driving force of which is Great Russian nationalism—in order to promote a greater sense of national unity. This is Russification of a more subtle variety.

China's nationality problem is of a different dimension because the minority peoples constitute only six per cent of the population. They are, however, a source of official concern because they inhabit sparsely settled and strategically vital areas amounting roughly to sixty per cent of China's total territory, much of which is reputedly rich in industrial resources.[4] Officially, Peking's policy is one of respecting local languages, customs, and religions (Reading 34). However, centralized control has been extended, often ruthlessly and militarily (as in Tibet), over the outlying regions of southwestern Yunnan, Tibet, Sinkiang, and inner Mongolia, and an active program of populating these areas with Chinese (Hans) has been initiated. Through intensive indoctrination, elimination of non-communist elders and local leaders, and resettlement of population, Peking hopes to discard its reliance on the loyalty and support of the non-Chinese peoples, thereby making its border areas politically reliable and militarily secure. Since the deterioration in relations with its principal neighbor and ideological rival, it has intensified the "Sinocization" drive. Meanwhile, charges of "great power chauvinism" are heard increasingly in the acrimonious dispute between Moscow and Peking, as each party seeks to establish itself the champion of the Turkic minority peoples (i.e., Uigurs, Kazakhs, Kirghizians, and Mongols) who live on both sides of the Sino-Soviet frontier in Central Asia.

In Eastern Europe the post-1956 spread of "national communism" resulted in a recrudescence of the nationality problem, which had lain dormant during the repressive Stalin era. The first phase in the withdrawal of pervasive Soviet domination occurred in the economic realm. Joint-stock companies were liquidated, trade treaties renegotiated, and investment plans redrafted to benefit national, not Soviet, needs. With increasing economic self-assertiveness and autonomy, East European communist

---

[4] Ho Kan-Chih, *A History of the Modern Chinese Revolution* (Peking: Foreign Languages Press), p. 558.

leaders moved to strengthen their popular base, while decreasing their former slavish reliance on the Red Army; they assiduously catered to nationalist feelings, much to the attendant disadvantage of minority groups. For example, in Czechoslovakia in 1960, the numerically dominant Czechs entrenched their power position by adopting a new constitution which changed the governmental structure to a unitary form, thereby giving Prague (and the Czechs) an even greater influence in the planning and management of the economy. There are indications that the four million Slovaks, who comprise about 20 per cent of the population, are growing restive and critical under the procuracy of the Czechs. In Rumania, the leadership's treatment of the Hungarian minority of 1.5 million people has stirred nationality unrest and strained relations between Rumania and Hungary (Reading 35). Ethnic nationalism seems to be overshadowing communist solidarity.

Of all the countries of the region, none has been as bedeviled by the problem of national minorities as Yugoslavia; and yet, possibly because the survival of the state hung in the balance, she has made the most impressive advances, by mitigating the political tensions between the major nationality blocs and by promoting widespread social and economic reforms for the smaller minorities. The 1945 organization of the state along federal lines appears to have effectively solved Yugoslavia's most divisive pre-war political problem, the implacable enmity between the Serbs and the Croats, and provided the other nationality groups with equitable representation. The six federal republics—Bosnia and Herzegovina, Croatia, Macedonia, Montenegro, Serbia and Slovenia—were established along ethnic lines to forestall any return to the pre-war dominance of the Serbs. The federal solution has also been the political vehicle by which the concept of a Yugoslav, as opposed to any particularist, nationalism has been promoted. To encourage national integration, which is admittedly a long-range process, the federal government has embarked on an ambitious program of economic development in the more backward areas of the country.

In addition to the major nationality groups, Yugoslavia has a number of smaller minorities, of which the Albanians and the Hungarians are the most numerous and the most difficult to assimilate.[5] After Belgrade's split with Moscow in 1948, the Cominform's efforts to incite these minorities failed. The Yugoslav government took appropriate security measures against these provocations, and refrained "from large-scale action against the minorities."[6] This restraint very likely enhanced the effectiveness of the far-reaching reforms that were adopted: e.g., the establishment of the

---

[5] For a judicious and interesting analysis of this complex subject see Paul Shoup, "Yugoslavia's National Minorities under Communism," *Slavic Review*, XXII, No. 1 (March, 1963), 64–81.

[6] *Ibid.*, p. 73.

autonomous areas of Kosovo-Metohija for the Albanians, and of Vojvodina for the Hungarians, within the territorial confines of the republic of Serbia; the grant of state financial aid to raise the educational and cultural level of the Albanians; and "the recruitment of 'national cadres' from the minorities for the party and state administration."[7]

The nationality problem remains a continuing headache for communist societies. Notable improvements have been wrought in the socio-economic positions of many of the minorities, but inherent in this strengthening is a heightened sense of national identity, with all its manifold political complications for Communist rulers. Writing of Yugoslavia, Professor Paul Shoup observed:

> Most of the minority population take no national pride in the achievements of the regime, associate communism with the Slavs, and in varying degrees remain unreconciled to their position. . . . The Communists, for their part, cannot completely avoid treating the minorities as second-class citizens. Repressive measures, carried out in the population generally to assure the security of the regime, always fall most harshly on the minorities because of their political attitudes. Granting cultural autonomy, on the other hand, corrects an old injustice but does not satisfy national aspirations.[8]

These perceptive remarks can apply to any communist country.

---

[7] *Ibid.*, p. 75.
[8] *Ibid.*, p. 79.

32 THE TASKS OF THE PARTY AND SOVIET NATIONALITIES

Programme of the Communist Party of the Soviet Union (Moscow: Foreign Languages Publishing House, 1961), pp. 102–5.

The Program of the C.P.S.U., adopted at the Twenty-second Congress in October 1961, states: "The boundaries between the Union republics of the U.S.S.R. are increasingly losing their former significance, since all the nations are equal. . . . Full-scale communist construction constitutes a new stage in the development of national relations in the U.S.S.R. in which the nations will draw still closer together until complete unity is achieved."

But this expectation does not lead the Party to overlook the existing nationality differences in the U.S.S.R. The nationalities are given reassurances that they will be permitted to retain their cultural and linguistic distinctiveness for the foreseeable future.

Under socialism the nations flourish and their sovereignty grows stronger. The development of nations does not proceed along lines of strengthening national strife, national narrow-mindedness and egoism, as it does under capitalism, but along lines of their association, fraternal mutual assistance and friendship. . . . The boundaries between the Union republics of the U.S.S.R. are increasingly losing their former significance, since all the nations are equal, their life is based on a common socialist foundation, the material and spiritual needs of every people are satisfied to the same extent, and they are all united in a single family by common vital interests and are advancing together to the common goal—communism. . . .

Full-scale communist construction constitutes a new stage in the development of national relations in the U.S.S.R. in which the nations will draw still closer together until complete unity is achieved. The building of the material and technical basis of communism leads to still greater unity of the Soviet peoples. The exchange of material and spiritual values between nations becomes more and more intensive, and the contribution of each republic to the common cause of communist construction increases. Obliteration of distinctions between classes and the development of communist social relations make for a greater social homogeneity of nations and contribute to the development of common communist traits in their culture, morals and way of living, to a further strengthening of their mutual trust and friendship.

204

With the victory of communism in the U.S.S.R., the nations will draw still closer together, their economic and ideological unity will increase and the communist traits common to their spiritual make-up will develop. However, the obliteration of national distinctions, and especially of language distinctions, is a considerably longer process than the obliteration of class distinctions.

The Party approaches all questions of national relationships arising in the course of communist construction from the standpoint of proletarian internationalism and firm pursuance of the Leninist nationalities policy. The Party neither ignores nor over-accentuates national characteristics.

The Party sets the following tasks in the sphere of national relations:

a. To continue the all-round economic and cultural development of all the Soviet nations and nationalities, ensuring their increasingly close fraternal co-operation, mutual aid, unity and affinity in all spheres of life, thus achieving the utmost strengthening of the Union of Soviet Socialist Republics; to make full use of, and advance the forms of, national statehood of the peoples of the U.S.S.R.;

b. In the economic sphere, it is necessary to continue the line of comprehensive development of the economies of the Soviet republics, effect a rational geographic location of production and a planned working of natural wealth, and promote socialist division of labour among the republics, unifying and combining their economic efforts, and properly balancing the interests of the state as a whole and those of each Soviet republic. The extension of the rights of the Union republics in economic management having produced substantial positive results, such measures may also be carried out in the future with due regard to the fact that the creation of the material and technical basis of communism will call for still greater interconnection and mutual assistance between the Soviet republics. The closer the intercourse between the nations and the greater the awareness of the country-wide tasks, the more successfully can manifestations of parochialism and national egoism be overcome. . . .

The Party will continue its policy ensuring the actual equality of all nations and nationalities with full consideration for their interests and devoting special attention to those areas of the country which are in need of more rapid development. Benefits accumulating in the course of communist construction must be fairly distributed among all nations and nationalities;

c. To work for the further all-round development of the socialist cultures of the peoples of the U.S.S.R. The big scale of communist construction and the new victories of communist ideology are enriching the cultures of the peoples of the U.S.S.R., which are socialist in content and national in form. There is a growing ideological unity among the nations and nationalities and a greater rapprochement of their cultures. The historical experience of socialist nations shows that national forms do not ossify; they change, advance and draw closer together, shedding all out-dated traits that contradict the new conditions of life. An international culture common to all the Soviet nations is developing. The cultural treasures of each nation are increasingly augmented by works acquiring an international character.

Attaching decisive importance to the development of the socialist content of the cultures of the peoples of the U.S.S.R., the Party will promote their further mutual enrichment and rapprochement, the consolidation of their international basis, and thereby the formation of the future single world-wide culture of communist society. While supporting the progressive traditions of each people, and making them the property of all Soviet people, the Party will in all ways further new revolutionary traditions of the builders of communism common to all nations;

d. To continue promoting the free development of the languages of the peoples of the U.S.S.R. and the complete freedom for every citizen of the U.S.S.R. to speak, and to bring up and educate his children, in any language, ruling out all privileges, restrictions or compulsions in the use of this or that language. By virtue of the fraternal friendship and mutual trust of peoples, national languages are developing on a basis of equality and mutual enrichment.

The voluntary study of Russian in addition to the native language is of positive significance, since it facilitates reciprocal exchanges of experience and access of every nation and nationality to the cultural gains of all the other peoples of the U.S.S.R., and to world culture. The Russian language has, in effect, become the common medium of intercourse and co-operation between all the peoples of the U.S.S.R;

e. To pursue consistently as heretofore the principles of internationalism in the field of national relations; to strengthen the friendship of peoples as one of the most important gains of socialism; to conduct a relentless struggle against manifestations and survivals of nationalism and chauvinism of all types, against trends of national narrow-mindedness and exclusiveness, idealisation of the past and the veiling of social contradictions in the history of peoples, and against customs and habits hampering communist construction. The growing scale of communist construction calls for the continuous exchange of trained personnel among nations. Manifestations of national aloofness in the education and employment of workers of different nationalities in the Soviet republics are impermissible. The elimination of manifestations of nationalism is in the interests of all nations and nationalities of the U.S.S.R. Every Soviet republic can continue to flourish and strengthen only in the great family of fraternal socialist nations of the U.S.S.R.

Hugh Seton-Watson

33 SOVIET NATIONALITY POLICY

Hugh Seton-Watson, "Soviet Nationality Policy," *The Russian Review*, XV, No. 1 (January, 1956), excerpted from pp. 3–12. Footnote references have been deleted.

Hugh Seton-Watson is Professor of History at the University of London and the author of a number of books on Soviet and Communist affairs.

At the outset it should be stated that I do not believe that Russia and her problems are unique. They have, of course, their special features, but in many ways they are comparable with other peoples and other lands. I do not believe that Russian nature is something that human reason cannot penetrate. . . .

. . . For the problem of Soviet nationality policy I suggest that it is worth looking at the experience of Austria-Hungary and of the small Balkan states, and on the other hand at the British and other European colonial empires. If one can separate those features of Soviet national policy which are characteristic of all multi-national states or colonial empires, from those which are peculiar to the Soviet regime, one will have made some real progress.

Lenin's doctrine on the national question is no doubt so well known that I need spend little time on it. He upheld in principle the right of every nation to self-determination, including the right of secession. At the same time he upheld the international solidarity of the proletariat, and the consequent duty of every working class to prefer the working class of a neighboring nation to the bourgeoisie of its own nation. The contradiction between these two principles could not be, and has not been, resolved either in theory or in practice.

Whether, during the stormy years after the October Revolution, any given nationality remained within Soviet Russia or had an independent state of its own, was decided not by theoretical examination of the conflicting principles, but by the geographical position of the respective nationality and by military force. Thus the Poles, Finns, Lithuanians, Letts, and Esthonians established independent states because they were first occupied by the invading German army and then defended by the victorious Western Powers, whose naval might was dominant in the Baltic

Sea. The Georgians, Azerbaidjanis, and Armenians had a few years of independence, but they were conquered because Soviet Russia and Turkey had a common interest in their suppression, because they quarrelled with each other, and because they antagonized the Western Powers. The other main nationalities of the Russian Empire, Ukrainians, Volga Tatars, and Central Asians, were inaccessible to western help and were conquered in turn by White and Red armies.

Once the Bolshevik regime was established, its official policy, as we know, was based on the principle of "a culture national in form and socialist in content." In theory, there were two dangers, to be combated with equal energy and vigilance. One was Great Russian Great Power chauvinism, the other, local bourgeois nationalism. In actual fact however, Bolshevik treatment of the nationalities after 1921 was as opportunist as it had been during the Civil War. The most important single fact about the history of Bolshevik nationality policy is that its phases coincide with, and were determined by the phases of Stalin's general policy.

The years of N.E.P. were a period in which, though the Bolsheviks held dictatorial power, they exercised it with relative mildness. This was true not only in the peasant economy but also in religious and cultural life and in nationality policy. During these years some of the nationalities enjoyed a real measure of self-government. In the Ukraine, the official policy of Ukrainization enjoyed true popular support. In Transcaucasia, though the vindictive intrigues of Stalin caused injustice and discontent, at least it was true that power was held by local men. But in the other parts of the Soviet Union conditions were different. After the disgrace of Sultan-Galiev the Volga Tatars lost most of their autonomy. In Central Asia, official Soviet sources show beyond doubt that power was concentrated in the hands of the local Russian minority, and the Asian peoples were kept in subjection. Occasional interventions by Moscow did not substantially change this state of affairs.

Stalin's second revolution of 1929, with its drive for collectivization of agriculture and rapid industrialization, brought a fundamental change of nationality policy, as of all other departments of policy. Ruthless centralization in the economic field was not compatible with self-government for the nationalities. Economic misery and political oppression created bitter hatred, and in the national areas this inevitably took the form of national hatred.

.   .   .

The war brought not only an understandable exaltation of patriotism in official propaganda, but a rigid identification of patriotism with subservience to the Stalinist totalitarian regime and ruthless punishment as traitors not only of the regime's enemies, but of whole nations regarded as potentially disloyal. To this period belong the genocide of the Volga Germans, Crimean Tatars, Chechens, Karachays, and Kalmyks.

The post-war period is marked by the emergence of the Soviet Union as one of the two giant powers of the world, with an imperialist policy affecting every part of the globe. This new phase of Soviet imperialism has required still further blows to the national individuality and national traditions of all the peoples of the Soviet Union. The most striking examples of this phase are the suppression of the national epics of the Moslem peoples and the falsification of the history of North Caucasians, Kirgiz, Ukrainians, Rumanians of Bessarabia, and other nations. The campaign against "cosmopolitanism" has the same significance. For example, Tadjiks must not show pride in the common culture which they share with Persians; rather they must stress the links between Tadjik and Russian culture.

This brief survey of the past leads to the important question: Is the nationality policy of the Soviet Union to-day one of Russification?

This raises two separate questions. The first is, "Does Russification exist?" The second, "Is Russification the driving force of Soviet nationality policy? Is it the motive of this policy, or only its result, or its instrument?"

The answer to the first question must be "Yes."

There are great differences between different parts of the Soviet Union. In Georgia and Armenia there has hitherto been absolutely no Russification. These republics are ruled exclusively by their own nationals. In the Ukraine and Azerbaidjan the problem is more complicated. On the whole it would seem to me that the Ukraine is ruled by Ukrainians, though the formerly Polish provinces form an exception and though, in general, the Russian resident element in the Ukraine certainly possesses influence out of proportion to its numbers. In Azerbaidjan, the city of Baku has a large Russian population, which no doubt is well represented in the state and party apparatus. But the study of such sources as have been available— admittedly imperfect—suggests that even in Baku most important posts are held by Azerbaidjanis, and that in the rest of the republic this is definitely so.

A special case are certain border provinces. Here there have been massive deportations of local people and massive colonization of Russians. This is true in the Western Ukraine, the Baltic states, and probably Western White Russia. It is also true in Bessarabia. In the Far East the same is true of Sahalin and the Kurile Islands. The motives of these actions are clearly strategic.

But the most important examples of Russification are to be found in the economically developing regions of Asiatic Russia, inhabited by Moslem, Buddhist, or Shamanist nations. Here Russification takes several distinct forms.

Colonization of Russians and Ukrainians affects in the first place the new industrial centers. The capitals of the Central Asian republics are largely Russian cities—Tashkent rather less so than the others. So are Izhevsk, capital of the Udmurt A.S.S.R.; Ufa—capital of Bashkiria; Ulan Ude—capital of Buryat Mongolia. But in certain areas colonization extends even to the countryside. After the mass starvation in Kazakhstan during collectivization, Russian and Ukrainian peasants were brought in. Khrushchev's new drive to develop the agriculture of Kazakhstan will take the process further.

To insist that Russian should be taught as a compulsory second language in national schools, does not seem to me to be unreasonable. Every great state must have a first language and in the Soviet Union it is obvious that this must be Russian. Much more dubious is the tendency to make Russian the only language in secondary and higher education in areas of mixed population. The universities of Central Asia, of which Soviet propaganda to Asia makes so much use, have for the most part Russian as the language of instruction and a very large proportion of their students are not Asians but resident Russians. Another element of Russification is the imposition of the Cyrillic alphabet for Asian languages and the systematic introduction into those languages of Russian words, which goes far beyond technical vocabulary in the strict sense.

. . .

Of the subordination of the republican governments to the Union government there is of course no doubt. It is clear even in the text of the Constitution and it is clearer still if one takes into account the hierarchy of the Communist Party. But here too the problem of Russification arises. In Central Asia the Second Secretaries of the Central Committees of the republican parties and in most cases the Second Secretaries of *oblast* committees are Russians. In Kazakhstan, of course, at present both the First and Second Secretaries are Russians, but this is perhaps due to temporary exceptional circumstances. It is interesting to note that post-war purges in the Central Asian parties appear to have affected Russian Second Secretaries more than Asian First Secretaries. This would seem to show that it is the Second Secretaries who wield the real power. In the case of the Ukraine the problem is not that the Ukrainian party is run by Russians—this does not seem to be the case—but that the Ukraine is extraordinarily under-represented in the leadership of the All-Union party.

Now comes the second question—"Is Russification the driving force, the motive, of Soviet nationality policy?": It is tempting to argue that Bolshevik policy is a continuation of the Russification policy of Alexander III and Nicholas II. There are some striking similarities. I have already mentioned the imperialistic interpretation of the suppression of Shamil and the Kirgiz. I am myself inclined to the view that the dominant social type which is emerging in the Soviet Union is a kind of bureaucratic state bourgeoisie, whose ideas and general mentality are a curious combination of those of the nineteenth century European capitalist bourgeoisie and the nineteenth century Russian bureaucracy. One might thus argue that there is likely to be a continuity of outlook between Plehve and Khrushchev.

Nevertheless I believe this idea to be wrong. I do not think that the Soviet government is interested in Russian nationalism. The conflict is not between the Russians and the smaller nationalities, but between these nationalities and a centralized totalitarian regime. The regime suppresses the nationalities as it suppresses all groups not created by itself. For the suppression of the nationalities it uses Russians as its instruments. It does this because the Russians are the most numerous, and culturally and economically the most advanced, of the peoples of the Soviet Union and because Russians, as Russians, are less likely to be disloyal to the regime. It may well be that individual Russians used by the regime in national areas, act in a contemptuous and chauvinistic manner towards members of other nationalities. The sum total of such arrogant actions may produce a very large volume of indignation. But Russification is not the government's aim.

The government's aim is total power. It intends to exploit every human being, and every economic resource in the country. If there is oil in the territory of Bashkiria or Azerbaidjan—that oil must be made available for the purposes of those who control the totalitarian machine centered in Moscow. If it is to their advantage that Uzbeks and Tadjiks should grow more cotton and less grain, they will be made to do so. When the British ruled Egypt, they developed cotton at the expense of grain and have been severely criticized for doing so. But there are three important differences between British treatment of Egypt and Bolshevik treatment of Turkestan. Firstly, the greater part of the profits of Egyptian cotton growing went to Egyptians, while all the profits of Uzbek cotton *kolkhozy* go to Moscow. Secondly, no British government would ever have considered, or did consider, withholding grain supplies from Egypt to starve its people into submission, whereas this threat was used by the Soviet government. Thirdly, Egyptians could and did bitterly attack not only British cotton policy but British rule itself. For Uzbeks or Tadjiks such criticism would be fatal.

In order to achieve total power over its subjects, the Soviet regime systematically atomizes society. All associations of citizens for whatever purpose must be directed by the Party and infiltrated by the M.V.D. This applies as much to groups of musicians or sportsmen or butterfly-lovers as to political groups. The regime has a special distrust, which, granted its premises, is perfectly just, for any association derived from some principle that is independent of, and older than the regime. The two most important associations of this kind are religious communities and nations. By its very nature the regime is unable to tolerate the existence of either. It is determined to destroy the nationalities, not in the interest of the Russian nation, but because the totality of its power demands it. It will not be content until no Uzbek feels that he is linked to another Uzbek, because he is an Uzbek, by a link stronger than that which binds him to his hierarchical superior in the totalitarian power system.

Soviet policy is a war of extermination against the principle of nationality. It can also fairly be described as imperialism. But it is not inspired by the desire to Russify the nationalities.

It would, however, be quite wrong to deduce from this that Soviet policy does not appear to the nationalities that suffer from it as a policy of deliberate Russification. . . .

In the Soviet Union the famines in the Ukraine and Kazakhstan seemed to their victims to be measures of extermination directed against their nations, though this was not in fact the conscious aim of Stalin.

The attitude of the Moscow government to Islam seems to be especially important. Bolshevik persecution of Orthodoxy was persecution by Russians of Russians. Persecution of Islam is persecution by Russians of Asians. The evidence shows without doubt firstly—that ever since 1917 the number of Communists among the Moslem nations of the Soviet Union has been very small, and secondly—that these Asian Communists have always been most reluctant to attack Islam, even though they personally may have ceased to be believers. The campaigns against Islam have always come from Moscow and their active exponents in the Moslem areas have been the resident Russian elements. Those Asian Communists who have supported the campaign have appeared to the population as mere puppets of the Russians. The attack on Islam in fact has been imposed from outside, by members of another nation with other religious traditions. Such a situation inevitably creates nationalist reaction.

There is a special problem to be considered—the formation of new intelligentsias among the nationalities. It is beyond dispute that the Soviet regime has given the nationalities greater opportunities of education and of careers for their talents than could have been dreamed of under the Tsars. Ukrainians, Transcaucasians, Tatars, and Central Asians now have hundreds of thousands of university students, teachers, engineers, scientists, and bureaucrats of all sorts. These men owe their careers to the Soviet regime. It is often assumed that they are grateful for this and that they form most loyal and reliable support for the Stalinist regime among their compatriots.

In my view this opinion is quite wrong. In the Kingdom of Hungary before 1914, Slovaks or Serbs or Rumanians who learned the Hungarian language and went to a Hungarian university, could acquire the best education and make good careers. But those who did this, did not become exponents among their own peoples of the Hungarian regime to which they owed their careers. On the contrary, they used their new knowledge and skill to make themselves leaders of the struggle of their peoples for independence from Hungary. The intelligentsia of the Asian nations was created by the opportunities of modern secular education created by the European Powers. Moslems, Confucians, and Buddhists of course had had schools of their own type, with their traditional form of culture, which may have been equal or superior to ours for centuries. But for survival in the modern world, modern secular education is needed. This was imported by the Europeans. The new Asian intelligentsia which arose from study in the schools and universities of the West, or in schools of the western type created in their countries, owed their careers entirely to the Westerners. But this did not make them exponents among their own peoples of western colonial rule. On the contrary, like the intelligentsia of the subject peoples of Hungary, they became leaders of their peoples' struggles for independence. Pandit Nehru was educated at Harrow, one of the best schools in England (which had among its pupils Sir Winston Churchill), and at Cambridge University. Ho-Chi-Minh studied in France, loves French literature and civilization and has had many French friends. The pioneers of the small Communist parties of the Arab lands include many former students of the American University of Beirut.

I do not believe that the same result is not also produced among the intelligentsia of the nationalities of the Soviet Union and especially among the Asian element. It is of course true that there are no independence movements in Central Asia like the Indian National Congress or the Egyptian WAFD or the Tunisian nèo-Destour. But, as we all know, this proves only that totalitarianism is different from democracy, that the M.V.D.'s function in Soviet society is different from that of the police in Britain or France. It does not prove that the Central Asian intelligentsia are not thinking in terms of nationalist movements. The campaigns of the Soviet Communist Party against "bourgeois nationalism" with all their fantastic excesses, provide indirect evidence.

In conclusion, a few words about the future. The record of Russian imperialism before 1917 was, it seems to me, neither worse nor better than that of other European imperialism. Bolshevik imperialism is a horrible tyranny, but the Russians are its victims as well as the other nations of the Soviet Union. There are positive elements in the historical relationship between the Russian people and their neighbors, at least in the east and south. Strong arguments can be found in favor of preserving a single great state, reorganized on a genuinely federal principle. But there is no iron law of history that states must be big.

Wang Feng

34 THE GREAT VICTORY IN OUR NATIONALITIES POLICY

Wang Feng, "The Great Victory in Our Nationalities Policy," *Current Background,* No. 609 (January 14, 1960), American Consulate-General, Hong Kong. Excerpted from pp. 3–8.

Wang Feng is Vice-chairman of the Nationalities Affairs Commission of the People's Republic of China.

Regional autonomy for the nationalities is the Party's basic measure for solving the nationalities question of the country.

The Constitution of the People's Republic provides for autonomy to be instituted in the regions of the minorities, setting them down as an inseparable part of the Chinese People's Republic. On the basis of that provision, the minorities areas (autonomous regions, autonomous *chou,* autonomous *hsien*), aside from functioning as local government organizations under the unified leadership of the Central People's Government, have various rights of autonomy.

Autonomy for the nationalities means that each of the areas big enough to be a first-grade administrative autonomous unit has the right to administer its own local affairs in the big family of the motherland. It is intended to safeguard the equality of the minorities, increase their activism in the country's political life and socialist construction and increase the mutual trust and friendly cooperation among the various nationalities of the country.

The provision of regional autonomy as a basic means of solving the nationalities problem of China is based on the relevant theoretical principle of Marxism-Leninism with due regard for the historical background and the present situation of the various nationalities in China.

. . .

China is a country composed of many nationalities with the Han people as the main constituent. It has a large population and vast land and has been existing in the world for a long time as a country of unified multi-nationalities. The following points are conspicuous in respect to the composition, distribution and relationship of its nationalities:

1. The Han people account for 94 per cent of the national population with over 50 minority nationalities including the Mongol, Hui, Tibetan, Manchu, Chuang, Uighur, Miao, Yi, Puyi, Korean and other people making up the remaining six per cent. These nationalities are, nevertheless, widely distributed in the country, occupying from 50 to 60 per cent of its land.

2. The situation of commingling is most conspicuous. Most of the minorities mingle with the Han people in large or small communities where the latter serve as the main constituent with whom close economic, political and cultural ties are established.

3. In the long period of historical development, economic relations and cultural intercourse were developed among the people, forming a country of centralized power composed of various nationalities with the Han people acting as the main constituents. Under that feudal centralized power system, although there were wars between the nationalities resulting from oppression and discrimination with the Han rulers riding roughshod over the minorities or these treading the Han people underfoot, the economic and cultural relationships of the nationalities however developed unimpeded. This was the main current in the history of the relations of our nationalities.

4. When the imperialists invaded China about 100 years ago, turning her into a semi-feudal and semi-colonial country, the existence of our minorities was, without exception, seriously threatened. Brought closer together by the common destiny, our people waged a long struggle against the domestic and foreign enemies, especially in the past 30 years in which the revolutionary struggle, led by the Chinese Communist Party, has forged an unbreakable relationship among our nationalities.

5. As a result of the historical development, the Han people have not only become the main constituents of our country, but have led the other nationalities in economic, political and cultural development.

6. For a long period of time, the imperialists have launched sabotaging activities in an attempt to alienate the relationship of our nationalities, and to instigate the so-called "national independence" designed to enslave the people of China through the policy of "divide and rule."

．　．　．

There are now in our country the Inner Mongolia Autonomous Region, the Sinkiang Uighur Autonomous Region, the Kwangsi Chuang Autonomous Region, the Ninghsia Hui Autonomous Region, and the Preparatory Committee for the Tibet Autonomous Region, 29 autonomous *chou,* and 54 autonomous *hsien.*

．　．　．

There is no doubt that all nationalities must undergo social reform and take the socialist road, this being the universal law governing the development of human society. In our country, the social reform of the nationalities areas is divided into two stages—the stage of democratic reform and the stage of socialist transformation. The aim of democratic reform is to redistribute the land and abolish the oppression and exploitation which took shape before the commencement of the capitalist system. The aim of socialist transformation is to eliminate the exploitation existing under capitalism, change the system of private ownership of means of production and establish the system of socialist collective ownership and eventually the system of ownership by the whole people.

Social reform is an internal matter of the nationalities, and since their historical conditions are different, it must be carried out with due regard for the wishes of the people and the desire of the leaders who have strong ties with the people. In other words, there must be differences in the time, method, and speed of the reform for the various nationalities. As early as the time before the October Revolution, Lenin pointed out: "It is inevitable that all nationalities must take the socialist road. But they will differ in the method to be adopted. Each of them will have its own characteristics reflected in one way of democracy or another and in one method of dictatorship of the proletariat or another as well as in its social life and the speed of its socialist transformation."

.   .   .

The political and economic conditions of the minorities areas are complicated. Not only the stages of social development but also the inter-area social economic structures of a number of the minorities people are different. For example. . . . in the Mongol, Tibetan, and Kazak nationalities areas, the whole population of 2,200,000 are still engaged in backward animal husbandry and are widely different from the people of the agricultural areas in both production and livelihood. At the same time, the minorities people are highly religious and practically all of them are followers of Lamaism and Islamism. The upper strata of the minorities and the religious personages have a strong influence over the broad masses. Rooted in the policy of oppression and alienation carried out by the reactionary ruling class, certain misunderstandings persist among the nationalities. In many of the areas, contradictions exist and disputes are frequent between the sects and the tribes. The imperialists and the remnants of domestic counter-revolutionaries are sparing no effort to make use of these religious relations to sabotage our country.

[In view of the foregoing situation] . . . the Party and the Government have adopted for the grazing areas of the minorities measures different from those applied to the agricultural areas. The social revolution for the agricultural areas generally starts with a land reform in which the lands of feudal lords and slave owners are seized and redistributed to the poor peasants who have little or no land, the privileges of the feudal lords and slave owners are abolished, and the toiling masses are liberated. Then on the basis of the successful land reform, the socialist transformation of the private ownership of the means of production is carried out to eliminate capitalist exploitation and ownership of means of production in order that the system of socialist collective ownership and ownership by the whole people may be established. However, in the social reform of the pastoral areas, cattle and sheep are not redistributed, but in its first step, the democratic reform, feudal privileges and exploitation are eliminated, and ranches are placed under public control, permitting, however, private grazing as a measure of mutual benefit to the herdowners and hired hands, and insuring the steady development of animal husbandry. On that basis, different measures are then adopted for the socialist transformation of the herdowners and hired hands in order to establish the system of socialist collective ownership and ownership by the whole people. . . . So long as the upper strata of the minorities area give up exploitation and accept reformation, the Government sees to it that they have the same political position and living standard after the reform and that the masses wage no intense struggles against them. For example, in the democratic reform of Tibet, we seized or confiscated no land or means of production of all those upper strata elements who refrained from participating in armed rebellion or in any other recalcitrant action; we pursued a policy similar to the buy-out measure adopted for capitalists in the Han people areas, allowing them to retain their civil rights and negotiating with their representatives on the time, steps and measures for reform. Though its concrete measures vary in the different areas, the essence of the peaceful way of "buying out" the upper strata of the minorities politically and economically is abided by. The peaceful reform is a revolution without bloodshed and is a special form of class struggle under specific conditions. . . .

. . . But a word of caution is necessary. Whether or not peaceful reform can be successfully carried out cannot be decided by the policy of the Party and the Government and the desire of the toiling masses alone. It depends much on the attitude which the upper strata of the exploitative class in the minorities areas adopt toward the reform. If elements of these strata follow the wishes of the people and accept the Party policy, then complete success will be possible. If they disregard the will of the people and the policy of the Party to such an extent as to put up resistance, then it will not be possible to continue the peaceful form and the alternative will be to crush this resistance in order that reform may go on. In either way (by force or through peaceful means), the masses must be fully mobilized and relied upon, and the Party's class line must be fully carried out to insure the successful realization of the reform. This is supported by the experience gained in the social reform of minorities areas.

In our numerous minorities areas, the upper strata of religious circles and the temples enjoy a wide range of feudal privileges, brutally exploiting and oppressing the people, and seriously obstructing development. The policy of the Party and the Government in this connection is to abolish the privileges and stop the exploitation. But where religious problems which the Party and the Government frequently meet in carrying out the reform are concerned, they are handled with caution and treated separately; clear lines of demarcation are drawn between the feudal privileges of the temples and religious habits, between normal religious activities and extortions and cruel treatment of followers, and between patriotic law-abiding religious workers and counter-revolutionaries operating under the cloak of religion. So, on the one hand, determined efforts are made to eradicate the feudal oppression and exploitation and suppress the counter-revolutionaries under the guise of religious workers, and on the other, care is taken that freedom of religion is fully safe-guarded, religious documents and structures are protected, and patriotic religious people are won over. The principle is to avoid any interference in the normal religious activities and to implement the Party's policy of freedom of religion. . . .

For a complex of reasons mainly historical—sparse population, backward economy and culture, the absence of industrial workers and the dearth of cadres and intellectuals—our minorities areas, even after they have completed the socialist revolution in the system of ownership of means of production, cannot change their backward state by their own efforts. They must have regular and valid help from the state and the advanced people—the Han people—to solve this problem. Obviously, the state's help to the minorities areas can only be gradual, very much subject to its current capacity. But that there has been and will continue to be help for them is beyond any doubt. . . .

Thanks to the leadership and help of the Party and the Government as a result of the close co-operation extended by the other areas, the economic and cultural aspects of the minorities areas have been markedly changed. The pace of improvement has been particularly rapid since 1958 when under the illumination of the Party's general line for socialist construction and with the sky-rocketing zeal of the people, a high tide in the general leap forward of socialist construction came into being. . . .

It is because the Han people are relatively numerous and ahead of the other nationalities in economic, political and cultural development that they play the guiding role in the national life and have therefore the responsibility of giving more help than they get in return.

The Party and the Government are opposed to chauvinism and local nationalism detrimental to the unity of our people, and make sure that Han cadres show no tendency toward greater Hanism. So, since the liberation, they have carried out broad education of the nationalities cadres and people in patriotism and socialism as well as in proletarian internationalism.

George Bailey

35 TROUBLE OVER TRANSYLVANIA

George Bailey, "Trouble Over Transylvania," *The Reporter,*
XXXI, No. 9 (November 19, 1964), excerpted from pp. 25–30.
Copyright 1964 by *The Reporter Magazine Company.*

George Bailey writes for The Reporter *and other journals on Eastern Europe.*

Romania, in its own inimitable fashion, offers an instructive sampling of
the tensions and contradictions that are tearing the Communist world
apart. In this country, a general restiveness and political opportunism have
gone so far that criticism of Moscow's leadership has taken more or less
official forms. . . .

In fact, the Romanian Communists have outwitted and outmaneuvered
the Soviet Union at virtually every turn in a long course of events extending
at least as far back as the 1952 ouster of the Moscow loyalist Ana Pauker
and her clique. Then, or not long afterward, they reverted to their native
tradition of circumspect double-dealing and discreet intrigue. Among the
switches and shifts of the ideological shell game that ensued, there was
none more successful than the Romanian substitution of de-Russification
for de-Stalinization. To the delight of the Russophobe populace, by 1963
the Romanian authorities had liquidated the Gorki Institute of Russian
Studies, the Russian bookstore, the Romanian edition of the Soviet magazine *New Times,* and the obligatory study of the Russian language in all
schools and universities. Since then virtually all Russian street and place
names have disappeared.

But de-Russification is merely one of the many negative aspects of
Romanization. Acting ostensibly as the honest and impeccably Communist
broker between the Soviet Union and China, the Romanians have actually
cleared the way for their own traditional brand of supernationalism.
"Greater Romania," said a Communist diplomat recently, "is the whore of
the Socialist camp, a Balkan whore bent on Balkanizing the Communist
bloc." The Romanian talent for divisiveness has nowhere been more
evident than in the handling of the oldest Balkan problem of them all:
Transylvania.

Graustarkian Showpiece

It has long been axiomatic that great powers adjust Balkan borders to suit their own purposes. This is particularly true of Transylvania, which has been passed back and forth almost as often as a bottle at a Balkan party. In the Treaty of Trianon, 1920, the Western Allies dismantled the Austro-Hungarian Empire, stripping Hungary of two-thirds of its territory and almost one-third of its population and ceding the greater part of both to Romania. With the Vienna Award of 1940, Hitler gave the northern half of Transylvania, including its capital city of Cluj, back to Hungary and so stimulated a competition between Hungary and Romania for Nazi favor in the field against the Russians, the Hungarian troops fighting for the addition of the southern half of Transylvania, the Romanians fighting for the return of the northern half. Similarly, the Soviets at the close of the Second World War restored the Trianon border between Hungary and Romania, calculating that this would tend to offset the Soviet Union's annexation of Bessarabia and the Bukovina from Romania on the east and provide a popular national issue favoring the Communist-dominated government in Romania; furthermore, the consequent failure of the not-yet Communist Hungary to obtain any sort of satisfaction on Transylvania might weaken the leading Smallholders' Party, which was the main obstacle in the way of a Communist take-over in Hungary. Like Hitler, the Soviets sought to use the Transylvanian issue as a means of keeping both Hungary and Romania under control.

Naturally, there are a great many people who consider themselves Hungarians now living in Romanian territory. More than half a million of them inhabit the strip of territory some thirty miles wide along the Hungarian-Romanian border. This area, properly speaking, is not and never was part of Transylvania. It is made up of four counties of the old Kingdom of Hungary and is geographically an extension of the central Hungarian plain. The other main concentration of Hungarians in Romania is the solid block of Szeklers, some seven hundred thousand strong, who have inhabited most of eastern Transylvania since the tenth century. The Szekler area lies almost exactly in the center of Romania, more than one hundred miles to the east of the Hungarian border. King Carol had agreed to cede the border area—the so-called "Partium"—to Hungary even before the Vienna Award was forced upon him, and the Hungarians had great hopes that the Soviets would undertake some doctoring of the border, especially after Hungary became Communist.

Instead the Soviets chose to provide an object lesson in Marxism-Leninism by applying the principle of "genuine proletarian internationalism for all Communists" to the 1,700,000 Hungarians in Romania, who constitute the largest ethnic minority in Eastern Europe. Thus, Article 82 of the Romanian constitution of 1952 provides that "Every individual national group may freely make use of its own language, and may freely visit at every level those institutions of general education in which instruction is given in its mother tongue . . . ," and Articles 19, 20, and 21 attempted to solve the millennial problem of the Szeklers through the creation of the Autonomous Hungarian Region. Modeled on the autonomous regions within the individual Soviet Republics, it was clearly meant to serve as a showpiece of "genuine proletarian internationalism." Communist functionaries from Moscow, Bucharest, and Budapest converged on the region. Stakhanovites from all three countries were sent to instruct and inspire the workers, youth brigades were organized, factories and roads were built, farmers were persuaded or forced to join collectives. But then came the Hungarian revolt.

In retrospect, it is apparent that the Hungarian revolt in the fall of 1956 was the turning point in the course of Communism in Europe. Establishing the Hungarians as the arch culprits in the eyes of the Soviets, it provided the Romanian Communist Party with a classic opportunity to demonstrate its loyalty to the Soviet Union. The Romanian Communists were in a position to render the Soviet Union a signal service in playing host to Imre Nagy, Pal Maleter, and other leaders of the Hungarian revolt during their long incarceration and subsequent execution, relieving the Russians of the onus of deporting the rebels to the Soviet Union. They were also able to help the Soviet Union in Hungary by sending Hungarian-speaking goon squads to Budapest and the provinces to reinforce the decimated and thoroughly demoralized Hungarian Security Service.

At the same time, the Hungarian revolt thoroughly alarmed the Romanian Communists. The reason was simple enough: the same anti-Communism that exploded in Hungary immediately spread to the Hungarian minority in Romania. As in Hungary, students, teachers, and university professors were in the forefront of the action. There were student demonstrations in Cluj, in Medias, in Timisoara, and in the administrative center of the Hungarian Autonomous Region, Tirgu Mures—in fact in every area where there were Hungarian students in any numbers. Furthermore, the revolt threatened to catch fire among the Romanian peasantry and the country's intellectuals. Some of the more circumspect Romanians were only waiting to see whether the West would support Hungary. When that didn't happen, the Hungarians were obviously doomed.

There followed the Soviet isolation of Hungary and the branding of the Hungarians as fascists and chauvinists. The Romanians were quick to take the Soviet cue, exploiting the official condemnation of the Hungarians to the hilt and applying it particularly to the Hungarian minority in Romania. For the moment the Hungarian minority in Romania rose in sympathy with the Hungarian revolution, Romanians tended to see the whole thing as part of the old campaign for the annexation of territory in Transylvania to Hungary. Thus the Romanian Communist Party was not only fighting for its life, it was also fighting for what every Romanian considers Romanian national territory.

Russian troops put down the disorder in Romania and thousands of Hungarians were arrested, perhaps hundreds put to death. In one trial alone in Cluj, thirteen out of fifty-seven accused were executed. This year some eight thousand political prisoners were released with considerable fanfare by the Romanian government in a general amnesty. But as far as I could ascertain in my recent travels through Transylvania, not one of the Hungarians arrested during the revolt has yet been released.

The Capital of Limbo

Two years after the revolt, the Romanian government received the great and all-important prize for loyalty and services rendered to the Soviets— the withdrawal of the Red Army. "Genuine proletarian internationalism" is also gone, and the Romanian desire to keep the Hungarian minority in its place has found more and more ways of expressing itself. In 1959, the rector of the Bolyai University, Professor Lajos Takacs, expressed his regret over the "nationalist isolation" of the Hungarian minority and requested the ministry of education "to examine the advisability of having two universities in Cluj." In June 1959, the students and the professors "unanimously approved" the merger of their university with the Romanian Babes University.

Late in 1960, the Romanian government undertook the administrative reorganization of the entire country, ostensibly to effect a more rational economic division among the various territories. Actually, the reorganization achieved the ethnic gerrymandering of the Autonomous Hungarian Region, and the authorities have used economic measures to break up the Szekler communities and disperse the fragments throughout the country. The closing of Hungarian cultural institutions has also continued. The six-hundred-year-old Hungarian college at Aiud was closed and its library impounded. In 1962 the last Hungarian institution of higher learning, the Institute of Medicine and Pharmacy at Tirgu Mures, was liquidated outright; the Romanian authorities did not even bother to cloak the operation as a merger. The liquidation was officially described as "the reduction of Hungarian-language classes" at the institute.

It was in 1962 that the Romanians launched their main administrative assault against the Autonomous Region. All key positions in administration and industry were taken over by Romanians. Dimitru Puni, a Romanian, was appointed chairman of the regional people's council. The Hungarian Writers' Association in Tirgu Mures was merged with a Romanian

Writers' Association imported for that purpose. In the same way, the Szekler State Theatre was enlarged by the addition of a Romanian section. The most far-reaching measure, however, was the merging of Hungarian with Romanian schools. By the end of 1962 there was no longer a single wholly separate Hungarian school in Romania. Within two years the new dispensation had made a mockery of the constitution's guarantee of access to schools where instruction is given in each people's "mother tongue." Romanian has effectively replaced Hungarian at every level as the language of official and public life. This is not only because the leaders and key functionaries of the region are all Romanians who know no Hungarian; employees throughout the region have been put on notice that if they fail to use Romanian in public they will be summarily dismissed. . . .

Romania's transformation from an obsequious satellite practicing "genuine proletarian internationalism" to a fiercely independent national state pursuing a policy of forcible assimilation of minorities is accompanied by a propaganda offensive on a broad front that includes the reinterpretation of history as a method of furthering the Romanization of Romania. Romanian writers have taken issue with Soviet historians on the apportionment of roles in the liberation of Romania from the fascist yoke and won their point. The spate of articles and brochures produced to document the party's leading role in the "victorious armed uprising of August, 1944," and the exploits of "the new Romanian Army" is often supplemented with situation maps giving the positions and movements of the Romanian units and "patriotic battle groups" in overrunning the "German-Hungarian forces" in Transylvania. . . .

The main target for historical revision, however, is what Romanian writers refer to as "the Habsburg occupation," especially during its final period. At a conference of historians held in Hungary [in May 1963], Romanians expounded their theory of "double exploitation and oppression of the masses by the dominant nations of Austria-Hungary." The great majority of landowners, they said, had been Hungarian and German; the great majority of peasants had been Slavs and Romanians. This had resulted in a double burden of national as well as social oppression. The Hungarian hosts, a West German, and a Soviet historian denied the validity of the theory, which not only equates classes with nations but also distinguishes between the nationalism of dominant nations ("imperialist chauvinism") and the nationalism of suppressed nations ("national liberation movements"). The theory was not designed merely to denigrate the Hungarians retroactively as chronic imperialist chauvinists and justify Romanian possession of Transylvania; it was also the academic celebration of Romania's right to develop its entire range of basic industries as a unitary, independent, and fully equal state, not to be exploited by industrially dominant countries such as the Soviet Union, Czechoslovakia, and East Germany within Comecon.

The Hungarian Handicap

There is no doubt that the legacy of the Habsburg Empire and its hangnail Horthy "regency" of 1920–1944 has weighed heavily on the Hungarian Communists. As model proletarian internationalists, they have been constrained from the first to single out Hungarian history for special censure, an exercise in which they found themselves enthusiastically abetted by Romanians, Czechs, and Yugoslavs, all of whose countries have large Hungarian minorities. For faithful Communists, the Hungarian revolt only proved that the Hungarians have still not managed to outlive their fascist-chauvinist past. In his preface to the new two-volume *History of Hungary,* which appeared early this year, Eric Molnár states that the purpose of the work is "to expound Hungarian history in connection with the histories of our neighbor nations and by this means liquidate the Magyar global Hungarocentric, nationalistic point of view."

Even for Communists, it is difficult to promote their national interests while decrying the national character. The Romanians can—and repeatedly do—tie the Hungarians in knots merely by reminding them of the Leninist rules by which the Hungarians (but not, apparently, the Romanians) are bound. Thus the world was treated in early 1962 to the spectacle of the Hungarian government prosecuting Hungarian patriots on Hungarian soil at the insistence of the Romanian government. A group of refugee Transylvanian intellectuals—there are many such in Hungary—had been holding regular meetings to consider what could be done to relieve the plight of the Hungarian minority. The Romanian government learned of the activity and demanded that the Kadar régime make an example of the group's leaders or bear responsibility for the breakdown of "Hungarian-Romanian friendship." Three of the former Transylvanians were tried and sentenced. One, Dr. Sándor Püski, was sentenced to four and a half years in prison; the others got off a little lighter.

In retrospect, we can see that the Hungarian revolt, whose first demand was the withdrawal of Soviet troops from Hungary, made the continued presence of Soviet troops in Hungary essential to the existence of a Communist régime. Furthermore, the revolt virtually stripped the Kadar régime of any room for diplomatic maneuver inside as well as outside the Soviet bloc—particularly since the Romanian Communist Party was able to turn the revolution to its own nationalistic purposes. And in the process, not surprisingly, Hungary's unequal struggle with Romania has strained many a prominent Hungarian Communist's doctrinal allegiance to the breaking point. . . .

Meanwhile relations between Hungary and Romania have deteriorated still further. Traditionally the churches have played a signal role in the alternate Magyarization and Romanization of Transylvania; in general, the Catholic and Protestant Churches reflect Hungarian and German interests, while the Orthodox Church has always embodied the ethnic state religion of the Romanians. As a result, Romanian Communists have taken to supporting the Orthodox Church as their pawn in the struggle and persecuting the Catholic and Protestant Churches as Hungarian pawns. . . .

The greatest single source of irritation to the Hungarians is the state cultural agreement with Romania. Strict Romanian application of the terms of the agreement has prevented the Hungarian government from establishing any sort of cultural link between the homeland and the minority. Hungarians in Romania are restricted to a mere half dozen classical Hungarian authors such as the nineteenth-century epic poet János Arany and the lyricist Endre Ady. Most other books in Hungarian are translations of Romanian authors. According to the terms of the agreement, no book concerning Transylvania may be published in Hungary without the approval of the Romanian censors. Radio and television broadcasting are not restricted by the agreement, and here the Hungarians enjoy a geographical advantage since most of Transylvania is closer to Hungary than to Bucharest, which is on the other side of the Transylvanian Alps in any event. However, Radio Bucharest competes with Radio Kossuth in Hungarian-language programs, and the Romanian authorities advise against listening to the Hungarian state radio.

The only comic relief in the situation is provided by the use both sides have made of the Hungarian-Romanian film-exchange program. The Hungarian government always takes the maximum of eight films a year—even though the notoriously poor Romanian films are box-office poison—in order to insinuate an equal number of Hungarian films into Romania. The Hungarians were incensed, however, when the Romanians dubbed in Romanian-language sound tracks and then added insult to injury by providing the minority with Hungarian subtitles. When the Hungarian government protested, the Romanians stopped the dubbing and provided Romanian subtitles—but then deliberately desynchronized the Hungarian sound tracks. The old subtitles in Hungarian were at least legible.

· · ·

A hopeless dilemma confronts the once powerful Hungarian wing of the Romanian Communist Party: its members must support, if not actively implement, the Romanian government's anti-minority policy. As a result, the Hungarian wing has been purged by the Romanian party leadership and ostracized by the Hungarian minority. As nearly as I could make out, the only crumb Hungarian Communists in Budapest can proffer to Hungarians in Romania is the advice that they should infiltrate the Romanian Communist Party in order to promote the practice of Leninist principles, particularly as regards minorities.

According to one historian I talked with, the organization of the Szekely area as an autonomous region put the Russians in a position "to balance the old Transylvanian question between Romania and Hungary." But the position was abandoned with the withdrawal of Soviet troops from Romania. Since then, the Soviet Union has kept pretty much out of the situation. . . .

The Romanians were among the first to recognize "genuine proletarian internationalism" as merely a Soviet device to justify maintenance of military bases in Eastern Europe and so secure Soviet economic exploitation. And even this Soviet desire has been skillfully used by the Romanians in the service of their own national cause, leaving others to make the sacrifices for the sake of international Communism. In effect, Romania capitalized on the misconceived gallantry of the Hungarians, whose revolt gave their neighbor a chance to win concessions from the Russians.

And through it all, the Romanians clearly foresaw the re-emergence of nationalism, which Communist theoreticians used to call "the main danger to the successful construction of the new state system." Far from being surprised by the Sino-Soviet split, the Bucharest government was banking on it. As a widely quoted Romanian proverb has it: "In time the waters recede, the rocks remain."

Bibliography

U.S.S.R.

Armstrong, J. A., *Ukrainian Nationalism: 1939–1945* (2nd ed.). New York: Columbia University Press, 1963.

Bennigsen, A., and C. Quelquejay, *The Evolution of the Muslim Nationalities of the U.S.S.R.* Paris: Mouton, 1961.

Caroe, O., *Soviet Empire: The Turks of Central Asia and Stalinism.* London: Macmillan & Co., Ltd., 1953.

Conquest, R., *The Soviet Deportation of Nationalities.* London, Macmillan & Co., Ltd., 1960.

Dmytryshyn, B., *Moscow and the Ukraine, 1918–1953: A Study of Russian Bolshevik Nationality Policy.* New York: Bookman Associates, 1956.

Kolarz, W., *Russia and Her Colonies.* London: George Philip & Son, Ltd., the London Geographical Institute, 1952.

Park, A. G., *Bolshevism in Turkestan: 1917–1927.* New York: Columbia University Press, 1957.

Pipes, R., *The Formation of the Soviet Union: Communism and Rationalism, 1917–1923* (2nd ed.). Cambridge, Mass.: Harvard University Press, 1964.

Rywkin, M., *Russia in Central Asia.* New York: Collier Books, a division of Crowell-Collier Publishing Co., 1963.

Schlesinger, R., *The Nationalities Problem and Soviet Administration.* London: Routledge & Kegan Paul, Ltd., 1956.

Smal-Stocki, R., *The Captive Nations: Nationalism of the Non-Russian Nations in the Soviet Union.* New York: Bookman Associates, 1960.

Wheeler, G. E., *Racial Problems in Soviet Muslim Asia.* New York: Oxford University Press, Inc., 1960.

————, *The Modern History of Soviet Central Asia.* New York: Frederick A. Praeger, Inc., 1964.

Zenkovsky, S. A., *Pan-Turkism and Islam in Russia.* Cambridge, Mass.: Harvard University Press, 1960.

CHINA

De Francis, J., ed., "National and Minority Policies: The Various Nationalities in China and the Policy of the Communist Government," *The Annals of the American Academy of Political and Social Science,* CCLXXVII (September, 1951), 146–56.

————, *Nationalism and Language Reform in China.* Princeton, N.J.: Princeton University Press, 1950.

Lattimore, O., *Inner Asian Frontiers of China.* Boston: Beacon Press, 1962.

Li, T., *Tibet: Today and Yesterday.* New York: Bookman Associates, 1960.

EASTERN EUROPE

Djilas, M., *Montenegro.* New York: Harcourt, Brace & World, Inc., 1964.

Janowsky, O. I., *Nationalities and National Minorities.* New York: The Macmillan Company, 1945.

Kostelski, Z., *The Yugoslavs: The History of the Yugoslavs and Their States to the Creation of Yugoslavia.* New York: Philosophical Library, Inc., 1952.

Lettrich, J., *History of Modern Slovakia.* New York: Frederick A. Praeger, Inc., 1955.

Shechtman, J. B., *Postwar Population Transfers in Europe.* Philadelphia: University of Pennsylvania Press, 1962.

Chapter Seven

The Politics of Development: Reconstituting the Economic Base

In the process of becoming world powers, the Soviet Union and China have gone through two revolutions: the first, political; the second, economic. Through political revolution, their Communist Parties seized and consolidated the *power* necessary to build a socialist society. But the establishment of the *material basis* for socialism took a second, or economic, revolution from which emerged the present totalitarian institutional framework. The considerations resulting in the economic alternative which was adopted are the focus of this chapter.

The Bolsheviks surmounted the trials of "war communism," defeating the conglomeration of White armies and interventionist forces and rendering ineffectual the residue of non-communist opposition. They then undertook to entrench their political rule. To provide a respite for the population and encourage economic recovery, Lenin took "two steps backwards" in order to advance "one step forward" and adopted the New Economic Policy (NEP) in 1921. This policy remained in effect for seven years and succeeded in restoring the economy to production levels approximating those of 1914. In China, too, the revolution went through several stages. By late 1949, the Communists had defeated the Kuomintang and established political rule over the mainland. Notwithstanding their involvement in the Korean war in November 1950 and their need to eliminate the still existing scattered pockets of Kuomintang resistance, they moved expeditiously to curb inflation, end administrative corruption, and carry out a program of land reform. It was only in 1953, with the introduction of the First Five Year Plan, that they embarked on a program of planned economic development.

Both Soviet and Chinese leaders believed in the overriding necessity for heavy industry as the key to socialist transformation. As the first communist elite to come to power, the Bolsheviks had to pioneer the way to socialism. Differences inevitably arose over the best path to take. From 1924 to 1928, there was an "industrialization debate" which involved not only contrasting views of how best to transform Russia into an industrial and modern state, but also a bitter intra-Party struggle over the succession to Lenin's mantle, questions of Party democracy, the role of the trade unions in a socialist state, and issues of foreign policy. Economic arguments became inextricably interwoven with political alignments, at least until Stalin emerged in 1929 as master of the Party apparatus. A comparable debate occurred in China between 1950 and 1957, but with these differences: It did not involve a fundamental struggle for power within the Party, nor were contrasting positions aired openly, as they had been in the Soviet Union prior to 1929; also, the Chinese had the Soviet model and experience to guide them.

Stalin launched the second, or economic, revolution in 1928 to accelerate industrialization and to transform the mixed economy of 1921–1928 into a planned socialist economy. A number of considerations were instrumental in shaping his policy. First, Stalin realized that large capital outlays were urgently needed for the construction of new plants. These could come from only two sources: from abroad in the form of credits, loans, grants, and earnings from exports; or internally, from expanding the gross national product and instituting a policy of enforced savings, which entailed keeping consumption low while investing great amounts of capital in new physical plant and infrastructure. Convinced of the hostility of the capitalist world, and recognizing that the industrial recovery which had taken place under NEP had been possible "because it had been based on the utilization of the old industrial capacity [built during the Czarist period] and *not* on the creation of the new,"[1] he decided to abandon NEP and adopt five-year plans which emphasized the accelerated accumulation of capital and enforced savings.[2]

Second, a policy of enforced savings in an agrarian country necessitated bending agriculture to the needs of industrialization. A steady supply of

---

[1] Alexander Erlich, "Stalin's Views on Economic Development," in *Continuity and Change in Russian and Soviet Thought,* ed. Ernest Simmons (Cambridge, Mass.: Harvard University Press, 1955), p. 87.

The Soviet economy recovered during NEP because it had available the pre-war physical plants, entrepreneurial groups, banking system, and so forth. Thus, small investments brought forth an immediate outflow of goods, as the factories were put back into use. But by 1926–1927, the pre-war structure had been restored. The Party then faced the problem of creating new physical plant.

[2] Foreign developments, particularly the worldwide depression of the early 1930's, underscored the essential correctness of Stalin's insistence that Soviet economic development rest largely on Soviet resources. Under the First Five-Year Plan, 10 per cent of Soviet capital requirements was to be supplied by imports of agricultural and industrial machinery which would be financed through exports of Soviet grain and

food had to be assured for the urban population, and the rural unemployed and underemployed had to be moved to the cities, trained, and integrated into the industrial labor force. Stalin believed that this could best be accomplished by a high degree of centralized planning, allocation of resources, and extensive governmental control over the economy. The bitter resistance of the peasants and their destruction of livestock, crops, and machinery, jolted Soviet leaders to the realization that *rapid* collectivization and industrialization required more pervasive controls over the economy and society than had originally been foreseen.

Third, the widespread concern in the Communist Party over the prosperity and recovery of the dominant private sector of agriculture and over the State's dependence on the private peasant for surpluses of grain (Reading 36) contributed to the adoption of Draconian measures. Large segments of the Party feared that the "kulaks," as all the peasants who were opposed to collectivization were labelled, might be able to thwart the construction of socialism. Collectivization was therefore to serve a double function. Politically, it would destroy the kulak class and socialize the peasantry within a more readily controlled and managed collectivist institutional framework. Economically, it would increase agricultural production through mechanization, large-scale farming, and the use of more scientific methods; ensure a steady flow of food and labor to the cities; enable the government to utilize kulak holdings to strengthen the collectives; and facilitate socialist planning (Reading 37).

Fourth, there were considerations of national security. Given their fear of another intervention, and the reinforcement of this fear by their ideological outlook, Soviet leaders looked to heavy industrialization as the key to the economic transformation which was prerequisite to military strength. In a speech in February 1931, Stalin stressed the urgency of accelerating the rate of industrial growth:

> To slacken the tempo would mean falling behind. And those who fall behind get beaten. . . . One feature of the history of Old Russia was the continual beatings she suffered because of her backwardness. . . . We are fifty or a hundred years behind the advanced countries. We must make good the distance in ten years. Either we do it, or we shall be crushed.[3]

In the process of carrying out his economic revolution, Stalin totalitarianized Soviet society. Industrialization rests on the modernization of other aspects of society, e.g., education, socialization, and transportation; and this, in the eyes of some, can be accomplished more easily and quickly by the imposition of totalitarian controls over the entire society. There is no general agreement on the question of how far the state should intervene

---

lumber. With the plummeting of world commodity prices, the U.S.S.R. had to export ever-larger quantities merely to pay for modest amounts of machinery.

[3] Joseph Stalin, *Problems of Leninism* (Moscow: Foreign Languages Publishing House, 1953), pp. 455–56.

to set in motion a self-generating process of growth and modernization (Readings 38 and 40). But we know that the Soviet Union did succeed in the economic transformation of a relatively weak, backward, essentially peasant society via totalitarianism.

Many of the features of present-day Soviet society were shaped and tempered during the First Five-Year Plan. The use of terror on a mass scale, for example, began in response to the peasants' resistance to collectivization. The Party used terror to pacify the countryside. Then, having set up a growing number of prison camps, the leadership found in the exploitation of slave labor a convenient method of exacting a high rate of involuntary saving, of building factories, roads, and machinery with a labor force that could be kept at a marginal level of existence. This gave rise to the systematic use of slave labor during the Stalin era and to the expansion of the powers of the secret police which administered these camps. Between 1929 and 1933, the trade unions were emasculated, as responsibility for production shifted to management. No longer were trade unions permitted a policy-making function; their primary task was now the raising of production. They became a tool of management. Wages were set by Moscow, and collective bargaining was eliminated. In the "Workers' State," the trade unions were without power or influence.

The Chinese launched their second, or economic, revolution in 1958. The decision to take the Great Leap Forward was dictated by the agricultural stagnation that had set in. According to one Western economist:

> Farm production was growing only slowly, possibly just sufficiently to keep pace with population growth. Moreover, the harvest was subject to sharp fluctuations in response to changing weather conditions. This in turn led to marked annual fluctuation in the rate of industrial growth.[4]

Between 1950 and 1957, the Chinese communist regime compiled an impressive record of economic performance. It curbed inflation, nationalized industry, and expanded industrial production. By 1952, land reform was completed, the landlord class eliminated, and landholdings equalized. Smoothly, quickly, with minimum dislocation, the regime moved in 1953 to collectivize agriculture, to shift landholdings from private to collective ownership, in part, out of a growing concern over the spread of peasant elements who aspired to self-enrichment; in a word, it feared the growth of a kulak class much as had the Soviet leaders in the late 1920's. In 1955, in a statement rationalizing collectivization, Mao Tse-tung noted:

> Everyone has noticed in recent years there has been a spontaneous and constant growth of capitalist elements in the countryside and that new rich peasants have sprung up everywhere. Many well-to-do middle peasants are striving

---

[4] Alexander Eckstein, "On the Economic Crisis in Communist China," *Foreign Affairs*, XLII, No. 4 (July, 1964), 656.

to become rich ones. Many poor peasants, lacking sufficient means of production, are still not free from the toils of poverty; some are in debt, others selling or renting their land. If this tendency goes unchecked, the separation into two extremes in the countryside will get worse day by day.[5]

Yet agricultural productivity remained low between 1952 and 1957 and was a drag on the development of industry and on the economy as a whole. Furthermore, by 1957 it had become evident to Mao that, in consequence of the growing rift between the two countries, no additional economic aid could be expected from Moscow. The stagnation of agriculture, the mediocre harvests, and the withering of foreign aid, led the leadership to introduce the communes and intensify the pace of industrialization. The Chinese sought to maximize the economic value of their vast reservoir of manpower by utilizing it more efficiently for large-scale irrigation and flood control projects and by applying labor-intensive methods to the raising of agricultural yields. The commune program of 1958 was intended to give the state greater control over the peasantry, its output, and its consumption.

Several contrasts may be noted between the Soviet and Chinese strategies of forced and accelerated economic development (Reading 39). First, in the Soviet Union, totalitarian control over the entire society was both a concomitant and a consequence of collectivization and rapid industrialization; in China, totalitarianization preceded the communization and forced industrialization drive of 1958. Second, as Professor Benjamin Schwartz has written, the Chinese attempt to apply the Stalinist model of economic development has forced Peking to face up to "certain intractable facts":

> In the Soviet Union the population problem was not a factor of any importance. In China it is a factor of overwhelming importance. The pre-Stalinist industrial base of the Soviet Union was much more considerable than the industrial base of China before 1950. The reservoir of available industrial skills and probably of natural resources was much larger in the Soviet Union.[6]

Professor Schwartz also suggests that the outlook of the Chinese leadership differs significantly from that held by Stalin and his entourage on the eve of the Soviet First Five-Year Plan in that an underlying feature of Chinese thinking is the assumption that:

> . . . Totalitarian collectivism can be internalised as it were into the very soul of a whole people by prescribed techniques of psychological "persuasion" and that specific therapy is available for the cure of all ideological "sickness" (the therapy may, of course, involve physical labour).[7]

---

[5] Mao Tse-tung, *The Question of Agricultural Cooperation* (Peking: Foreign Languages Press, 1959), pp. 31–32.
[6] Benjamin Schwartz, "Totalitarian Consolidation and the Chinese Model," *The China Quarterly*, (January–March, 1960), p. 19.
[7] *Ibid.*, p. 20.

He notes that "even though the initial pressures behind the 'commune' were probably economic, the ideological framework into which it has been set has a significance of its own." The Chinese leaders believe that there is a direct correlation between socialization and production, and they proceed on the assumption that both can be achieved through a combination of coercive persuasion and ideological remolding. The Chinese drive to establish communes elicited severe criticism from Premier Khrushchev, who observed that the U.S.S.R., too, had started to set up communes after the Civil War but had quickly abandoned them because they were unsuited to "the material and political conditions" of the time. By implication, the Chinese were following an erroneous and uncommunist course.

The experience of the Soviet Union and Communist China indicates that a backward, friendless, peasant country, intent upon modernization and military security, and indifferent to the human cost, can achieve rapid economic development within a totalitarian framework. In both countries, economic transformation strengthened the power of the Party, the military establishment, and the economic system, and made possible further socialist construction. Although centralization brought increasing bureaucracy and its attendant problems, and although the problems of agriculture resisted solution, industrialization has reached impressive levels, investment is high, and political control is assured.

Joseph Stalin

36 ON THE GRAIN FRONT

J. Stalin, *Works,* Vol. XI (Moscow: Foreign Languages Publishing House, 1954), excerpted from pp. 85–100.

In this speech, delivered on May 28, 1928, Stalin presented the economic data and arguments for collectivization.

What should be considered as the basic cause of our difficulties in the matter of the grain supply? What is the way out of these difficulties? What, in connection with these difficulties, are the conclusions that must be drawn as regards the rate of development of our industry, particularly from the point of view of the relation between the light and heavy industries? . . .

The basis of our grain difficulties lies in the fact that the increase in the production of marketable grain [grain actually available to the leadership for the cities or for sale abroad] is not keeping pace with the increase in the demand for grain. . . .

Here are a few figures illustrating the structure of grain production in the past, in the pre-war period, and at present, in the post-October period. . . . they are quite adequate to enable us to understand the difference between the pre-war period and the post-October period as regards the structure of grain production in general, and the production of marketable grain in particular.

What does this table show?

It shows, firstly, that the production of the overwhelming proportion of grain products has passed from the landlords and kulaks to the small and middle peasants . . .

It shows, secondly, that in our country the principal holders of marketable grain are the small and, primarily, the middle peasants. This means that not only as regards gross production of grain, but also as regards the production of marketable grain, the U.S.S.R. has become, as a result of the October Revolution, a land of small-peasant farming, and the middle peasant has become the "central figure" in agriculture.

It shows, thirdly, that the abolition of landlord (large-scale) farming, the reduction of kulak (large-scale) farming to less than one-third, and the passing to small-peasant farming with only 11 per cent of its output

234

	GROSS GRAIN PRODUCTION		MARKETABLE GRAIN (I.E., NOT CONSUMED IN THE COUNTRYSIDE)		
	Millions of poods	*Per Cent*	*Millions of poods*	*Per Cent*	*Percentage of marketable grain*
Prewar					
1. Landlords	600	12.0	281.6	21.6	47.0
2. Kulaks	1,900	38.0	650.0	50.0	34.0
3. Middle and poor peasants	2,500	50.0	369.0	28.4	14.7
Total	5,000	100.0	1,300.6	100.0	26.0
Postwar (1926–27)					
1. State farms and collective farms	80.0	1.7	37.8	6.0	47.2
2. Kulaks	617.0	13.0	126.0	20.0	20.0
3. Middle and poor peasants	4,052.0	85.3	466.2	74.0	11.2
Total	4,749.0	100.0	630.0	100.0	13.3

marketed, in the absence, in the sphere of grain production, of any more or less developed large-scale socially-conducted farming (collective farms and state farms), were bound to lead, and in fact have led, to a sharp reduction in the production of marketable grain as compared with pre-war times. It is a fact that the amount of marketable grain in our country is now half what it was before the war, although the gross output of grain has reached the pre-war level.

That is the basis of our difficulties on the grain front.

That is why our difficulties in the sphere of grain procurements must not be regarded as a mere accident. . . .

What is the way out of this situation?

Some people see the way out of this situation in a return to kulak farming, in the development and extension of kulak farming. These people dare not speak of a return to landlord farming, for they realise, evidently, that such talk is dangerous in our times. . . . These people think that the Soviet regime can rely simultaneously on two opposite classes—the class of the kulaks, whose economic principle is the exploitation of the working class, and the class of the workers, whose economic principle is the abolition of all exploitation. A trick worthy of reactionaries. . . . Talk about the kulak being "no worse" than the urban capitalist, about the kulak being no more dangerous than the urban Nepman,[1] and therefore, about there being no reason to "fear" the kulaks now—such talk is sheer liberal chatter which lulls the vigilance of the working class and of the main mass of the peasantry. It must not be forgotten that in industry we can oppose to the small urban capitalist our large-scale socialist industry, which produces nine-tenths of the total output of manufactured goods, whereas in the countryside we can oppose to large-scale kulak farming only the still weak collective farms and state farms, which produce but one-eighth of the amount of grain produced by the kulak farms. . . .

What, then, is the way out of the situation?

1. The way out lies, above all, in passing from small, backward and scattered peasant farms to united, large socially-conducted farms, equipped with machinery, armed with scientific knowledge and capable of producing the maximum amount of marketable grain. The way out lies in the transition from individual peasant farming to collective, socially-conducted economy in agriculture . . .

2. The way out lies, secondly, in expanding and strengthening the old state farms, and in organising and developing new, large ones. . . .

3. Finally, the way out lies in systematically increasing the yield of the individual small- and middle-peasant farms. We cannot and should not lend any support to the individual large kulak farms. But we can and should assist the individual small- and middle-peasant farms, helping them to increase their crop yields and drawing them into the channel of co-operative organisation. . . .

Should not, in addition to these measures, a number of other measures be adopted—measures, say, to reduce the rate of development of our industry, the growth of which is causing a considerable increase in the demand for grain, which at present is outstripping the increase in the production of marketable grain? No, not under any circumstances! To reduce the rate of development of industry would mean to weaken the working class; for every step forward in the development of industry, every new factory, every new works, is, as Lenin expressed it, "a new stronghold" of the working class, one which strengthens the latter's position in the fight against the petty-bourgeois elemental forces, in the fight against the capitalist elements in our economy. On the contrary, we must maintain the present rate of development of industry: we must at the first opportunity speed it up in order to pour goods into the rural areas and obtain more grain from them, in order to supply agriculture, and primarily the collective farms and state farms, with machines, in order to industralise agriculture and to increase the proportion of its output for the market.

---

[1] Nepman refers to the private trader and businessman who arose and flourished during the NEP period.

Joseph Stalin

37 ON THE NEED FOR RAPID INDUSTRIALIZATION

Joseph Stalin, *Problems of Leninism* (Moscow: Foreign Languages Publishing House, 1953), excerpted from pp. 309–11, 332–37.

In this speech delivered at the April 1929 Plenum of the Central Committee and the Central Control Commission of the Communist Party, Stalin denounced the defeated "Right Deviation" group, led by Bukharin, Rykov, and Tomsky, for opposing the program of rapid industrialization and forced collectivization of agriculture then being undertaken. This speech signified the start of what was to soon develop as the Stalinization of Soviet society.

We are now at a new stage of development, distinct from the old period, from the period of restoration [the NEP period]. We are now in a new period of construction, the period of the *reconstruction* of the whole national economy on the basis of socialism. This new period gives rise to new class changes, to an intensification of the class struggle. It demands new methods of struggle, the regrouping of our forces, the improvement and strengthening of all our organizations.

The misfortune of Bukharin's group is that it is living in the past, that it fails to see the specific features of this new period and does not understand that new methods of struggle are needed. Hence its blindness, its bewilderment, its panic in the face of difficulties.

What is the theoretical basis for the blindness and bewilderment of Bukharin's group?

I think that the theoretical basis for this blindness and bewilderment is Bukharin's incorrect, non-Marxian approach to the question of the class struggle in our country. I have in mind Bukharin's non-Marxian theory that the kulaks will grow into socialism, his failure to understand the mechanism of the class struggle under the dictatorship of the proletariat. . . .

Hitherto, we Marxist-Leninists thought that between the capitalists of town and country, on the one hand, and the working class, on the other, there is an *irreconcilable* antagonism of interest. This is exactly what the Marxian theory of the class struggle rests on. But now, according to Bukharin's theory that the capitalists will *peacefully grow* into socialism, all this is turned topsy-turvy; the irreconcilable antagonism of class interests

237

between the exploiters and the exploited disappears, the exploiters grow in socialism. . . .

Either one thing or the other: either there is an irreconcilable antagonism of interests between the capitalist class and the class of the workers who have assumed power and have organized their dictatorship, or there is no such antagonism of interests, in which case only one thing remains: to proclaim the harmony of class interests.

Either one thing or the other:

Either Marx's theory of the class struggle, *or* the theory of the capitalists growing into socialism;

Either an irreconcilable antagonism of class interests, *or* the theory of harmony of class interests. . . .

. . .

Finally, as to the question of the rate of development of industry and of the new forms of the bond between town and country. This is one of our most important points of difference. The importance of this question is that it is the converging point of all the threads of our *practical* differences on the economic policy of the Party.

What are the new forms of the bond, what do they signify from the point of view of our economic policy?

They signify, firstly, that besides the old forms of the bond between town and country, whereby industry chiefly satisfied the *personal* requirements of the peasantry (cotton textile, footwear, and manufactured goods in general), we now need new forms of the bond, whereby industry will satisfy the *productive* requirements of peasant farming (agricultural machinery, tractors, improved seed, fertilizers, etc.).

. . .

As long as it was a question of *restoring* agriculture and of the peasants assimilating the landlords' and kulaks' land, we could be content with the old forms of the bond. But now, when it is a question of *reconstructing* agriculture, this is not enough. Now we must go further and help the peasantry to reorganize agricultural production on the basis of a new technique and collective labour.

Secondly, they signify that simultaneously with the re-equipment of our industry, we must seriously begin to re-equip agriculture too. We are re-equipping, and have already partly re-equipped our industry, placing it on a new technical basis, supplying it with new and improved machinery and new and improved cadres. We are building new factories and plants and are reconstructing and extending the old ones; we are developing the iron and steel industry, the chemical industry and the machine-building industry. On this basis new towns are springing up, new industrial centres are multiplying and the old ones are expanding. On this basis the demand for food products and for raw materials for industry is growing. But agriculture continues to employ the old equipment, the old methods of tillage practised by our forefathers, the old, primitive, now useless, or nearly useless technique, the old small-peasant, individual forms of farming and labour.

Take the mere fact that before the revolution there were nearly 16,000,-000 peasant households, and now there are no less than 25,000,000! What does this indicate if not that agriculture is assuming a more and more scattered, fragmentary character. And the characteristic feature of scattered small farms is that they are unable sufficiently to employ technique, machines, tractors and scientific agronomic knowledge, that they are farms with a small output for the market.

Hence, the insufficient output of agricultural products for the market.

Hence, the danger of a rift between town and country, between industry and agriculture.

Hence, the necessity for increasing, whipping up the rate of development of agriculture to that of our industry.

And so, in order to avoid the danger of a rift, we must begin thoroughly to re-equip agriculture on the basis of modern technique. But in order to re-equip it we must gradually amalgamate the scattered individual peasant farms into large farms, into collective farms; we must build up agriculture on the basis of collective labour, we must enlarge the collective farms, we must develop the old and new state farms, we must systematically employ the contract system on a mass scale in all the principal branches of agriculture, we must develop the system of machine-and-tractor stations which help the peasantry to assimilate the new technique and to collectivize labour—in a word, we must gradually transfer the small individual peasant farms to the basis of large-scale collective production, for only large-scale production of a socialized type is capable of making full use of scientific knowledge and modern technique, and of advancing the development of our agriculture with seven-league strides. . . .

Failing this it will be impossible to develop agriculture to any extent. Failing this it will be impossible to solve the grain problem. Failing this it will be impossible to save the weaker strata of the peasantry from ruin and distress.

Finally, they signify that we must develop our industry to the utmost as the principal source from which agriculture will be supplied with the means required for its reconstruction: we must develop our iron and steel, chemical and machine-building industries; we must build tractor works, agricultural-machinery works, etc. . . .

[It] will be impossible to supply the rural districts with machines and tractors unless we accelerate the development of our industry. Hence, the speedy development of our industry is the key to the reconstruction of agriculture on the basis of collectivism.

Such is the meaning and significance of the new forms of the bond.

Bukharin's group is obliged to admit, in words, the necessity of the new forms of the bond. But it is an admission only *in words,* with the intention, under cover of a verbal recognition of the new forms of the bond, of smuggling in something which is the *very opposite.* Actually, Bukharin is opposed to the new forms of the bond. Bukharin's starting point is not the speedy rate of development of industry as the lever for the reconstruction of agriculture, but the development of individual peasant farming. He puts in the foreground the "normalization" of the market and permission for the free play of prices on the agricultural produce market, complete freedom for private trade. Hence his distrustful attitude to the collective farms which manifested itself in his speech at the July Plenum of the Central Committee and in his theses prior to the July Plenum of the Central Committee. Hence his disapproval of every and any form of emergency measures against the kulaks during grain-purchasing campaigns.

We know that Bukharin shuns emergency measures as the devil shuns holy water.

We know that Bukharin still fails to understand that under present conditions the kulak will not supply a sufficient quantity of grain voluntarily, of his own accord.

That has been proved by our two years' experience of grain-purchasing campaigns.

But what if, in spite of everything, there will not be enough grain marketed? To this Bukharin replies: "Do not worry the kulaks with emergency measures; import grain from abroad." Not long ago he proposed that we import about 50,000,000 poods of grain, i.e., to the value of about 100,000,000 rubles in foreign currency. But what if foreign currency is required to import equipment for industry? To this Bukharin replies: "Preference must be given to imports of grain—thus, evidently, relegating imports of equipment for industry to the background."

It follows, therefore, that the basis for the solution of the grain problem and for the reconstruction of agriculture is not the speedy rate of development of industry, but the development of individual peasant farming, including also kulak farming, on the basis of a free market and the free play of prices in the market.

Thus we have two different plans of economic policy.

THE PARTY'S PLAN:

1. We are re-equipping industry (reconstruction).
2. We are beginning seriously to re-equip agriculture (reconstruction).
3. For this we must expand the development of collective farms and state farms, employ on a mass scale the contract system and machine and

tractor stations as means of establishing a *bond* between industry and agriculture in the sphere of *production*.

4. As for the present grain-purchasing difficulties, we must admit the necessity for temporary emergency measures that are bolstered up by the popular support of the middle- and poor-peasant masses, as one of the means of breaking the resistance of the kulaks and of obtaining from them the maximum grain surplus necessary to be able to dispense with imported grain and to save foreign currency for the development of industry.

5. Individual poor- and middle-peasant farming plays, and will continue to play, a predominant part in supplying the country with food and raw materials; but alone it is no longer adequate—the development of individual poor- and middle-peasant farming must therefore be *supplemented* by the development of collective farms and state farms, by the contract system applied on a mass scale, by accelerating the development of machine-and-tractor stations, in order to facilitate the squeezing out of the capitalist elements from agriculture and the gradual transfer of the individual peasant farms to large-scale collective farming, to collective labour.

6. But in order to achieve all this, it is necessary first of all to accelerate the development of industry, of metallurgy, chemicals, machine building, of tractor works, agricultural-machinery works, etc. Failing this it will be impossible to solve the grain problem just as it will be impossible to reconstruct agriculture.

Conclusion: *The key to the reconstruction of agriculture is the speedy rate of development of our industry.*

BUKHARIN'S PLAN:

1. "Normalize" the market; permit the free play of prices on the market and a rise in the price of grain, undeterred by the fact that this may lead to a rise in the price of manufactured goods, raw materials and bread.

2. The utmost development of individual peasant farming accompanied by a certain reduction of the rate of development of collective farms and state farms (Bukharin's theses of July and his speech at the July Plenum).

3. Grain purchasing on the spontaneity principle, precluding under all circumstances even the partial application of emergency measures against the kulaks, even though such measures are supported by the middle- and poor-peasant masses.

4. In the event of shortage of grain, to import about 100,000,000 rubles worth of grain.

5. And if there is not enough foreign currency to pay for imports of grain and equipment for industry, to reduce imports of equipment and, consequently, the rate of development of our industry—otherwise our agriculture will simply "mark time," or will even "directly decline."

Conclusion: *The key to the reconstruction of agriculture is the development of individual peasant farming.*
This is how it works out, comrades.
Bukharin's plan is a plan to *reduce* the rate of development of industry and to *undermine* the new forms of the bond.
Such are our divergencies.

Herbert J. Ellison

38 THE DECISION TO COLLECTIVIZE AGRICULTURE

Herbert J. Ellison, "The Decision to Collectivize Agriculture," *The American Slavic and East European Review* (now published as the *Slavic Review*), XX, No. 2 (April, 1961), excerpted from pp. 191–97. Footnote references have been deleted.

Herbert J. Ellison is Associate Professor of History at the University of Kansas. Professor Ellison is one of those specialists who feel that the economic reasoning behind the decision to collectivize was unwarranted and that the decision was primarily a political one.

Western scholars have produced a variety of interpretations of the Soviet decision to collectivize agriculture, and these interpretations are sufficiently distinct that one cannot place them in a few neat categories without misrepresenting the intentions of individual analysts. But it is possible to make comparisons between interpretations in terms of the presentation of the reasons for collectivization on the one hand, and the alternative possibilities on the other.

There are, first of all, some who present the Soviet rationalization of the collectivization decision—the inevitability of agrarian socialism, the class struggle and economic analysis—in more or less full form. This is true of such prominent interpreters of Soviet economic development as Alexander Baykov and Maurice Dobb. It is also true of E. H. Carr, at least so far as he has developed the subject chronologically in his masterful analysis of the Bolshevik Revolution. These works—especially Carr's—are generally more literate and thorough than the Soviet studies, and lack the polemical tone so often characteristic of the latter. On the major points of interpreting this question, however, there is implicit agreement.

Most Western analysts, however, appear to reject the materialistic determinism on which the Soviet interpretation is founded. Indeed, they switch the argument decisively to emphasize the causative role of the Communists' desire for socialist agriculture so that Communist ideology is seen as a vital force in the transformation of reality, not a simple reflection of it. With such an approach the political, or ideological, inspiration for collectivization can be placed alongside a description of the economic developments which also helped effect the decision. In most studies the economic and political "factors" are simply listed without any explicit rating of the importance of either, though occasionally one finds a cryptic judgment, such as Michael Karpovich's statement that "one might even say that politics predominated over economics in the motives for its adoption." There are, however, implicit differences of interpretation evident in the relative emphasis given to ideological and economic influences.

One school of thought emphasizes the economic reasons for the decision to collectivize, sometimes giving them an almost independently decisive role. Thus one writer emphasizes the economic developments which brought the Soviet government to the conclusion "that its only way out of the ever more menacing grain crisis was the collectivization of the great bulk of Soviet agriculture and the wiping out of the independent kulaks." Another, having listed the economic problems of agriculture in the late 1920's, concludes: "Hence the decision to launch the collectivization program . . . and thereby to make possible the agricultural surplus necessary for an industrialized country." Other scholars plainly see political commitment as the more important influence in the making cf the decision and therefore give primary attention to the political debates and to the power struggle between groups offering rival interpretations of party doctrine. The assumption in such cases seems to be that ideology is the decisive factor, setting the goal of full socialism (industrial and agricultural), and that economic developments are important as they influence the course of the debate and help to precipitate a decision.

.   .   .

Both the official Soviet rationalization and many Western studies paint a picture of Soviet economic life in the late 1920's which suggests that there was no feasible alternative to the collectivization of agriculture. In the official analysis this is the key point, the economic demonstration, as it were, of the will of history made manifest. The analysis insists, first of all, that by 1927 it was plain that industrial development was being retarded by agriculture. Industrialization depended on funds from agriculture, for such means as the government had at its disposal for this purpose came largely from the agricultural tax and from surcharges on industrial commodities. But the peasant wished to eat more and get his industrial goods more cheaply, aspirations at odds with the government's industrialization objectives. A special villain of the Soviet (and many Western) versions is the kulak, for he wished to exploit his neighbor's labor and coveted his land. He also produced most of the surplus grain and hoarded it in order to charge the state an inflated price.

The policy of the government for this situation was to use all available means of "alienating" whatever surplus product the peasant possessed so as to assure a steady growth of industry without at the same time causing the peasant to balk and refuse to sell his produce (or even curtail production) because of a high grain tax or unfavorable terms of trade for industrial products. . . .

By 1925, however, it was plain that agricultural production and agricultural deliveries to government procurement agencies and to urban markets were too small. After cautiously trying a policy of concessions to the peasants from 1925 to 1927, the government was forced to recognize that the policy had failed. The annual grain collection crises remained, socialist agriculture was more remote than before because of the strengthening of the kulaks through the concessions on leasing land and hiring labor, and industrialization was proceeding at a "snail's pace." According to the official analysis, therefore, collectivization was the only means of improving agricultural efficiency and of getting more grain for the cities and for export.

Criticism of the economic rationalization of the collectivization decision can be pursued initially simply in terms of the accuracy of the picture of economic conditions on which it is based. Then can one question whether it was true that there was no alternative to collectivization.

The Soviet leaders were not empirical economists. Their theoretical commitments led them to distort economic realities and to overlook or misunderstand the effects of their own measures. An example of outright distortion—and one very widely repeated in Western works—is the claim that the peasants hoarded a grain surplus. Grain production had not regained prewar levels even in 1925–27 and "there was not the slightest reason to expect marketings of farm products to reach pre-war magnitudes." The production of grain—the mainstay of the diet—was still below the prewar level, while the population had grown, and the problem was not hoarding but low production. However, when low production was discussed at all, it was explained as deriving from the inevitable inefficiency of small-scale peasant farming (an assumption contradicted by West European experience) and remediable by the transition to large-scale socialist farms which would be more efficient (an assumption contradicted by the experience with the sovkhozes).

It was indeed true that Soviet peasant agriculture was backward. Land tenure rights were vague, and with the persistence of communal tenure and the strip system over most of Great Russia the individual holder had no security of tenure. Efficient farming was frustrated by the constant division of households and multiplication of ever smaller holdings. Nearly half of the households lacked draft animals; technique was generally at an exceedingly low level, and poverty was more the rule than the exception.

It is also true that most of these conditions were inherited from the prerevolutionary era. The point is, however, that before World War I there was a wide range of programs in effect aimed at rationalization and modernization of agriculture: the land tenure reforms for the provision of security of tenure, consolidation of landholdings, and abolition of communal land controls; arrangements to facilitate the leasing and selling of land so that owners of excessively small holdings might migrate to free land areas or resettle in the cities; improvement of technique through demonstration stations; growth of credit societies to provide cheaper short- and long-term loans; encouragement of the co-operative movement for the development of the profitable sale of agricultural commodities and economical purchase of industrial goods, and so forth. These were programs which called forth the energy and leadership of the most vigorous and able elements in the villages and brought a steady increase in agricultural production and peasant prosperity in the years before the war.

But the firm sense of direction in agricultural policy—so long in developing—was negated by the contrary purpose of the Soviet government in the era of War Communism—the erection of a socialist agricultural system. With the frustration of this purpose by peasant opposition, Soviet agricultural policy reached an impasse. According to the code of 1922 the agrarian commune was neither encouraged nor discouraged. There was no consolidation of landholdings; instead, peasants were encouraged to split up their landholdings into ever more uneconomic holdings because of the official persecution of "kulaks." The agrarian resettlement scheme never regained its prewar vigor, and opportunities in the cities were at a minimum with unemployment always at a high level. The co-operatives, having been converted into a brittle, centralized bureaucratic apparatus during War Communism, never managed to regain their independence or the peasant's confidence. . . . The terms of trade for industrial goods were less favorable than they had been since the 1890's, and agricultural implements were both scarce and expensive. If a peasant managed to overcome this impressive array of obstacles and achieve a modest prosperity he was open to the danger of being branded a kulak and relieved of his gains. As one well-informed observer of Soviet agriculture in the 1920's put the question simply, "How can he be expected to do productive work under such conditions?"

Thus, not only did Soviet agricultural discussions tend to ignore or misrepresent the problem of production, but Soviet agricultural policy tended gravely to aggravate it, contributing handsomely to the creation of a situation where it was a miracle that agricultural production was as high as it was . . .

Seen from this perspective, collectivization cannot be described "as the only solution to the riddle of how to industrialize on the basis of NEP . . . the only release from that closed circle of interdependent limiting factors." On the one hand, many of the economic circumstances which purportedly compose the "closed circle" were either created or in one way or another affected by politically inspired policies. And on the other, collectivization was by no means an obvious or exclusive solution to these problems, unless one was already committed to agrarian socialism. Political doctrine, then, played the vital role in making the decision. One is obliged to conclude that the primary force behind the decision was not impersonal economic "forces" but rather preconceived political objectives and economic experience politically interpreted.

Nicolas Spulber

39 CONTRASTING ECONOMIC PATTERNS: CHINESE AND SOVIET DEVELOPMENT STRATEGIES

Nicolas Spulber, "Contrasting Economic Patterns: Chinese and Soviet Development Strategies," *Soviet Studies*, XV, No. 1 (July, 1963), excerpted from pp. 1–5, 14–16. Footnote references have been deleted.

Nicolas Spulber is Professor of Economics at Indiana University and the author of a number of works on Soviet and Communist economies, including The Soviet Economy: Structure, Principles, Problems.

Strategies are ways of allocating resources in order to reach a long run objective, political, economic or military. A common objective for all underdeveloped areas is industrialisation in the shortest possible period. But this objective is always accompanied by a number of proximate ends, each of which may be furthered or hindered according to the ways in which each and all of the other ends are pursued. For instance, since the mid-

1920's the Soviet leaders have set for their backward economy the bold objective of "catching up with and surpassing in the shortest historical period the highest indices of capitalism." Simultaneously the Russians aimed at the liquidation of the rich peasants, the rapid collectivisation of agriculture and the elimination of market relations in certain sectors— objectives which in certain ways impeded their main goal. Their economic strategy was thus shaped not only as a function of the ultimate goal, but also as a function of a number of proximate goals, each of which reflected both objective possibilities and subjective interpretations of what was necessary and feasible for reaching the main goal.

Since the early 1950's, the leaders of Communist China have decided to aim high and boldly: their first goal is to surpass Great Britain's industrial development, but they add their intention "to leave Britain and even the whole capitalist world behind" once a "socialist industrial China, mighty, prosperous and unshakeable" has been established. While taking Britain's outputs as their first target, the Chinese naturally and continuously compare their own problems, solutions and achievements with those of the U.S.S.R. during its own industrialisation drive. Both countries are vast in size, both started from very low levels of development, and both have the same ultimate goal. But if the ultimate goals of the two giant Communist powers are identical, their strategies differ significantly. This is due not only to crucial differences in factor endowments but also to subjective interpretations concerning the utilisation of peasant manpower in the process of industrialisation, the "optimal" correlation between the growth rates of industrial and agricultural outputs, the ways of spreading modern technology in a vast and extremely backward economy, and planning principles and methods. The rationale of the two strategies is of interest, I believe, for those who follow not only developments in the Communist bloc but also the efforts at industrialisation of all newly emerging nations. . . .

. . .

When the U.S.S.R. was launched on the path of all-out industrialisation in 1928, the U.S. was producing 16.9 times the U.S.S.R.'s coal output, 11.8 times its pig-iron output, 12.2 times its steel and 20.0 times its electricity. In agriculture the U.S. produced 1.4 times the Soviet output of wheat, 1.1 times of rye, 1.8 times of barley, and 1.3 times the output of oats. The Soviet per capita outputs ranked much lower because the U.S.S.R. had a population of over 150 million as against less than 120 million in the U.S.; the per capita income was probably 5.3 times higher in the U.S. than in the U.S.S.R.

Not being plagued by insuperable problems of natural resources—except locational problems—the Soviet Union could rapidly erect a new, modern industrial and military structure on a rather limited domestic foundation. In 1928 its industrial plant consisted of a total of 9,190 "large" enterprises with an installed capacity of 2.5 million H.P. and a gainfully employed total of some 2.2 million. Within these totals, the producer goods industries —fuel and power, iron and steel, machine construction, chemicals and building materials—included only 3,019 plants with 1.4 million H.P. and 1.2 million workers. Small industry, including handicrafts, employed some 3.9 million workers, 76.2% of whom were in rural areas. On this foundation only, and for a long time with very limited imports of machinery and equipment from abroad, the Soviet leadership built a respectable industrial and military power in some twelve years (1928–1940).

While the rural population was 4.4 times as large as the urban population, the Soviet leaders placed the former, from the early 1930's on, within the tight organisational framework of peasant collectives, a framework which made the peasant a residual claimant to his own output and allowed both a sharp step-up in the rate of savings in agriculture and the channelling of most of these savings by the state into the planned expansion of heavy industry. The Soviet leaders regarded the peasants as a passive element to be dragged along while the process of industrialisation proceeded to reach full speed. The peasants were to be a docile ally, patiently cooperating with the state, while a growing army of industrial workers erected a powerful industry—a mighty industry of producer goods. After the development of industry on a large scale, peasant agriculture and the villages would be deeply changed: the expanding domestic producer goods industry would mechanise fully all agricultural work, while cheaply re-equipped consumer goods industries would cover all mass-consumption needs.

Notwithstanding the general acceptance of the idea that the peasantry could not change in any significant way through its own efforts, divergent views arose as to what was both feasible and appropriate in order to accelerate the industrialisation of the country. Three main positions emerged during the Soviet debates carried on during the mid-1920's regarding the rate of growth, the intensity of industrialisation, the strategy of development and the principles and methods of planning.

Some economists, such as Lev Shanin, affirmed that in a backward country like the U.S.S.R. the most rapid industrialisation would be achieved through a rapid rise of agricultural productivity. Massive channelling of investment into this sector, and the ensuing expansion of output, would guarantee rapidly increasing savings which could subsequently be channelled into industry. The growth of agriculture would expand capabilities for importation of equipment from abroad and would at the same time secure adequate raw materials for domestic light industry. All this, added Shanin, would prevent the disruption of trade between town and countryside, would further the processes of urbanisation and industrial growth, and would in time allow the growth of a domestic heavy industry, providing for uninterrupted and harmonious development.

The second position on the way to achieve industrialisation was formulated by N. Bukharin, leader of what later became the Right wing of the party. Bukharin stressed the need of developing industry (light as well as heavy) and agriculture simultaneously. According to him, industry and the towns depended both on agricultural supplies and on the rural market; since agriculture needed producer as well as consumer goods from the towns, Bukharin rejected the postponement of the development of producer goods industries which was implied in Shanin's reasoning.

The third position taken in the debate was propounded by the so-called Left wing of the party. The Left emphasised, for both political and economic reasons, what it called "the dictatorship of industry" and the absolute primacy of heavy industry in any rapid, autarkic economic development. In a crucial document of the 1920's E. A. Preobrazhenski, the economic spokesman of the Left, affirmed that the rapid industrialisation of the country and the mechanisation of its agriculture—in Soviet parlance, the shifting of the national economy as a whole onto a higher technological level—could be achieved only if a massive and sustained effort was made to develop the domestic producer goods industries. Asserting that the existing under-development forced a skewed type of growth—with industry expanding faster than agriculture, and heavy industry expanding faster than light industry—Preobrazhenski affirmed that for a long period agriculture would have to pay a "tribute" to industry as the lever for the rapid economic transformation of the country as a whole.

After hesitating between the Right and the Left position, Stalin finally chose to implement the latter, while smashing both factions politically. In order to force the peasants to cooperate with the bureaucracy and the industrial workers, that is, "to feed them gratis while building up Soviet industry" (to use the apt expression of L. E. Hubbard), Stalin's party-state machine forcibly collectivised the peasants within a few short years. At the height of the drive, during the first three months of 1930, millions of peasants were forced into collectives, and in the process an enormous amount of rural capital was annihilated.

The basic characteristics of the Soviet strategy of development are by now quite familiar. Throughout the all-round planning era opened at the turn of 1928, the Russians systematically allocated from 40 to 50% of all their investible resources to industry, 80% of which were in turn concentrated in heavy industry and particularly in the "key" group of electricity, iron and steel and machinery construction. The most advanced technological processes were introduced on a large scale in this group, while the lowest priorities in investment were assigned to light industry and agriculture. The Russians did introduce tractors into agriculture when they proceeded to collectivise it—in part to offset the losses of draft animals killed by the peasants during this forced drive; but even after the introduction of tractors on a large scale, many aspects of agricultural work and of livestock husbandry remained highly labour intensive and farming continues to absorb, up to now, close to half of the total labour force.

Since 1928 no debates on this path of development have taken place in the U.S.S.R. While at certain times—in 1953 particularly—the rate of investment has briefly been brought into question, a massive shift in the basic pattern of investment chosen in the late 1920's has never been advocated. The Soviet literature on growth presents this pattern of allocation as the embodiment of "universal laws" of economic development, and presents the Soviet economic strategy and planning procedure as a model valid for any underdeveloped area—*a fortiori* for Communist-led backward countries.

Compared with China at the beginning of its industrialisation drive in 1952, the U.S.S.R. produced at the inception of its accelerated industrialisation process, in 1928, 1.7 times China's pig-iron output, 3.3 times its steel, 1.5 times its coke, and 29.0 times its oil output. In relation to the production levels of the industrial giants, China's industrial posture was even more precarious than that of Russia in the 1920's. To take some basic intermediate products, Great Britain, the U.S.S.R. itself and the U.S. produced in 1952, 5.7, 6.3 and 30.2 times China's pig-iron output; 12.8, 16.8 and 65.0 times its steel; 6.2, 5.6 and 22.1 times its coke; 65.2 times (U.S.S.R.) and 784.5 times (U.S.) its oil; and 8.8, 11.4 and 64.5 times, respectively, its electricity.

.   .   .

The Chinese Communists shaped their strategy of industrialisation not in open debates—as did the Russians in the mid-1920's—but in closed meetings of their top leadership. We cannot, therefore, ascertain the alternatives which were rejected. Scattered references to "impatience of leftists" and to "conservatism of the rightists" indicate the existence of divergences and strains, but there is as yet no way of examining the proposals and views of the defeated.

In terms of the Soviet debates on a strategy of development, the Chinese approach comes closest to Bukharin's preoccupation with both agricultural supply and peasant demand, his insistence that the countryside needs both agricultural machinery and manufactured goods of mass consumption,— i.e., the products of both heavy and light industry—and his understanding that the limits of industry's growth are directly governed by the growth of the output of grain, cotton, hides, wool and flax. But the Chinese have acted to further industrial and agricultural output simultaneously in a way not clearly perceived in the 1920's. They understood—as Professor Nurkse put it—"that the state of disguised unemployment implies at least to some extent a disguised saving potential as well" and that the use of rural "unproductive" labour for work on capital projects, fed by the rural "productive" labourers, would transform the latter's "virtual" savings into "effective" saving. They opted for technological dualism, i.e., for the simultaneous development of two industrial sectors, a modern, capital-intensive one based on fixed factor proportions and a small scale, labour-intensive one based on variable factor proportions. Conditions for implementing this "Nurkse cum Eckaus model of economic development," as Professor Eckstein has rightly called it, were in preparation from the early 1950's.

Throughout the 1950's the Chinese hoped that the small-scale sector would be able to cope with the needs of agriculture for both implements and consumer goods, so that the largest part of the centralised investments could be fed massively into the modern sector. For a while the two emphases—on heavy industry and on multi-purpose developments in agriculture—were not in conflict, since the scarce inputs they claimed were in many respects dissimilar. But the Chinese could not seriously hope either for a continuous "orderly advance" on all sectors—since the planners and organisers were dealing with numerous unknowns in this phase of the economy's development—or for a lasting separation between the modern sector and the rest of the economy, because small-scale industry could not be expected to provide the machinery with which to mechanise agriculture. The advance in all directions proceeded often blindly and wastefully; on the other hand, the need to divert a substantial part of the output of the modern sector to the rest of the economy soon became pressing and unavoidable.

Notwithstanding their over-ambitious goals, their ruthlessness, their uncoordinated advance in several competing directions, and their gross miscalculations in planning, the Chinese leaders' approach to economic development exercises today an unmistakable impact particularly in the densely populated, very backward Asian or African areas: this approach may be summed up as reliance on the mobilisation of vast masses of labour for capital construction work in heavy industry, light industry and multi-purpose projects in agriculture; simultaneous expansion of a modern and a small scale industrial sector; postponement of the mechanisation of agriculture until the domestic industry is able to supply a substantial quantity of tractors and fuel. In fact, some of the tenets of the Soviet method of industrialisation—the unstinting emphasis on certain branches and on a certain output mix, the exclusive preference for the most advanced production techniques in the top priority branches and the downgrading of small plants and of handicraft production, the doctrinaire approach to the role of the peasantry in furthering economic growth—are brought under scrutiny even in eastern Europe.

Not withstanding their tight organisational set-up, the Chinese have probably not reached the rates of savings achieved by the Russians—or for that matter, more recently, by other Asiatic countries with special advantages, such as Japan or Burma. The Chinese rate of savings from current output has been only about 16.8% for 1950–1959 as compared to 19.5% for Burma and 28.9% for Japan. These figures, however, exclude the unpaid contributions of the mass mobilisation of under-employed rural labour, contributions which are difficult to evaluate. The crux of the problem is the growth of population and the fact that the planners continue apparently to believe that on balance an expanding population is an asset for a country relying on massive mobilisations of its under-employed rural labour. The failure of agricultural output to grow rapidly may force the planners to become aware of the mounting pressures which the population growth puts on the country's slim savings from current output.

In spite of very significant strides, China is still far removed from its goal, and is still far behind the main industrial countries. While pushing vigorously ahead in the development of certain basic intermediate products China still has to catch up with Great Britain, not to speak of the U.S.S.R. at the latter's level of 1940. Even after a spectacular growth in steel output in 1960, Great Britain, the U.S.S.R. and the U.S. exceeded the steel output of China 1.3, 3.5, and 4.8 times; moreover, China is far behind in some crucial modern industries, such as nucleonics, electronics and plastics. In agriculture, in spite of the turn toward mechanisation, by the beginning of the 1960's China possessed only as many tractors as Russia did in the early 1930's. But the Chinese leadership does have the ruthless power to rely on massive mobilisation for carrying out the further industrialisation of the country.

The Chinese profited from Soviet errors; e.g., they avoided pushing the peasants into collectives before an active psychological and organisational campaign had been undertaken. But they have committed new and no less disastrous errors of their own; e.g., overstraining and physically exhausting their human resources, blunting agricultural incentives, overestimating the results achieved, and drawing erroneous sowing plans. The current "New Course" is, however, not likely to cripple indefinitely their advance, though growth will necessarily continue to be both "unstable and subject to periodic setbacks" because the Chinese economy is still strongly tied to a backward agriculture, and because it depends now almost exclusively on its national resources to further industrialisation.

Josip Broz Tito

40 CONSTRUCTION AND CONTRADICTION

Josip Broz Tito, *Forty Years of Revolutionary Struggle of the Communist Party of Yugoslavia* (Belgrade: Publishing House Yugoslavia, 1959), excerpted from pp. 30–37.

On the occasion of the Fortieth Anniversary of the founding of the Communist Party of Yugoslavia, Tito delivered this speech in which he reviewed the problems that Yugoslavia had faced after the war in building up the country, the need to go it alone after the break with Stalin in 1948, and the far-reaching liberalization of the economy and the society which was adopted in 1952. Tito also discussed the major problems which emerged during Yugoslavia's Stalinist phase of development.

It is well known that, at the end of the war, we inherited a completely devastated and plundered country, economically backward, with virtually no industry or advanced agriculture, and with a corresponding social and cultural backwardness. We were without material reserves on which we might have been able to rely, at the beginning, at least for the rebuilding of the country, not to mention the construction of socialism. . . .

What measures was it necessary to undertake, in such an unfavourable situation as that in which we found ourselves at the end of the war, in order to realize the ideals and desires for which hundreds of thousands of our fighters gave their lives? It was necessary gradually to create conditions for the socialist construction of the country, and we unhesitatingly set about this difficult task. It was vital to create, as soon as possible, the economic preconditions for the building of socialism. For this purpose, revolutionary measures were undertaken with regard to social relations; in the first place, all means of production, which until then, although on a limited scale, had served to enrich private owners, were confiscated and placed in the hands of the state; not only the basic means of production, but also the commercial and credit banks, transport and the whole mineral and other wealth of the country were turned over to the state; the agrarian reform was so thoroughly carried out that the creation of capitalist elements in the village became impossible, since the size of the holdings was limited by law to ten hectares.

In the initial period of the construction of our socialist country, the need for the best possible use of very limited material resources and social forces in the building up of the economy, the inadequate training of the working class and the working people in general, the lack of specialized bodies for the implementation of economic tasks and other causes and conditions, demanded centralized control and management of the production process, as well as detailed planning of production of the execution of planned tasks.

These conditions and tasks demanded the strengthening and expansion of the leading role of the Communist Party in the government apparatus and the more direct guidance of the activities of this apparatus. In these very difficult initial conditions of construction, the members of the Party once more loyally carried out their tasks.

With great efforts, the economy was rebuilt. By the building of new, large, industrial and power capacities, the foundations were laid of the socialist economy, which became the paramount factor in our country.

The country's social structure was also changed. The working class has greatly increased in number as a result of the large influx of workers from the villages into industry; the percentage of the peasant population has fallen from 76 per cent before the Second World War, to something over 50 per cent.

The building up of the economy and the political and cultural activities played their part in the very rapid raising of the political and cultural level of the masses. Thus the necessary conditions were formed for the strong creative drive of the working people.

The Communist Party strengthened numerically and organizationally, qualifying itself for the execution of complex tasks—for the direction of the process of the construction of socialist Yugoslavia. Even under conditions when its direct management of the government mechanism was a necessity, it paid constant attention to the need for the closest possible links with the masses, continually stressing the importance of and the need for democratic forms in the mechanism of government authority.

The mass social organizations—the People's Front, Trade Unions, USAOJ and others—became a force, numbered in millions, which also showed great initiative in the solution of the economic, political, social and cultural tasks of rebuilding and construction. The great energy shown by these organizations was not the result of their passively carrying out the directives of the Party, but stemmed from the fact that their aims and activities were in complete accord with aims and activities of the Party, which means that the programme of the Party became their own programme and the aims of the Party their own aims.

However, the excessively important role of the state apparatus in the management of the economy and other fields of social life, under conditions of still great economic and other backwardness, the high degree of concentration of authority in the central organs of state and the direct management of the state mechanism by the Party, resulted in the spontaneous appearance of certain negative phenomena: bureaucracy, the danger of the Party and state apparatuses merging, the danger of the government apparatus becoming too independent and thus placing itself above society, the danger of the social and political workers becoming administrators and of turning the working man into the mere executioner of directives, instead of making him an active and conscious participant in socialist construction, and so on. All this threatened to bring about the separation of the political leadership from the masses and was leading to the stagnation of the creative initiative of the workers and the stagnation in social and economic life. But the tendency towards bureaucratic distortion and the merging of the Party with the administrative apparatus did not originate on our soil, despite the economic backwardness of our country, but was transplanted from abroad, as an ideological and material influence of Stalinist practice, by copying everything from that practice. This resulted in considerable damage to our economic development.

Although the Yugoslav Revolution, by its constant underlining of the need for democratization and of our specific character, resisted bureaucratic degeneration, the complete meaning and danger of bureaucratism only became clear to us through the conflict with Stalin and resistance to his pressure. Hegemony revealed itself as the foreign manifestation of bureaucratism, and the internal bureaucratic elements as its active support in the endangering of the achievements of the revolution and socialist development.

Thus the conflict with bureaucratism on the foreign plane imposed the need for radically clearing out the bureaucratic elements in the country. The predictions of Marx, Engels, and Lenin that the socialist revolution would be threatened not only with the restoration of capitalism, but also by bureaucracy, has been borne out in the experience of our development. . . .

The Communist Party of Yugoslavia understood in time the need for a decisive struggle against the dangers of bureaucratic deformations and also the necessity of preventing them by the introduction of measures for the creation of new relations in production and social life.

In 1949 and 1950, the Party undertook a whole series of new steps directed towards the creation of a new economic and social system.

Measures were undertaken towards decentralization, the limitation of the functions and competence of the central organs and the reduction of their apparatus. The role of the local government bodies was increased (by the Law on People's Committees, 1949), and the direction was clearly laid down towards democratization, the establishment of social self-government and the transference of the functions of management from the central government to the republic, district and municipal bodies.

Together with this, decisive steps were undertaken against the tendency of the Party and state apparatuses to merge. The view was stressed that the leading role of the Party and its members could not be a social privilege, but the result of social, political and ideological activity, and it was emphasized, at the same time, that by this the responsibility of Communists for the successful development of socialism was not diminished but attained even greater importance.

Changes were carried out in the methods of economic planning, and conditions were gradually prepared for freer and more independent action by socialist economic factors. The social and economic interests of the working class were expressed, above all, in various measures: the abolition of rationing, the gradual transference to a freer market, the introductions of the element of economic stimulus in working collectives, and so on.

The passing of the Law on Workers' Management in 1950, marked another big step forward in the development of a socialist democracy. This clearly paved the way for the further development of socialist, social relations in our country. . . .

Our social development after the Sixth Congress [November 1952] showed tremendous results. However, its movement was not in a straight line. It was developing through a process of contradictions, out of which negative, accompanying phenomena appeared that had to be overcome.

The basic contradiction was that encountered in the building of the system of a socialist economy, expressed as a contradiction between the need for the completion of "key capital projects" and the need for decentralizing financial resources and giving greater freedom to the independent socialist economic factors, the working collectives and communes, in the disposal of these resources. The tasks of completing the key projects demanded great economic effort and the concentration of financial resources in a narrow economic sector, as well as the retarding of the development of a whole series of branches of production and the living standard of the masses. The conditions under which this was carried out, particularly between 1949 and 1954, were the most difficult in the postwar period in our country.

The second contradiction resulted from the undeveloped socialist consciousness and from the need that, in the conditions of advanced forms of democratic management in the economy and society, this consciousness should be such as would enable our whole social development to move more rapidly along the road towards the development of socialist relations. The inadequately developed socialist consciousness led to the emergence of unsocialist attitudes towards the disposition of social resources and appearances of particularism and localism, while in the ideological and political fields it occasionally expressed itself as petty bourgeois anarchism.

In the process of carrying out the line laid down by the Sixth Congress, through the struggle and creativeness of the working masses, under the leadership of the League of Communists of Yugoslavia, these negative tendencies were successfully overcome, and the basic features of a new social, economic and political system have been constructed.

Bibliography

U.S.S.R.

Baykov, A., *The Development of the Soviet Economic System.* New York: The Macmillan Company, 1946.

Dobb, M., *Soviet Economic Development since 1917.* New York: International Publishers Co., Inc., 1948.

Erlich, A., *The Soviet Industrialization Debate: 1924–1928.* Cambridge, Mass.: Harvard University Press, 1960.

Gerschenkron, A., *Economic Backwardness in Perspective.* Cambridge, Mass.: Harvard University Press, 1963.

Jasny, N., *The Socialized Agriculture of the U.S.S.R.* Stanford, Calif.: Stanford University Press, 1949.

Maynard, J., *Russia in Flux.* New York: The Macmillan Company, 1948.

Spulber, N., *Soviet Strategy for Economic Growth.* Bloomington, Ind.: Indiana University Press, 1964.

————, *Foundations of Soviet Strategy for Economic Growth: Selected Soviet Essays: 1924–1930.* Bloomington, Ind.: Indiana University Press, 1964.

Swianiewicz, S., *Forced Labour and Economic Development: The Experience of Soviet Industrialization.* New York: Oxford University Press, Inc., 1965.

CHINA

Adler, S., *The Chinese Economy.* London: Routledge & Kegan Paul, Ltd., 1957.

Barnett, A. D., *Communist Economic Strategy: The Rise of Mainland China.* Washington, D.C.: National Planning Association, 1959.

Eckstein, A., *Conditions and Prospects for Economic Growth in Communist China.* Cambridge, Mass.: Massachusetts Institute of Technology Press, 1954.

Li, C., *Economic Development of Communist China.* Berkeley, Calif.: University of California Press, 1959.

EASTERN EUROPE

Sanders, I. T., ed., *Collectivization of Agriculture in Eastern Europe.* Louisville, Ky.: University of Kentucky Press, 1958.

Chapter Eight

Operational Characteristics and Problems of Communist Economies

The outstanding economic fact about the Soviet Union is its achievement in creating a substantial and impressive industrial base. Rapid industrialization has helped to make it a global power, a feat China seeks to emulate. Though the decades since the introduction of the First Five-Year Plan in 1929 have been harsh and trying, the Soviet leadership has in large measure realized its objectives—to transform and modernize Soviet society, to overcome Soviet economic weakness and military vulnerability *vis-à-vis* the capitalist countries, and to improve the standard of living. By instituting a system of central economic planning and allocation of resources, and by restricting consumption, new housing, and welfare services, the regime was able to invest a high proportion of the national income in industrial plant. This "primitive accumulation of capital," i.e., the construction of physical plant and infrastructure, was accomplished ruthlessly at enormous human and economic cost. Much that had been built during the 1930's was destroyed during World War II, but by 1950 the Soviet economy had regained pre-war production levels.

Post-Stalin leaders have faced a different problem: the need to maximize efficiency and productivity. They are confronted with different types of resource and investment problems. Because the economy is more complex than in the 1930's and 1940's, when priority was easily given to the expansion of physical plant, particularly for heavy industry, the guidelines are less clear. On one occasion, Khrushchev ridiculed the economic planners for "wearing steel blinkers," for wastefully continuing to accord top priority to steel at a time when the chemical industry, for example, was lagging far behind the needs of the economy. The industrial machine is available (Reading 41), but how can it be made to function most efficiently? The eminent Soviet mathematician, L. V. Kantorovich, "estimates that the introduction of more rational methods of economic planning and administration would raise Soviet industrial output by as much as 50 per cent without additional inputs."[1] Aware of the shortcomings of their planning mechanism, the Soviets have moved forcefully to improve it. For example, mathematical economics, long in disrepute as un-Marxist, is again coming into favor. Particular attention has been accorded to input-output analysis (a technique for obtaining a comprehensive mathematical picture of the economy in terms of a series of equations relating the output, or production, of an enterprise or industry to the input, or resources, required for that production) and to linear programming (a mathematical method facilitating the solution of intricate problems of economic operations). Both techniques require electronic computers, which are still in short supply despite increased investment by the State Committee on Automation and Machinery Building.

To cope with the intricate and interrelated economic problems, three general approaches have been used in ever-changing combinations: (1) frequent reorganizations of industry and agriculture; (2) a differentiated and manipulated incentive system; and (3) hortatory appeals to idealism and patriotism. During the 1953–1965 period, when reorganization was being stressed, there were a number of accomplishments. It must be noted, however, that in the Soviet Union, and indeed in all communist societies, administrative tinkering is not without political content. Soviet leaders may agree on the need for reforms, but there are usually divergent views of the proper character and timing of the reforms, which are, in turn, linked to the continual jockeying for political power. Though the secretiveness of political struggle in the Soviet Union makes a precise charting impossible, it is reasonable to assume that positions on economic questions bear a close relationship to intra-Party alignments and factions.

Several examples may be cited. In May 1957, Nikita S. Khrushchev, First Secretary of the Central Committee of the CPSU, reorganized Soviet industry by transferring considerable control from the central ministries in Moscow to approximately 100 newly established regional administrative areas (*Sovnarkhozes*). Industry had been organized along product or sectoral lines, and control concentrated in one All-Union Ministry in Moscow; Khrushchev reorganized it along geographical lines which, not unfortuitously, coincided roughly with territorial subdivisions coming un-

---

[1] Leon Smolinski, "What Next in Soviet Planning?" *Foreign Affairs*, XLII, No. 2 (July, 1964), 603.

der the authority of regional first secretaries who were mostly Khrushchev appointees.

There were also cogent economic reasons for this industrial reorganization of 1957. The ministries had become veritable independent empires, annexing to themselves all the sources of supply needed to meet their production quotas without regard for the requirements and problems of other ministries or sectors of the economy. This *departmentalism* bred insularity and promoted an economically irrational use of resources. Khrushchev noted that since each ministry was concerned only with its own supply problems, it was not uncommon to have materials transported thousands of miles, even though in the immediate locality ample supplies were available under the control of another ministry which would not part with its surplus materials for fear of running short at some future time. This *hoarding* led to uneconomic and inflated inventories, statistical duplicity, and gross waste, the inevitable consequences of a system in which ministries were production-oriented, not cost-oriented, and in which production quotas were cast in physical, not price, terms. Khrushchev also criticized the excessive *bureaucratism* that abounded. Innovation and initiative diminished; indeed, were often discouraged, as communication between the center and the factory became more cumbersome and time-consuming. Clearly, some economic reform was required. But its ultimate form, i.e., the particular cluster and timing of the alternatives adopted, was intimately related to Khrushchev's triumph over his principal competitors, Malenkov, Kaganovich, Molotov, and others.

The 1957 industrial reorganization reapportioned political as well as economic power. The regional Party secretaries, who generally supported Khrushchev, gained the upper hand over the local managerial elite, who previously had been a major source of political power to those controlling the central ministries. In retrospect, it is possible that, in the 1953 division of authority, Malenkov *preferred* to be Premier rather than First Secretary of the Party because domination of the 52 central ministries (25 were abolished by the 1957 reform) may have seemed then the more promising avenue to full political power.

In February 1962, the country was consolidated, this time into 17 economic regions. The original 1957 reorganization had given rise to a diffusion of decision making and to *localism,* which is the placing of local interests above those of the nation. Each of the 100-odd economic regions had begun to compete for scarce capital and resources, much as had the central ministries before 1957. A major reform was instituted in November 1962. However, as far as can be determined, this reform was intended primarily as an administrative corrective, a larger regional operational and planning unit being necessary for optimal efficiency. No major struggle for power seems to have been at stake. In October 1964, however, the frequent economic reorganizations were a factor in the deposal of Khrushchev by his "own" lieutenants, who had become gravely concerned over the deleterious and disruptive effects that these were having on the economy, the administrators, and the Party.

In September 1965, the Central Committee approved a series of extensive economic reforms that called for the abolition of the *sovnarkhozes* which were established by Khrushchev in 1957 and the reinstitution of a ministerial system of industrial administration. Though linked with measures designed to stimulate the initiative of factory managers, these reforms signify a possible shift in the power alignment in the Central Committee. It is yet too early to foresee the effect of the reforms on the decentralization-centralization issue.

Frequent reorganizations are perhaps endemic and inevitable under the Soviet system because they are so often linked with the struggle for power and because the regime is constrained by its ideology and political values from discarding centralized control and planning. The commitment to "social engineering" confronts the leadership with a basic dilemma: How can effective Party control over industry be maintained without intruding a political influence that hinders management from achieving maximum economic performance? In practice, the line between a recommendation and a directive from a local Party official is a thin one—undefined and ever-shifting—and engenders administrative confusion. The establishment, in 1959, of special Party control commissions in Soviet factories has helped somewhat, but the conflict between managerial responsibilities and Party authority remains. Quite common are "family circles," which involve collusion among local Party, government, and management officials to conceal irregularities and corruption.

Successful though the innovations and improvements effected by the periodic administrative reorganizations have been, each Soviet leadership has comprehended also the logic of arguments for an improved *incentive system* as a way to achieve greater efficiency, goods of higher quality, and more economical production. Illustrative of this second approach to the problem of raising production and productivity has been the introduction by the post-Khrushchev Soviet leadership of some of the proposals of Yevsei G. Liberman, Professor of Economics at Kharkov University. "Libermanism," as the plan put forth in 1962 by the Soviet economist has come to be known, is an ambitious and far-reaching attempt to restructure the system of incentives; it seeks to make the entire price and planning mechanism more orderly and economically rational. Liberman suggested that the central planning authorities continue to set the quantitative or physical production targets, the assortment of output, and the delivery schedules to be achieved by the different sectors, but that the individual factory manager be permitted more leeway in fulfilling his quotas and setting the general investment pattern of the factory. The "what" would be determined by the political leaders; the "how" by the managers. Bonuses for management and higher wages for the workers would be determined, not by mere fulfillment of physical quotas but by the actual profit level (to be fixed for each industry). Because of widespread misconceptions regarding the Liberman proposals, it may be appropriate to cite the views of one American economist who emphasizes the fact that:

> . . . the Kharkov professor did not submit a program intended to replace central planning by the automatic functioning of market forces. The major economic objectives were still to be determined by the central planning agency. Increased freedom for managers to make subsidiary plans, a more meaningful price structure, and an enhanced role for profits *at the enterprise level*—these all were to be instituted for but one purpose: the more efficient performance of the tasks prescribed by the government.[2]

In early 1965, the regime announced that some 400 textile, clothing, and footwear factories would go over to a new basis of production: goods would be produced to fill orders received directly from retail outlets, profits would be established by the enterprise itself, and the profits earned by the enterprise would be the basis of its reward. This innovation is a limited form of Libermanism.

There are two distinct aspects to the over-all economic problem of devising a suitable incentive mechanism: the problem of providing more adequately for the consumer (Libermanism), which affects only a narrow segment of the economy; and the problem of allocating resources for the producers'-goods section of the economy. The latter problem is by far the more crucial and basic. It is the one that Soviet leaders have been most wary of attacking, for it involves a fundamental reevaluation of the Party's role in directing the economy and of the relationship between political power and economic control.

Soviet leaders expect the administrative reforms and the new incentives to spur the economy to new levels of quantitative and qualitative achievement; nevertheless they have not discarded an old standby from the Stalin era: exhortations to those in the population who respond to nonmaterial rewards such as medals and public recognition. The third general approach to raising production, which was introduced during the 1930's when the regime was unable or unwilling to raise living standards for the general population, is designed to stimulate the individual worker to outpace production norms and to promote "socialist competitions" between brigades or factories. Under Komsomol or Party aegis, activists urge workers to overfulfill production targets, holding out the promise of prestige as well as bonuses.

Stakhanovism, which made its debut in 1935 and involved the organiza-

---

[2] Harry G. Shaffer, "Ills and Remedies," *Problems of Communism*, XII, No. 3 (May–June, 1963), 24.

tion of shock brigades of outstanding workers who were encouraged to compete with one another and spur others to new production records, was buttressed by Gaganovism in 1958. Named after Valentina Gaganova, an outstanding worker who voluntarily transferred to a lagging work brigade at a loss of pay in order to raise its production level, it has been hailed as the start of "a great movement for a Communist attitude toward labor," as a demonstration that the Soviet citizen is capable of socialist idealism, and as an indication that workers are not stimulated primarily by material motives. But a large segment of the population will not respond over a long period of time to manipulated moral symbols. The leaders understand this, and while such activities remain a characteristic feature of Soviet life they are to be complemented by material rewards.

Maximum industrial growth is a key Chinese objective, also. Since 1953, industrialization has been promoted by a variety of methods. During the 1953–1957 period, material incentives were generally stressed: bonuses, piece-rate wage systems, and so forth. Desirous of maintaining a very high rate of capital investment—about 20 per cent of national income—and confronted with a deterioration in relations with the Soviet Union, Peking embarked in 1958 on an accelerated program of socialist transformation. Material incentives yielded to nonmaterial incentives, replete with socialist competitions, socialist emulations, and exhortations. Communal organizations and communal living were forcibly established; even backyard steelmaking was briefly encouraged. The masses were called upon to sacrifice for socialism. But inefficiency and waste grew, and the leadership shifted back, in 1961, to a system emphasizing incentives. According to one Western economist, "The fundamental dilemma still faces them: to raise output material incentives must be heightened and consumption increased, but increased consumption means reduced capital accumulation—a reversal of basic communist economic strategy."[3]

The establishment of the People's Liberation Army style of "political departments" in factories and enterprises, in 1964 and 1965, signified a tightening of discipline and a return to revolutionary *élan* as a way of exacting more from the workers while keeping consumption low (Readings 42 and 43). It also aimed at coping with wide-spread corruption, especially in the countryside, which remains relatively immune from day-to-day Party control. To reach the stage where it can "take off" economically, the leadership has embarked on a program of Stalinizing China's society and economy.

Yugoslavia, which elected to stress efficiency rather than control, has reached a level of economic decentralization unrivalled anywhere in the communist world (Reading 45). But eddies of change are appearing

---

[3] Charles Hoffmann, "Industrial Work-Incentives in Communist China," *Current Scene*, II, No. 13 (May 1, 1963), 11.

througnout Eastern Europe. After two years of discussion, Czechoslovakia, for example, seems about to alter its rigidly centralized planning and production system. Under the new plan, individual enterprises will determine their own production within state-approved limits. Thus, once again, as so often in the past, Czech authorities appear ready to follow in Moscow's footsteps. They say that:

> Except in special cases, every enterprise will have to pay its own way. Its gross income will consist of the proceeds from the sale of its products after the costs of materials, transport, and amortization have been deducted. From its gross income each enterprise will cover its capital investment, interest charges, credit repayments, and payments to the State. What remains will constitute the wage fund. While basic wages will have to conform to national wage policies, the enterprise will be free to grant bonuses according to the level of its own earnings.
>
> While price policy will continue to be set centrally, the present rigid price system will be replaced by one which will adapt more readily to supply and demand. There will be fixed prices for raw materials, power, and basic necessities, minimum and maximum prices for some commodities, and, for a limited range of goods, free prices which will be determined entirely by market conditions.[4]

In addition, subsidies for inefficient plants are scheduled for elimination, and central planning is to be placed on a suggestive not prescriptive basis. It remains to be seen how drastically Czechoslovak communism will in fact move in the direction of economic overhauling.

In Hungary, in 1964, the regime took the significant non-Marxist step of charging factories 5 per cent interest on the gross value of their net worth. It was the first Soviet-bloc country to adopt on a national scale a policy that Yugoslavia had introduced in 1961. The purpose is to reduce waste and hoarding, and utilize labor and capital more efficiently. As part of its quest for a larger share of non-communist world markets, the Kadar regime has initiated a number of reforms to improve the quality of Hungarian manufactures. Managerial personnel are no longer appointed solely on the basis of Party loyalty. In Kadar's view, "He who is not against us is with us." On this basis, professionally competent non-Marxists are being entrusted with responsible positions if they can help the economy.

By contrast, in Poland, where liberalization in 1956–1957 had proceeded further than anywhere else in Eastern Europe except Yugoslavia, the Party leadership has moved cautiously in recent years to reestablish tighter controls in an effort to end the poor performance of various sectors of the economy (Reading 44).

For the student of politics the recent economic developments in the

---

4 *Prague News Letter,* November 7, 1964.

communist world raise a number of important questions: Are gross inefficiencies and waste an institutionalized aspect of a centrally planned and controlled economy? Will these economies evolve toward greater decentralization? Will China be able to avoid the economic ills that have plagued Soviet planners and Party leaders? Will increasing reliance on market techniques along the lines of the Liberman proposals have political consequences? Will the quest for greater *economic* rationality necessarily have consequences for the *political* decisions and development of society? How far can a communist economy be decentralized without placing in jeopardy the traditionally central political role and control of the communist Party?

The failures of repeated reorganizations and inadequate incentives have nowhere been more glaring and protracted than in the field of agriculture (Readings 46, 47, 48). No communist country, although Rumania may become the first, has yet developed into a major producer of surplus food. Farm yields are low for many reasons: insufficient investment; lack of chemical fertilizers; low level of mechanization; meager research; bureaucratic controls which engender widespread resentment; uncooperative weather (the droughts and floods which have afflicted communist countries in recent years could be overcome by vast irrigation and flood control projects, but this would require a far higher level of investment than communist countries have been willing to allocate); and finally, yields which are low because of the unfavorable socio-political conditions under which collectivization was introduced.

The hostility and apathy of the peasantry have thus far barred the emergence of an efficient and enthusiastic peasantry. In China, for example, agricultural production made spectacular progress from 1950 to 1957. But when the Great Leap Forward was launched in 1958, food production slumped sharply, as the peasants resisted with indifference, inefficiency, and "petty-bourgeois" obstructionism. To accelerate the socialization of the peasantry and to make the most of available rural resources, more than 100 million peasant households were forced in a few months into 26,000 people's communes. Organizational zeal was buttressed by ideological militancy, and excessive egalitarianism, centralization, and activism quickly deprived the peasant of the last vestiges of individualism. As a result, production plummeted, waste and resentment abounded, and equalization of income embittered the disappropriated peasants.

The regime was soon forced to make concessions, retreating by 1960 from the militant phase of the Great Leap to communism. Specifically, it again permitted the peasant to cultivate a small plot of ground for private use, to resume the familiar pattern of family life, and to be relieved of some of the oppressive aspects of regimentation. In practice, there is considerable similarity between the Soviet collective farm and the Chinese commune, although the institutions themselves are based on markedly differing theoretical assumptions.

The peasant poses the greatest challenge for communist regimes. Rooted to the land, accustomed to reaping the tangible benefits of his backbreaking labor, he cherishes his individual plot, lavishing on it care and effort which he begrudges the collectivized sector. He is regarded by the communists as a petty bourgeois who resists change; change, for him, has become synonymous with deprivation, upheaval, and suffering. As a group, the peasant has benefitted least from improved living conditions. He has come to view governmental concessions as short-lived and expedient, as granted only under duress. The resolution of the agrarian problem demands a revised system of rewards and an assurance to the peasant that improvements will not be taken away by the regime in its drive for ideal organizational models. There is a gap in outlook and values which will not soon be bridged. Yet, until communist regimes win the support of the peasantry, they will not be able to shape societies of plenty.

41 OPERATIONAL CHARACTERISTICS OF THE SOVIET ECONOMY

Joint Economic Committee of the Congress, *Dimensions of Soviet Economic Power*, 87th Cong., 2nd sess., 1962 (Washington, D.C.: Government Printing Office, 1962), pp. ix–xiv.

The following is from an essay that served as Introduction for a compendium of reports, submitted to the Joint Economic Committee of the United States Congress, on significant aspects of contemporary Soviet economic developments.

For the purpose of its effective management from a single command post, the economy of the U.S.S.R. has been organized, since the beginning of Soviet rule, along the lines of a military establishment. Economic decisions, large and small alike, are made by agencies of the state, responsible only to the central authorities. Everything, from the volume of steel smelting to the manufacture of rubber pacifiers for babies, is ordered and controlled by a designated commission, ministry, or council, as the case may be, responsible only to the top for the production of the commodity in question. In all cases, the purpose is the same, namely the exclusion of private citizens and groups from direct access to any resources used in the production of goods and services.

Economic enterprise in the Soviet Union is considered too important a matter to be left to "unauthorized" entrepreneurs. State enterprise is total. Presumably, only the central agencies of the state can be entrusted with the secret of the exact schedule of priorities of the regime. As a practical matter, too, when only state agencies are involved in the process, the assortment of output can be more readily controlled or, if necessary, reversed by direct order from the supreme authority. Over the past 45 years, therefore, the political authorities of the country have assumed responsibility for all major decisions in the economic sphere, including the programing of the production of goods and its distribution on the basis of a complex system of directives issued from the center.

This form of organization has made it possible for the political oligarchy to retain in its hands, at all times, the key levers of control necessary to assure a flow of economic goods that will provide added strength for the state—primarily heavy industrial materials, production equipment, and military end products. Inevitably, too, the goals of production and the method of economic management have come to influence each other reciprocally over the years in the U.S.S.R. The continued insistence on a high level of output of the implements of war and maximum expansion of productive capacity in the heavy industries had made necessary the perpetuation of an economy organized on a war footing.

A prominent partisan of the political order of the U.S.S.R., the Polish economist Oskar Lange, has publicly expressed his own carefully weighed judgment of the Soviet economic system, as recently as 1957, in the following words: "I think that, essentially, it can be described as a *sui generis* war economy." His judgment was based, he explained, on the continued predominance of the following features of economic life in the U.S.S.R.: (1) The high degree of centralization of the process of decision-making in all phases of economic activity: planning, investment, materials allocation, and plant management; (2) the centralized disposal of resources on the basis of administratively established priorities; (3) the replacement of economic incentives by political incentives motivating the ruling elite. Broadly speaking, he characterized the economy of the U.S.S.R. as "a highly politicized economy, both with regard to the means of planning and management, as well as the incentives it utilizes."

This characterization has probably come as no surprise to the Soviet leaders, who are well aware of the conditions under which their production system works. They know that their own overriding long-term political goals have impelled them to employ this cumbersome wartime method of economic decisionmaking. The only alternative to this method is a system of decentralized decisions, in which the current needs of the population would inevitably emerge as the prime source of influence on the pattern of production. From their viewpoint, this would mean a calamitous surrender to the status quo. It would involve a decision to stand by and watch the whole elaborate mechanism of economic controls, built into a vast patchwork apparatus since the civil war years, slip out of the hands of the history-minded oligarchy and fall under the influence of nonpolitical groups and organizations concerned with the immediate needs of production and distribution for the welfare of the citizen.

Under the prevailing system, however, the same closed circle of party chieftains who enjoy a monopoly of political power in the U.S.S.R. also exercise absolute authority over the economic assets of the nation. In order to stimulate the growth of "hard" lines of production at a forced pace, the Soviet leaders begin by extracting an unusually high rate of savings from current consumption. This is clearly reflected in the allocation pattern developed by the regime. In 1960, for example, 31.3 per cent of the gross national product of the U.S.S.R. was allocated to investment, as compared with a proportion of 17.9 per cent in the United States. Once this huge investment fund is accumulated (equal to $42 billion), it is so distributed as to channel some 40 per cent of all new capital into industry. Furthermore, when it comes to allocating shares within industry, the branches devoted to capital goods production receive 88 per cent of all new industrial investments, leaving only 12 per cent for the branches producing consumer goods.

Much in the same vein, the regime deploys the labor force of the industrial sector with a strong bias in favor of the heavy branches of production. Seventy per cent of all workers in industry are employed in the production of capital goods destined for the expansion of plant capacity rather than for the output of finished goods for the use of the mass of consumers.

For operational purposes, therefore, the Soviet economy is directed as a single nationwide enterprise, approximately as envisioned by Lenin, with the Presidium (the renamed Politbureau) of the party, serving as its board of directors. The Presidium has assumed for itself exclusive authority for programing the various individual levels of output in the economy under a series of production schedules, called plans, each schedule covering a period of one, five, or more years. These plans are unique, in the sense that they are neither forecasts nor recommendations as is often the case in other countries. Rather, they serve as directives, operational orders, or commands that are legally binding upon all active participants in the production process.

The same central political authority, moreover, finds that the preparation of this type of plan serves as the beginning rather than the end of its involvement in the business of economic administration. Having set up a scale of priorities in national production, by administrative procedures, the political center has to proceed to enforce its choices by taking two more essential steps: (*a*) dividing the total investment pie among the various claimants within the economy, by rank of its strategic importance; and (*b*) allocating, in physical quantities, the whole spectrum of input materials required by the economic enterprises across the country.

Another basic characteristic of the Soviet economy that has a bearing on the outside world is the fact that it is not responsive to the demand for goods generated by the population. Purchasing power in the hands of the public cannot, in the U.S.S.R., influence the pattern of either investment or production. In these critical areas, as elsewhere, only one will prevails, namely the will of the political high command, regardless of what the public wants. The annual investment plans, as prepared by the leadership behind closed doors, continue to stress the expansion to the hilt of facilities for the production of goods considered essential for the economic ambitions of the regime. The goods considered to be "vital" by the regime are typically the means for expanding the industrial base: machine tools, turbines, presses, forges, and rolling mills; not textiles, refrigerators, meat, or automobiles. As a result, the industrial base continues to be expanded, at the highest possible rate, despite the chronic conditions of underproduction in agriculture, housing, consumer goods, child care facilities, retail trade facilities, public services, and other essential needs of the mass of citizens.

The central fact that needs to be borne in mind is that what happened in the economy of the U.S.S.R., following the Communist seizure of power, was not simply that productive property was taken away from private individuals and groups and placed under government ownership. This was merely the formal condition of the establishment of a state-operated economy. What happened, in a fundamental sense, was that, as a direct result of total confiscation, the public itself was forcibly and permanently deprived of all influence over the assortment of goods produced by the economy. Overnight, as it were, all economic affairs of the nation were pulled behind the same curtain of secrecy that shrouded the activities of the political oligarchy in all other spheres. Thereafter, all decisions related to the range of goods to be produced were "off limits" for the public, reserved as the sole, private responsibility of the high command of the Communist Party.

At present, this high command alone determines the basic proportions along which the economic resources of the country are to be distributed, and issues directives to the administrative agencies of the government aimed at the enforcement of these proportions. The supreme leaders of the party apparatus, who also occupy all the key posts in the government structure, do not, it should be noted, consider themselves accountable to the mass of citizens for their authority. They are not in the habit of going to the nation to renew their mandate to govern. They prefer to work with the kind of mandate that cannot be recalled. Accordingly, they claim to have been brought to their position of power by the very force of the process of "history" rather than by the will of a majority of the citizens who make up the nation. And history, they allege, has endowed them with all the authority they need: not only to seize and hold power in their own country, without the consent of the governed, but also to expand the grip of communism to all other independent nations regardless of the expressed intent of the population of these countries.

Under these conditions, the ruling oligarchy has succeeded in effectively destroying the power of the public over the direction of economic development in the U.S.S.R. Given their own scale of priorities, strictly controlled and enforced, money in the hands of the citizen does not give him a vote for a product mix of his own choosing. All that money can give him in these circumstances is the right to roam about the stores, the right to stand in line to buy the kind, the amount, and the quality of goods that the appointed planners have approved for production. In short, they have succeeded in producing a system of public ownership of the means of production in which the public is effectively excluded from the area of decisionmaking in production.

This profound bias against the public will has given rise to a conspicuous paradox in Soviet economic practice. On the one hand, the regime has firmly achieved the ability to plan its own requirements, in military strength and in widening the industrial base in particular, with a high degree of accuracy. The targets in steel or machine tool production, for example, are generally met in full in Soviet long-term plans. At the same time, however, most of the families of the nation have been left without the power to plan their own future, not only in regard to housing, furniture, consumer durables, or location of residence, but also in the procurement of their daily necessities. The question of "what will the stores have today," familiar to all people in time of war, is forever haunting the citizen of the state-dominated economy of the U.S.S.R. The same uncertainty also drives him to the stores every day. He lives in an economy that produces annually one refrigerator per 100 families. Working without a refrigerator, the housewife cannot plan her daily menu; she must depend on what she can find in the store.

The conflict inherent in the commitment of the Soviet leadership to an awe-inspiring military posture commensurate with its worldwide ambitions rather than with the size of its economy emerges into the open from time to time with painful clarity. A recent development may be cited as an illustration. In 1957, Chairman Khrushchev turned the spotlight on a brand new promise to provide a vast increase in meat production, announcing that he expected to catch up with the United States in the per capita output of meat by 1961, at the latest. The promise proved to be immensely popular. The party chieftain undoubtedly enjoyed the pleasant echo of the popular response. At the same time, however, he continued to dispose of the capital resources of the nation in the manner to which he had long become accustomed, assigning the lion's share to heavy industry and military technology. The collective farms, on the other hand, continued to be paid for their meat by the state at a price that fell far short (by 50 per cent) of covering average cost of production. Naturally enough, meat production failed to increase. By mid-1962, it became quite clear that the prices paid by the consumers for meat would have to be raised.

In the upshot, the Communist Party was forced to issue a wordy proclamation to the people, on June 1, 1962, to explain the painful decision. The explanation stressed the obvious fact that it was necessary to improve incentives on the collective farms by paying them higher prices for livestock products. Then, it added, that it was also necessary to pass the burden of higher prices on to the consumer, explaining that the party cannot "transfer funds to this area at the expense of strengthening our defense capability and the expansion of our industry." Whatever happens in this economy, in short, the proportions favored by the oligarchy in the pattern of allocation of resources are not subject to change.

42 POLITICAL WORK FOR ECONOMIC GROWTH

"Political Work is the Lifeline of All Work," *Red Flag* (*Hung-ch'i*), No. 6 (Peking, March 31, 1964), as translated in *Current Scene*, Supplement, I, No. 1 (Hong Kong, 1964). Excerpted from pp. 2–9. Footnote references have been deleted.

In keeping with its recent exhortations to the Chinese people to intensify socialist education, to study the thought of Chairman Mao Tse-tung, and to emulate the loyalty and diligence of the People's Liberation Army, the Party leadership has extended the People's Liberation Army type of political commissar system into offices and areas concerned with economic affairs. This is an extension of a method of dual leadership employed in the armed forces for nearly 40 years. Political commissars have served beside military commanders at all levels of the army to indoctrinate troops and to ensure that it is "the Party which directs the gun" and not "the gun which directs the Party."

On March 31, 1964, the Party Central Committee declared, in its magazine Red Flag, *that politics must be placed in full command of the economy. The article, which was reminiscent of the 1958–1960 Great Leap Forward, when "Politics takes command" was a major slogan and "redness" took precedence over "expertness," sets forth the rationale for the political commissar movement, and promises to have an enormous impact on domestic developments.*

The article indicates that two motives underlie the drive to create a special political network in economic organizations. By reinforcing controls, the Party hopes to halt a disturbing decline in revolutionary ardor and quell the growth of "spontaneous capitalistic tendencies"; it hopes also to stimulate an upsurge in "socialist construction."

Following the seizure of political power by the proletariat, the main task is economic reform and economic construction. We should undoubtedly concentrate our principal energies on economic work and fight for the successful building of socialism and communism. However, it is completely inadequate merely to point out our main tasks. We must not only put forward tasks but also solve the problem of the fulfilment of these tasks. How should economic construction in a socialist country proceed? What are the direction, line and policy in accordance with which economic construction should be conducted? What attitude and viewpoint should we take in dealing with this work? Unless these questions are settled first and settled satisfactorily, the economic tasks will not be fulfilled and a socialist economy will not be built.

This is to say that, as in the past when victory in military struggle was primarily determined by the Party's political leadership, success of socialist economic construction is also primarily determined by Party leadership, by the State leadership of proletarian dictatorship, by the correctness of the Party's lines, principles and policies, and by our ability to deal with problems correctly from the political angle. Here politics remains the supreme commander, the basic guarantee and premise for the fulfilment of economic work.

.   .   .

Lenin said, "The whole question is this (and can only be this from the Marxist viewpoint): If a class does not deal with its problems correctly from the political angle, it will not be able to maintain its rule and consequently cannot solve its production tasks."

The question is quite clear. The socialist economic base must have the service of such a superstructure as socialist politics. Socialist economic construction must be ensured by the systematic political work of the proletarian party.

In the period of socialism, politics and political work play a new, historically unprecedented, special role in relation to the economy and economic work.

First, socialist, communist economy is unlike any other economy. It is not spontaneously generated or spontaneously developed. Socialist economy, an economy which can be created only by a proletarian regime led by the vanguards of the proletariat, the Communist Party, lacks any ready-made germs not only in the old society. Even after the birth of a socialist economy, its consolidation and development and its transition to a communist economy cannot be spontaneous and unplanned, but can take place only through Communist Party leadership and the unified, planned management and adjustment of the proletarian government. To manage and lead a socialist economy, it is necessary to observe and follow the laws of development of socialist economy itself, and only the proletarian party and the proletarian state under its leadership can consciously master the laws of socialist economy and apply them in formulating correct lines and policies. All those who are engaged in economic work in all sectors or the heads of economic departments and units should make the Party's lines and policies the starting point of their every action, consciously execute the Party's lines and policies, and submit themselves to the unified plans of the State, which means submission to the whole by the parts. Such mindfulness of the whole is the political viewpoint. If those engaged in socialist economic work lack such a conscious attitude and mindfulness of the whole, and if this [consciousness and mindfulness] is not ensured by systematic political work, economic work will not be done well. Here any spontaneous action, letting people do what they choose, and departmentalism will seriously harm the cause of socialist construction.

Second, socialist economic construction and transition from socialism to communism proceed in complex circumstances of class struggle. The socialist economic system can be established and developed only in an unceasing struggle against the vestiges of various old forces and the old system. These old forces and ideas which reflect the old system will not give way easily. The struggle will necessarily be protracted and devious. The reason why the proletariat lead the people of the whole country in economic construction is because they want to ensure the fulfilment of the great historic mission which they have taken up, that is, they want to abolish all exploitation, eliminate class distinctions, establish a communist society, and realize the liberation of all mankind. Accordingly, in socialist economic construction, we cannot start from the purely economic viewpoint or that of simple development of productivity. Instead, we must start from the political viewpoint of the proletariat, analyse, with the Marxist-Leninist class viewpoint and method of class analysis, our own circumstances, the situation of economic development, and various trends in economic work, and find the correct way to help the proletariat to overcome the bourgeoisie. On the other hand, the bourgeoisie and all internal and external enemies are trying their utmost to resist and reverse the direction of the development of a socialist economy. With this end in view, they will make the utmost use of all forces of spontaneity, of all forms of a purely economic viewpoint or the viewpoint of economism which is divorced from politics, and of any tendency which would weaken the ideological and political leadership of the proletariat, so that the socialist economy may gradually change its nature and "peaceful economic construction may be changed into peaceful disintegration of the social regime." Therefore, it will be highly dangerous if the economic departments of socialism do not strengthen their political work, fail to give the great numbers of cadres and the masses proletarian political-ideological education, tend to lay emphasis on business rather than politics, incline to the pursuit of only "material incentives," and fail to check the growth of revisionist tendencies.

Third, in its economic construction, a socialist country should firmly carry out the guideline of self-revival through its own efforts, and build and develop socialism by relying on its own labouring people and its own resources. . . .

Comrade Mao Tse-tung has said, "Political work is the lifeline of all economic work. This is so particularly in a period when the social economic system is undergoing radical reform." Obviously, if revolutionary political work is not strengthened in accordance with the principle of having politics lead and command economic affairs throughout the entire period of socialist construction, when this social economic system undergoes radical changes it will be impossible to do our construction work well.

As in the founding of the people's army in the past, when emphasis was placed at the very beginning on building the army on a political foundation, so when our state organized an army for socialist economic construction, Comrade Mao Tse-tung pointed out with equal emphasis that this largest of all armies must be built and regulated on a political basis. He repeatedly reminds us to insist on criticizing the tendency to remain indifferent to politics. On the one hand we must oppose those impractical politicians and on the other hand we must oppose those practical-minded persons who have lost their bearings. By paying no attention to thought and politics but by busying oneself all the time only in business matters, one may become an economist or technologist who has lost his bearings. That is highly dangerous. Ideological work and political work are guarantees for the fulfilment of economic and technical tasks. They serve the economic base. Thought and politics are also the supreme commander and the soul. As soon as our ideological work and political work are slightly relaxed, economic work and technical work will certainly go the wrong way.

Comrade Mao Tse-tung points this out specially: All economic, industrial, agricultural and commercial departments of our state must establish and strengthen political work by emulating the Liberation Army before we can rouse the revolutionary spirit of the millions of cadres and the masses on the entire economic front.

Ralph L. Powell

43 COMMISSARS IN THE ECONOMY: "LEARN FROM THE PLA" MOVEMENT IN CHINA

Ralph L. Powell, "Commissars in the Economy: 'Learn from the PLA' Movement in China," *Asian Survey*, V, No. 3 (March, 1965), 134–38. Footnote references have been deleted.

Ralph L. Powell is Professor of Political Science and program chairman of the School of International Service of American University. He recently did research in the Far East on a Ford Foundation grant.

The campaign to learn from the PLA continued throughout 1964, but it received much less publicity than during the spring. Such "movements" are not meant to be permanent campaigns. They can be revived when needed. Apparently this drive has essentially served its purpose of intensively publicizing the virtues of the armed forces and of informing the cadres regarding aspects of the PLA that should be emphasized in economic institutions. By the fall of 1964 the slogan "Learn from the PLA" had largely been replaced by the theme "Depend on the Poor and Lower-middle Peasants." Nevertheless, at the end of the year Premier Chou En-lai again called on the Party, the government and all cadres to learn from the "thoroughly revolutionary spirit and style of work" of the armed services. The policy of establishing political departments and of increasing political control and activities in economic institutions is obviously meant to be a long-term program. Nevertheless, its durability will probably depend on the degree to which it achieves the Party's multiple objectives.

Official mass media have made exaggerated, as well as some realistic assessments of the effectiveness of the program to learn from the PLA and establish new political departments. Despite a general note of official enthusiasm, the Party press and radio have admitted that there have been some criticisms of the policy and certain faults in its administration. In the application of the "five-good" campaign, some units grasped the concept of "good at production," but neglected the other four "goods," especially the idea of "good in political thought." The military cadres who had been sent to finance and trade departments in 1963 all had "fine" characteristics, but they were not qualified for work in those specialized agencies. There were "some defects" in their activities and they developed "various states of mind." It was necessary to explain to these representatives of the favored PLA that although their new tasks were "common place," they were important. Another report stated that although political cadres had a firm grasp of the routine and administrative aspects of political work, they were "divorced from reality" and it was necessary for them to develop a knowledge of production. It was also admitted that there are natural "contradictions" between political campaigns and the needs of production, as well as between political, administrative and technical personnel, who see things from different angles. The approved solution is for everyone to be broadminded—red and expert. It is considered to be even more important to strengthen the "unified leadership" of the Party committees.

An Appraisal

The leaders of Communist China have adopted a dubious policy that involves economic risks. Outwardly, the concept of nation-wide learning from the armed forces and the establishment of military-style political departments by all elements of the industrial and commercial economy appear to be almost as radical and dogmatic as the ill-fated major campaigns of the Great Leap, and indeed some of the extravagant terminology of the Leap has been employed in the new campaign. Nevertheless, the new drive involves less emotionalism and somewhat greater prudence. The sense of urgency is not as high and the officials and cadres are not being urged to create miracles, as they were in 1958. Furthermore, there are some important limitations on the program. The Party is not again attempting to militarize the whole populace, or even the industrial and commercial elements of the economy. Although there have been references to an industrial army, the policy does not order the already highly regimented economic institutions to adopt the military organization and structure of the armed services, only their political apparatus and techniques. During the Great Leap, the Party tried to militarize the whole adult population, especially the peasants, in a universal labor militia, under the slogan "Everyone a Soldier." That major experiment ended in serious failure.

Also, although the campaign to learn from the armed forces applies to all farm labor and rural organizations, the program to establish PLA-type political sections does not include them, at least not yet. Rural institutions have their own forms of Party machinery. Either the Party leaders realistically judge that a politico-military apparatus is not suitable for the great masses of the peasantry or they prudently believe that the system could not now be effectively applied.

In terms of their own interests there are several positive reasons why the Party leaders adopted the program to learn from the PLA and transplant its political departments. Obviously, by 1963, Mao Tse-tung and his lieutenants were convinced that, outside the Party itself, the armed forces furnished the most advanced form of inculcation and application of the omnipresent "thought of Mao." Also, forms and procedures created for the PLA had largely permitted the Party to close the gap that had developed between its ideological and organizational leadership roles. The revitalized politico-military machinery of the armed services provided in addition a more effective relationship between Party control and professional administration than was true in economic institutions. Finally the Party chiefs believed that not only the system of indoctrination of the PLA, but also its current management practices were superior to those of industry and commerce.

There are also less tangible reasons for the new policy. The official press indicates that the aging Party leaders are worried about the future of their revolution. Being historically minded they are aware of the effect that time has had on other revolutionary and ideological movements. They are disturbed by the subversive influence of "modern revisionism." The impact of traditional Chinese loyalties and customs, as well as what the Party calls "bourgeois remnants," also worry them. In this sense the "Learn from the

PLA" campaign is symptomatic of a state of mind. It is closely related to the tremendous emphasis placed on the "thought of Mao," the great campaign of socialist education and the drive to promote worthy revolutionary successors.

The campaign to learn and borrow from the armed forces has increased the influence and prestige of the PLA. But certainly the new program does not signify a seizure of power by the military, nor does it even indicate that the Party's senior military specialists are now playing a dominant role in the Party. What the new political program does indicate is that the Party now believes that the armed forces are an "obedient tool," whose political machinery and techniques can be transferred to other organizations and whose degree of loyalty and professional competence are worthy of emulation.

Insofar as the program to learn and copy from the PLA represents the desire of the Party to tighten its control over the economy and improve its machinery and techniques for indoctrination in economic institutions, it may be quite successful. Certainly this was true of the application of these apparatus and techniques to the armed forces. The emphasis placed on improving basic-level offices and enterprises seems sound and the Party admits that it is necessary.

However, as the *People's Daily* has stated in a different context, "The army is indeed different from a factory." Forms and procedures that functioned satisfactorily in a military establishment to improve efficiency will not necessarily have the same result in economic institutions or among civilian bureaucrats. Management systems appropriate for a disciplined military establishment will not necessarily operate well in an economic system. It is doubtful that non-material incentives that stimulated self-sacrifice in the armed services will be as effective in shops, factories and banks. The new staffs of political departments and the numerous "instructors" have added thousands of economically non-productive cadres to the already bloated bureaucracy of ministries and enterprises. Their propaganda campaigns and meetings detract from production time. Also, the establishment of a military-type political commissariat has already created friction in economic organizations.

The concept of "Politics in Command," with its connotations of total Party domination and the supremacy of ideological and political considerations, had a disastrous effect on the economy during the Great Leap. So far the present application of this concept has been more restricted and less fanatical than in 1958–60. Still it is a dangerous and tempting policy for a regime as ambitious and ideologically inclined as that of the Communist Party of China.

Furthermore, the constant demands to apply the thought of Mao Tsetung to industry and commerce, as well as to the armed forces, is a dubious prescription for a troubled economy. Most of Mao's important writings were produced in the 1930's and 1940's and were devoted primarily to the revolutionary seizure of power. His extensive works constitute an outstanding revolutionary doctrine, but even some of his military concepts can no longer be effectively applied in a nuclear era. Certainly, the thought of Mao has less applicability to a modernizing economy, even if his views are "flexibly" applied.

Finally, since the policy of learning from the armed services and the program of establishing military-type political departments in economic institutions are attributed to Mao, they officially become part of his "enrichments" of Marxism-Leninism. Hence, they become a part of the Chinese revolutionary model and another variation from "communism" as practiced in the Soviet Union. In the still continuing struggle for the leadership of the international communist movement, such radical concepts provide another distinction and thus a further source of friction between parties.

44 THE PARTY AS MANAGER AND MANIPULATOR: THE POLISH EXPERIENCE

Excerpted from *Economic Problems 1964: Materials and Documents* (Warsaw: Department of Information for Abroad, 1964).

In late November 1963, the Fourteenth Plenum of the Central Committee of the Polish United Workers' Party (Communist Party) was convened to discuss the shortcomings and problems of Poland's economy. Some of the problems discussed have relevance for other countries of Eastern Europe as well.

The tasks of our economic policy mapped out in the present report call for the mobilization of all the forces of the Party, raising its political activeness and forms of Party work to a higher level, as well as improvement of the methods applied by Party authorities managing the national economy, above all, increasing the sense of responsibility for the situation in the national economy of all Party bodies and organizations on all levels. It must be pointed out that a number of Party bodies and authorities, and basic Party organizations, have not conducted a sufficiently energetic campaign to ensure the full implementation of the planned economic targets, in line with the principles of maximum economy, as recommended by the resolutions of the Central Committee. Glaring facts of priority being given to the local interests of an enterprise, an industrial branch or a region are sometimes tolerated. This is seen in failure to bring to light all the existing production reserves, in the endeavours made to bring the production plan down to the minimum and the wages fund up to the maximum, and also in the efforts made to get the maximum investment credits, although these credits are not always earmarked for really indispensable investments.

As regards the policy of the Party in matters of personnel, particularly the evaluation of managerial staff and the promotion of certain people to leading posts in the national economy, more consideration than so far should be given to the results attained by the candidates in their work to date, apart from their vocational qualifications and political merits. The practice of transferring people from one leading post to another if they fail to put the Party directives into practice should be discontinued.

All the basic Party organizations and authorities, and all Party members, must do their best to ensure the implementation of general social targets and explain properly to the personnel and the entire community that the economic policy of the Party is correct, decidedly coming out against any attempts to give priority to local interests over the nation-wide aims.

Along with the unsatisfactory level of propaganda and organizational activity, yet another fact deserves notice in the work of many basic Party organizations and in the attitude adopted by some Party members: the fact of yielding to the tendencies to take a liberal attitude to infringement of the principles of thrifty economy by enterprises and their workers.

The Party activists in their everyday work should show concern for technical progress, for rational management, for thrift and financial discipline, for work discipline. They should actively combat waste of production materials, absenteeism, substandard production, and any liberal attitude towards people neglecting their duties. They should make people realize that all of them are responsible for the work done.

Workers should be informed as to how the enterprises are using the wages fund, who and for what are being awarded prizes and bonuses, what the trend of employment and production costs is, how the plan for the production of various articles is being implemented, what is made of raw materials and production materials, how export production is being developed, how the plan for technical progress is being implemented, what new departments or factories are being put in motion, etc., etc.

At the same time more attention than so far should be given to the correct shaping of socialist relations and the creation of a socialist atmosphere in the enterprise. First of all, Party organizations must take care that the rights of the personnel are duly observed, and combat all signs of bureaucracy and red tape and an indifferent attitude towards proposals and postulates submitted by the personnel, they must take energetic steps to combat all signs of mutual backing and the formation of cliques.

The Party authorities should on no account tolerate any costly initiatives that have not been given due consideration and do not always correspond to the real needs of the region. Initiative in the direction of performing voluntary social deeds should be duly appreciated and supported but at the same time it is necessary to direct this initiative into the right channels and properly control the real possibilities and the economic advantages to be gained from voluntary actions.

The Party authorities should adopt the principle of frequent—at least once a month—public appearances of members of the given Party organization to provide information at work meetings, Party and trade union meetings, at meetings of people representing various milieus and at conferences of Party activists. At all these meetings, comprehensive and convincing answers should be given to all direct questions and all doubtful matters and questions that may seem obscure to anybody should be elucidated.

The work of the Party authorities and of the basic Party organizations after the 14th Plenum should concentrate on improving methods of inner-Party work and the work of the Party leadership in economic matters and social relations within the enterprise. This can only be achieved by a critical evaluation of the shortcomings existing in the enterprise.

. . .

The tasks resulting from the economic situation of the country are not easy. Their implementation requires a strengthening of the responsibility of all sections of state and economic administration for the results of the work they are entrusted with, for the observance of work and wages discipline, for the implementation of the planned tasks according to the basic economic and technical indices.

. . .

The implementation of the resolutions of the Plenum calls for the conscious engagement of the whole Party, of all Party bodies and organizations and of all the members of the Party.

At conferences and meetings of the basic Party organizations the Party bodies and organizations should inform Party activists and Party members as to the present economic situation of the country and point out to them the absolute necessity for the personnel to make a general drive for the full utilization of reserves, for the maximum savings in the management of social means, for a more rapid growth of labour productivity, for better financial discipline, work discipline and good organization of work.

Attention should be concentrated mainly on the following key problems:

1. Fixing the level of employment at the minimum necessary for better organization of work, taking into account the reserves existing in this sector; the

correct application of the wages system and observation of the principles of grading of work and individual qualification groups of staff, and also seeing to it that bonuses and other awards are granted openly and only for real achievements;

2. Analysis of the planned range of goods to be produced, particular attention being paid to export production;

3. Analysis of the technical progress plan of the enterprise, particularly schemes which guarantee the implementation of the planned increase in labour productivity and the reduction of material costs;

4. More efficient management of materials, elimination of waste of raw materials, of fuels and power; analysis of the norms of consumption of raw materials and other materials per production unit which should be brought up to date; improvement of the organization and methods of storage;

5. More rational management of investment means, the elimination of unnecessary investment schemes, reduction of building costs and shortening of the period of building work and speedier achievement of the planned effects;

6. Improvement of the system of work organization based, among others, on constant control to reveal the causes of disturbances and stoppages in production, and the reasons for working over-time.

The decisive measure of Party activity should be an energetic attitude in the face of difficulties, combating wastage, absenteeism, poor workmanship, tolerance of neglect, and lack of a proper sense of responsibility.

All the basic Party organizations, all the Party bodies and every member of the Party should, above all, make it his task to see to it that the general social aims are implemented and should energetically combat tendencies towards particularism in enterprises, branches of industry and local areas.

As regards the policy of the Party in evaluating the managerial staff and making appointments to leading posts in the national economy, more attention should be paid than so far to the results of the candidate's work in the posts previously held, apart from his vocational and political qualifications.

The effectiveness of the efforts made by the Party will be all the greater, the closer the links the Party bodies and organizations establish with the workers and the more they show themselves capable of creating an atmosphere conducive to the development of the initiative of the workers. The Party organizations must see to it that the rights to which the personnel are entitled are in fact given them, they must eliminate all signs of a bureaucratic, indifferent attitude towards the problems, suggestions and postulates of the staff, they must conduct an unyielding fight against all manifestations of mutual backing and the formation of cliques. Far more attention should be paid to the problems of youth, to teaching them a conscientious attitude towards their work and giving them the proper conditions for improving their professional qualifications, as well as to the question of proper mutual relations between youth and the older members of the staff. . . .

The Workers' Self-Government Conferences have a big role to play in the implementation of the tasks facing the enterprises. . . . [They] should lay particular stress on determining the organizational and technical measures to be taken to ensure the attainment and surpassing of the indices for labour productivity. . . .

In the course of their activities the Workers' Self-Government Conferences should control the way the enterprise is managing the wages fund, inquiring for what and to whom prizes and bonuses are awarded, what the employment situation is, and what the production costs are; they should examine the way the assortment plan is being realised, ascertain the position as regards management of raw materials, and other materials, see how the export of products is developing in the enterprises and how the plan of technical progress is being implemented, including newly installed production means. . . .

Socialist work competitions should be developed, as should the Socialist Work Brigade movement and the work of rationalization clubs and teams. Control of the correct implementation of the resolutions of the Workers' Self-Government Conferences by the management of the enterprise should be conducted through the Workers' Councils, and the personnel should be informed of the results and conclusions of the control. . . .

In the work of Party bodies the principle should be accepted that more frequent information should be given by their members at party and trade union meetings at factories and institutions, meetings of various social groups and at conferences of Party activists. A system of economic information inside the Party itself should be elaborated, enabling quick and proper information to be supplied to Party bodies concerning the way the current tasks of the plan are being implemented.

The level of current economic information given by the press, the radio and television should be improved; this information should be presented in a more interesting form, e.g., more frequent appearances and speeches by economic and social leaders both at the central and local level.

In making more generally known the production achievements of the enterprises, more attention and more space should be given to the people who made these results possible by their conscientious and devoted work.

Anthony Sylvester

45 YUGOSLAVIA'S
TRIUMPHANT REFORMERS

Anthony Sylvester, "Yugoslavia's Triumphant Reformers," *East Europe*, XIV, No. 2 (February, 1965), excerpted from pp. 8–10.

Anthony Sylvester is a British journalist who specializes in East European affairs.

At present the [Yugoslav] leaders seem determined not to yield to those who advocate greater centralization and a partial return to the planning system prevailing in the U.S.S.R. and other communist countries. Most Yugoslav economists seem to have nothing but contempt for that system, even though they are aware of the shortcomings of their own. A member of a recent economic delegation to Rumania told me, "They are where we were in 1948. We can't learn much from them." If anything, the government seems anxious to increase the scope and effectiveness of decentralization so as to allow a greater interplay of economic forces and encourage local initiative. Economic enterprises now have greater freedom to dispose of their funds—although according to some press reports the process is slow and painful and some managers, particularly those of the more profitable enterprises, are complaining that local authorities and other government agencies are finding ways of extracting money from them by means of taxation, social contributions, etc., to an extent not substantially different from that which prevailed before the reform.

The law reorganizing the banking system represents a major departure. Edvard Kardelj, who is regarded as second in the line of succession to the Yugoslav leadership, and who has been behind all the crucial political decisions and reforms in Yugoslavia, played a major role in drafting it. Banking in Yugoslavia, as in all communist countries, has been a vehicle for state control of the nation's economic life. Decisions whether or not to lend money, for example, were made on the basis of arbitrary criteria by men who were, in effect, civil servants. Now the banks are to stand on their own feet financially. The state will, of course, continue to exercise a major influence on the banks. It will provide the initial funds and will be represented in the governing bodies of the banks. But local economic enterprises will also be represented in the banking administrations. The draft law stipulates that state organs (or, to use the official jargon, "the political-territorial units") must in no case have more than 49 per cent of all the votes held by the banks' governing boards. The law has met some opposition, and it is not without significance that leading officials in the Federal Chamber of Commerce, who consider any restriction of the state bureaucracy inadvisable, have been among the critics.

Ideologically, the banking law is seen as further affirmation of the "withering away of the state" and of "self-management by producers themselves." Practically speaking, it represents a qualified victory for those forces that have long been struggling for more rational management of resources and a closer relationship between costs and results. This policy, if carried out, may indeed mean that grandiose projects in the less developed parts of the country will be abandoned as uneconomical and that unemployement will increase. Any attempt to put Yugoslavia's industrial life on a sound economic basis—which is unthinkable at present—would inevitably produce widespread shutdowns of factories; while it is clear that the government is not contemplating any major reorganization, some steps in that direction are considered necessary.

Titoism Appraised

In the search for more efficient ways of running a nationalized economy, Yugoslavia continues to remain the trail blazer. Whatever the shortcomings of their system, the Yugoslavs have discredited the notion that good economic results can be achieved by exhortation, by "socialist emulation," or by pushing people around. Recognizing the prime importance of profitability in economic activity, they have moved in the direction of common sense.

The various reforms which go by the name of "Titoism," such as insistence on the independence of local authorities and economic enterprises, are significant on a number of levels. For it is these reforms which will finally make possible a rational dialogue between East and West, that is, a reasoned comparison between Western and communist methods. Certainly no dialogue was possible previously when, enraptured with their giant industrial projects, the communists claimed that they were creating an entirely different human being and that their schemes could only be carried out because they had done away with capitalist exploitation.

The communists are now being forced to admit that economic laws were operating despite their attempts to deny or ignore them. The emphasis on huge construction projects which brought no immediate returns has, for instance, generated powerful inflationary pressures. In Yugoslavia rising consumer prices are one indication of this fact. In the U.S.S.R., inflationary symptoms are often suppressed because the state fixes prices. But any visitor who has had young Russians offer exorbitant prices for his clothing, or who has seen Russian housewives standing in long queues outside shops, knows that inflation exists. During a recent visit to Volgograd I counted over 200 people in a queue outside a shop selling sugar.

Throughout the communist world there is too much money chasing too few goods. The Yugoslavs have apparently drawn the logical conclusion from this fact and are therefore prepared to allow some measure of freedom with respect to prices, wages, etc. The other communist governments are suppressing the visible symptoms of inflation without removing its underlying causes. Which way is better is a matter of argument, but the Yugoslavs must be given credit for recognizing the facts of life.

There are limits, of course, to what can be done under any communist regime. "Don't you believe it is difficult to achieve a proper degree of responsibility in business life when all enterprises are nationalized?" I asked a Yugoslav economist. "We are aware of the problem," he answered. "But we are trying to achieve through the system of worker management what is achieved in capitalism when the management of a company is responsible to its shareholders." Although this places a heavy burden on the Yugoslav industrial worker, who is more often than not barely literate, it is typical of the current thinking in official Yugoslav circles. Indeed, it is impossible to avoid reference to "self-management" in any broad discussion of Titoist reforms, this being the center of Yugoslav revisionist philosophy. In a literal sense, worker-management is hardly taken seriously by anyone in Yugoslavia, and it is, in fact, one of those concepts which, like democracy, mean one thing within the framework of Marxism-Leninism and quite another outside it. To understand what the Yugoslav leaders mean by worker-management, it is necessary to understand the role given in Yugoslavia to the League of Communists.

It is the League and its million or so members which is supposed to represent the "conscious" force in Yugoslavia's domestic development. The League must retain leadership and ultimate responsibility by the very definition of the system. Ideally, there can be no conflict between the League's interests and those of the nation. If such conflicts arise, they presumably stem from "bureaucratic distortions" or lack of education among the masses. In this essential there is little difference between Yugoslav communism and communism elsewhere in Europe.

But the Yugoslav communists are reluctant to use direct methods of control, preferring to work by means of "persuasion." The leaders constantly insist that administrative methods be avoided—and in fact they are used only when things get out of control. That is, "administrative methods" are applied when workers' councils fail to toe the party line, when the party organization in a given enterprise is weak or lacking in unity, and when the workers' councils or other organs of workers' management assume the character of unruly parliaments. Such instances, however, are not considered normal—and prompt intervention by outside authorities is demanded.

Yet the Yugoslav system does allow a fairly broad range of interpretations with respect to what is in the national interest or in the interest of a particular enterprise. A resourceful director of an enterprise will know how to fight for his own interests while remaining on good terms with the central authorities. And he will maintain close contact with the party and will very often be a member himself. All this, however, is a far cry from the "industrial democracy" dreamt of by Western socialists.

46 CONTINUING CRISIS IN SOVIET AGRICULTURE

The 1965 Eastern Europe Agricultural Situation (Washington, D.C.: Department of Agriculture, 1965), excerpted from pp. 10–16. Footnote references have been deleted.

1964 witnessed the end of the Khrushchev era and the beginning of gradual readjustment under his successors. Thus ended a decade of Soviet agricultural policy dominated by Khrushchev.

This analysis, prepared by the East European Branch of the United States Department of Agriculture, under the editorship of Dr. Lazar Volin, provides a retrospective picture of Khrushchev's efforts and of the direction being taken by his successors.

[1964] opened with a spate of conferences, addressed by Khrushchev, and devoted to spurring agricultural production, which had lagged for several years behind Soviet goals and had declined dramatically in 1963. Late in the summer, Khrushchev toured the eastern and southern agricultural regions ending up in the heart of the New Lands area. He inspected a number of collective and state farms, held many discussions with farm managers, specialists, and workers, and made several speeches. Khrushchev characteristically dispensed criticism and praise, offered suggestions for improvement, and sought "advice."

He was obviously stung into this restless activity by the agricultural fiasco in 1963, but his last agricultural tour was, no doubt, a rewarding experience because of the generally good crops he found in the eastern and southeastern regions, which had been so drought-stricken the previous year. Khrushchev undoubtedly considered the improvement in the New Lands, a project he masterminded, as a personal vindication.

The jolt of the 1963 disaster, however, made the problem of more stable and expanded production uppermost in his mind. Both these objectives . . . were to be achieved through intensification of agriculture, designed to raise productivity per acre, per animal, and per worker. This policy received strong impetus and additional emphasis in 1964. It was in sharp contrast to the extensive method of agricultural expansion previously pursued. Reliance had been placed chiefly upon bringing under cultivation a large area of marginal land, with low and highly fluctuating yields, and on increasing livestock herds, regardless of their productivity. Except for some industrial crops like cotton and sugar beets, resources were used mainly for extensive programs in agriculture. The sown area increased between 1953 and 1958 by 95 million acres and by another 57 million by 1963. The results in terms of production, however, were disappointing after the record crop of 1958. Poor weather aggravated the organizational shortcomings of collectivist agriculture. Soviet leaders began to stress the fact that a large area of land is no longer available for agricultural expansion, and further production increases must come from higher productivity.

Mineral fertilizer . . . was selected as the principal vehicle for such agricultural intensification, and Khrushchev transferred to fertilizer much of the enthusiasm formerly lavished on other projects. He addressed a meeting of the Central Committee of the Party in December 1963, which dealt with expansion of the chemical industry and devoted much attention to fertilizer. More attention to agricultural intensification was given in another session of the Central Committee in February 1964. A program was initiated to step up production and use of fertilizer, and capital investment for this purpose was significantly increased. . . . Much fertilizer was wasted because of inefficient transportation, lack of storage, and mishandling. . . .

The Khrushchev fertilizer program called for concentrating the application of fertilizer in areas where it could be used to the greatest advantage in terms of crop output, avoiding the dry regions where the value of fertilizer is marginal. The program also recognized and tried to remedy the inferior quality and the great waste in fertilizer transportation, storage, and handling. An educational campaign was initiated on efficient application of fertilizer, for which the know-how in many areas is lacking. A new "agro-chemical" (soil) service to survey farms and determine the most effective use of fertilizers was inaugurated. This attempt to improve the effectiveness of the fertilizer program is likely to be a slower process than the growth of fertilizer output.

The fertilizer program has apparently survived the downfall of Khrushchev. The economic plan for 1965, approved by the new leadership, calls for an output of 33.5 million tons of fertilizer, a reduction of only 1.5 million from the Khrushchev 1965 goal of 35 million tons. Thus an increase in output even larger than in 1964 is projected for 1965.

Next to fertilizers and other chemicals in Khrushchev's intensification program was the new emphasis on irrigation, particularly growing more grain under irrigation. Interest in irrigation in the Soviet Union has waxed and waned as devastating droughts have been followed by better weather. Traditionally, Soviet irrigated farming is concentrated in the cotton-growing Central Asian republics, and to a lesser extent in the Caucasian republics. Only a small proportion of the irrigated acreage has been used for grain. It was Khrushchev's aim to obtain higher and more stable grain yields by using more irrigated land and thus provide a "kind of insurance reserve." He stressed particularly the growing of corn under irrigation. The irrigated grain area increased only slightly in 1964, when it was over 5 million acres. There seems to be an opportunity of improving the utilization of irrigated areas apart from the planned irrigation construction. Reportedly 16 to 17 per cent of the 23.2 million acres of land with irrigation networks in collective and state farms in 1962 was either not utilized at all, or was not irrigated for various reasons.

More intensive farming generally requires, under modern conditions, increased capital inputs and investment which were supplied by the Soviet Government during the Khrushchev administration, though not on a scale considered adequate.

Increased investment in agriculture is likely to continue under the new leadership. It is planned to increase state investment in 1965 for production purposes to a record of 5.7 billion rubles, compared with 4.8 billion in 1964. Long-term state credits to collective farms are to be increased 19 per cent to a record high of 1.5 billion rubles. This is exclusive of investment in industries manufacturing agricultural machinery, fertilizer, etc., and of investment by collective farms on their own account.

On the organizational side, another effort was made by the government in 1964 to insure greater flexibility in agricultural planning. This was also the aim of legislation in 1955, which was supposed to abolish the highly detailed centralized agricultural planning, confining the role of the government to planning of procurements. Collective farms, on the basis of procurement quotas, were to plan their own production without interference by authorities. There was, however, a loophole in the law; the plans prepared by the collective farms were to be reviewed by local authorities, primarily to examine whether procurement goals could be met. Actually, the authorities widely used this provision to significantly change the plans. Often they did not even wait for the farms to prepare their own plans, but confronted them, as in the past, with ready-made acreage and production goals. The Soviet press and official pronouncements, including those of Khrushchev, criticized for years such violations, but this apparently did not have any effect. On March 20, 1964, a decree was issued confirming the farm planning procedure established in 1955 and castigating its widespread violation. The decree made one significant amendment by providing that, in case of disagreement between authorities and collective and state farms regarding their plans, the "last word" remains with the farm management. It is too early to say how the new law will work, particularly what the relationship will be between farm management and the district agricultural administrations, which have wide powers of supervision over collective and state farms. Old bureaucratic traditions and habits of interference with collective farms may die hard.

In line with Khrushchev's renewed emphasis on the much-touted agricultural specialization, the decree of March 1964 required republic and local authorities to determine, during 1964–65, the specialization of each collective and state farm, providing for "the most effective combination of the various branches of production in accordance with natural and economic conditions." Such determination of farm specialization was to be made by the authorities, jointly with the managers, specialists, and activists in each collective and state farm. How far this operation had actually proceeded by the time of Khrushchev's ouster and whether it will be continued under his successors is not known.

.   .   .

Serious attention was focused on the so-called backward or weak farms. This subject has been much to the fore for many years in Soviet agricultural and economic literature and official discussion. But despite the many reforms of the Khrushchev era—increased government procurement prices, improved managerial personnel, increased investment and credit—a serious economic gap still exists between different farm units. During the past year, the government decided to strengthen weak collective farms by using long-term credits, reducing taxes (deduction of 75 per cent of the income tax obligation) and granting money for such operations as liming of acid soils and drainage construction.

Increased economic incentives to farmworkers continued to be stressed in 1964 by the Khrushchev administration and the press. One significant step in July 1964 was the establishment of pensions on a national scale for aged and invalid members of collectives, paid maternity leave, and some other social security benefits. Previously, each collective farm was supposed to have its own pension plan, but many had none and there was considerable variation in existing plans. Some categories of workers, transferred to collective farms after liquidation of machine-tractor stations, and workers in state farms were covered by the national social security system. Beginning January 1965 a unified collective farm social security system was established, separate from the national system. A centralized fund was created for this purpose; most money will be contributed by collective farms—1 billion rubles—while the state will provide 400 million rubles. The number of collective farm pensioners in 1965 is estimated at 6.8 million. The pensions will vary from a minimum of 12 rubles per month to a maximum of 102 rubles, which is also the maximum for state farmworkers under the national system. Collective farms are permitted to pay additional benefits from their own treasuries. Paid maternity leave will be granted for 56 calendar days before and after childbirth. The new farm social security law is a modest yet significant step toward equalizing the economic status of collective farmers and workers in state enterprises.

It appeared from various statements by Khrushchev during the last months of his leadership that he was ready to tackle the crucial question underlying increased economic incentives to farmers and the more general problem of improving the national standard of living, which he so often stressed. This is the question of providing an adequate supply of manufactured consumers' goods at reasonable prices and tolerable quality. For unless there is an adequate supply of goods to meet the demand resulting from larger incomes generated by increased economic incentives, an inflationary situation of "rubles chasing goods" is bound to occur.

. . .

While there were significant clues to Khrushchev's increasing consumer-mindedness and a changed attitude on the question of industrial priorities, there were no firm quantitative commitments before his ouster which would indicate how far he was prepared to go. His successors, however, while less positive in their statements, made decisions with respect to industrial growth which appear to be along Khrushchev's lines. The revised economic plan for 1965, adopted in December 1964, stipulated the same rate of growth in 1965 as in 1964 (8.2 per cent) for heavy industry, while it increased the growth rate of light industry from 6.5 per cent in 1964 to 7.7 per cent in 1965.

. . .

Though Khrushchev's name usually has not been mentioned since his ouster, he was nevertheless publicly castigated for his stewardship of agriculture—and this despite the good 1964 harvest. Sometimes his own criticisms were turned against him. Thus, an editorial in *Pravda* of December 15, 1964, had the following indictment:

In the management of agriculture there were made serious mistakes. The basic principle of socialism—the economic interest of collective farmers, the remuneration of people according to their work—was violated. The passion for administration by ordering about, for continuous reorganizations without anything useful being accomplished, for boasting, and for empty talk had a detrimental effect on agriculture.

As if to emphasize the contrast with Khrushchev, his successors proceeded cautiously in matters of agricultural policy. Premier Kosygin specifically rejected any haste in agricultural reorganization. However, some steps were taken and certain tendencies became discernible during the first months of the new regime. The splitting of the party and the government apparatus on the local level into agricultural and industrial segments, carried out by Khrushchev in 1962, with consequent close involvement of party officials in the operational aspects of agriculture and industry, was abandoned and the separate segments united.

A more liberal policy was proclaimed toward the private sector; livestock raising was particularly encouraged. The extra restrictions placed upon private plots and livestock numbers during the past few years were lifted. The special taxation of city inhabitants possessing livestock was abolished. The sale of feedstuffs for private livestock was organized in some areas by the state.

The rationale of these measures is two-fold: to stimulate increased livestock production after the distress slaughter of 1963, and to win popularity for the new regime. Such liberalization has occurred in the past—the last time in 1953–54 under Khrushchev and Malenkov—but usually the period of relaxation was followed by a tightening of the screw, as was the case under Khrushchev after 1956.

The new regime also proceeded in the footsteps of its predecessor by raising the procurement price of milk without, however, increasing the retail price to the consumer as was done in 1962, when both producer and consumer prices of meat and butter were raised sharply. At that time the seasonal reduction in milk prices paid to the farms in the summer was abandoned, which had the effect of increasing the average price of milk over the year.

Among the tendencies which have become evident since Khrushchev's downfall is what seems to be a campaign in the Soviet press against Lysenkoism. Lysenko is the acknowledged leader of the Michurinist (or Lysenkoist) school of biology, which adheres to the discredited doctrine of the inheritance of acquired characteristics, rejects modern heredity theory, and wages war on genetic science. In recent years, Lysenko's stock was apparently high with Khrushchev, and this had detrimental influence on biological research.

Another tendency is the mounting criticism of Khrushchev's pressure to grow corn—"the queen of the fields"—in many areas which were not climatically suitable or did not possess the resources for successful corn production. This is paralleled by increased interest in grasses (hay crops) in the northern and north central regions. Grasses were tabooed by Khrushchev, despite their suitability to these areas. But a number of Khrushchev's innovations, such as increased use of fertilizers, social security benefits, emphasis on economic incentives, seem to be retained by the new leadership.

Leonid I. Brezhnev

47 URGENT MEASURES FOR THE FURTHER DEVELOPMENT OF SOVIET AGRICULTURE

Excerpted from L. I. Brezhnev, "Urgent Measures for the Further Development of Soviet Agriculture," *Soviet Documents*, III, No. 17 (April 26, 1965).

This report was delivered by L. I. Brezhnev, First Secretary of the Central Committee of the Communist Party of the Soviet Union, at the Central Committee Plenum on March 24, 1965. Brezhnev, a close associate of Khrushchev from 1938 to 1964, was one of those responsible for the deposal of the former First Secretary. In 1954, he was placed in charge of the "Virgin Lands" project in Central Asia. He successfully carried out this agricultural innovation and was made President of the U.S.S.R. in 1960, a post he relinquished in July 1964.

Comrades! We are confronted by the fact that in recent years agriculture has slowed down in its development, and our plans for increasing agricultural production have remained unfulfilled. . . .

What are the main reasons for such a situation?

First, the weak spot in agricultural management is the fact that the demands of the economic laws of the development of the socialist economy have not been fully taken into account and quite often have even been ignored altogether. We have in mind, first of all, such laws as those of planned and proportional development, expanded socialist reproduction, and also the principles of combining social and personal interests, of material incentives, and others. But life, as we know, severely punishes those who do not take these laws into account, who ignore them and take a subjective approach.

Actions of a purely arbitrary character have increasingly prevailed in the practical leadership given to agriculture in recent years, especially in the fields of planning, price formation, and finance and credit. It cannot, for example, be considered normal that purchase prices for a number of agricultural products do not cover production costs. This resulted in great losses for collective and state farms.

The frequent and, at times, far-fetched reorganizations created an atmosphere of nervousness and commotion, made it impossible for managers to look ahead, and undermined their faith in their own abilities. Quite often, it became the practice to run collective and state farms by issuing bureaucratic instructions and peremptory orders, instead of by doing thoughtful and painstaking work and making a deep analysis of the situation.

Second, quite considerable tasks were set before agriculture, but they were not sufficiently backed up by the necessary economic measures, in particular, by the correct fixing of prices for agricultural produce and manufactured goods, the allocation of the appropriate capital investments, and the improvement of material and technical supplies. State capital investments in agriculture, for instance, were 11.3 per cent of the total investments in the economy in the five-year period 1954–1958, while the target figures for the Seven-Year Plan (1959–1965) put them at only 7.5 per cent of the whole.

.   .   .

Third, very little was done in practice to achieve an improvement in methods of farming and to raise soil fertility. Many collective and state farms violated the rules of crop rotation and the elementary rules of agronomy. Central bodies issued many different stereotyped directions on cultivating the land, the crop pattern, the switch-over from one system of farming to another, and the keeping and feeding of cattle, without allowing for the natural and economic conditions of production and local experience. All these things impeded the planned management of the economy, reduced the role of agricultural organs, and did not lead to a productive use of the land.

Finally, when speaking about the reasons for the lag in agriculture, we must also recognize that there were serious shortcomings in the work of party, soviet, and agricultural bodies. Of course, the work was more complicated for our cadres in an atmosphere of frequent reorganizations. Nevertheless, we did not make use of all the possibilities at our disposal. We did not work well enough with people, did not make sufficient use of experts and agricultural science, and did not succeed in properly organizing the analysis and dissemination of advanced experience.

Comrades! We are encountering the consequences of errors in agricultural management in all zones of our country, but they have had a particular effect in the non-black earth areas. Let us take, for example, the Smolensk Region. The gross output of agriculture in that region has increased by only one per cent in the last five years. The region has still not reached even the prewar level of production of the most important field crops.

The crop yields in the region remain low. The average amount of milk obtained per cow on collective and state farms has decreased by nearly 400 kilograms. The only branch of agriculture that is showing a profit is flax-growing.

We cannot help being seriously concerned about the state of affairs in agriculture. . . .

We must rectify the mistakes made in agriculture quickly and put an end to subjectivism. We must make use, on a broad economic basis, of material and moral stimuli in the development of production. Great efforts and a radical change in methods of work are demanded from the party, soviet and economic bodies, from all of us.

The System of Agricultural Procurements Must Be Improved

Comrades! The Presidium of the Central Committee attaches great importance to the question of improving the system of procurements and purchases of agricultural products. It has many shortcomings and must be improved.

Its basic fault is that it creates uncertainty on collective and state farms and prevents proper planning of production. Collective and state farms get purchase plans for a period of only one year, and frequently after great delay. Furthermore, these plans are often amended during the procurement process, and collective and state farms are given additional assignments which often exceed those planned.

Collective and state farms have been known to appeal to the state for seed after completing grain deliveries. In 1962 the state sold them 1,373,-000 tons of seed. This year requests have again been received for two million tons of seed.

In a number of zones, the price for the purchased grain does not cover the cost of its production. Such a practice is detrimental to the state, undermines the economy of the collective and state farms, and provides no incentive to the farmers.

We all know from our own experience what difficulties we have had to cope with during grain procurements. How faulty and unreal the grain purchasing plans were is seen in the fact that in the last ten years these plans have been fulfilled only three times—in 1956, 1958, and 1964.

Life demands insistently that we improve our entire system of procurements. First of all, we need to switch over to stable procurement plans that cover several years. These plans must harmoniously combine national interests with those of the farms concerned. . . .

Consolidation of the Material and Technical Base of Agriculture

Comrades! . . . [The] machinery per unit of labor at the collective and state farms is still inadequate. We still do not have the necessary numbers of tractors, automobiles, combines and other complex farm machines, or cultivators, harrows and seeders. This leads to the slowing down of field work and to reductions in yields.

It can be hardly be regarded as natural for autumn plowing to last, as frequently happens, not 18 to 20 days, but up to two months, and to stop when the frost starts, whereas every peasant knows that a good crop can be obtained only if the autumn plowing is completed early. Owing to insufficient numbers of combines and other machines, the harvesting of grain crops not infrequently takes from 30 to 40 days, causing great losses in the harvest.

In the interests of advancing agriculture, there must be a decisive increase in the material and technical supply of collective and state farm production, a radical increase in the output of farm machinery, and improvements in its quality, reliability, and durability.

While developing the production of tractors and other machines, it is essential to guarantee a unification of machine parts, units, and mechanisms. We can no longer tolerate a situation in which the appearance of every new machine creates a problem of spare parts, and the list of spare parts grows from year to year.

Workers, engineers, technicians, and party organizations at industrial enterprises should do everything necessary to supply machinery to agriculture on time and to radically improve the quality of agricultural machinery. In turn, the agricultural authorities should do away with the practice of making repeated alterations in the orders they place with industry for farm machinery.

The question of the efficient utilization of the machinery available and of its careful preservation is also a very pressing one. It is essential to heighten responsibility for the correct use of machinery, to increase the material incentive for the engineers, technicians and machine operators in agriculture, and to improve the work of supplying spare parts and materials to collective and state farms. . . .

Certain Questions Concerning the Organizational and Economic Strengthening of the Collective and State Farms

Comrades! A major condition for the advancement of the productive forces of agriculture is the correct development of socio-economic relations in the countryside. As is known, two types of socialized farming have developed historically in the agriculture of our country—collective farms and state farms, based on two forms of socialist ownership—state ownership and collective farm-cooperative ownership.

Experience has shown that a skillful combination of the development of these two types of farming enabled us to reorganize agriculture on a socialist basis. It must be assumed that the two types of socialized farming will continue to exist and progress for a long time. *Our duty at the present stage is not to accelerate the transformation of one form into the other, but to do everything to enable both types to develop and flourish.* . . .

The Level of Party Work in the Countryside Must Be Raised

Comrades! The great tasks of economic and cultural development in our country enhance immeasurably the leading role played by the Communist Party and its cadres in the life of society. The building of communism is based on the mighty creative forces of the people. This puts a special responsibility on the party—constantly to improve organizational, political, economic, and ideological work. . . .

We must admit, however, that some party organizations are still exercising little influence over the economic activities of collective and state farms and are overlooking major shortcomings, and that the standards of their work with the people, with the masses, are low. In the work of some party organizations there is not the necessary militancy and purposefulness. . . .

. . . There must be an end to peremptory orders and bureaucratic instructions, petty tutelage, and the usurping of the function of the leaders and experts of collective and state farms. We must root out all manifestations of showiness and ballyhoo. . . .

Special attention must be paid to strengthening and increasing the role of the primary party organizations on collective and state farms. They are on the front line of the struggle; they are directly carrying out the policy and directives of the party. At present there are 50,000 primary party organizations in the countryside, with a membership of more than two million. That is a great force, comrades, which is capable of solving the problems posed by the party in a militant way.

48 AGRICULTURAL POLICY IN EASTERN EUROPE

The 1964 Eastern Europe Agricultural Situation (Washington, D.C.: Department of Agriculture, 1964), excerpted from pp. 24–25, 36–37, 41, 49, 51, 55–56.

The following summary statements are taken from a publication of the Economic Research Service of the United States Department of Agriculture. The data on the agricultural condition of Eastern Europe were collected and analyzed under the general editorship of Dr. Lazar Volin, a distinguished expert on Soviet and East European affairs.

Poland

Since the decollectivization of agriculture in 1956, Polish farmers have been permitted to retain their freedom of choice regarding joining collectives. As a result, small privately owned farms predominate. Compulsory deliveries from private farms remain in effect, although quotas are smaller than in the mid-1950's. The quantities of fertilizer and improved seed available to private farmers have been increased substantially.

Elimination of the immediate threat of collectivization has given private farmers a greater incentive to produce, as reflected in output statistics of recent years. Nevertheless, the private farmer continues to work at considerable odds compared with state and collective farms and agricultural circles.

Private farms account for 86 per cent of total arable land area and produce over 85 per cent of all crop and livestock products. The average size of the individual farm is about 5 hectares. . . . State farms currently account for 12 per cent of the arable land area and collectives for only a little over 1 per cent. Agricultural circles are the means employed by the Government to educate farmers in collective principles, for agricultural collectivization remains an ultimate goal of Polish agrarian policy.

Most agricultural produce moves to market through state channels, either by compulsory deliveries or contractual sales to the Government. Compulsory delivery from private producers is the major mechanism by which the Government maintains its hold on agriculture. Fulfillment of compulsory delivery quotas, which are based on farm size and productivity, is a prerequisite to other off-farm sales, including direct sales to consumers on a free-market basis. The low prices paid by the Government are essentially a form of taxation. In addition to compulsory deliveries and contractual procurements the Government also purchases agricultural commodities on the free market at prices higher than those paid for compulsory and contractual deliveries.

Land taxation is another means by which the Government controls private farming. Since the tax rate has increased progressively with the size and productivity of farms, it has been a major factor in restricting the size of private farms. . . .

A significant new policy development during 1963 was the introduction of the "Agrominimum," a complex of improved farm practices which are to be employed on every farm to increase output. Agricultural circles are the main channels through which this new law is to be effected. That the Government is strongly intent on implementing this policy is evidenced by the fact that farmers who fail to cooperate will not be able to obtain building materials, feed, seed, fertilizer and other inputs.

Agricultural investment in Poland has been continually rising. Between 1955 and 1962 the annual allocation of state funds for developing agriculture has nearly doubled. Deliveries of tractors, machinery, mineral fertilizer, and insecticides have been increasing, but in quantities insufficient to meet requirements. The private farmer remains reluctant to make long-term investments because of his continued fear of eventual collectivization. . . .

Czechoslovakia

The Government in 1963 continued its drive to consolidate collective farms into larger units. During the last 5 years the number of collective farms has been drastically reduced. In 1959 there were 12,560 collective farms with an average of 354 hectares of agricultural land. By early 1963 the number had been reduced to approximately 4,500 of which more than half were the consolidated type with an average of more than 700 hectares of agricultural land. State farms also have been undergoing consolidation, but at a much slower rate. In 1963 there were 359 state farms with an average of 3,552 hectares of agricultural land. As of January 1962 the socialist sector (collective and state farms) held 83 per cent of all agricultural land and 87 per cent of the arable land. Thus, only a small portion of the agricultural land remains in private ownership—small garden plots of members of collective farms and small individual farms. As stated by Jiri Hendrych, Secretary of the Central Committee, "The process of socializing agriculture has more or less been completed and state and collective farms are absolutely decisive in agriculture."

In addition to the continuing consolidation of state and collective farms, a second major government effort in 1963 was the reorganization of agricultural administration. Until 1963, district committees were responsible for overseeing agricultural production. Because of other duties, however, their role in farm management was limited.

Responsibility for agricultural production was assigned in April 1963 to a newly created Agricultural Production Administration (APA), directly responsible to the Ministry of Agriculture. The initial task of the APA was to prepare annual production and procurement plans for each district and region, subject to approval of the respective district and regional committees and the Ministry of Agriculture. The principal responsibility of the new administration is to ensure that production and procurement plans are met. Other responsibilities include better land utilization and consolidation of the remaining small collectives.

Another important change in agricultural policy during 1963 was in regard to compulsory deliveries from small landholders and the private plots of collective farmers. Under the new regulation small landholders with less than 0.3 hectares are released from obligatory deliveries. Deliveries from landholders with 0.3 to 0.5 hectares will be based on agreements between the producer and the local procurement organization. After fulfillment of obligatory delivery quotas, any remaining fruit and vegetables may be sold to consumers at prices not to exceed state retail prices. Each household may slaughter one of its own hogs without restrictions. A second hog may be slaughtered only when the collective farm has fulfilled its pork procurement goal. Five kilograms of fat must be delivered to the State from the second hog slaughtered.

For collective farmers, marketable surpluses must be first offered to the state procurement organization. Produce not purchased by the State may be sold directly to the consumer.

Hungary

There were no major changes in agrarian policy in [1963–1965] with the continuation of the policy of some liberalization within the framework of collectivization. With the consolidation phase of collectivization well underway, the major emphasis now is on streamlining the administrative structure of agriculture and increasing production.

The 1964 plan calls for an increase of 4 to 5 per cent in agricultural output. This is much more realistic than the targets set in the preceding 2 years. The original 1965 agricultural plan was officially abandoned in late 1963. In reality, however, it was abandoned a year earlier. This does not indicate a de-emphasis of agriculture but a more realistic approach to planning. Agricultural development has been singled out by Hungarian officials as the key to economic development in the coming years, and the proportion of state investments in agriculture and the chemical industry is to increase again in 1964 [and 1965]. . . .

Bulgaria

The Bulgarian Government in February 1963 reversed its policy of discouraging the legal minimum of private property permitted in agriculture. Private plots of collective farmers, permitted by law but heretofore frowned upon in practice, were to be assigned to those collective farmers not having plots, and plots under the minimum legal size were to be enlarged. Furthermore, collective farms were advised to supply collective farmers with the legal minimum of livestock, to assist them with feed supplies, and to permit grazing on communal pastures. One published report indicated that the permissive policy may have been extended even to workers on state farms.

State farm workers and part-time farmers among the urban population were included in a follow-up decree in August concerning the encouragement of private hog raising. Two government agencies were to contract with farmers for the purchase of privately owned hogs the farmers had fattened. Other government agencies were designated to supply the necessary feed and breeding services. Efforts to increase poultry raising were also made, including the supply of a given amount of feedstuffs for each egg obtained from the collective farmers. These decrees implicitly attest to the superiority of private over collectivized care of livestock. Their success will depend significantly, however, upon the availability of additional feed supplies.

. . .

A series of decrees emanating from the May Plenary Session of the Bulgarian Communist Party Central Committee dealt with problems of agricultural organization and planning. These adjustments followed the general direction set forth by the Soviet Union with the reorganization of the Ministry of Agricultural Production and the establishment of Administrations for Agricultural Production on the local government level in place of the former agricultural sections. The tendency of this and other decrees is towards centralization and greater control by specialists.

Yugoslavia

A primary goal of Yugoslav agrarian policy is increasing agricultural production through the modernization of production practices on large socialist farms. A basic factor underlying this policy is the necessity for expanding the commercial output of agricultural products. Yugoslav leaders have become increasingly convinced that in the long run only large-scale mechanized farming can supply the increasing market demands of this unique economy. To this end, the goal of 30 per cent of the arable area in the socialist sector by 1970 has been announced.

Estimates of land in the Socialist sector at the end of 1963 ranged from 15 to 18 per cent of the arable area which is a slight increase over 1962. The socialist sector has a considerably larger share of productive land, as almost half of the holdings are in the Vojvodina, the most fertile region of the country. The purchase of private land by socialist farms again exceeded 100,000 hectares in 1963.

Cooperation between private peasants and agricultural cooperatives showed a marked increase in 1963. This was especially true in wheat production where the area planted cooperatively was double that of 1962. In the Vojvodina, 70 per cent of the private land in wheat was farmed under cooperative arrangements in 1963.

The policy of mechanization and state purchase of land to increase the area in large farms has accelerated the migration of unskilled rural people to urban areas. As a result, more than half of the unemployed in Yugoslavia are from rural areas. As this problem continues to grow, it may affect the policy of enlarging the state sector of agriculture.

Probably the most noteworthy trend in recent years has been the increase in government purchase prices of agricultural products.

Bibliography

U.S.S.R.

Bergson, A., *The Economics of Soviet Planning*. New Haven: Yale University Press, 1964.

———, and S. Kuznets, eds., *Economic Trends in the Soviet Union*. Cambridge, Mass.: Harvard University Press, 1963.

Berliner, J., *Plant and Manager in Soviet Industry*. Cambridge, Mass.: Harvard University Press, 1957.

Campbell, R. W., *Soviet Economic Power*. Boston: Houghton Mifflin Company, 1960.

Degras, J., ed., *Soviet Planning: Essays in Honor of Naum Jasny.* New York: Frederick A. Praeger, Inc., 1965.

Dinerstein, H. S., *Communism and the Russian Peasant.* New York: Free Press of Glencoe, Inc., 1955.

Goldman, M. I., *Soviet Marketing.* New York: Free Press of Glencoe, Inc., 1963.

Granick, D., *The Red Executive.* New York: Doubleday & Company, Inc., 1961.

Holzman, F. D., *Readings on the Soviet Economy.* Chicago: Rand McNally & Co., 1962.

Joint Economic Committee of the Congress, *Dimensions of Soviet Power,* 87th Cong., 2nd sess., 1962. Washington, D.C.: Government Printing Office, 1962.

Laird, R. D., and E. L. Crowley, *Soviet Agriculture: The Permanent Crisis.* New York: Frederick A. Praeger, Inc., 1965.

Nove, A., *Economic Rationality and Soviet Politics.* New York: Frederick A. Praeger, Inc., 1964.

———, *The Soviet Economy.* New York: Frederick A. Praeger, Inc., 1962.

Schwartz, H., *The Soviet Economy Since Stalin.* Philadelphia: J. B. Lippincott Co., 1965.

———, *Russia's Soviet Economy.* Englewood Cliffs, N.J.: Prentice-Hall, Inc., 1954.

Spulber, N., *The Soviet Economy: Structure, Principles, Problems.* New York: W. W. Norton & Company, Inc., 1962.

Vakar, N. P., *The Taproot of Soviet Society.* New York: Harper & Row, Publishers, 1961.

Volin, L., *A Survey of Soviet Russian Agriculture.* Washington, D.C.: United States Department of Agriculture, 1951.

CHINA

Chao Kuo-Chun, *Agrarian Policy of the Chinese Communist Party: 1921–1959.* New York: Asia Publishing House, 1960.

Eckstein, A., *The National Income of Communist China.* New York: Free Press of Glencoe, Inc., 1961.

Gluckstein, Y., *Mao's China: Economic and Political Survey.* Boston: Beacon Press, 1957.

Hughes, T. J., and D. E. T. Luard, *The Economic Development of Communist China: 1949–1958.* New York: Oxford University Press, Inc., 1959.

Li, C., *Industrial Development in Communist China.* New York: Frederick A. Praeger, Inc., 1964.

Perkins, D., *Price Policy in Communist China.* Cambridge, Mass.: Harvard University Press, 1966.

Rostow, W. W., *et al., Prospects for Communist China.* New York: John Wiley & Sons., Inc., 1954.

Szczepanik, E. F., ed., *Symposium on Economic and Social Problems of the Far East*. New York: Oxford University Press, Inc., 1963.

Wu, Y., *The Economy of Communist China: An Introduction*. New York: Frederick A. Praeger, Inc., 1965.

———, *An Economic Survey of Communist China*. New York: Bookman Associates, 1956.

EASTERN EUROPE

Balassa, B. A., *The Hungarian Experience in Economic Planning*. New Haven: Yale University Press, 1959.

Hoffman, G. W., and F. W. Neal, *Yugoslavia and the New Communism*. New York: Twentieth Century Fund, 1962.

Kolaja, J., *A Polish Factory: A Case Study of Workers' Participation in Decision-Making*. Lexington, Ky.: University of Kentucky Press. 1960.

Korbonski, A., *Politics of Socialist Agriculture in Poland: 1945–1960*. New York: Columbia University Press, 1965.

Macesich, G., *Yugoslavia: The Theory and Practice of Development Planning*. Charlottesville, Va.: University of Virginia Press, 1964.

McVicker, C. P., *Titoism: Pattern for International Communism*. New York: St. Martin's Press, Inc., 1957.

Montias, J. M., *Central Planning in Poland*. New Haven: Yale University Press, 1962.

Waterson, A., *Planning in Yugoslavia: Organization and Implementation*. Baltimore, The Johns Hopkins Press, 1962.

Zauberman, A., *Industrial Progress in Poland, Czechoslovakia, and East Germany: 1937–1962*. London: Oxford University Press, 1964.

Chapter Nine

The Shaping of Consensus

Once entrenched in power, communist elites embarked on the rapid economic and social transformation of society, undissuaded by the staggering toll in human life and resources. Particularly in the beginning stages of "socialist transformation," as in the Soviet Union from 1929 to 1931 and in China from 1951 to 1953, they used organized terror extensively in order "to alter the structure of society at a rapid rate and from above through forceful administrative devices."[1] Communist leaders were impelled by their vision of the future, as well as by their quest for economic and military security, to uproot and destroy established social and political elements. Out of a sense of fanatic "self-righteous utopianism"[2] they were prepared to pay any price. Through terror, communist leaders eliminated their opponents, atomized society, and extended the unquestioned authority of the Party over the whole of society; they ruthlessly imposed the discipline and mass deprivation required by the "primitive accumulation of socialist capital," by the overriding objectives of a collectivized agriculture, an accelerated pace of industrialization, and a centralized and planned economy.

Having achieved these goals, Soviet and Chinese leaders now seek, by non-coercive persuasion, to enlist popular support, inculcate loyalty, and stimulate the productivity and creativity upon which their regimes depend for economic, technological, and scientific advances. Though the threat of terror is ever present in the background, control and consensus are being managed through an elaborate system of interrelated, Party-dominated mass organizations, e.g., youth organizations, trade unions, people's militias, and cultural groups.

The focus is on the youth. In them the leaders place their hopes for the

---

[1] Barrington Moore, Jr., *Terror and Progress U.S.S.R.* (Cambridge, Mass.: Harvard University Press, 1954), p. 172.

[2] *Ibid.*

future of communism. Believing that man is a perfectible creature and that through education and science he can realize the secular ideals posited in communist ideology, communist revolutionaries from Marx to Lenin to Mao retained the optimism of the nineteenth-century liberal European outlook. However, as rulers they find it difficult to transfer their revolutionary and puritanical zeal to the next generation. The socialization of the youth is beset by many problems, especially in the Soviet Union where communism has been in power for the longest period (Reading 49). As the training ground for future Party leaders, the Soviet Communist Youth League (Komsomol) is the core of indoctrination and involvement. Its more than 53 million members are organized for recreation and trained for citizenship. But play is becoming a less important function, as the emphasis is shifting to ideological training, "volunteer" work on various projects, and the development of vigilant wardens of the public morality. The realization that educational and professional opportunity depend in large measure on receiving a clean bill of health from Komsomol authorities has led to increasing careerism, cynicism, or apathy.

With the post-Stalin shelving of terror, Stalin's successors turned to non-coercive persuasion to curb the rising "anti-social" and aberrant behavior. They adopted a series of extra-judicial practices designed to supplement the activities of existing mass organizations. And through voluntary public organizations—the prototypes of "communist self-government"—social and public pressure is brought to bear on individuals to make them mend their socially unacceptable ways, i.e., behavior that is not criminal but which is deplored by the regime as contrary to the norms of communist morality and idealism.

One of the voluntary public organizations, the Comrade Courts, has been established in places of residence and work, to try a variety of minor offenses. The enabling statute clearly expresses the purposes for which the Comrade Courts were created:

> Comrades' Courts are elected public agencies charged with actively contributing to the inculcation in citizens of a spirit of a communist attitude toward labor and socialist property and the observance of the rules of socialist society, and with developing among Soviet people a sense of collectivism and comradely mutual assistance and of respect for the dignity and honor of citizens. The chief duty of the Comrades' Courts is to prevent violation of the law and misdemeanors detrimental to society, to educate people by persuasion and public influence, and to create an intolerant attitude toward any antisocial acts. The Comrades' Courts are invested with the trust of the collective, express its will and are responsible to it.[3]

Volunteer police brigades (*druzhiny*) have been constituted to help clear the streets of delinquents, drunks, and trouble-makers, and to assist the militia in maintaining public order and social discipline. Yet, the Soviet

---

[3] *Current Digest of the Soviet Press*, XIII, No. 33 (September 13, 1961), 8–9.

experience with such quasi-judicial instruments of social management since 1958 (Reading 50) has not been a complete success, to judge from the continued intensive campaigns against "anti-social" elements.

Another measure—the "anti-parasite" laws—was adopted in 1957 to root out "idlers," drunkards, speculators, and citizens shirking "socially useful work." The Propaganda and Agitation Department of the Party's Central Committee has waged an unremitting struggle against these "parasitical elements," particularly those engaged in the accumulation of private property. Numerous articles have urged militant campaigns against "those who refuse to work yet succeed in eating" and against "all private-ownership tendencies, indifference to politics, lapses into nationalism, religious prejudices and other forms of bourgeois ideology." The frequency of such articles indicates that these phenomena have become particularly worrisome to the Party.

To a degree not approached by the Soviet Union, communist China has blanketed the country with mass organizations, reaching down into the smallest hamlet and group. No one is forgotten, no one is excluded. The organizations have been developed to a point where:

> . . . every individual . . . is a member of some organized association brought into existence by the Communists themselves, . . . [i.e., he must participate in some "small" group which is organized] around a principal activity, namely, "study" (*Hsueh-hsi*), the activity commonly referred to as "brainwashing."[4]

These small groups are designed to accomplish nothing less than the total restructuring of personality and personal values, attitudes, and behavior. Through endless sessions of criticism and self-criticism, of explanation and argument, of persuasion and ideological remolding, they aim at bringing the thinking of members "into line with that of the Party. Complex interplay of psychological and personal factors gives the technique its special character and power"[5] (Reading 51):

> First, the study group is official. The leader represents and reports to higher authorities. Every member knows that evaluation of his thinking as reactionary, backward, bourgeois, apolitical, progressive, or zealous materially affects his future for better or for worse.
>
> Second, everyone must express an opinion; there is no freedom of silence. In a small, intimate group, whose members know each other well and work and sometimes even live together, it can be very embarrassing to express an incorrect idea, yet over a long period it is virtually impossible to dissemble.
>
> Third, parroting theory or the official line is not enough. . . . The important thing is to apply correct theory so as to discredit one's previous incorrect

---

[4] H. F. Schurmann, "Organization and Response in Communist China," *Annals of the American Academy of Political and Social Science,* CCCXXI (January, 1959), 52–53.

[5] Harriet C. Mills, "Thought Reform: Ideological Remolding in China," *Atlantic Monthly* (November, 1959), p. 72.

conceptions so thoroughly in one's own eyes that one gladly discards them and accepts the new.[6]

Believing that nonantagonistic contradictions can be rectified by discussion and persuasion, the Chinese leaders inaugurated the *Cheng-feng* movement as far back as 1942 in order to indoctrinate the new recruits who had joined Mao's revolutionary army, many of whom were considered to have "brought with them the vestiges of the evil ideology of the old society, namely, remnants of petty-bourgeois individualism."[7] *Cheng-feng,* or "rectifying the work style," has also been translated as "ideological remolding," particularly for "the correction of unorthodox tendencies in learning, the Party, and literature." The rectification program is not a purge in the Stalinist sense of having great numbers expelled from the Party and executed. Instead, it seeks to reeducate the remnants of China's former commercial and feudal classes (Reading 52). According to Mao:

> . . . in exposing errors and criticizing defects, our whole purpose is the same as the doctor's in treating a case; namely to cure the patient but not to kill him. A person suffering from appendicitis will recover if his appendix is removed by the surgeon. Any person who has committed errors is welcome to treatment until he is cured and becomes a good comrade, so long as he does not conceal his malady for fear of taking medicine or persist in his errors until he becomes incorrigible, but honestly and sincerely wishes to be cured and made better. You cannot cure him by subjecting him to hearty abuse or giving him a sound thrashing. In treating a case of ideological or political illness, we should never resort to violence, but should adopt the attitude of "treating the illness in order to save the man," which alone is the correct and effective method.[8]

One of the most important ways Communist Parties dominate society is by their monopoly of the educational system and the means of communication (Reading 53). The Party controls the press, the radio, television, and all publications; no ideas or policies may be discussed publicly unless they bear its imprimatur. Through education and the indoctrination that is implicit in any monistic system of education, and the network of mass organizations, it hopes to "educate" the masses to communism (Reading 54). But the proof of the pudding is in the eating, and the experience of the Soviet Union with its almost two generations under communism suggests that human nature is not readily altered by totalist persuasion, indoctrination, and isolation. There are limits to the efficacy and permanence of totalism because there persists in the spirit of man a hope for individual dignity and differentiation that is antithetical to the policies of the social engineers of communism.

---

[6] *Ibid.*

[7] Mao Tse-tung, *Rectify the Party's Style in Work* (Peking: Foreign Languages Press, 1955), p. 22.

[8] *Ibid.,* pp. 28–29.

Allen Kassof

49 REGIMENTATION AND REBELLION AMONG SOVIET YOUTH

Allen Kassof, *The Soviet Youth Program: Regimentation and Rebellion* (Cambridge, Mass.: Harvard University Press, 1965), excerpted from pp. 171–75; 183–86. Footnote references have been deleted. Reprinted by permission of Harvard University Press. Copyright 1965 by the President and Fellows of Harvard College.

Allen Kassof is Assistant Professor of Sociology at Princeton University and an Associate of the Center of International Studies, Princeton University.

The central fact about the Komsomol and Pioneers is that they are not organizations of or for youth, but agencies of the Communist Party and the Soviet government. They are controlled and staffed by political personnel in the interests of an authoritarian regime. Therein lie both the strength and the weakness of the program. This highly centralized and coordinated effort contributes substantially to the maintenance of Soviet totalitarianism. Because they block the open formation of dissident youth groups, the Komsomol and Pioneers must be counted as important assets to the Soviet leadership. Although the program does not enable the regime altogether to escape the disruptive consequences of the Soviet variety of youthful rebellion and unrest, it does contain them to a significant degree by closing off legitimate channels of protest. This in itself is no small accomplishment.

The program also successfully fulfills a number of positive purposes. Imperfect as it is, it is still an important medium for communicating to the new generations a monolithic political ideology, a consistent world view, and basic values useful in an expanding industrial order. If the content of its message at times appears to the outsider to be unsophisticated and naive, it should be kept in mind that the Soviet audience has very little opportunity for comparative evaluation.

Certainly the program's incessant indoctrination accurately finds the mark in part of the new generation. Although the distribution of "types" in the youthful population is impossible to derive in the absence of accurate quantitative data, those who are thoroughly convinced by the program's message must be counted as heavily as those who are turned away or discouraged by the repressive tactics of the youth organizations. Even if we dismiss the notion of the New Soviet Man as sheer propaganda, there are ample numbers of ordinary humans who are convinced by the slogans of the youth program and thoroughly dedicated to the values they embody.

. . .

Nor is it necessary that the youth program produce only enthusiasts. Indeed, the presence of too many true believers may be undesirable in a system where the persistent emphasis on formal values is likely to draw attention to the gap between the ideal and the actuality. An effective balance, instead, consists of enough such paragons to set the tone and a larger mass of the mildly committed who do not invest so much faith in literally interpreted doctrine that the inevitable departures of daily life from the golden image cause wholesale disillusionment. In this respect the Soviet regime may actually profit from its partial failure to arouse a universal and passionate acceptance of official views. The question of how to evaluate the youth program, then, centers not so much on its success among the minority of enthusiasts as on the way it affects the larger contingent of ordinary members. This study has attempted to provide a balance sheet of assets and deficits in the program as they affect this group.

In the credit column, I have already mentioned the usefulness of the program in repressing dissident tendencies (or at least in hindering their coalescence) and the fact that it does provoke positive reactions in a part of the new generation. A less easily demonstrated but equally major strength of the program—when the Komsomol and Pioneers operate according to plan—is that it gives official recognition to youth as a partner in the larger societal undertaking and thereby provides a sense of identification and purpose that so often is lacking among youth in modern societies. Granted that this recognition is in large part a disguise for an extreme form of tutelage by politicians and administrators, it is recognition nonetheless and should not be underestimated. Moreover, by dealing with youth in adult terms—that is, by insisting that young people function according to rules rather than in terms of an adolescent or youth subculture—it may be that the new generations are more readily incorporated into the "serious" concerns of a growing industrial order.

These strengths are partially offset by a number of pervasive weaknesses. There are extremely serious problems of internal organization: excessive bureaucratization, the virtual exclusion of the rank and file from responsible decision making and sometimes even from participation, the deadening consequences of boredom and indifference, the partial displacement of the program's long-range goals by its role of hiring boss and disciplinarian, the resentment aroused by the youth organizations' invasions of privacy, the adherence to routine at the cost of imaginative and productive innovations. In addition, the program is partially undermined by the inconsistencies between its content and the competing influence of reality—resulting, for example, in *bezdelnichestvo* [idling]. More generally, these inconsistencies may be said to stem from the effort to indoctrinate youth with highly orthodox, almost sacred convictions at a time when the development of the Soviet industrial system, the spread of mass education, and the growing sophistication of an urban population increasingly lead to a secularization of values. Even in highly favorable circumstances, the maintenance of a revolutionary élan is difficult. As the Revolution itself recedes into the distant past and the needs of the system come increasingly to center on the more routine needs for technical rationality, organizational skill, and occupational performance, the youth program is faced with the unhappy task of purveying a partially outdated message. Or, from another point of view, the advent of relative affluence in the U.S.S.R. is creating new diversions, new aspirations, and new forms of emotional investment that conflict with the old single-minded focus on self-sacrifice and future-orientation.

. . .

We know that the Soviet youth program . . . specifically seeks to avoid the development of a youth culture through its monopoly over the time and energy of young people in supervised activities; instrumental values are heavily stressed in the Soviet training literature as well as in the daily activities of Komsomol and Pioneer members. There appear to be two possible consequences of these efforts to hold Soviet youth to a straight and narrow path. One is that, in the absence of alternative outlets in the form of a generally accepted youth culture, there is an intensive focus of motivation toward achievement and performance in terms of adult and "serious" standards. The other possibility, ironically enough, is that natural pressures toward the development of a distinctive youth culture, since they are shut out of the official program, come to be expressed in deviant and (from the regime's point of view) illegitimate forms of behavior. This may well be the source of the stilyagi and others: in their efforts to disassociate themselves from the conventional morality of the youth program, they create a distinctive badge of allegiance to the "wrong" attitudes.

The Soviet youth organizations are imposed by adults. Without the backing of the party, they would very probably lose all but a hard core of faithful followers. This does not necessarily signify widespread dissatisfaction with the larger system or demonstrate that Soviet youth, even if given the opportunity to do so, would actively attack the program. But it does appear to be true that the overwhelming majority of citizens who are old enough to have formed an opinion view the program with great indifference at best. Although the junior organization is spared the more severe hostility experienced by the Komsomol, it is not immune. But the young person who is not attracted by the youth program, or who refuses to accept its values, cannot easily find a legitimate alternative; the formation of competing groups, even if they are informal, is strongly discouraged by the youth organizations. Thus, the individual who rejects the program must rely heavily upon his own internal resources in working out personal standards of behavior. One Komsomol member, whose comment was reported in the youth poll cited above, put the situation this way:

> The desire to prevent young people from making mistakes sometimes leads to depriving them of the right to think independently, leads to thinking in formulas and stereotypes unregulated by debate, proof, or life itself. Sometimes individual young people, failing to receive answers to sharp questions, become distrustful and reserved. Their social interests shrink, turning often into a kind of nut—often with a rotten center. Some take the path of hypocrisy, and split personalities appear—persons who are quite different when alone than when among people.

Split personalities, of course, are a very real danger in the Soviet system, for they are a potential source of accumulated pressures toward unplanned and unanticipated innovation and change. And it would be strange indeed if the relatively laissez-faire approach to youth training in American and other pluralistic societies were to produce conformist personalities, while a rigidly imposed youth program in the Soviet Union produced a generation of hardened rebels.

These and other inviting speculations must remain untested against fact until it becomes possible to study Soviet society from within, free of political and ideological restrictions against objective social inquiry. But they do suggest that, even with the full resources of an authoritarian regime available, it is not easy to control or to raise new generations in accordance with a prescribed pattern or to create a new society by revolutionizing the minds of the young. The changes that have been wrought over the generations since the Bolshevik Revolution are profound, yet they seem to stem as much from the general influences of industrialization and modernization as from the programmatic efforts to transform youth through a system of all-encompassing organizations.

Above all, we must remember that the youth program does not operate in a vacuum. Despite its enormous scope, it has not succeeded in insulating youth from contact with life. In particular, the Soviet regime has neither destroyed nor replaced the family as an influential source of early attitudes, values, and sentiments that sometimes compete with those of the official youth program; nor is there any sign that Soviet leaders are prepared to incur the enormous liabilities that would be involved in the kind of major internal revolution required to replace the family altogether—if, indeed, this were at all possible. The establishment of the boarding schools is an important step in extending the influence of the program, but it falls far short of the total envelopment of entire generations in a manipulated training environment.

For the next decade or two at least, there is little probability of important alterations in the established youth program. Trends now in evidence, such as the expansion of membership and the efforts to include still younger members in the organizations, will continue. Certainly there is no prospect that the organizations will revert to their earlier status as exclusive groups of elite youth, for there is no longer a place for them. Moreover, as long as the plans for rapid industrialization and capital development remain in force, the central values of the program, emphasizing achievement, self-sacrifice, and the suppression of independent attitudes and behavior, will persist. At the same time, the program will be faced with more counter-pressures generated by its own internal deficiencies as well as by the accelerating dynamism and complexity of an industrialized modern society. The growing demand to enjoy the fruits of a productive economy, already felt to some extent, increased contact with heretical ideas from the outside world, the subtle problems of controlling a literate populace, will all aggravate tendencies now faced by the youth program.

The more distant prospects depend in part upon how rapidly and how far Soviet society continues in the direction of liberalization that has taken place since the death of Stalin. I believe it would be a serious error, however, to expect the Soviet regime to abandon or modify its efforts to draw new generations into the system through a comprehensive, official youth program. Liberalization has involved the diminishing resort to mass terror and brute physical coercion that we usually associate with totalitarianism. But this change should not be confused with a surrender on the part of the dictatorship of its claim to ultimate scientific knowledge about society or of its belief in both the practical necessity and the moral desirability of planning and direction from above. There is little prospect, then, that certain social functions—including the training of youth—incorporated under Stalin into the public realm, will be returned by a Communist regime to the status of voluntaristic or private concerns. At best, the Soviet youth program will become more benign and less repressive, though no less total in its coverage. The day when there will be free and autonomous organizations of Soviet youth is not yet on the horizon.

Robert G. Wesson

50 VOLUNTEERS AND SOVIETS

Robert G. Wesson, "Volunteers and Soviets," *Soviet Studies,* XV,
No. 3 (January, 1964), excerpted from pp. 231–49. Footnote
references have been deleted.

*Robert G. Wesson is Associate Professor of Political Science at the University
of California, Santa Barbara. The author of* Soviet Communes, *he has written
extensively on Soviet affairs.*

In recent years, much of the task of keeping order among Soviet citizens
and disciplining minor offenders has been given to volunteer police brigades (*druzhiny*) and "comrade" courts composed of associates of the
accused. . . . But *druzhiny* and comrade courts are only part of a
multiform movement. Unpaid workers have been mobilized in a host of
varied organizations and in sundry ways to guide and control others, to
exert pressure for better conformity to Soviet morality and laws, in case of
need to correct and punish or to denounce to other authorities, and otherwise to fill functions ordinarily pertaining to the state. There are street and
apartment committees, parents' committees, commissions on juvenile
affairs, diverse semi-official volunteer commissions and councils, "social"
inspectorates, "social" bureaux of local soviets, etc., some new and others
enlarged and strengthened, all to work freely for the building of communism.

Communists have always thought highly of unpaid labour, and from the
beginning the Soviets have called upon the willing not only to help in
reconstruction, to build subways or settle Siberia, but also to carry out such
governmental activities as the collection of grain from peasants. Volunteer
fish-warden groups, under the state inspectors, were started long ago. But
the movement which has gone full spate since the Party Congress of
February, 1959, and more so since the Party Programme of 1961, calls
upon volunteers not to meet a specific temporary need but permanently to
assume a variety of official or semi-official tasks; the general rationale is
movement toward the communist society wherein work generally is to be
without monetary reward and all share in the administration of government. Moreover, the volunteers, instead of merely putting themselves at the

314

disposal of the government or the Communist Party, are now organized into a multitude of special groups. Before 1959 there were some helpers of the regular militia under the procurator; the *druzhiny* since 1959 have been given greater authority, set off by themselves immediately under the party. Comrade courts at work-places are almost as old as the Soviet system, but since 1959 they have been organized on a residential basis with new authority. Previously limited to labour discipline, they now deal with a great variety of minor infractions and disputes, from malicious gossiping to quarrels over the use of housing. Usually a new organization has been built upon the nucleus or the precedent of an old one, as were the *druzhiny* and comrade courts. For example, the apartment committees were developed from councils attached to local offices of the housing administration. The result has been a massive proliferation. Thus Rostov, by no means a model city, was in 1962 credited with more than 2000 "social" organizations, including 380 apartment and street committees, 700 comrade courts and 152 volunteer bureaux of local soviet executive committees (*ispolkomy*), all for a population of 660,000.

. . .

Among the host of volunteer organizations, the *druzhiny* and comrade courts are perhaps the most publicized in the Soviet Union as well as abroad. But important and basic are the apartment committees, or street committees where individual houses prevail. These date back to the needs of postwar reconstruction and have existed in many places since 1955, but were not made general until after 1959, when sanctioned by a RSFSR decree. Their increased role was in part made possible by the establishment of corresponding party cells, which are vital for their proper functioning. An apartment committee corresponds not to a single building, but to a block (*kvartal*) or section under an office (*kontor*) of the housing administration; however, there are sometimes committees for smaller divisions. The members, numbering from 3 to 25, should be elected by a general meeting for two-year terms, subject to confirmation by the city or raion soviet. They have a president, vice-president, and secretary, and may divide into numerous sections, such as for culture, sanitary affairs, upkeep of grounds, and the like. Meetings should be at least monthly.

The duties of apartment and street committees are many. Working under the local *ispolkom,* or executive branch of the soviet, they organize volunteer work of various kinds in and around dwelling-places. Besides obvious duties in connection with the repair and appearance of buildings, they are to work closely with the housing administration in all its tasks. They help to start and they co-operate with women's councils, which treat matters of special concern to women and children, with parents' councils, and sundry cultural or protective societies. They help to establish and co-operate with comrade courts and organize *ad hoc* anti-parasite meetings, an undertaking which they share with presidents of comrade courts. They are to fight juvenile and other delinquency, to foster political education and general morality, to see that children go to school, to keep watch over buildings and socialist property, to organize socialist competitions with other street or apartment committees, to nudge householders to keep up sidewalks and pay rents, to act on complaints, to bring any necessary matters to the attention of authorities, to persuade dwellers to paint and repair, to exert moral pressure on violators of rules of good conduct and proper use of buildings. In case of need, if moral pressure proves insufficient, they turn miscreants over to comrade courts or to state authorities. For this purpose they may draw up an accusatory act.

More solid powers are vested in the commissions on juvenile affairs, established in the RSFSR by authorization of August, 1961. Made up of volunteers approved by the local *ispolkom,* to which they are responsible, their chief task is to combat juvenile delinquency. They should find out persons under 18 years of age who are out of school but not at work and get them properly occupied, attack gambling and other vices and conditions which lead astray, organize leisure activities and educate and admonish parents concerning the treatment of their children. They may act as wards for minors turned over to them by regular courts, or themselves may serve as tribunals to judge minors sent to them from the procuracy, the militia, *druzhiny,* or regular courts. They can issue binding orders on matters within their competence and can reprimand offenders, turn them over to a comrade court, require payment of damages caused by a minor up to 20 rubles, or levy a fine in this amount. Like apartment committees, they should work closely with parents' committees. These, with many of the same objectives, but without official powers, are organized for an apartment block, a school or a single grade; for liaison, the director of the school is a member of the parents' committee while a representative of the parents' committee sits with the school council.

Apartment and street committees, comrade courts, etc., are separate from the local soviet although under its jurisdiction. Administrative commissions, on the other hand, are directly attached to the *ispolkom.* These bodies have long existed but had no great powers until 1961; in the 1931 law their powers were: warnings, fines and compulsory labour (at the normal place of work). For most of the period the law was probably dormant. Now they, like the comrade courts, are virtually a new arm of law enforcement. . . .

. . .

It cannot be assumed that all these volunteers are vigilant guardians of Soviet order and active civic improvers. If they were, Soviet society would be indeed exemplary. On the contrary, there are indications of some lack of zeal and assidity. . . .

It is not remarkable that many volunteers should be less than diligent. Leaders and officials, the successful and ambitious, have little free time. One committee was criticized for inviting the collaboration of a man who was already director of a sugar factory, member of the city party committee and vice-president of one of its commissions, member of a committee of the sovnarkhoz, president of a section of the atheist group, general propagandist, member of the staff of the *druzhina,* etc. However, it seems that very often the leaders of the older social organizations are pulled into the new; activists of trade unions, Komsomol, Communist Party and other organizations are usually candidates for the responsible posts. It is easiest to call upon those who have already proved themselves. When invited or elected, they may well find it difficult either to decline or to give much attention to the new post.

Consequently, most of the active volunteers seem to be retired persons, civil or military. In Moscow, more than 125,000 pensioners were reported in 1962 to be working for the soviets. Many inspectorates are made up entirely of pensioners, and the head, who will be expected to give most time, often is such. The composition of the staff may depend to some extent upon the leader; if a full-time worker is named to head the bureau, he is likely to get other employed persons to help, while a pensioner will get other pensioners; but the latter do more work.

Elderly citizens are also desired for their experience and judgment. Retired teachers are recruited for the education bureau, former trade workers to inspect shops, engineers to examine buildings, etc. The doctrine is that volunteer organs should be composed of a mixture of old and young, to join sober knowledge with youthful enthusiasm. The older workers, however, may prefer their own organization. In the case mentioned above where a volunteer militia bureau was set up alongside the *druzhina,* the only discernible reason was that, whereas the *druzhiny* are filled with young people, the militia bureau was formed by a retired army officer, other pensioners and elderly workers.

For the ambitious, volunteer work is a merit badge. It is likely to appeal for other reasons to those who have abundant free time. The tasks assigned are generally popular. Social workers try to see that stores get fresh merchandise, handle it properly and treat customers efficiently and courteously; most attention is given to foodstuffs, a particularly sore point. They are also expected to propose improvements, to try to make the distribution network more effective, not only pointing out shortcomings but helping to correct them. They inspect unsatisfactory repair services. They cannot much alleviate the housing shortage, but they can help to keep buildings presentable and habitable. Volunteers are to scrutinize the operation of schools, clinics, libraries, local transport, sanitary services and the like, all of which directly interest many persons. They are called upon to organize playgrounds, fix sidewalks and improve the handling of milk; if they can do these things, society must approve, as it must if the *druzhiny* make the street safe.

The volunteers also generally have the pleasure of working with people, rather than with papers or things. One of their frequent functions is to hear complaints, a task which the regular bureaucracy is doubtless glad to shed. The volunteer worker usually cannot take action, but he passes the complaint on with his recommendation and should follow up its disposition, perhaps taking satisfaction in the results achieved. A volunteer financial bureau is concerned not with the city books but with explaining the tax laws to the citizens and seeing whether they pay properly. Volunteer inspectors in the social security bureau deal directly with recipients of pensions. For example, citizen Frolov, retired, working under the guidance of an official inspector, holds office hours from nine to two once weekly in each of three villages assigned to him. There he helps people to make out forms, checks their documents and affidavits and forwards these with his opinion, examines witnesses and reviews doubtful cases. Since pensioners no longer go to headquarters, he must have considerable effective powers of decision. He and other such inspectors also visit pensioners occasionally and procure assignments for those who are willing, like himself, to do something for the cause. Thus the volunteer should have an interesting and significant task for which he feels responsible and the results of which he can see.

While the duties are probably not very burdensome unless ardour should make them so, there are charms of variety and the dignity of a position and a badge. The retired get a chance to remain usefully active, housewives have opportunities for social and sociable undertakings. There is the pleasure not only of serving the community but of a little use of power, the satisfaction of checking and finding fault with others. Many may delight in showing up the shortcomings of the bureaucracy, while others correct their humbler neighbours. Volunteer groups recruited by apartment committees hold inspections not only of communal areas, halls and public facilities, but of living quarters, and scold the occupants for poor maintenance or uncultured sloppiness. *Izvestiya* reported that an apartment committee, on denunciation by a volunteer, charged a woman with immorality merely for holding family gatherings on Sunday afternoons. . . .

Thus appealing to human instincts, the volunteer movement can probably mobilize a good deal of labour for the Soviet economy with little cost and perhaps some political benefit. It may bring some savings to the budget; Sevastopol claimed a 16 per cent economy in municipal salaries by getting a large part of the population into volunteer work. But it is possible that volunteers are most useful in checking the bureaucracy. Amateurs seemingly may be sometimes more zealous than professionals in peering into dark corners. They may also be more honest, relatively immune to bribes and stricter in censure of the cheaters. It is not surprising that they should be, so far as they have different interests and attitudes from those whom they are set to control. Pensioners in particular are less subject to reprisals and devoid of careerist motives, hence readier to uncover corruption and misdeeds.

A volunteer staff of critics and controllers must thus be a nuisance if not a threat to careerist and self-seeking office-holders, and relations are evidently not always cordial between professionals and amateurs. Sometimes the former try to shut the latter out of the real business of the bureaux, keeping them in menial positions. Perhaps in self-defence, bureaucrats of the *ispolkom* often become social workers of the same. The secretary frequently names as volunteer controllers his own colleagues. This, of course, is highly undesirable.

The chief good which Soviet leaders claim from the use of volunteers to enforce rules and morality and assist in the management of the state is that it represents progress toward the planned communist society. When all citizens participate in administration, the state is expected to dissolve as a coercive force. This cannot be understood to mean that compulsion will be abolished, so that men are free as birds, but that psychological pressure should be substituted for force. Moral-ethical imperatives should then suffice to control behaviour, ethical prevailing over legal mandates, as in the Confucianist order or as in a well-bred family. This would plainly seem to require not only a great deal of education but universal or nearly universal participation of the people in the business of maintaining order. Indifference would be only a grade less than rebellion.

So far as they are successful, the volunteer organizations make their contribution to the communist order by accustoming people to apply social pressure and to respect and submit to it, as well as to work without specific monetary reward. That is, they tend to make the community more like a single family, or, one might say without implying moral judgement, like a beehive, wherein each does his duty because it lies in his character, and compulsion is needed only occasionally to exile the drones. The social organizations and volunteer control can progress in the Soviet Union and become more important so far as moral suasion is sufficient motivation; their progress or lack of it will indicate much regarding the ability of that country to reach its social goals.

However, to say that bringing volunteers into the management of local affairs is equivalent to democratization shows a use of the word "democratic" quite different from that usual in the West. Many of the more responsible volunteers are already recognized leaders in Communist Party, trade union, Komsomol or other Soviet agencies; to give them new assignments means no spreading of authority. Many deputies stay on with the soviets as aides or inspectors when their term expires, perhaps with nearly equal influence. The new organizations do not take over significant official functions, but assist in carrying them out. They do not decrease but in effect increase the authority of the centre. . . .

So far as the volunteer movement succeeds, it represents a strengthening of the communist order and Soviet leadership in the control of society.

Ezra F. Vogel

51 FROM FRIENDSHIP TO COMRADESHIP: THE CHANGE IN PERSONAL RELATIONS IN COMMUNIST CHINA

Ezra F. Vogel, "From Friendship to Comradeship: The Change in Personal Relations in Communist China," *The China Quarterly,* No. 21 (January–March, 1965), excerpted from p. 46, pp. 54–60.

Ezra F. Vogel, Lecturer at the Social Relations Department and Research Associate at the East Asian Research Center, Harvard University, is author of Japan's New Middle Class.

In the first fifteen years of communist rule on the Chinese mainland, personal relationships have undergone an important transformation, a transformation which testifies to the success of the regime in penetrating and influencing the private lives of its citizens. From the view of the individual, the change in personal relationships arises principally from the uncertainty as to whether private conversation will remain private or whether it will in some way be brought to the attention of the authorities. When one no longer confides in a friend for fear that he might pass on the information, either intentionally or unintentionally, an element of trust is lost. When a person no longer invites a friend to his home for fear the friend might see something that he would later be called upon to describe, the nature of the relationship is altered. When a person begins to watch carefully and think about what he might be revealing to his friend and wonders under what circumstances this information might be brought to the attention of the authorities, friendship as a relation of confidence and personal commitment is weakened. . . .

. . . In place of friendship as a relationship of mutual trust and privacy or as a "feudalistic" relationship between benefactor and recipient, the concept of comradeship has become gradually diffused throughout the population. Originally the term "comrade" was used among the members of the loyal band of Communists to signify a faithful and trusted follower in the context of a wider society in which many people were not comrades. It implied a fundamental equality, and even today in Party meetings, Party members are regarded as fundamentally equal, even though in their work units they would have superior-subordinate relationships to carry out their activities.

With the takeover of the mainland and the enunciation of the New Democracy in 1949, the term "comrade" was gradually extended in practice to include the population at large. At first it was used for officials, and then perhaps gingerly and almost playfully (as with any group learning new terms) it was gradually used by people in talking to each other until it became fairly widespread. It was not used, however, among close friends. It was used to describe the relationship of one person to another in their role as fellow citizens. As one's activities and responsibilities as a citizen of the state came to play an important part in one's life, so did the relationship between citizens become a critical mode of interpersonal relations. It became the dominant basis for all interpersonal relations and was supported by propaganda and by the very small group discussions that played such a key role in the weakening of friendship.

The essence of the term "comrade" lies not only in the loyalty to Communism (counter-revolutionaries, landlords and other "enemies of the people" would not be addressed as comrades) but in the universal nature of comradeship. In a very fundamental sense, every citizen is a fellow comrade, and there is no longer such a sharp line even between friends and comrades. Part of the ethic underlying the concept of comrade is that there is an important way in which everyone in the society is related to every other person. Hence it is perfectly natural for people to address others whom they never met before. The other side of the concept is that one should not have special relationships with certain people which would interfere with the obligations to anyone else. A special relationship between two people is not considered sacred and not even praiseworthy; this would not be a comradely relationship and it would be considered suspect and illegitimate.

An important element in "comradeship" is the accent on "helping" other people. "Helping" is at times a euphemism for getting another person to fall in line and do what is expected of him, whether by logical arguments, forceful persuasion, or repeated reminders. This kind of "helping" is something that one should do for a comrade, for anyone else in the society. But "helping" also means spending time to be of assistance to a person in need. A student who is having trouble with his lessons should be helped by someone who can give the assistance. An old person on the street should be given assistance by someone located conveniently nearby. A newcomer to a group should be helped by someone already on hand to become acquainted with the new place, to find all the facilities that he will need.

There is a positive value placed on being of assistance to others, on spending time and energy to make things easier for them. Indeed, some refugees from mainland China find it difficult to adjust in Hong Kong to the fact that no longer are people really looking after them and caring for them.

Although activists are likely to be the best informers, they are also likely to be the best comrades. Activists are expected to and do in fact spend considerable time assisting their colleagues and neighbours. They assist new arrivals, they make suggestions for how to do things, they try to arrange help for the needy. Comrades are concerned for their fellow citizens, and this concern includes both seeing that they stay in line and that they be given assistance when they need it within the limits of the possibilities of the time and place.

Comradeship is also strongly egalitarian in its underlying ethic. Because of their work position, some people have considerably more authority and power than others. But as fellow citizens, as comrades, they are in many fundamental respects regarded as equals. A person who is a Party member or who has more education or a higher status in his personal relations with others is supposed to behave as an equal. Of course, this does not entirely work out in practice, but the underlying ethic is clear, and a case where it was not practiced would be considered an abuse.

The pattern of caution and reserve in personal relationships paradoxically is probably the greatest among Party members, whom the régime considers very reliable, and the intellectuals, whom the régime considers very unreliable. What is common to these two groups is that they are subjected to more study meetings, self-criticism, and criticism. The Party members are subjected to intense control because of their power and responsibility. Because of their power, the régime demands of them a much higher level of loyalty and discipline than it demands of ordinary citizens, and it exercises constant vigilance lest impure elements or impure thoughts affect the ranks of the Party. The intellectuals are subjected to intense control because of their unreliability, their lack of discipline, and because the régime recognises their potential for influence, especially influence on the minds of youth.

Party members who are least in danger of being rightists, *i.e.,* those with the purest backgrounds and thoughts, may have a feeling of security and camaraderie unknown anywhere else in the society. The Party, being the one organisation where frequent meetings and organisational strength are not suspect, gives its members a group spirit in place of more intimate friendship.

Factory workers and peasants are less subject to pressures, not only because they have a "good" class background but because the demands of keeping up production place some limits on the frequency and length of meetings. Since educational institutions can tolerate more political meetings without clearly and visibly affecting the results, they are more prone to such intrusions.

Peasants are subject to less intrusion than are factory workers partly because the rural organisation, even under the commune, is not as tight and highly controlled and structured as factory organisation. Partly peasants are less controlled because the distance from political power centres is farther and because the proportion of Party members, Youth Leaguers, etc., is less. Peasants may be just as reticent to express criticism to authorities, but the concern about private conversation being brought to the attention of authorities is certainly not as great as in other groups, and the extent to which opinions could deviate before being reported is undoubtedly much greater. This is not to say that peasants have not been affected by the same pressures; the régime's exploitation of local community cleavages, the sending in of outsiders into rural areas, and the informing activities of Youth Leaguers and local Party members have affected friendship patterns even in remote rural areas.

Although comrades are theoretically equal and close companions, in practice some are more close than others. While they would be reluctant to admit it, people who grew up under certain economic conditions and have been assigned a certain family status do tend to feel more comfortable with comrades who have been assigned the same status. When a comrade goes to the city or is assigned with other comrades to go to a rural area, he is likely to associate with comrades from his same area who can speak the same dialect and share the same local tastes in food and opera and join in discussion of local news or mutual friends. A comrade may feel tense in talking to a comrade who has power over him and become somewhat stiff and formal when talking to a comrade under him, but will relax with a comrade of about his own level. Though more intimate with comrades in his own small group, a person may feel freer with an acquaintance in another group because there is less danger that their conversation will have to be reported and discussed in a meeting. Young people of the same sex do not sense the slight embarrassment and reserve that can characterise relations between men and women. A better-educated person may feel somewhat cautious with a less-educated comrade because he cannot display his inward feeling of superiority, and the less educated may try to suppress the embarrassment he feels in trying to behave like an equal when he in fact feels inferior. Comrades of the same educational level do not have this problem.

So prominent are political considerations that subtle shadings in political attitudes often separate closer comrades from other comrades. Often these political shadings are not discussed openly, but they are sensed and understood. A comrade who was criticised in a campaign several years ago feels closer to another comrade who was criticised in the same campaign. An activist is more likely to feel comfortable with another activist; a League member can talk more easily to another League member. And, even within the Communist Party, a mildly enthusiastic Party member is more likely to feel closer to another who is mildly enthusiastic, a former rightist is likely to feel closer to another former rightist.

There are many ways to express this closeness. Comrades can talk together, go to movies, or go on walks together. While they are not in the position to do big things for each other like offer major financial assistance or find jobs, there are many little favours they can do for each other. They can share their tight rations, they can help each other with their washing or sewing. They can share their books or their clothes. They can assist each other with their lessons or their work. A comrade who has some special political information might in the context of some casual conversation simply say that it is not wise to do such and such, thereby indirectly warning of some impending political campaign. They would ordinarily avoid any kind of political discussion that might conceivably be embarrassing if later discussed with authorities, but they can make subtle criticisms in ways that would later be defensible. Within the confines of not discussing items which might be politically embarrassing later, there can be considerable loyalty between comrades, and the easy-going affability, kindness and considerateness which characterise friendship in other parts of the world are also found among comrades in Communist China.

Within certain confines, the régime has gradually grown to accept the existence of closer comradeship. The programme of having everyone discuss almost everything about himself and his friends which characterised China in the early period after takeover, has generally given way to a sharpening of the line between what the régime needs to know and what it doesn't need to know. As long as these relationships do not seem threatening to the régime and are kept within bounds, comrades are given freedom to be closer to some comrades than others. While comrades may associate fairly freely on an individual basis, they rarely assemble in a large group except under official auspices. Large groups are inevitably anathema since their potential for damage caused by unified opposition is much greater. Hence, any sizeable group must have its activities very carefully authorised, and its activities must be reported in great detail by very reliable comrades. Because their friendships are potentially more dangerous, men are watched more carefully than women, and old women are perhaps given more leeway in their friendships than any other group in the population.

The practice of not interfering with non-threatening relationships inevitably involves a distinction between the politically reliable and the politically unreliable. Comrades with very clean records of continued activism and support for the régime are given considerable leeway in forming close relationships. But the régime is much more suspicious of budding friendships when one of the pair has some "problems in his background." More frequent observations and reports are required of associates of suspects. Even without any special reason, suspects may be called upon to report on their activities and engage in criticisms of themselves and their comrades. Special meetings may be called, and if these friendships appear too close, they may suffer all the more and even be assigned to different (and often lower) positions in places where they could not possibly have contact with each other. Hence, those who have suspicious backgrounds must be much more cautious in forming relationships and more reserved even in seeing the same person too many times lest it lead to further suspicions. They are in fact, as the régime wishes them to be, relatively isolated.

While some comrades are in fact closer to other comrades, there is a limit as to how close they can become. The limit is dictated partly by fear, but it is supported by the ethic of comradeship which demands that friendships do not interfere with one's role as a citizen, that an individual's commitment with another individual not interfere with his commitment to the collectivity.

As a moral ethic, comradeship is very similar to the moral ethic governing work relationships in the West. One is expected to be friendly but not to form such deep friendships that they interfere with doing the work. In work relationships one can be considerate, kind and relaxed without developing a special private relationship and commitment to the other person. One can discuss some limited personal matters, but it is inappropriate to talk too much about one's personal tastes. If two people are continually together, whispering, going everywhere together, it is regarded as lack of consideration for the rest of the group.

What is unique about Communist China is not the presence of a universalistic ethic governing personal relations, but the absence of a private ethic to supplement the public ethic and support the commitment of the individual to his friend. In most Western countries, close personal relationships may exist outside of a work context giving personal support to the individual for the tensions which exist in his more formal work requirements. In Communist China, the universalistic ethic penetrates much more deeply into personal lives so that it is difficult to gain personal support from the tensions generated in the more formal relationships. This is not as severe a problem as one might imagine. For the citizen who is bitterly attacked by comrades, the combination of criticism and avoidance by friends can be devastating. But most Chinese people do not seem to require as high a level of personal support as people in many other societies. Their needs for dependent gratification are not so great, and the support of friends and especially of family members, even if expressed only by attitude rather than by potentially dangerous conversation, appears to be sufficient. But the individual is also tightly integrated into his small group, whether it be at work or in the neighbourhood, and to the extent that he cannot stand completely independent of social pressures and requires some support, he is dependent on his small group which is closely integrated with the régime, and this support is conditional on his showing the proper political attitudes, a situation which gives the régime considerable leverage in getting the individual's co-operation. The general small group support for being a good comrade is not the same as the relatively unconditional support which a friend offers his friend, but it has become an important psychological substitute. A person relies on his comrades not only for expediency but to satisfy his desires for personal companionship.

The growth of the new universalistic ethic has been important to the régime not only because it reduces the threats to political control. It is important because a modernising society undergoing rapid social change and reorganisation requires a basis of personal relations which makes it possible for people of different social backgrounds, from different geographical areas, with different personal tastes to have relationships with each other. This can only be supplied by a universalistic ethic. But the all-pervasiveness of the universalistic ethic, its penetration into private lives can only be understood in terms of the régime's desires for the power to be able to influence people even in small matters of their daily lives. Because people rise into membership in the Young Communist League and the Communist Party partly because they have proved their willingness to place the goals of the Party above the goals of friendship, it has assured that the leaders, even more than the average people, will be comrades first and friends second.

Ho Kan-Chih

52 SOCIALIZING THE BUSINESS COMMUNITY

Ho Kan-Chih, *A History of the Modern Chinese Revolution* (Peking: Foreign Languages Press, 1959), excerpted from pp. 556–59.

Ho Kan-Chih is a Chinese Communist historian.

In the relations between capital and labour, deviations on both sides had occurred in the early years after the liberation. On the one hand, some capitalists had stubbornly refused to concede to the workers their essential democratic rights; on the other hand, some workers had put forward excessive demands. To rectify both, it was necessary to induce the capitalists to recognize the workers' essential democratic rights and the benefit that the development of production would bring to the people's economy. The tension between capital and labour was eased by consultation, and the relations between them normalized by contracts.

To readjust the relations between production and marketing, all the private and public sectors of the economy were urged to strengthen their planning, overcome blindness and anarchy in production and keep a balance between production and marketing.

At the Third Session of the First National Committee of the People's Political Consultative Conference convened in October 1951, it was resolved that in order to embark on large-scale economic construction, the People's Government should devote its main efforts to launching a nation-wide movement for increasing production and practising economy.

To further such a movement, a relentless struggle had to be waged against corruption, waste and bureaucracy, for corruption and waste held back the increase of production and practice of economy, while bureaucracy was the hotbed where corruption and waste were fostered. To eliminate these evils, the *san fan* movement[1] was carried out among government employees in the winter of 1951 and the first half of 1952.

Corruption, waste and bureaucracy had continued to exist under the

---

[1] A movement against what was known as the "three evils"—corruption, waste and bureaucracy.

revolutionary regime. There were two main reasons for this. First, after the victory of the revolution, the Party had adopted a policy of taking over all the personnel of Kuomintang government organs and enterprises, many of whom had not had time to remould themselves ideologically. Then, a considerable number of cadres failed to have a clear perception of the change in class relations after the victory of the revolution and were not vigilant enough against the corrosion and attack by the decadent bourgeois ideas. They neglected or ignored the warning given by the Second Plenary Session of the Seventh Central Committee of the Party that it was imperative to guard against the "sugar-coated bullets" of the bourgeoisie. As corruption, waste and bureaucracy were expressions of a decadent bourgeois outlook, the *san fan* movement was virtually a struggle against this outlook.

Parallel with the *san fan* movement, the *wu fan* movement[2] was carried out among industrialists and businessmen. This was a counter-blow at the repeated onslaughts made by the bourgeoisie against the working class during the three years after liberation. Many capitalists had been kicking at the Party's policy of restricting capitalist industry and commerce. They were only ready to take government orders for processing and manufacture when the market was dull and the supply of raw materials short. But when the market was brisk and raw materials easily obtainable, they would attempt to shake off all restrictions and seek high profit in the free market. Some of them had actually gone so far as to make super-profits by illegal means. Employing as their weapons the "five evils," they made a furious assault on cadres in government organs and enterprises. Most cases of large-scale corruption and embezzlement were committed by agents of the bourgeoisie inside government organs or enterprises in collusion with law-breaking capitalists. This state of affairs was not merely a question of violation of law and discipline on the part of the offenders, but was chiefly the upshot of the corrosive influence of the bourgeoisie and their furious onslaught on the revolutionary camp. The bourgeoisie had fondly hoped to rob the people of the fruits of their revolution. This was tantamount to making a frontal attack on the leadership of the working class. Hence the *san fan* and *wu fan* movements were essentially struggles for the preservation and consolidation of the leadership of the working class.

The *san fan* movement cleansed government organs, established closer ties between the government and the masses, strengthened discipline and increased efficiency in government work, and greatly reduced government expenditure. The *wu fan* movement curbed substantially the illegal activ-

---

[2] A campaign against the "five evils"—bribery of government personnel, tax evasion, theft of state property, cheating on government contracts and stealing economic information.

ities among the capitalist industrialists and businessmen and brought capitalist industry and commerce within the orbit of state plans.

Edward Taborsky

53 CONTROL OF EDUCATION AND MASS MEDIA IN CZECHOSLOVAKIA

Edward Taborsky, *Communism in Czechoslovakia: 1948–1960* (Princeton, N.J.: Princeton University Press, 1961), excerpted from pp. 541–43, 589–91. Reprinted by permission of Princeton University Press. Copyright 1961 by Princeton University Press. Footnote references have been deleted.

Edward Taborsky is Professor of Government at the University of Texas. He was Secretary to the Foreign Minister of Czechoslovakia in 1938. After the Nazi take-over, he joined the government-in-exile in England. As Personal Aide, he accompanied President Beneš to the 1943 conference with Franklin D. Roosevelt and to the 1943 and 1945 conferences with Stalin and Molotov. From 1945 to 1948 he was Czechoslovak Envoy to Sweden.

The whole educational establishment is permeated, as is every other sphere of activity in the communist state, by a thorough system of interlocking checks and controls governed by the notorious principles of democratic centralism and one-man management. The supreme controller is the Minister of Education. As a plenipotentiary of the Party leadership in the most crucial sector of the battle for men's minds he wields an almost absolute authority over every important facet of the country's education. While the actual operation of all schools below the college level, including the power to appoint and dismiss teachers and to create new schools, is in the hands of the school departments of the people's committees, these are bound in every phase of work by a maze of detailed directives and regulations that leave them little discretion.

The principal instrument of the Minister of Education in the exercise of his control is a nation-wide network of regional and district school inspectors who, as their instruction specify, "are responsible for the work of the principals, teachers, and other school workers entrusted to their supervision from the political, professional, pedagogical, and administrative viewpoint." The school principals in their turn are personally responsible for the work of all the teachers attached to their schools. . . .

. . . Another useful device of control over the teachers, as well as the pupils' classwork, are the "pupil's books" in which are kept a regular record of the pupil's work, his failures and success, and his "socialist commitments."

Together with these official or formal controls are multiple informal controls involving school administrators, teachers, and pupils, as well as outsiders. The key role in this respect is assigned to the KSČ's primary units in the schools. . . .

. . . communist teachers check on their non-communist colleagues to help them "fulfill their tasks in an exemplary fashion." By using the prescribed devices of criticism and self-criticism they must see that the education of youth is carried out in the Marxist-Leninist spirit. They must report shortcomings to the proper authorities. Although they may not replace the principal, they have the right and the duty to criticize him whenever necessary and to make recommendations for improvement in school work. They are instructed to gather information from selected communist students in the Pioneer and Youth Union organizations who bring them "a view from below" regarding the teacher's work. As reported from many different sources and implicitly confirmed from communist quarters as well, these informers from among the communist pupils are a constant menace both to their classmates and to the teachers, particularly in the upper secondary schools. They engage in conversations with other pupils, especially those of bourgeois origin, during school intervals. They keep close watch over the teachers' lectures and behavior as well as the pupils' reactions. Sometimes they remain in classrooms, locked during the noon interval, for the purpose of searching through other pupils' satchels and papers. Information obtained through such spying activities is handed over to the secretaries of the Party units in the schools and finds its way eventually into the cadre reports of the pupils and teachers.

Finally, these intramural Party controls are supplemented by frequent informal checks from the outside. "Friends of the school" participate through the Associations of the Parents and Friends of the School, in meetings of pedagogical councils, and through other contacts with the schools. Party units and work councils of various socialist enterprises visit classrooms and pupils' and teachers' gatherings, organize discussions with the pupils, and invite them to their plants. An additional avenue of outside check has also been opened by the recent inclusion of actual work in factories and collective farms as a substantial part of the school curricula.

. . . [W]hat have thus far been the other results of the communist battle for the adult mind?

To begin with, the system of controls over, and the degree of regimentation of, all the media of adult indoctrination follow closely those of the
U.S.S.R.; and so does the over-all pattern of development. When regimentation was at its peak in the Soviet Union, so was it in Czechoslovakia. The
mollifying effects and after-effects of the post-Stalin thaw were much the
same in Czechoslovakia as in Russia. . . .

The Soviet trends are also reflected in the degree to which the controls
are applied to the various indoctrination media. They are most complete in
broadcasting and in libraries. Being administered directly by the State
under the supreme and constant direction of the Ministry of Education and
Culture, these two institutions remained under strict control even during
the post-Stalin relaxation. This is true also of the Society for the Dissemination of Political and Scientific Knowledge which belongs among the most
orthodox and most doctrinaire of the Party's transmission belts.

Next in line in the thoroughness of communist control are the newspapers. But for a few flashes of nonconformism at the height of the post-
Stalin thaw, the Czechoslovak daily press has ever since the communist
coup of 1948 kept within the prescribed bounds of Party directives, even
though it did so with an obvious lack of enthusiasm. . . .

Although the motion picture industry is as fully government-controlled
as the radio, it has nevertheless withstood the onslaught of ideological
regimentation somewhat better. Having had no previous experience in the
field of film production, the Party controllers have evidently found it more
difficult to impose their will there than in the operation of the air waves. As
a consequence, Western influence and the traditional concept of the motion
picture as a means of entertainment rather than a medium of indoctrination
have lingered on despite persistent communist efforts to weed them out.
The Czechoslovak film industry had to be warned repeatedly against such
gross ideological *faux pas* as a "superficial and narrow portrayal of the role
of the KSČ," "inaccurate portraiture of the types of the middle peasants
and of the village rich" or plain "escaping from reality." . . .

Similar difficulties confront the regime in the live theater area which
continues, according to communist complaints, to be plagued by unhealthy
individualism and leftovers of bourgeois attitudes. In spite of stiff communist controls the theaters still somehow manage to show socially neutral
plays without an appropriate ideological message. One way of doing this is
to include in the repertoire a disproportionate number of classical plays.
Another method, scored recently by a Czech communist broadcast as "a
clever move designed to circumvent the crux of socialist problems," is the
"exaggerated staging of progressive plays by authors writing within a
capitalist society."

54 THE ROLE OF SOCIAL ORGANIZATIONS IN THE CONSTRUCTION OF COMMUNISM

The Road to Communism: Documents of the Twenty-second Congress of the Communist Party of the Soviet Union, October 17–31, 1961, (Moscow: Foreign Languages Publishing House, n.d.), pp. 553–56.

In his report "On the Programme of the Communist Party of the Soviet Union" at the Twenty-second Party Congress in October 1961, Premier Nikita S. Khrushchev expressed his belief that a communist society would be built within 20 years. He noted that as the dictatorship of the proletariat developed into "a state of the whole people" there was still a strong need for the maintenance of public order and legality. To assist the state organs of government in "a further strengthening of legality and of law and order," Khrushchev stated that "public organizations of working people will play an increasing role in combating antisocial and criminal elements. The fight against misappropriators of public property, against parasites and rowdies will be waged still more effectively, since it will have become the business of all working people and their organizations." This greater reliance on quasi-governmental bodies to regulate and mold social behavior is a characteristic feature of Soviet everyday life and an increasingly important Party preoccupation since 1962.

The role of social organisations increases in the period of the full-scale construction of communism. The *trade unions* acquire particular importance as schools of administration and economic management, as schools of communism. The Party will help the trade unions to take a growing share in economic management and to make the standing production conferences increasingly effective in improving the work of enterprises and exercising control over production. The trade unions shall:

1. Work constantly to increase the communist consciousness of the masses; organise an emulation movement for communist labour and help the working people in learning to manage state and social affairs; take an active part in controlling the measure of labour and the measure of consumption;

2. Encourage the activity of factory and office workers, enlisting their aid in the work for continuous technical progress, for higher productivity of labour, for the fulfilment and overfulfilment of state plans and assignments;

3. Work steadfastly for the improvement of the skill of factory and office workers and their working and living conditions; protect the material interests and rights of the working people;

4. Ensure that housing and cultural development plans are fulfilled and that public catering, trade, social insurance, and health resort services are improved;

5. Ensure control over the spending of public consumption funds and over the work of all enterprises and institutions serving the people;

6. Improve cultural services and recreation facilities for the working people; encourage physical training and sports.

The *Young Communist League,* an independently acting public organisation of the youth which helps the Party to educate young people in a communist spirit, enlist them in the practical job of building the new society and train a generation of harmoniously developed people who will live, work and manage public affairs under communism, will play a greater role. The Party regards the youth as a great creative force in the Soviet people's struggle for communism.

The Y.C.L. must display still greater initiative in all spheres of life, must encourage the activity and labour heroism of the youth. Y.C.L. organisations must concentrate on educating the youth in a spirit of utmost devotion to their country, the people, the Communist Party and the communist cause, constant preparedness for labour for the good of society and for overcoming all difficulties and improving the general education and technical knowledge of all young men and women. It is the sacred duty of the Y.C.L. to prepare young people for the defence of their socialist country, to educate them as selfless patriots capable of firmly repelling any enemy. The Y.C.L. educates the youth in a spirit of strict adherence to communist moral principles and standards. Its activities in the schools and Young Pioneer organisations must contribute to the moulding of a buoyant, industrious, and physically and morally sound generation.

A greater role will be played by *co-operatives*—kolkhozes, consumers', housing and other co-operative organisations—as a form of drawing the masses into communist construction, as media of communist education and schools of public self-government.

Other social associations of the working people—scientific, scientific-technical and popular-science societies, rationalisers' and inventors' organisations, associations of writers, art workers and journalists, cultural-education organisations, and sports societies—will likewise be developed.

The Party regards it as a major task of the social organisations to promote labour emulation in every possible way, and to encourage communist forms of labour, to stimulate the activity of working people in building a communist society, to work for the improvement of the living conditions of the people and the satisfaction of their growing spiritual requirements. Mass organisations should be given a greater part in managing cultural, health and social insurance institutions; within the next few years they should be entrusted with the management of theatres and concert halls, clubs, libraries, and other state-controlled cultural-education establishments; they should be encouraged to play a greater part in promoting law and order, particularly through the people's volunteer squads and comradely courts.

To extend the independent activities of mass organisations, the Party considers it necessary further to reduce their salaried staffs from top to bottom, to renew each elective body by roughly as many as one-half of its membership at the regular election. It is advisable for the leading functionaries of social organisations not to be elected, as a general rule, for more than two consecutive terms.

As socialist statehood develops, it will gradually become *communist self-government* of the people which will embrace the Soviets, trade unions, cooperatives, and other mass organisations of the people. This process will represent a still greater development of democracy, ensuring the active participation of all members of society in the management of public affairs. Public functions similar to those performed by the state today in the sphere of economic and cultural management will be preserved under communism and will be modified and perfected as society develops. But the character of the functions and the ways in which they are carried out will be different from those under socialism. The bodies in charge of planning, accounting, economic management, and cultural advancement, now government bodies, will lose their political character and will become organs of public self-government. Communist society will be a highly-organised community of working men. Universally recognised rules of the communist way of life will be established whose observance will become an organic need and habit with everyone.

Historical development inevitably leads to the withering away of the state. To ensure that the state withers away completely, it is necessary to provide both internal conditions—the building of a developed communist society—and external conditions—the victory and consolidation of socialism in the world arena.

Bibliography

U.S.S.R.

Alt, H., and E. Alt, *Russia's Children*. New York: Bookman Associates, 1959.
Bauer, R. A., *The New Man in Soviet Psychology*. Cambridge, Mass.: Harvard University Press, 1952.
————, A. Inkeles, and C. Kluckhohn, *How the Soviet System Works*. Cambridge, Mass.: Harvard University Press, 1956.
Berman, H. J., *Justice in the U.S.S.R.* (2nd ed.). Cambridge, Mass.: Harvard University Press, 1963.

Brzezinski, Z. K., *The Permanent Purge: Politics in Soviet Totalitarianism.* Cambridge, Mass.: Harvard University Press, 1956.

Buzek, A., *How the Communist Press Works.* New York: Frederick A. Praeger, Inc., 1964.

Cantril, H., *Soviet Leaders and Mastery Over Man.* New Brunswick, N.J.: Rutgers University Press, 1960.

Counts, G. S., *The Challenge of Soviet Education.* New York: McGraw-Hill Book Company, 1957.

DeWitt, N., *Education and Professional Employment in the U.S.S.R.* Washington, D.C.: Government Printing Office, 1961.

Feifer, G., *Justice in Moscow.* New York: Simon and Schuster, Inc., 1964.

Fisher, R. T., Jr., *Pattern for Soviet Youth.* New York: Columbia University Press, 1959.

Inkeles, A., *Public Opinion in Soviet Russia: A Study in Mass Persuasion.* Cambridge, Mass.: Harvard University Press, 1951.

————, and R. A. Bauer, *The Soviet Citizen.* Cambridge, Mass.: Harvard University Press, 1959.

Kassof, A., *The Soviet Youth Program: Regimentation and Rebellion.* Cambridge, Mass.: Harvard University Press, 1965.

Mace, D., and V. Mace, *The Soviet Family.* New York: Doubleday & Company, Inc., 1963.

Mehnert, K., *Soviet Man and His World.* New York: Frederick A. Praeger, Inc., 1962.

Moore, B., Jr., *Terror and Progress U.S.S.R.* Cambridge, Mass.: Harvard University Press, 1954.

Morton, H., *Soviet Sports.* New York: Collier Books, a division of Crowell-Collier Publishing Co., 1963.

CHINA

Fraser, S., ed., *Chinese Communist Education: Records of the First Decade.* Nashville, Tenn.: Vanderbilt University Press, 1965.

Kuo-chun Chao, *The Mass Organizations in Communist China.* Cambridge, Mass.: Massachusetts Institute of Technology Press, 1953.

Labin, S., *The Anthill: The Human Condition in Communist China.* New York: Frederick A. Praeger, Inc., 1960.

Lifton, R. J., *Thought Reform and the Psychology of Totalism: A Study of "Brainwashing" in China.* New York: W. W. Norton & Company, Inc., 1961.

Schein, E. H., I. Schneier, and C. H. Barker, *Coercive Persuasion.* New York: W. W. Norton & Company, Inc., 1961.

Schurmann, H. F., *Ideology and Organization in Communist China.* Berkeley, Calif.: University of California Press, 1965.

Yu, F. T. C., *Mass Persuasion in Communist China.* New York: Frederick A. Praeger, Inc., 1964.

EASTERN EUROPE

Reisky de Dubnic, V., *Communist Propaganda Methods: A Case Study on Czechoslovakia.* New York: Frederick A. Praeger, Inc., 1960.

Szirmai, Z., ed., *Law in Eastern Europe: Studies in Polish Law,* Vol. VII. Leiden, Netherlands: A. W. Sijthoff, 1963.

Chapter Ten

The Cultural Condition under Communism

"Communism," someone once remarked, "may die of boredom." And indeed at the height of Stalinism, life was drab and devoid of hope; a stifling sense of fear pervaded Soviet and East European societies; people were fatigued not only from physical overwork but from the grayness of life and the jaded reiteration of official promises for a better world. A monotonous bleat echoed across the Soviet empire. It was a time of external conformity and internal withdrawal.

But in the period following the death of Stalin, and especially since the halcyon days of 1956, voices of dissonance and unrest have been heard in the Soviet Union and Eastern Europe, and the key word appears to be "alienation" (Readings 55 and 56). Though its causes and symptoms vary, alienation appears to afflict the youth of all countries, and in an age when youth has never been more courted, self-conscious, unsure, or rebellious. One psychiatrist has observed:

> The youth rebellions opposing totalism in Eastern Europe, Russia, and China seem to combine urges toward privacy, personal freedom, and self-expression (frequently manifested by interest in non-Communist literature, art, and jazz music, or by "bourgeois romance"), with patterns of nihilism not too different from those in the United States and among youths throughout the world.[1]

More than just the proverbial "conflict of generations," these rebellions are symptomatic of a deeper *malaise*—disillusionment with the failure to

---

[1] Robert Jay Lifton, *Thought Reform and the Psychology of Totalism* (New York: W. W. Norton & Company, Inc., 1961), p. 471.

337

practice the humanism implicit in communist ideals and ideology. The leaders are seriously concerned because apathy and estrangement are greatest among segments of the youth and intelligentsia, the very groups most favored by communist regimes.

The intelligentsia is described as a "social stratum consisting of people who are occupied professionally with mental labor." Composed of the "brain workers" of socialism, it is not a class in the Marxist sense of the word "because it does not hold an independent position in social production, although it plays a big part in the life of socialist society."[2] It is supposed to disappear as a distinct social group because, according to the 1961 Party Program, "With the victory of communism mental and physical labour will merge organically in the production activity of people. . . . Workers by hand will have risen in cultural and technological standards to the level of workers by brain." But there are few signs of such a trend, for the specialized skills necessary for industrial society tend to breed their own socio-economic stratification. Although the Soviet intelligentsia is more diverse in background, distribution, and function than its pre-1917 counterpart, it seems as self-conscious of the social gulf separating it from the rest of society. The composition and character of the intelligentsia, both in Russia and China, have altered considerably during the past few decades (Reading 57), but as a social group it continues to pose a problem for communist societies.

Soviet writers classify about 20 per cent of the working population as intelligentsia, but a distinction may be made between the "technical" intelligentsia and the "creative" intelligentsia. The former comprises the overwhelming majority; it includes the scientists, engineers, educators, administrators, and so forth, who are interested primarily in material and social advancement, and who accept the Party's judgment on all matters. Having acquired sufficient education to qualify as "brain-workers," they are proud of having transcended their lower-class origins and associate their rise in station with the leadership and the system. They are apolitical, loyal, and self-satisfied.

It is with the creative intelligentsia that communist regimes have their main difficulties. Among this group is found the corpus of nonconformist, questioning, and bold artists and writers. And it is to this group that the alienated youth gravitates, finding in its work the treasured concern for humanist values, for decency, democracy, and respect for the individual in everyday life.

Communist regimes believe that art and literature must serve socialism and conform to officially sanctioned criteria because they are ideological weapons to be deployed in the education of the masses and against "all

---

[2] O. W. Kuusinen, ed., *Fundamentals of Marxism-Leninism* (Moscow: Foreign Languages Publishing House, 1960), pp. 730–31.

wrong tendencies and ideological vacillations." On December 17, 1962, L. Ilyichov, a member of the Party Secretariat, told a conference of writers and artists:

> We should bear in mind as an immutable truth the fact that art always has an ideological-political tendency and that in one way or another it expresses and upholds the interests of definite classes and social strata. And when we encounter this or that tendency in art, the first questions which naturally arise are: Whose interests does it serve? Where is it asking people to go? What social ideals does it assert? . . . Art that is divorced from life is incapable of serving the transformation of life. . . .
>
> [Furthermore], good intentions on the part of an artist do not by any means exclude the possibility that objectively his works may serve the interests of hostile forces.[3]

The difficulty arises over where the line between officially approved "socialist realism" and decadent "bourgeois formalism and abstractionism" is to be drawn. Khrushchev, for example, approved the publication of A. Solzhenitsyn's *One Day in the Life of Ivan Denisovich* (a stark portrait of life in a slave-labor camp during the latter years of the Stalin era), but he denounced and forbade the publication of Pasternak's *Doctor Zhivago* (which had initially been accepted by a Soviet publishing house). His diatribe against artists "who produce 'paintings' of such a kind that it is hard to say whether they have been produced by a man's hand or painted by a donkey's tail" is often quoted. Composers have been attacked for "cacophonous" music; and writers, for "anti-Soviet misanthropic verses, very much like the ravings of a lunatic."

In art, as in politics and morals, the Party is the final arbiter. It has arrogated to itself the authority "to shape the results of the artistic process," because to relinquish its authority in one area might lead to erosion in other areas and because the Party fears the consequences of the free and critical questioning that underlies the "protest" literature of the post-Stalin period.

In China, the leadership has been ambivalent in its handling of the intelligentsia. Needing the intellectuals for "socialist construction," yet suspicious of their Western-shaped education and their individualism, it has fluctuated between benevolent accommodation and militant ideological remolding. In January 1956, for example, the Central Committee convened a special session to discuss ways of enlisting the support of the intellectuals in the drive for development. The principal speech, delivered by Chou En-lai, presaged Mao Tse-tung's "Hundred Flowers" venture, with its invitation to open criticism of existing shortcomings. Chou En-lai decried the Party's mistrust of the intellectuals and called on it "to improve the manner of employing and placing them, so that they can develop their specialized

---

[3] *Soviet News*, No. 4792 (January 4, 1963), p. 10.

skills to the benefit of the state."[4] He said that scientists who wished to undertake research should be permitted to do so, that they should not be assigned "administrative work in government organs and schools":

> Intellectuals outside the Party must not only enjoy our confidence, but also enjoy our support. That is to say, they must be given jobs and authority, their views must be respected, the results of their professional research and work must be valued. There must be promoted and extended academic discussions of Socialist construction. Their creations and inventions must be given opportunities for experiment and extension. A small number of Party members and League members do not respect the leadership of intellectuals who are non-members of the Party but occupy higher positions above them. This situation must be corrected.
>
> The failure to give due confidence and support to some intellectuals is the major manifestation of sectarianism in some of our comrades in dealing with the question of intellectuals. Not a few comrades are still not used to the practice of consulting intellectuals outside the Party on matters, or to give them timely guidance and assistance. Some comrades easily get themselves estranged from intellectuals outside the Party, and even adopt the attitude of respecting them but keeping them at a distance. In this way, there is a lack of mutual understanding, and estrangement becomes the easier. However, they are important workers of our State, the quality of their work will directly affect national construction, and so we have the responsibility to learn to use the attitude of dealing with our own comrades in our approach to them, in correctly understanding them, and to give them guidance and assistance so that they may promote their active role in work.[5]

During the 1957–1961 "anti-rightist" period, the Party shifted to an emphasis on ideological remolding of the intellectuals and "accelerated its campaign to transform the 'bourgeois intellectuals' into 'working-class intellectuals,' " to make them "both red and expert."[6] From 1961 to 1964, the Party again moderated its insistence on "political study"; then, late in 1964, it undertook anew a campaign of remolding the artists and intellectuals. Chou En-lai set the tone by asserting that "socialist culture must serve the politics of the proletariat, serve the workers, peasants and soldiers, and serve the economic base of socialism." It is clear that the Chinese communist leadership seeks to root out dissidence and nonconformity in all realms, lest they engender opposition to the regime's totalist drive to remake society; at the same time it does not wish to destroy the creativity of the intelligentsia until a new generation, presumably compliant and committed to socialism, has been trained.

---

[4] Chou En-lai, "On the Question of the Intellectuals," *Current Background,* No. 376 (February 7, 1956), p. 6.

[5] *Ibid.,* p. 6.

[6] Dennis J. Doolin, " 'Both Red and Expert': The Dilemma of the Chinese Intellectual," *Current Scene,* II, No. 19 (September 1, 1963), 5.

Among the social problems confronting communist regimes, none has proved more frustrating than religion. Religion is like a nail; the harder you strike it the more deeply imbedded it becomes. The traditional role, character, and attraction of religion and religious institutions have been markedly different in the Soviet Union and China (Reading 58).

Since January 1918, when all church property was nationalized in Russia, the Party has tried to eradicate religion by force, social pressure, education, and economic deprivation; it has indoctrinated the young in atheism and the "science" of dialectical materialism, and it has mounted repeated and virulent antireligious campaigns. There was a temporary relaxation during World War II, when Stalin perceived that the people would fight, suffer, and die for God and country, but not for the Politburo and communism. Believing that religion could provide the solace needed to sustain a heroic war effort, and that the church did not constitute any political threat, he permitted hundreds of churches to reopen. But since 1945, the regime has renewed its efforts to weaken the attraction of religion by ridiculing practitioners and denigrating the assumptions underlying religious belief. The Party Program states:

The Party uses ideological media to educate people in the spirit of a scientific material world conception, to overcome religious prejudices without insulting the sentiments of believers. It is necessary to conduct regularly broad atheistic propaganda on a scientific basis, to explain patiently the untenability of religious beliefs, which were engendered in the past when people were overawed by the elemental forces and social oppression and did not know the real causes of natural and social phenomena. This can be done by making use of the achievements of modern science, which are steadily solving the mysteries of the universe and extending man's power over nature, leaving no room for religious inventions about supernatural forces.[7]

But perhaps the ultimate indication of the persisting and *spreading* attraction of religion in the Soviet Union is that for the first time in the history of the Communist Party, the Rules of the CPSU, modified at the Twenty-second Congress in 1961, include the following provision in the section on "Party Members, Their Duties and Rights":

It is the duty of a Party member: . . . (*d*) to master Marxist-Leninist theory, to improve his ideological knowledge, and to contribute to the moulding and education of the man of Communist society. To combat vigorously all manifestations of bourgeois ideology, remnants of a private-property psychology, *religious prejudices,* and other survivals of the past; . . . [Italics added.][8]

---

[7] *Programme of the Communist Party of the Soviet Union* (Moscow: Foreign Languages Publishing House, 1961), p. 110.

[8] *Rules of the Communist Party of the Soviet Union* (Moscow: Foreign Languages Publishing House, 1961), pp. 6–7.

The situation in Eastern Europe varies from country to country. In Poland the population is overwhelmingly Roman Catholic. There the prestige of the church is, paradoxically, greater than it was before the communist take-over. The state's confiscation of large church landholdings, the elimination of the influence of the nobility on the church, and the open opposition of the church to the Communist Party have combined to eliminate the sources of peasant hostility to the church; as a result, the church has regained the esteem of the peasantry. The peasantry's deep-rooted commitment to Catholicism was never in question, and now it has become pro-clerical. But urbanization and industrialization are challenges to the church; it must now adapt its appeal to a new sociological situation in which the important group to reach is the restless, alienated youth.

In Yugoslavia, a functioning though uneasy accommodation has been reached between the Roman Catholic Church and the communist regime; there never was a serious problem with the Serbian Orthodox Church (Reading 59). Ideologically, the regime remains hostile to religion but does not now seek to destroy it; indeed, it contributes modest material support to various religious denominations. The centrally directed effort to promote atheism and antireligious propaganda has been largely muted, and the regime allows the overwhelming majority of the people, who are not communists, to consider religion a private matter.

The many changes in the Soviet Union and Eastern Europe have mellowed the political systems and improved the conditions under which their citizens live. Though not all social groups have benefited equally, the improvements have touched them all. The harshness of the Stalin era has been mitigated: the indiscriminate application of widespread terror has ended; the improved standard of living and the preoccupation with economic rationality have had salutary side-effects in the social and cultural areas; and communist regimes are giving some serious attention to the problem of safeguarding the individual against arbitrary administrative behavior by local officials. Political power, however, remains centralized and impervious to public influence. Still, social and economic pressures are leading communist regimes to tolerate moderate cultural dissonances and to refrain increasingly from a too-confining control over the personal lives of their people.

Peter Veres

55 ALIENATION: A HUNGARIAN VIEW

Peter Veres, "Alienation: A Hungarian View," *East Europe*, XIV,
No. 3 (March, 1965), excerpted from pp. 23–26.

*Alienation is currently a favorite topic of discussion among East European intel-
lectuals. Peter Veres, a writer and former chairman of the Peasant Party of
Hungary, explored this subject in the December 1964 issue of the literary magazine* Kortars (*Budapest*), *and came to the conclusion that the Hungarian problem is not alienation but "indifference." His commentary illumines the nature
and dimensions of alienation, both in communist Hungary and in the non-
communist West.*

Alienation? Too much is being said nowadays on this topic. Sooner or
later alienation will become the chief preoccupation of our thinking
community. (I purposely did not say "philosophical" community, which is,
by the way, very inept.)

I would like, in this letter, to put aside the question of whether "alienation" is the same, and to what extent it is the same, as that mentioned by
Marx. A discussion is already under way on this question among persons
better informed than myself. I am not so worried about the concept of
alienation as I am about the following: how much of the discussion relates
to us Hungarians, to our present state of affairs, our situation and future?

Let me first explain why I exclude here the discussion on alienation
pursued in the West. I do this because I do not know anything essential or
truly authoritative about today's Western society. I do not know anything
about its deeper reality. As regards the surface, some of its aspects are
brought to us by the whirlwind of civilization. I feel—only "feel" and do
not "know"—that if a statistician were to examine the financial means of
"alienated" men in the West, it would turn out that they are not exactly
small.

The majority of these people have something to turn to in their alienation. They retire into their own little house or castle and to their respective
"hobbies." Such an investigation would probably reveal that secluded and
embittered individualism is a rather costly way of life. It requires a secure
source of income. . . . I believe that in the West the frame of mind of a
true worker, especially one with a family, or of an unemployed person

could not be characterized as alienation, but as hostile relations to the ruling forces of state and society.

I have a suspicion that alienation is the disease of intellectuals who are individualists in their way of thinking and feeling about life; of pseudo-intellectuals, related to the former in a rather snobbish manner; of persons always initiated, always in the know; and, finally, of "intellectual petty bourgeois" persons who are strongly oriented toward "success" without the talent to achieve it.

Alienation is also, and naturally, the malady of childless people, of people who do not belong to a nation or a community. A really hard-working individual—be he worker, peasant or intellectual—absorbed with the worries of everyday living, with trying to do his work well, and with the natural desire for minor joys, does not as a rule "philosophize" about existentialist questions. . . .

This, I would like to repeat, is only my logic, because I really do not know what the truth is under the surface success of Western bourgeois societies. . . . What, in fact, do we know about today's Western society? What do we know about the peasantry or, for that matter, about the workers who are the so-called highest (I don't like the term "ruling") class of the new world order? I would go even further and ask: what do we know about the petty bourgeoisie in the West? I do not mean the "intellectual" petty bourgeoisie, but the hard-working, small "freedom maniacs?" The best picture of them is provided by the new Italian literature (Pratolini, Moravia, Italo Calvino, etc.), which naturally portrays its own society. Interestingly enough, the same could be said about Americans. Faulkner and Thomas Wolfe wrote about the older America; Salinger, who I feel is not a superficial "success," writes about contemporary America. (I trust him more than Tennessee Williams, who rummages in putrefaction, for after all America is not characterized only by putrefaction.) There can be no committed literature without sociological awareness, without a way of looking at things from the point of view of society, without a communal feeling, way of thinking, taste and attitude. If there is a literature without these things, it merely plays an empty role.

What Is Hungary's Problem?

But let us, at last, turn to our own affairs. Why do I believe that the alienation problem, which has become fashionable in the West, cannot be adapted to our country?

In an article published last fall ("Meetings of Writers and Readers" in *Nepmuveles*), I used the term "indifference" to describe the apathy, lethargy and lack of interest displayed by a fairly large number of workers, even including persons who attend evening courses in order to broaden their knowledge. This lack of interest is primarily evident in connection with true literature and deep thought, but it also manifests itself in respect to problems connected with the state, nation, community and with the socialist ideal and socialist construction.

A fairly large proportion of our youth, not the hooligans, but the quiet and reliable young men who study conscientiously and who for the sake of peace and in order not to be bothered have joined KISZ [the Communist Youth Association], have developed a kind of "apolitical" mentality. This, I believe, is less due to Western existentialist and nihilistic influences than to the general feeling of Hungarian youth that it is not being entrusted with any real tasks.

The "apolitical" attitudes of grownups, *i.e.,* middle-aged workers and older persons, is partly the result of the above feeling. But it is mainly due to weariness and disappointment—the rebound from Messianism! Taken together, these factors are so strong that, in my opinion, compared to the many other important and pressing economic or other questions, "apoliticalness" is the biggest and most difficult problem facing Hungarian society today.

Is the phenomenon which I call indifference not identical with what is labelled alienation in the West? My answer is: no. I do not give this answer to be eccentric, nor is it an attempt at originality. I could qualify this "no" by stating that alienation in the Western sense of the word could be applied to some intellectuals. It could also be applied to a certain extent to all the people who contribute to the building of a socialist society without having a socialist ideology, faith and conviction. The people I refer to here are not simply physical laborers, but men engaged in propaganda work who have to proclaim and preach the socialist faith and precepts, all the while not accepting that faith and belief, or holding to an opposing creed.

The Anatomy of Indifference

The indifference of the broad masses, however, derives from entirely different sources. It comes from dissatisfaction with the achievements and progress of socialist construction, with the prevalent housing conditions and with homelessness. These are the reasons for most of the unhappiness and ill feeling. This dissatisfaction grows along with "individualization," which today could be called a worldwide phenomenon. Dissatisfaction is also caused by present wages and working conditions; it includes the boredom of performing work without a feeling of vocation for the sole purpose of earning one's daily bread. (This is the point most closely approaching alienation in the Western sense of the word.)

Work is "monotonous," life is "hectic," both of them are exhausting, and this is why amusements, the "weekend," and "vacationing" degenerate into a mania. An old-time landlord or farmer never "took a holiday," because he could always refresh himself at home. (Traveling, "seeing the world," or going to spas were something other than weekending and vacationing.) There is also the dissatisfaction connected with nerve-racking commuting in general, and particularly in the mornings and evenings and on weekends.

· · ·

This could be one of the reasons, but let us abandon the digressions, even though they actually lead someplace, and let us concentrate on the main line, which I, in spite of the complexity of some of the digressions, consider to be the following: A fairly large part of the Hungarian population, which was very poor, without real means and without civic rights ("three million beggars" in the villages, the fourth million in the cities), awaited and welcomed socialism with a "Messianic" fervor. (I do not refer here to the hostile, incredulous and "class alien" persons, whom one cannot expect to sing the praises of socialism, but who, nevertheless, are coming along fine.)

After 1945, and for understandable propaganda reasons, we continued to strengthen this Messianic psychosis of happiness which, in fact, is a historical malady. Some journalists, radio and TV men are still strengthening it out of overzealousness, good intentions or merely because of an inherited "routine of style." Yet it is obvious that our task should be to liberate those of our people who were brought up in poverty and without civic rights, whose character contains a certain ephemeral enthusiasm and exhaltation, to liberate them from this Messianic psychosis so that they may regard everything in the world, their own fate as well as the construction of socialism, with a certain amount of historical realism. Without such realism it is simply impossible to live in today's world, let alone in tomorrow's world!

A Man Grows Tired

As I have said before, the problem is very complex, many-sided and intricate. A scientific analysis of it is the task of sociologists who have the necessary facilities. I can only enumerate a few of my impressions. For example, I would like to mention one of the most natural historical experiences, *e.g.,* that the people—their number in Hungary is not small—who have fought a great deal and for a long time, first for the revolution, then for the realization of the new order and the new way of life, have grown tired. They would have grown tired even if they had not been forced along the well-known, upsetting, winding detours, even if they had not been forced to obey the "random" measures of an antagonistic leadership. A man engaged in public affairs grows tired whether or not his work is successful. But perhaps the worst thing for him is for his faith to be upset, for the results of his work to be different from what he had believed, expected and desired. . . .

Finally, in order to make it clear to those who might fail to understand what proceeds from the above, as well as from that which has not even been said, let me try to explain where I find all this leading. The human being distinguishes himself from all other types of animals by his ability to influence his own fate and human existence, up to the limit to which the recognized truth leads him. It seems to me the road leading out of the difficulties, which though already announced has not yet been taken because of various major and minor impediments, is the one which stresses the necessity to find, work out and set up with the citizens—party members and non-party people alike—a frank, authentic, objective and just familiarization and understanding of public affairs.

Zbigniew A. Jordan

56 ALIENATION AND WITHDRAWAL AMONG POLISH YOUTH

Zbigniew A. Jordan, "The Ideologies of Polish Youth: From Revolution to Withdrawal," *East Europe,* **13,** No. 1 (January, 1964), excerpted from pp. 8–11. Footnote references have been deleted.

Zbigniew A. Jordan received his Ph.D. from Poznan University before World War II. He is the author of Philosophy and Ideology: The Development of Philosophy and Marxism-Leninism in Poland since the Second World War, *and a frequent contributor to scholarly journals.*

. . . [T]he ideology of withdrawal is not a thing of the past; it is part of the present-day urban adolescent culture in Poland. It puzzles the older and angers the middle generations, who severely criticize the culture of the youth in their teens and early twenties. . . . [T]here seems to exist a clear-cut ideological difference between the 16 to 24 age group and those 25 to 34 years old.

The "puzzling tribe of the young," as the practitioners of the ideology of withdrawal have been called by a Warsaw sociologist, made its appearance in the post-October 1956 period. Like the juvenile delinquent gangs a few years earlier, they first became identifiable by their style of dress. In the course of time, however, they developed fine variations in attire, which precluded categorical identification of all rebel youth groups as a single movement. Observers in Warsaw reported that particular "clans" of youth adopted different ways of dress to emphasize their separateness from other youth groups and at the same time to harmonize their outward appearance with their cultural aspirations.

The spread of a distinctive dress and hair style, often modeled on the fashion prevailing among the youth in *Quartier Latin* and *St. Germain,* the addiction to jazz and rock-and-roll, the popularity of "haunts" with background piano music, night caves and cabarets in vaulted cellars, all seemed to indicate that Polish youth had gone "existentialist." Although undergraduate theatres, coffee-rooms, dance halls, night clubs and other places of entertainment patronized by the young are nothing new in the youth culture, their extreme popularity is a novel phenomenon. They are manifestations of the younger generation's wish to disassociate themselves from the adult world.

The young also tend to assert their self-reliance and defiance by violating the accepted patterns of sexual behavior. "Among a certain section of our youth there exists a pugnacious nonchalance which demands trivialization of the affairs of the heart," wrote a Warsaw newspaper. "Swaggering vulgarity, insensitivity and brute force—in the mind of a certain type of man—are evidence of the modern approach to sex matters, of the disgust with prejudice and a new way of life." This apparently applies equally to both sexes. A seventeen-year-old girl is often referred to as a *kitten*—a coolly profligate creature, contemptuous of the morals and ways of life of the adults.

In the moral and sexual life of contemporary youth in Poland one may discern certain characteristic features. For one thing, sexual experiences begin early. "Today's sixteen-year-old children are grown-up people," wrote a journalist about the younger generation. They lead a full sexual life on the principle of casual gratification. To them, the distinctions between sentiment and the physiological urge are incidental and unimportant; freedom and sexual promiscuity are synonymous. Sexual contacts are, if the reports are correct, matter-of-fact and impersonal, for, to these young people, any deviation from cynicism is considered hypocritical or down-right dishonest.

In its main features this picture of youth is familiar to us from newspapers, books and films from Paris, London or New York. Just how faithfully they reflect the way of life of contemporary youth, and to what extent they are representative, we can never be certain. They are, however, accepted as such and interpreted as symptomatic of the difficulties of identity formation in a rapidly changing society. Since adolescent cultures everywhere seem to show a considerable similarity in their basic character-istics, it can be reasonably supposed that the disorientation from which they arise transcends national differences in political and social order. What this malaise is, however, has yet to be defined.

There is in Poland a group of young writers representative of the so-called "black literature." Marek Hlasko, the oldest among them, is well known abroad because his stories have been translated into many Euro-pean languages. The group is, however, very large and distinguished by talents. Some literary critics see in them a psychological and artistic kin-ship to the "angry young men" or to the beatniks. Like their counterparts abroad, the young Polish writers are accused of sometimes being unsure of what they are protesting about. To use G. K. Chesterton's quibble, they are said to have made *revolutionize* into an intransitive verb. Having no deep loyalty and rebelling against everything under the sun, they are considered incapable of performing any really useful social function.

According to other observers, these young writers express the world view of the contemporary Polish youth. What the latter feel, experience and demonstrate by their way of life, the artists formulate and convey in their works of fiction: a "tacit agreement with the beliefs and feelings of their contemporaries." As somebody else observed, the self-determination of this new generation as a mass phenomenon is accomplished not only by its mores but also through its artistic means.

The young writers do not think that their distinctiveness requires interpretations or justification; they take it for granted. They consider themselves to be members of a generation totally different from preceding ones.

> They do not find a place for themselves either in the mores or moral tradition of the bourgeoisie or in the theories and activities of (Marxist) ideologists. They isolate themselves in groups defined simply by age. The generational distinctiveness is regarded as a high value which needs not be demonstrated, since it appears to be self-evident. The adults are either considered as con-temptible creatures or ignored. . . .
>
> A young writer is likely to say that he does not intend to take part in the world made by the adults. He ridicules the sense of national identity, likes to return to his childhood and is always anxious to prolong youth as a state of secular grace. He seeks support, above all, in the disillusionment resulting from the bankruptcy of his adolescent or even childish dreams, which in an apparent way do not fit reality.

The representatives of the middle generation stress that they criticize the very young not for their immaturity but for what they call their infantilism, which reveals itself in various ways. For the writers of the "black litera-ture," adults are either fools or knaves. They never learn from experience. Hardly have they survived one crushing defeat of their high-sounding ideals, then they are ready to start afresh, to fall into new traps and suffer new debacles. The young wish to extricate themselves from this spiral of disasters, but in so doing they knowingly block all ways of escape. In order not to become contaminated by the world, they refuse to take risks as others do or to participate in what they call the "ideological fraud" or the "rat race." They indulge in cheap and naive sentimentalism, feel deserted, unhappy, helpless and hunted down. They turn their backs upon life, refuse to play its game and, having done so, torment themselves with vengefulness. They assume that youth alone is able to reveal what is hidden in the secret recesses of the human personality. They believe exclusively in their emotions from which they expect release from internal tensions, and ultimate salvation. They are disillusioned with the past, distrustful of ideology and convinced that the social order is transitory, neither better nor worse than what came before or what will follow. Since they show little appreciation of intellectual standards and cultural achievements but attach the highest value to instinct, they readily embrace various myths about themselves and the world which allow them to escape into despair, anarchy and irresponsibility.

"Holy Barbarians"

This portrait of the younger generation shows some obvious similarities between the "holy barbarians" in the United States and their counterparts in Poland. They share at least two important characteristics: they reject the world and are aggressively nonconformist. They reject the world because they conceive it as an inevitable fraud unredeemed by any distinctions which make one of its forms preferable one to another. Their nonconformism results from this conviction and from the sense that they are strangers in the world into which they were born.

In the case of the Polish beatniks, an important component of their outlook is the rejection of the values inherent in either the old or the new social order and their staunch refusal to cooperate in upholding either. Another important characteristic is their fascination with a personality pattern in which sentimentality and an existential sense of loneliness, despair or anguish are of a minor significance. The Polish beatnik seems to hold firmly to the belief that if the individual fails to understand and see meaning in the events in which he is involved, it is futile to pretend that the world makes sense. He makes much of his powerlessness in the face of events too complex to be influenced by him, and resigns himself to hopelessness. These are not necessarily, however, symptoms of infantilism. While it may be true, as Talcott Parsons—one of the leading American sociologists—suggested, that those who suffer acutely from this awareness constitute the inevitable quota of social casualties likely to occur in processes of drastic social change, the refusal to make compromises and to be deluded by "specious" arguments is a basic trait of every nonconformist.

The firm refusal to accept from adults their way of perceiving the world, the sincere determination to remain truthful to oneself and to make no concessions to conventions clearly belied by experience, are also shown by adolescents with no literary ambitions. This striking attitude among present-day youth is apparent in a letter written by a fourteen-year-old and published in the Catholic weekly *Tygodnik Powszechny*.

> We shun the habits and customs with which the older generation tries to present us and also the whole nonsense of more or less recent years. For this reason we are often in conflict with practically everything in our environment. We shun falsehood . . . we do not believe anybody's word. The whole world is mendacious. Also parents often tell lies. Therefore, we too tell them . . . but this does not mean that we are happy with it or that we don't see the lie . . . one has to be consistent and one has to make up one's mind one way or another: either to lie or not to lie. It is no use being indignant that others are mendacious while telling lies oneself.

The moral condemnation and the rejection of the adult world in the name of truth and consistency can be either a typical adolescent reaction or an intimation of the ideology of withdrawal. This is not meant to imply that the ideology of withdrawal is simply a continuation of the social psychology of adolescence. While the ideology of withdrawal originates in the experiences of adolescence and in the inter-generational differences, it also has its roots in the particular social situation and climate in Poland. It should be remembered that the disillusioned youth grew up in the stalinist period, and what they say in general terms about fraud and lies has for them a concrete and palpable content.

The younger generation is bound to be different from the older one; to find out that it is different is to discover the self-evident. The middle-aged reaction to those younger than themselves is largely caused by the contrast with their own youth. They themselves were deeply committed participants, totally engaged in the vast changes going on around them. They too viewed the world honestly, ardently and naively. They now see these qualities in others but in an inverted form resulting in withdrawal instead of commitment.

The ideology of withdrawal is the ideology of a highly articulate minority which, however, has many characteristics in common with other groups of their contemporaries. The attitudes and value orientations of its supporters are closely related to the characteristics of Polish youth in general. The findings of social research on youth, based on cross-national representative samples, seem to support the view that the ideology of withdrawal, reflected with varying intensity in different youth-groups, is actually the ideology of the whole social generation.

The Threats to Social Continuity in Poland

. . . With the ideology of withdrawal . . . there exists a serious threat to social continuity. By social continuity is meant the maintenance of the main institutional roles, of the orientations and values peculiar to a given society, in spite of changes in the composition of its membership. Generally, the conditions favoring the interaction of members of different age-groups also favor the continuity of the social system. On the other hand, if this interaction is severely strained or breaks down, social continuity and cultural transmission are endangered and are bound to suffer.

The question arises as to what are the causes of the alleged break in social and cultural continuity in Poland. In modern societies there are tendencies at work which enlarge and accentuate the break between the adult world and the world of youth, thus creating conditions favorable to segregation of youth into homogeneous groups according to age, disrupting social continuity, hampering cultural transmission, giving rise to ideologies of aggression or retreatism and to various forms of deviant behavior. Trends apparent in all modern societies were intensified in Poland by the various social effects of war and, in particular, by the social results of wartime and postwar upheavals.

To these general causes should be added three particular ones, which seem to give rise to the youth problem in Poland. The first of them concerns the discrepancy between family values and orientations and those accepted by the official communist ideology. The inevitable tensions and strains caused by this discrepancy are increased by the autocratic use of power, its encroachment upon privacy and its interference with the educational functions of the family. The reduced role which the family plays in the social structure accentuates the problems in the transition from adolescence to adult life and hampers the adjustment to extra-familial functions and activities.

The second major cause of the youth problem concerns that form of alienation which is defined as the non-availability of, or the discriminatory access to, the means by which socially approved goals can be attained. This is widely recognized to be one of the primary sources of various forms of deviant adjustment. It appears to be also an important contributory factor to normative disorientation, to an uncertain and ambivalent attitude toward the norms which regulate social interaction, define permissible and impermissible patterns of behavior and thus establish social coherence and solidarity.

A third, related cause is the conflict between individualistic and collectivistic systems of values. This conflict is perhaps now more apparent than ever before because the revolution in Poland has entered a stage of stabilization. Now traditional attitudes and value-orientations reassert themselves and press for the fulfillment of what are socially regarded as legitimate needs and aspirations.

All these causes have combined to produce a distinct social generation, marking the point when one era ends and another begins. The ideological peculiarities of today's youth, in particular their disengagement from any sense of social cause, make for an uncertain future for themselves and for succeeding generations.

Benjamin Schwartz

57 THE CHINESE AND RUSSIAN INTELLIGENTSIA: A TENTATIVE COMPARISON

Benjamin Schwartz, "The Intelligentsia in Communist China: A Tentative Comparison," in *The Russian Intelligentsia,* ed. Richard Pipes (New York: Columbia University Press, 1961), excerpted from pp. 172–81. Footnote references have been deleted.

Benjamin Schwartz is Professor of History and Government in the area of East Asian studies at Harvard University. He is the author of a number of books, including Chinese Communism and the Rise of Mao *and* In Search of Wealth and Power: Yen Fu and the West.

For convenience, we may divide the twentieth-century Chinese intelligentsia into three generations. There is the transitional generation of the late nineteenth and early twentieth century—men whose roots lie deep in the old culture, who have undergone the regimen of a traditional education, but who are already deeply shaken by the desperate plight of their state and society. They are already prepared to consider new institutions and foreign ideas, and yet are in many ways still part of the older literati. The crucial break comes with the student generation of the beginning of the twentieth century, many of whose members must be considered as the first truly "alienated" intellectuals of modern China. The third significant generation is the student generation of the May 4th period (1919), men now in their fifties and sixties. It is in this generation that the basic intellectual tendencies of recent decades crystallize.

The first generation is not yet alienated from the state. It still yearns to be "used," and still hopes to save the state from ruin. It is in the next generation that we see the emergence of the mystique of revolution. Only with this generation can we begin to speak with any assurance of a modern intelligentsia. It is also this generation which faces the enormous frustrations of the post-1911 period. There are many who enter political life in the sordid "warlord" period, but a clear cleavage appears between the "political opportunists" (*cheng k'o*) who serve, and the alienated intelligentsia who remain outside. The May 4th generation does become involved in the revolutionary activities of the Kuomintang-Communist alliance. Some of its members, in fact, become the bureaucracy of the Nationalist government. Yet many remain an alienated intelligentsia. The reasons for this are complex. The bulk of the intelligentsia had become committed in the period between 1919 and 1927 to a generally "left" and antitraditional stance. There were, to be sure, individuals like Liang Sou-ming, Feng Yu-Lan and others who may be considered the Chinese equivalents of the Russian Slavophiles. They continued to stress the validity, even the superiority, of certain Chinese values and often used Western conceptions to support their views. Like many of the Slavophiles, however, they carefully dissociated themselves from the official neo-traditionalism of the established regime and remained on the outside. The Nationalist government under Chiang Kai-shek attempted to create a neo-traditional underpinning for its nationalism and regarded the stance of the intelligentsia with profound mistrust. With the growth of the Maoist phase of Chinese Communism, we have a small segment of the intelligentsia who, as it were, simultaneously became professional revolutionaries and acting functionaries of a Communist state within a state.

In this light one does not feel that the alienation of the Chinese intelligentsia from the state is as decisive or as profound as that of the mid-nineteenth-century Russian intelligentsia. During the period between the 1911 revolution and the rise of the Nationalist government, the intelligentsia does not confront the massive power of a state from which it feels alienated. It rather confronts the disintegration of the state. Under the Nationalist government it is indeed alienated, yet the officialdom of that government is drawn from a background identical with its own, and there are many elements who live in a twilight world between government and intelligentsia, in spite of their mutual hostility. With the rise of the Communist state many of the intelligentsia were prepared to serve without undergoing the enormous adjustment from the life of "professional revolutionary" to bureaucratic functionary which we find among the old Bolsheviks in Russia. One can speak of the alienation of the twentieth-century

Chinese intelligentsia from the state. It is, however, a much more ambiguous and less decisive alienation than that of its Russian nineteenth-century counterpart.

Nevertheless, it is interesting to note that, as in the case of the Russian intelligentsia, the best of the Chinese intelligentsia do not turn their attention to the "practical" professions, in spite of a concerted effort on the part of the late Ch'ing government and later of the Nationalist government to channel it in this direction. A "bureaucratic" career, academic life or writing seem to be the major alternatives, and the choice determines one's future alignment as a conformist or as an alienated intellectual. To a considerable extent one must bear in mind the persistence of traditional habits of thought and behavior. Beyond this, we find, as in the Russian case, a reluctance among the more sensitive to commit themselves to specialized professions while the major agonizing problems of their society remain unsolved.

It is in terms of emotional attitudes and certain dominant strains of thought that the resemblance between the two intelligentsias becomes most striking. Thus the major general drift in the long run is toward "totalistic" attitudes. . . .

In the long run, the Marxist-Leninist claim to a monistic interpretation of the world and a monistic resolution of China's difficulties weighed heavily in its favor during the 'twenties and 'thirties. The widespread acceptance of a Marxist-Leninist world image, it must be added, however, did not imply a necessary commitment to the Communist party. To the very brink of 1949 a large part of the Chinese intelligentsia remained apart from the Communist movement itself. In China, however, as in Russia, the chiliastic view of "progress" was to dominate gradualistic, evolutionary views. . . .

Viewed from the vantage point of China, Russian culture, even in its earliest form, must be viewed as an "affiliate" of the West. The Orthodox religion draws on the same Judaic and Hellenic sources as does the Christianity of the West.

Furthermore, the Russian enlightened nobility of the eighteenth century was in sustained contact with Western ideas, while the Petrine state had taken on many of the aspects of contemporary Western states. The language itself with its Indo-European structure and its heritage of Judeo-Hellenic concepts lends itself easily to the transposition of Western ideas. Thus, in spite of the gloomy social and political scene, the nineteenth-century Russian intellectual and literary development seem to mark the culmination of a slow growth, rather than a complete traumatic break. The intelligentsia may be in revolt, but it is in revolt within a continuous historic process. This feeling of culmination is most spectacularly manifest in the magnificent literature of the nineteenth century, with its universal appeal.

Yet even the literature of ideas, whatever its lack of originality, is forceful, eloquent and self-assured. The Russian intelligentsia is reasonably at home in its intellectual and spiritual world.

In twentieth-century China we have not only a profound social and political crisis but also the seeming collapse of a culture and a whole system of values. The twentieth-century intelligentsia feverishly seeks Western values to fill the vacuum, and it must attempt to convey its ideas in a linguistic medium which is saturated with the categories of thought of an entirely different culture. It is no wonder that the writings of this intelligentsia frequently seem naïve and awkward to the Western eye. The Chinese *intelligent* is much less self-assured than his Russian counterpart, much less at home in the world of ideas he has come to embrace, much more in need of a new orientation.

One aspect of this cultural crisis is the burning need for a sense of national dignity. One of the striking aspects of the mid-nineteenth-century Russian intelligentsia is its disassociation from nationalistic aspirations. This intelligentsia may be nationalistic in certain senses of the word, but it is entirely divorced from the aspirations and ambitions of the Russian state. On the contrary, it deplores the success of Russian arms and the oppressive extension of the influence of the Tsarist state abroad. (The sense of deprivation of dignity deriving from the loss of a sense of identification with state power does not exist for this intelligentsia.) In China, the preoccupation with the weakness and decay of the state is a common denominator uniting the last generation of the literati with the "alienated" generations of the twentieth century. To use the old Chinese phrase, "enriching the state and strengthening the military" is an aim shared by the most diverse ideological commitments. The deep resentment and sense of deprivation of dignity which accompany China's political humiliation become the personal resentments of the whole articulate class.

This difference reflects an enormous difference in the objective situation of the two societies. In spite of Russian backwardness, the Petrine reforms had made Russia one of the great powers of nineteenth-century Europe. The economic bases of this power may have been woefully weak, but this did not prevent the chancelleries of Europe from dreading the expansion of Russia's might. At the very end of the nineteenth century, the Chinese reformer K'ang Yu-wei could still offer Peter the Great as a model for his emperor. Not until the rise of Stalin in the twentieth century did a new sense of Russia's weakness as a world power become felt, and this sense was closely associated with a consciousness of her economic backwardness. The spokesmen of Stalinism are acutely and morbidly concerned with building up the power and prestige of the Russian state. In this light, the new ruling class hardly resemble the spiritual descendants of the nineteenth-century intelligentsia. Even Lenin, in spite of his strategic use of nationalism, in this respect still seems to belong to the older intelligentsia.

In China, the growing success of Marxism-Leninism owed much to the appeal of the Leninist theory of imperialism, particularly those parts that are related most directly to national resentments. While Marxism had been accepted in Russia in its original cosmopolitan garb, Marxism-Leninism was widely received in China only after it had already been bent to the uses of a resentful nationalism.

Most of the factors discussed above would seem to argue for a more compliant attitude toward totalitarianism on the part of the Chinese intelligentsia. The ardent cravings for a sense of national dignity, the deep spiritual insecurity, the long tradition of authoritarianism, the orientation toward state service, the rejection of "capitalist" values, etc., would all appear to have created preconditions for a complaisant attitude toward the Communist state.

While such a conclusion would provide a neat ending to this paper and conform to our usual expectations concerning "Asia," life continues to be richer than gray theory, and the intelligentsia in China tends to betray the unpredictable qualities of the intelligentsia elsewhere.

It is true that a considerable portion of this intelligentsia either actively welcomed the Communist assumption of power in 1949 or acquiesced in it. This is in striking contrast to the situation in Russia during the October Revolution. There, a large part of the political intelligentsia was anti-Bolshevik, and a considerable body of non-political intellectuals was also anti-Bolshevik. These facts, of course, reflect the enormous changes in the intellectual evolution of Russia during the late nineteenth and early twentieth centuries. . . . In twentieth-century Russia, the intelligentsia as here defined had become only one strand in a variegated intellectual stratum that included nonpolitical intellectuals, professionals who certainly considered themselves *intelligenty,* and groups advocating a wide gamut of opinion among the more politically minded intelligentsia. There was certainly no automatic polarization toward Leninism. Whatever similar tendencies existed in twentieth-century China, they were inhibited by the dire conditions created by the Japanese War and by the polarization of power toward the two political forces which enjoyed a military base. Efforts on the part of intellectuals to create "third force" groups were rendered ineffectual by this situation.

It must also be emphasized that in committing itself to the new regime the Chinese intelligentsia as a whole had not necessarily committed itself to the type of totalitarianism which subsequently emerged. It had committed itself to the acceptance of certain Marxist-Leninist premises. Many hoped that the totalism of the new regime would remain within a more moderate "new democratic" framework. It is doubtful whether they anticipated the whole fantastic "thought reform" experience.

The regime itself directed some of its most concentrated efforts to the psychological transformation of the intelligentsia. The whole "thought reform" experiment would seem to reflect an ambition to achieve by new methods a form of monolithic "internalized" consensus such as the Soviet Union has never achieved. On the other hand, the fact that much of this effort has been focused on the intelligentsia would indicate a deep and abiding suspicion of that stratum in spite of its complaisant attitude.

In certain respects the present situations in Russia and China cannot be compared. In the forty years since the October Revolution there has emerged in the Soviet Union a new professional and managerial class that hardly remembers the past. The Soviet Union has attempted with some success to appropriate the word intelligentsia to designate this class. A similar attempt is taking place in China, but as of the present, the word intelligentsia still refers to the older intelligentsia, and whatever professional class exists is still drawn from "older cadres," who, in the view of the regime, share many of the shortcomings of the intelligentsia as a whole.

It has perhaps not been sufficiently noted that the redefinition of the term intelligentsia has not solved all problems even in the Soviet Union. The professional classes may be acquiescent but they nevertheless lay claim to private preserves of specialized knowledge which, in some sense, place them beyond the pale of party omniscience. There is, of course, a long history of efforts to "bolshevize" the professionals in the Soviet Union. At the moment, the regime would seem to have made a tacit surrender to the expertise of those professions it regards as essential, in return for unquestioning political loyalty.

In China, on the other hand, the renewed attack on the intelligentsia since 1957 has involved an attack on the pretensions of experts and professionals as one of its integral ingredients. At the moment, the Chinese regime is rather more impressed with the "defects" common to the literary and academic intelligentsia and the professionals than with the differences between them. Both groups have dared to pit their judgments against the judgments of the Party on the basis of criteria external to the Party line. At the moment a concerted effort is under way to reduce the stature of both the professional and the nonprofessional intelligentsia.

The particular animus of the regime toward the intelligentsia, however defined, reflects of course the shocking revelations of the "Hundred Flowers" episode of 1956–1957. This is hardly the place to consider the reasons behind this episode or the intentions of the Communist Party leadership. For our purposes it is sufficient to note that the official slogan, "Let the hundred flowers bloom, let the hundred schools contend," was meant to suggest to the intelligentsia that a certain undefined area of free discussion was now open to them. What emerged was highly revealing. Not only were the literary and cultural policies of the regime attacked; not only did professionals challenge the authority of the Party within their areas of competence; but there were even those who raised the dread question of power itself. The very grounds on which the Communist Party claimed political infallibility were challenged. In raising the question of political power, the "civism" of the Chinese intelligentsia went beyond anything that has occurred in the Soviet Union since the inauguration of the "Khrushchev era." The numbers involved were, of course, small. One may surmise, however, that those who had the courage to speak represented many more who were silent. It is also true that this is still the older pre-1949 intelligentsia. Yet it was also the intelligentsia who had embraced the new regime and gone through all the ardors of "thought reform." Any notion of a natural proclivity on their part for limitless dosages of totalitarianism must certainly be rejected after this episode. The regime may ultimately reduce this older intelligentsia to complete silence and create a completely conditioned "new intelligentsia." One can no longer speak, however, of any unlimited receptivity on its part to totalitarian control.

In the end, the intelligentsia in China as in Russia remains an incalculable and unknown quantity. Chinese totalitarianism, like Russian totalitarianism, may have had one of its roots in the past propensities of the intelligentsia of these countries. In China, in fact, the top leadership of the Communist Party itself derives from that stratum. Yet the relations of the intelligentsia as a whole to the regime remain a problem. A rejection of Western liberalism does not necessarily imply a willing acceptance of totalitarian extremism in all its forms. Between the two lies a whole spectrum of possibilities. If the intelligentsia in twentieth-century China dreamed of "totalistic" solutions, this does not mean that the form of totalism that actually emerged has proven completely palatable. If it rejected Western liberalism, its exposure to certain habits of thought derived from liberalism has made a certain impression on it.

Finally, as to the extent that the traditional culture of China has shaped the present scene, it must be pointed out that this culture contained many conflicting tendencies. It is easy enough to draw up a list of such predispositions as may have facilated the acceptance of totalitarianism, yet within the older culture one can also discern predispositions that run in quite another direction. These tendencies were not "liberal," or "democratic," or "individualistic," and it would be wrong to romanticize them. They did involve, however, the concept of moral norms that transcend the arbitrary will of the ruler, and even the concept of what might be called the civic obligation of the literati to defend these norms. In China, as elsewhere, the intelligentsia remains an unpredictable variable.

Rensselaer W. Lee III

58 GENERAL ASPECTS OF CHINESE COMMUNIST RELIGIOUS POLICY, WITH SOVIET COMPARISONS

Rensselaer W. Lee III, "General Aspects of Chinese Communist Religious Policy, with Soviet Comparisons," *The China Quarterly,* No. 19 (July–September, 1964), excerpted from pp. 161–73. Footnote references have been deleted.

Rensselaer W. Lee III has done research in Formosa, at the Inter-University Center for Chinese Language Studies, Taipei, and is specializing in the comparative study of Soviet and Chinese institutions.

The Chinese and Russian Communists, as Marxist-Leninists, are fundamentally hostile towards religion, and are committed to its ultimate eradication. Although their attitudes towards religion are similar, their prescriptions for dealing with it are different. In essence, this difference arises from two divergent conceptions, one optimistic, the other pessimistic, regarding the progress of religion towards oblivion in a situation where the Communist Party has assumed leadership and where the "social" roots of religion have supposedly disappeared. The Chinese hold the optimistic view, a position which may be explained in part by the fact that institutional religion has traditionally been weak in China. I quote here C. K. Yang's description of institutional religion in China as it emerged in the modern period:

> As an organised body, modern institutional religion had a very small priesthood, divided into minute units of two or three priests each, largely unconnected with each other. It had barely enough financial resources for subsistence for this scanty personnel. It was deprived of the support of an organised laity. . . . It did not participate in various organised aspects of community life such as charity, education, and the enforcement of moral discipline. There was no powerful centralised priesthood to dominate religious life or to direct operation of the secular social institutions.

360

When the Chinese Communists came to power, therefore, they were not confronted with indigenous religious institutions which could offer any effective resistance. A very different situation prevailed in Russia, where organised religion—especially the Russian Orthodox Church—was strongly entrenched. The only organised religion which the Chinese may have regarded as a threat is Christianity, particularly the Catholic Church, because of its long connection with the West and because of its alleged position as a bridgehead for imperialist espionage and subversion in China. The Christian group, however, is not strong enough in number to present many difficulties to the régime. Institutional religions such as Islam in Sinkiang and Lamaism in Inner Mongolia and Tibet may pose some difficulties, but these are "culturally beyond the confines of Chinese society."

The traditional weakness of institutional religion in China has been responsible, at least in part, for the relatively optimistic and even benign views which the Chinese Communists have adopted towards religion in their country.

Religion, according to the Chinese Communists, has two sets of roots: "social" and "cognitive." The social roots of religion are found in the class struggle. Religion is a weapon used by the exploiting classes to drain the masses of their revolutionary energy. In the Chinese context "exploiting classes" would mean the landlords, the upper bourgeoisie, and the agents of Western imperialism. The exploiters, speaking through the medium of priests or missionaries, tell the masses to be submissive to their fate, which is preordained in accordance with divine wishes. They also tell the masses that life on earth, although miserable indeed, is simply a way-station along the road to eternal happiness in the heavenly kingdom. These "pernicious" doctrines lull the masses into abandoning the class struggle waged for a better life . . . hence the phrase "opium of the people." The Chinese Communists, however, do admit that there have been several cases in the history of their own country where religion has not served as an instrument of the ruling classes or as an opiate of the people. In the Taiping rebellion, for example, religion was obviously a force which galvanised the masses to action against the ruling classes. The Communists hasten to say, however, that it is truly exceptional for religion to play a positive role in peasant wars; besides, they describe Taiping Christianity as a "superstition" and a "negative ideology" which "did not correctly explain or elucidate actual conditions." Above all, being Marxists, they stress that the Taiping rebellion was not caused by religion but by the acute social contradictions existing at the time.

Religion also has so-called "cognitive" roots: namely, extreme poverty or economic backwardness, and man's failure to understand or to conquer the forces directing nature and society. In the former case, the Chinese Communists consider that a rise in living standards will bring about a general weakening of religious faith among the masses. However, the ideological awareness of the masses often lags behind the improvement in their economic well-being. The Chinese point to the fact that in the Soviet Union the decline in religion has not kept pace with the achievements of "socialist" construction. In the latter case, the Chinese say that eventually "the most profound mysteries and the most dreadful natural forces will no longer be mysterious or dreadful." As man grasps and uses the objective laws which govern his existence, he learns to overcome his fear of nature. As his fear of nature disappears, he is able to view objective reality from a scientific and materialistic standpoint. As his ideological awareness grows, his propensity for religious belief dwindles. Ideally, when his ideological awareness—and his economic well-being—reach a certain level, he will be freed from religious influences.

The Chinese Communists feel that they have destroyed the social roots of religion in China by eliminating the exploiting classes. They believe that with the "eradication of exploitation of man by man" religious influence has steadily become weaker. They also feel that with a general improvement in living standards, the increased dissemination of knowledge of natural and social sciences, and the resultant emancipation of the masses from the "enthralment" of natural forces, religion will gradually "die a natural death." Religion, says the Chinese Communist Party, "like other things, including the Communist Party, and the State has to run through the process of growth, development and extinction." The current party line emphasises the naturalness or inevitability of the progress of religion towards oblivion. Unlike their Russian comrades, who do not accept any natural laws regarding religion (or, for that matter, the Communist Party, which they say will assume an increasingly important political role as the Soviet Union moves towards Communism), the Chinese Communists do not consider religion so dangerous a force that an intensive atheist propaganda struggle must be waged against it. On the contrary, they seem to feel that religion will disappear by itself with a minimum of conscious interference.

.   .   .

In contrast to the Chinese, Russian Communists do not profess to believe in the "law of development of religion," and do not base their religious policy on any such law. Their attitude toward religion is far from being either casual or permissive. The traditional power of institutional religion in Russia caused the Bolshevik régime at the very outset to adopt a position of uncompromising hostility towards religion, a position characterised by incessant and virulent attacks against religious manifestations throughout the 1920's and 1930's. During the war, however, anti-religious activity ceased, and in the post-war years, until 1958, was considerably below the pre-war level. Since 1958, the régime has embarked on a new anti-religious campaign of massive proportions. Current Russian attitudes toward religion are based on two considerations: first, the still considerable influence which institutional religion, notably the Russian Orthodox Church and certain Protestant groups, exerts over some sectors of the population despite forty-five years of Soviet rule; and second, the apparent revitalisation of religious activity in the post-war period in certain areas of the Soviet Union "where systematic, effective, educational work is lacking." As *Kommunist* pointed out in July 1959:

> In some party organisations in the post-war period, atheist propaganda was weakened. Churchmen took advantage of this and tried to increase their influence among the population, especially among the young.

By laying the blame for the increase of religious activity in the post-war period to the weakness of atheist propaganda, the Soviet Communist Party has introduced an element which clearly distinguishes its evaluation of why religion survives from that of the Chinese. The Russians, like the Chinese, link the existence of religion in the era following the abolition of exploiting classes with the interaction of several "cognitive" or, as the Russians choose to say, "objective" causes, including economic backwardness, lag of consciousness behind reality, and lack of understanding concerning the forces which control nature. The Russians, however, also link the existence or, rather, the strength or weakness of religion in a given area with certain "subjective" causes: namely, the weakness or strength of atheist propaganda in the area. The Chinese, on the other hand, seldom refer to atheist propaganda in their public statements on religion, and when they do so it is mainly in reference to eliminating certain superstitious practices which interfere with production.

In sum, we may state the Chinese and Russian positions as follows: the Chinese believe that religion will progress along the road to extinction naturally, in accordance with certain laws, and with a minimum of overt anti-religious activity. The Russians evidently do not believe in any "law of development of religion," and regard atheist propaganda as an essential factor in religion's ultimate disappearance. Expressive of the Russian position is an incident which took place in an eighth grade class in Latvia where a girl, questioned about religion, replied that "religion would die out of its own accord because in time people would become better educated, more intelligent and would stop going to church." Her reply was held up as an example of erroneous thinking on religion. Because the Russian Communists have little faith in the propensity of religion to wither away of its own accord, I call their position a "pessimistic" one—pessimistic because it stems from forty-five years of experience in dealing with strongly organised and tenacious religious institutions.

Phases of Transition

The Chinese Communist policy towards religion is officially described as one of "seeking common ground while retaining differences." In the old China, says the Chinese Communist Party, religion had a two-fold purpose: to serve the ends of Chinese reactionaries and foreign imperialists. Now, religion has "basically shaken off their influence," and the government solicits the "wholehearted co-operation" from religion in creating the new China. In the theoretical terms of Maoism, an "antagonistic" contradiction has been basically transformed into a "non-antagonistic" contradiction. The ideological difference between religion and "scientific" Marxism-Leninism is a contradiction among the people. Religion and the Chinese Communist Party can find a political basis of co-operation in building Socialism. Chinese Communist religious policy emphasises "the provision of a common political basis to enable the believer to join the people throughout the country in a grand union and render services to Socialism." This common political basis is "anti-imperialist and patriotic and follows the road to Socialism." The difference in "ideological awareness" between believers and non-believers must be "no deterrent" to their mutual relations within the framework of the struggle for socialist construction.

Religious associations follow the pattern of other Chinese mass organisations in that their main purpose seems to be both to exercise political control and to mobilise support for the State. The meetings of these associations are held primarily for the purpose of displaying adherence to the Communist Party's "general line" in domestic and foreign policy, and only secondarily, if at all, to discuss matters pertaining to religion. . . .

It might be useful here to introduce a comparison with Soviet religious policy. The Russians, unlike the Chinese, have continually stressed the need for "struggle" against religious ideology, which is "incompatible" and "irreconcilable" with Communism. They coupled their efforts to build "Socialism" with a policy of militant atheism—not one of seeking co-operation with religious groups on a common political basis. Today, in the era of so-called transition from Socialism to Communism, Russian anti-religious efforts take on a peculiar air of urgency, for Russian theorists regard the elimination of religious prejudices as a prerequisite for the successful creation of a Communist society. As the Soviet theoretical journal *Kommunist* puts it: "The formation of a scientific outlook and Communist morality is unthinkable without struggle against religious morality." . . .

The Reconciliation of Religion and Communism

The Chinese Communist régime's religious policy in a sense has been dualistic. The Party line makes a sharp distinction between "superstition," as manifested in the proliferation of local gods and spirits, and "integrated religious systems," as represented by Islam, Buddhism and Christianity. The policy of "freedom of religious belief," *i.e.*, of soft-pedalling atheist propaganda at least for the present, and bringing believers and non-believers into a common front for the task of Socialist construction, does not extend to "superstition." An article in *Red Flag* (*Hung Ch'i*) in March 1958, entitled "A Major Victory for Atheism," revealed that in the first part of that year the Communists had conducted an all-out campaign to "smash gods and spirits" and obliterate superstitious beliefs in the villages. *Red Flag* stressed that the anti-superstition struggle "grasped the basic desire of the masses" which was "to raise production and improve livelihood." Many superstitious practices, apparently, were extremely wasteful, and contributed to economic backwardness of the peasants by keeping them in a state of complete subservience to nature, *e.g.*, by causing them to take a passive attitude in the face of natural calamities. The constant reference, in the *Red Flag* article, to the wastefulness of certain kinds of superstition indicates that the motive behind the Communist campaign to eradicate superstition was primarily economic rather than atheistic.

The "integrated religious systems," such as Islam, Buddhism and Christianity, did, as I indicated earlier, enjoy a certain measure of official tolerance from the government. However, the policy of "freedom of religious belief," as defined by the Party, did not prevent the Communists from persecuting believers. Indeed, there was considerable religious persecution in China. But it is important to note that this persecution was not directed against religion in name. It was directed against that category of religious believers which was unwilling or unable to reconcile devotion to one's faith with loyalty to the Chinese Communist régime. Its basis was apparently political, not atheistic. The régime was extremely unsympathetic to anti-Communist elements within religious circles, and made every effort to crush these elements on the pretence that they were "counter-revolutionaries operating under cover of the cloak of religion." The Party considers that there is not only "no contradiction" between religion and "patriotism" (*i.e.*, loyalty to the Communist régime and support for its policies) but that the latter is a necessary precondition for the survival of the former. The Communists say pointedly: "It is the duty of every citizen to be patriotic and patriotism is in accord with devotion to one's faith. Only by being patriotic will it be possible to lead a good religious life." . . .

The Chinese Communist policy of "freedom of religious belief" is designed to purge religious groups of rightist or anti-régime elements—*e.g.*, "parasitic" monks, "reactionary" imams, and "imperialist" missionaries and their "running dogs" in China—and to spur believers to active and productive efforts on behalf of Socialism. To this end, the régime has instituted a sort of "brainwashing process" to force believers to "speed up self-remoulding and cultivate socialist ideology."

The ideological remoulding process which the Communists have instituted for believers has four interrelated objectives: first, to extirpate all remnants of feudalist or, in the case of Christianity, imperialist thought; secondly, to develop Socialist consciousness and love of country; thirdly, to stimulate the desire to participate in tasks of Socialist construction; fourthly, to eliminate those religious practices which interfere with Socialist construction, and, as far as possible, to harmonise religious teachings with Communist doctrine. Here the general pattern seems to be an attempt on the part of believers to play down the other-worldly aspects of religious teachings, and to stress instead the creation of an ideal state through the implementation of Communist principles. Religion in China is acquiring a strong activist emphasis, in response to the exigencies of Socialist construction.

The techniques used by the Chinese Communists to implement this ideological remoulding process follow a fairly well-defined pattern. First, there are the "accusation meetings" which are aimed at purging the most outspoken anti-Party elements. Following this preliminary cleansing process, the imams, monks, preachers or priests, as the case may be, are herded into study sessions where they "enhance their political awareness," "surrender their hearts to the Party," and "resolutely take the road to Socialism." The study sessions are also intended to expose remnant reactionaries and to destroy lingering tendencies among believers to follow reactionary, feudalist or imperialist channels of thought. The study sessions have the further effect of moulding or adapting religious thought to suit Communist ideology. This adaptation involves an increasing emphasis on salvation through material progress, and on unification of the concepts of Communism and paradise. . . .

Again, it would be instructive for comparative purposes to refer here to Russian religious policy. The Russian Communists, as I indicated before, emphasise the incompatibility and irreconcilability of religion and Communism. They unquestionably regard religion as an ideological rival, especially now that they are in the process of building a so-called Communist society which by their own definition must be free of religion. Unlike the Chinese, the Russians are openly hostile toward religion itself, and regard with the utmost suspicion any attempts on the part of religious organisations to "adapt to modern-day conditions" by maintaining that there is "no conflict between Communism and religion." Whereas the Chinese appear to encourage the reconciliation of religious faith and Communist doctrine as part of their policy toward religion, the Russians emphasise the contradictions between religion and Communism, denouncing the idea of reconciliation as a trick used by churchmen to increase their following. . . .

Summary and Conclusion

Chinese Communist religious policy, like Soviet religious policy, has been dictated by circumstance. The Chinese have not had to cope with strong institutional religion in their country and therefore, unlike the Russians, have never regarded religion as an ideological rival. The Russians feel that religion will not disappear without conscious anti-religious efforts on their part. The Chinese, by contrast, feel that religion will disappear in accordance with a natural law of growth, development and extinction, and in response to the exigencies of socialist construction.

Chinese Communist religious policy is at present aimed at creating a satisfactory working relationship with religion during the period of building Socialism. The Chinese hail the common front, muffle atheist propaganda, and emphasise that co-operation between believer and non-believer is more important than the contradiction between them. The Russians, on the other hand, have never advocated a common front, are engaged in an intensive anti-religious campaign, and try to magnify the contradiction between religion and Communism. The Chinese may some day, like the Russians, wage an atheist campaign against religious survivals. Whether or not they will, depends on the proclivity of religion to wither away "of its own accord." The Chinese Communists could very well mount a Soviet-style frontal attack against religion, should it prove to be more tenacious than they anticipate.

In order to integrate religion better into the framework of the struggle to create the new society, the Chinese have attached considerable importance to the ideological "remoulding" or thought reform of believers. The purpose of this thought reform movement is to eliminate rightist tendencies among believers, to instil Socialist awareness and patriotism, to stimulate production efforts and to remould religion to suit Communist ideology. I think that this last point is particularly significant in terms of understanding the régime's long-term policy toward religion. The key to this policy is the phrase, "handling of contradictions among the people." As religion begins to lose its other-worldly character and to emphasise the need for building a perfect society here on earth, the contradiction between religion and Communism will all but disappear—provided, of course, there is no conflict on the type of ideal state to be created. In any case, the amalgamation of religious teachings and Communist doctrine, with religion's ultimate disappearance, is almost certainly a major aim of Chinese religious policy. It is an aim which, in terms of traditional Chinese attitudes toward religion, should not be difficult to accomplish, for as Derk Bodde says, "The Chinese have been less concerned with the world of the supernatural than with the world of man. They are not a people for whom religious ideas and activities constitute an important part of life. It is ethics . . . and not religion of a formal organised type that has provided the spiritual basis of Chinese civilisation."

George W. Hoffman • Fred W. Neal

59 RELIGIOUS COEXISTENCE IN YUGOSLAVIA

George W. Hoffman and Fred W. Neal, *Yugoslavia and the New Communism* (New York: Twentieth Century Fund, 1962), excerpted from pp. 403–7. Footnote references have been deleted.

George W. Hoffman is Professor of Geography, University of Texas, and author of The Balkans in Transition. *Fred W. Neal is Professor of International Relations, Claremont Graduate School, and author of* Titoism in Action.

In Yugoslavia, the regime does not so much oppose religion as attempt to limit its influence and, where possible, utilize it. There is complete freedom of religion in the sense that public worship is permitted without interference but not in the sense that the religious organizations or clergymen as such may take stands on important public issues at variance with the state. The Titoist leaders frankly look forward to a time when religion will have died out, but they recognize that this time may be several generations hence, and meanwhile they are pledged not to force the issue. According to Kardelj, "social development itself, i.e., the development of material forces, will be the factor which will bring the final decision . . . , and not political or ideological forms, regardless of their character."

A law designed to "normalize relations between church and state" was passed in 1953. It provided for government assistance to the religious communities, the operation of theological seminaries and a religious press. Internal autonomy was guaranteed, interference with religious services prohibited and church rites following civil marriages permitted. Generally speaking, under this law an informal *modus vivendi* exists between the regime and Serbian Orthodox Church and the Moslem community, while there is an uneasy mutual toleration between the government and the Roman Catholic Church. Relations with the latter are complicated not only by its ties with Rome and the strongly anti-Communist tone of Roman

Catholicism generally but also by its traditional association with Croat nationalism.

To help the churches keep in mind lessons taught by strong-arm methods during the police state period, the authorities do not hesitate to crack down on any priest who gets out of line or on individual confessants who use religious ideas for political propaganda. No high church official has been jailed since 1954, when the Orthodox Metropolitan of Montenegro was convicted of "anti-state activities" for busying himself with local election matters. Occasionally priests, particularly Roman Catholics, are imprisoned.

Until his death early in 1960, Monsignor Stepinac, the Yugoslav primate, was a focal point of the hostility existing between the regime and the Roman Catholic Church. When the Archbishop was released from prison at the end of 1951, church-state relations appeared to be on the mend. But when the Vatican followed this move by presenting him with a cardinal's hat, Yugoslavia angrily broke off relations and closed the Papal nunciature. Cardinal Stepinac had been restricted by government decree to his native Croatian village. Both he and the Holy See steadfastly ignored a standing Belgrade offer to allow him to leave the country provided he did not return. The cardinal shunned the regime. Although a number of Yugoslav bishops visited Rome in 1958, Monsignor Stepinac did not ask to be present at the Papal election later that year. Unlike many other Roman Catholic prelates, he refused to vote in either local or national Yugoslav elections.

Church and state tolerate each other but little more. High Roman Catholic churchmen in Zagreb complained to the authors in 1958 that threats by local Party officials against village priests "frequently occur as a result of our struggle with Communism." Indicative of the problem of national particularism involved, these Croat prelates tended to blame "Serbian influences" for at least part of their troubles.

The government has usually avoided formal hostility because of the strong position of Roman Catholicism in Croatia. Although the Zagreb Church officials cited above said they saw "no end" to their struggle with Communism, they also agreed that outward manifestations of regime hostility were less than at any time since the end of the war. In the fall of 1959, Vladimir Bakarić, the leading government and Party official in Croatia, indicated that Cardinal Stepinac would be permitted to resume his duties as primate when the sentence passed on him in 1946 had expired. On February 9, 1960, the Roman Catholic Archbishop of Belgrade, Josip Ujčić, received the Tito government's highest civilian decoration, the People's Order of Merit, First Class, on his eightieth birthday. The next day Cardinal Stepinac died, and Archbishop Ujčić became the acting head of the Roman Catholic Church in Yugoslavia. Later that year Archbishop Franjo Seper of Zagreb was named as the new primate.

A persistent issue plaguing relations between the Roman Catholic

Church and the regime has been the refusal of the hierarchy to authorize its priests to join government-approved clerical associations. There are five of these for Roman Catholic priests, and, despite episcopal opposition, about 40 per cent of the Catholic prelates in Yugoslavia are members. Importance is attached to the clerical associations because they enable the government to get its ideas across to the clergy and indicate a degree of acceptance of the regime on the part of the churches. Priests benefit through social insurance only if they are members of the clerical associations. The Orthodox Church and the Supreme Vakuf Assembly, ruling body of the Moslem community, permit their clergy to join similar associations. . . .

While the regime does not directly interfere with internal administration in any of the churches, it does not hesitate to do so indirectly when political considerations are involved. A good example is the manner in which the Holy Synod of the Serbian Orthodox Church was pressured into accepting Macedonian demands for an autocephalous church in that republic in 1958. The government was anxious to accommodate the Macedonian clergy in order not only to limit the power of the Serbian Church but also to mend its fences in Macedonia and minimize the impact of Bulgarian irridentist claims to that area.

In return for its toleration and material aid, the Tito regime receives formal tokens of support in a number of ways, at least from the Orthodox and Moslem organizations. One form consists of admonitions to the faithful to be loyal to the government. Usually the basis of this is along the line of giving "unto Caesar that which is Caesar's" but sometimes it goes further. The supreme Moslem Assembly, for instance, in 1957 declared its "greatest gratitude to our state leadership, with you at its head, Comrade Tito," for the fact that the Moslems were enabled to have "a completely free religious life, and, with the material aid of the state, to achieve their aims." The annual conference of Moslem priests of Serbia went even further, pledging "to continue fighting tirelessly for the development of Socialist democracy and for the future development of Socialist Yugoslavia."

Another area of support which the regime receives from the religious organizations is in foreign policy. The Serbian Moslem priests mentioned above, for example, denounced Albanian claims about the Albanian minority in Yugoslavia. Hadji Sulejman effendi Kemura, as the press deferentially refers to the Reis Ul Ulema, or chief, of the Moslem community, has toured the Middle East amid great fanfare both there and in Yugoslavia. Both Russian and Rumanian Orthodox Church leaders have exchanged visits with their opposite numbers in Yugoslavia, each time issuing joint statements calling for peace and international cooperation. The Serbian Orthodox clergy also maintains traditional ties with the

Church of England and usually plays host to visiting churchmen from the West. These are not unimportant services for a small, isolated country steering a perilous course between Moscow and the West.

While there is no continuing campaign against religion in any formal sense, there are from time to time anti-religious articles in the press. The newspapers are quick to attack such things as time utilized for religious holidays and to cast a scandalized eye at such bacchanalian revels as sometimes occur on feast days in the villages. Overzealous priests are likely to find their faults magnified and their efforts publicly derided.

Religion is still a force in the lives of a majority of the people. Women remain the backbone of both Christian and Moslem congregations. There are some evidences of a falling off of young people at services, particularly at the mosques, and older people invariably predominate among those active in all the faiths. However, there seems to have been no sharp change in the age composition of either Orthodox or Roman Catholic confessants during the past decade.

Bibliography

INTELLECTUAL FERMENT

Alexandrova, V., *A History of Soviet Literature*. New York: Doubleday and Company, Inc., 1963.

Brown, D., *Soviet Attitudes toward American Writing*. Princeton, N.J.: Princeton University Press, 1963.

Chao Chung, *The Communist Program for Literature and Art in China*. Hong Kong: Union Research Institute, 1955.

Chen, T. H. E., *Thought Reform of the Chinese Intellectuals*. New York: Oxford University Press, Inc., 1960.

Crowley, E. L., and M. Hayward, eds., *Soviet Literature in the 1960's*. New York: Frederick A. Praeger, Inc., 1964.

Fischer, G., *Science and Politics: The New Sociology in the Soviet Union*. Ithaca, N.Y.: Cornell Center for International Studies, 1964.

Friedberg, M., *Russian Classics in Soviet Jackets*. New York: Columbia University Press, 1962.

Hungary Today, by the Editors of *Survey*. New York: Frederick A. Praeger, Inc., 1962.

Kuncewicz, M., ed., *The Modern Polish Mind: Anthology*. Boston: Little, Brown & Co., 1962.

Johnson, C. A., *Freedom of Thought and Expression in China: Communist Policies toward the Intellectual Class*. Hong Kong: Union Research Institute, 1959.

Johnson, P., *Khrushchev and the Arts: The Politics of Soviet Culture, 1962–1964.* Cambridge, Mass.: The Massachusetts Institute of Technology Press, 1965.

Laqueur, W. Z., and G. Lichtheim, eds., *The Soviet Cultural Scene 1956–1957.* New York: Frederick A. Praeger, Inc., 1958.

MacFarquhar, R., *The Hundred Flowers Campaign and the Chinese Intellectuals.* New York: Frederick A. Praeger, Inc., 1960.

Mu Fu-sheng, *The Wilting of the Hundred Flowers: The Chinese Intelligentsia under Mao.* New York: Frederick A. Praeger, Inc., 1963.

Pipes, R., ed., *The Russian Intelligentsia.* New York: Columbia University Press, 1961.

Roucek, J. S., and K. V. Lottich, *Behind the Iron Curtain.* Caldwell, Idaho: Caxton Printers, 1964.

Schneiderman, S. L., *The Warsaw Heresey.* New York: Horizon Press, 1959.

Shteppa, K. F., *Russian Historians and the Soviet State.* New Brunswick, N.J.: Rutgers University Press, 1962.

Swayze, H., *Political Control of Literature in the USSR: 1946–1959.* Cambridge, Mass.: Harvard University Press, 1963.

Vickery, W. N., *The Cult of Optimism: Political and Ideological Problems of Recent Soviet Literature.* Bloomington, Ind.: Indiana University Press, 1963.

Yarmolinsky, A., *Literature under Communism: The Literary Policy of the Communist Party of the Soviet Union from the End of World War II to the Death of Stalin.* Bloomington, Ind.: Indiana University Press, 1960.

RELIGION

Bach, M., *God and the Soviets.* New York: Thomas Y. Crowell Company, 1958.

Benz, E., *The Eastern Orthodox Church: Its Thought and Life.* New York: Doubleday & Company, Inc., 1963.

Bissonnette, G., *Moscow Was My Parish.* New York: McGraw-Hill Book Company, 1956.

Curtiss, J. S., *The Russian Church and the Soviet State: 1917–1950.* Boston: Little, Brown & Co., 1953.

Kolarz, W., *Religion in the Soviet Union.* New York: St. Martin's Press, Inc., 1961.

Pollock, J. C., *The Faith of the Russian Evangelicals.* New York: McGraw-Hill Book Company, 1964.

Schwarz, S., *The Jews in the Soviet Union.* Syracuse, N.Y.: Syracuse University Press, 1951.

Spinka, M., *The Church in Soviet Russia.* New York: Oxford University Press, Inc., 1956.

Timasheff, N. S., *Religion in Soviet Rusia: 1917–1942.* New York: Sheed & Ward, 1942.

Yang, C. K., *Religion in Chinese Society*. Berkeley, Calif.: University of California Press, 1961.

Zernov, N., *The Russian Religious Renaissance of the Twentieth Century*. New York: Harper & Row, Publishers, 1964.

SCIENCE AND SOCIAL PROBLEMS

Bauer, R. A., ed., *Some Views on Soviet Psychology*. Washington, D.C.: American Psychological Association, 1962.

Field, M., *Doctor and Patient in Soviet Russia*. Cambridge, Mass.: Harvard University Press, 1957.

Joravsky, D., *Soviet Marxism and Natural Science: 1917–1932*. New York: Columbia University Press, 1961.

Levine, I. R., *Main Street: U.S.S.R.* New York: Doubleday & Company, Inc., 1959.

Levy, M. J., *The Family Revolution in Modern China*. New York: Octagon Books, 1963.

Miller, W. W., *Russians As People*. New York: E. P. Dutton & Co., Inc., 1960.

Rounds, F., *A Window on Red Square*. Boston: Houghton Mifflin Company, 1953.

Slamecka, V., *Science in Czechoslovakia*. New York: Columbia University Press, 1963.

———, *Science in East Germany*. New York: Columbia University Press, 1963.

Slonim, M., *Russian Theatre: From the Empire to the Soviets*. New York: Harcourt, Brace & World, Inc., 1961.

Chapter Eleven

Whither Communism?

More than one-third of the world lives under a communist political system. Whereas in the U.S.S.R. the engineers of the revolution have long since passed from the scene, in China and Yugoslavia they still rule, even as the post-revolution generation comes of age and waits impatiently in the wings. Communist political systems are young, and it is premature to make generalizations concerning their probable evolution; nonetheless, some observations about key attributes of communist systems may be useful.

First, communist elites have demonstrated a remarkable facility for retaining political power. Except for the notable but temporary disintegration of communist power in Hungary in late October of 1956, the internal viability of communist regimes has not been seriously threatened. Since legitimacy is at least partly a function of time, the longer the communist elites remain in power, the less likely is the prospect of counterrevolution and the more apt they are to gain local acceptance. Barring a nuclear cataclysm, which presumably would render anachronistic the current configuration of political systems, communist oligarchies seem firmly entrenched and generally accepted by their populations—even in Hungary, where political oppositionists learned through bitter experience that the Western powers were unable to intervene effectively for fear of precipitating a general war. In Eastern Europe, the proximity of Soviet military power and the strategic importance of the area to Soviet national security militate against the success of any noncommunist or anti-communist political group, for, in the improbable event that such a group did seize power, it is unlikely that Moscow would remain inactive. The Polish and Hungarian experiences of 1956 will tend to keep any struggle for power confined within a communist framework (Reading 60). Accordingly, "liberation" from without is no longer a credible alternative. To the extent that liberation can be realized, whether in the form of greater autonomy from Moscow, or of further relaxation internally, or both, it is likely to come as a consequence of an erosion and transformation of communist rule, and not of open revolution.

The political stability of communist regimes is reinforced by their mastery of organization: the monopolization of political power; the ability to implement reform through bureaucratic structures; the management, direct and indirect, of the economic, educational, cultural, and social aspects of life; the monopolization of mass media, which facilitates indoctrination and the manufacture of consensus; and the ability to atomize potential opposition. This capacity to wield power and manage society is a hallmark of communist elites which portends a lengthy period of rule.

One element of potential political instability inhering in communist systems stems from the absence of any institutionalized or proven procedure of ensuring an orderly succession. Yet the Soviet Union has weathered three major succession crises without any visible challenge to continued Party domination or to the communist character of society. The Chinese and the Yugoslavs still have to demonstrate that they, too, can withstand the strains of a major transfer of power. But if the Soviet experience has any relevance, the presumption must be that they will be able to surmount such crises, though these be protracted and involve considerable bloodshed. The instability which might result would involve the upper echelons of the power structure, but not the foundations of society. There is no apparent institutional or ideological rival capable of supplanting the Communist Party.

Second, communist regimes in the U.S.S.R. and China have brought about a renaissance of national power. Through their revolutions, they have promoted modernization and a national revitalization, and made their countries into great powers once again. In Yugoslavia, Poland, Hungary, Rumania, and Bulgaria, Communist Parties have swept aside backward, feudalistic oligarchies and have forcibly imposed essential economic, educational, and social reforms. Their modernization seems well under way, much needed and long overdue.

The political impact and implications of modernization are not yet clear. Over the past few decades, new social groups (i.e., scientists, technicians, and managerial personnel) have emerged, with a stake in the system and a desire for personal and material security; the level of education and welfare has risen, creating a higher level of expectations; and industrialization and urbanization have intensified the pressures for a more rational and sophisticated system of controls. These factors contributed to the post-Stalin liberalization in the U.S.S.R.; de-Stalinization was necessary because Stalinism had become counterproductive. Thus, it seems unlikely that mass terror, which was a concomitant of the consolidation of political power and

of enforced modernization during the initial stages of accelerated industrialization, will again be employed against the population at large, as it
was in Stalin's Russia of the 1930's, Mao's China of the early 1950's, or
Tito's Yugoslavia after the war. Communist regimes are seeking to cajole
rather than coerce their peoples; to raise living standards and minimize the
exercise of arbitrary power. They have shown their skill at managing
power; they have still to demonstrate their ability to run a flourishing
society (Reading 62).

Third, we do not expect to see any uniformity of development in
communist countries. While most observers would agree that all communist systems are characterized by Communist Party control, by authoritarian and hierarchical bureaucratic institutions, and by a shared core of
ideological beliefs, differentiation is a demonstrable political fact. For an
understanding of this phenomenon we look to other factors: nationalism
and the quest for national identity, however that may be interpreted by the
given national group; the style of political and cultural life that distinguishes a people; the "personality" and predilections of an oligarchy; and
geographic size and location. Though the intensity and impact of any of
these factors are impossible to measure, the experience of communist
societies in recent decades indicates, for example, that nationalism, in
paradoxical fashion, transcends communism as an emotional and integra-
tive force in societies *living under communism*. This suggests that
nationalism indelibly shapes the character and style of communism.
Through the internal pressures which it engenders among the leadership,
nationalism influences the evolution of individual communist systems in
ways that have been, and are now, largely unanticipated, and strengthens
differentiation within the communist world.

Fourth, speculations concerning the evolution of communist systems
must consider the unresolved and intensely debated relationship between a
country's level of economic development and the character of its political
system. Is totalitarianism the twentieth century variant of historial absolutism and tyranny? Or does it represent a phase of political evolution
through which a society passes when it is industrializing and modernizing
rapidly? What is the impact of industrialization on a totalitarian political
system? The essentially economic determinist arguments of some social
scientists hold that the *embourgeoisement* of communist systems will, in
the foreseeable future, result in the diminution of Communist Party
hegemony; that economic development will give rise to influential interest
groups outside of the Communist Party; and that industrialization, urbanization, and affluence will mellow totalitarianism, erode communist rule,
and produce a meaningful "democratization" of communist systems,
thereby making them more akin to the Western democracies. The contrary
view has also been persuasively argued:

. . . the changes that have taken place in the Soviet Union may in some part be "managed" changes, not reluctant concessions which weaken the rule of the Party, but deliberate steps taken to strengthen it, although it is possible that even "managed" changes may have effects which are not wholly anticipated.[1]

An American sociologist has suggested that a new concept, the "administered society," may prove useful in analyzing recent changes in Soviet society (Reading 61). Clearly, conflicting interpretations are possible.

Finally, though all communist societies are committed to the building of communism, it is only in the U.S.S.R. that the leadership claims to have built socialism and to have entered the initial stages of communism—"the period of the full-scale construction of communism." It is also the Soviet leaders who have given the most detailed picture of the future communist society. There have been reports that Peking, too, is preparing a blueprint for communism, as part of its ideological rivalry with Moscow. In Eastern Europe, one sees few signs of such eschatological exercises; there the focus is on limited, tangible, and realizable goals.

Communist eschatology received considerable attention in the *Program of the Communist Party of the Soviet Union,* adopted in October 1961. The specific goals of the future society are described in terms of affluence for all within a generation; of planned, regulated activity which "leads to a natural fusion of rights and duties to form single standards of communist behavior"; of "universally recognized rules of the communist way of life . . . whose observance will become an organic need and habit with everyone"; of "harmonious relations" which will "be established between the individual and society on the basis of the unity of public and personal interests"; of growing administrative authority being delegated to the local Soviets (Councils); and of "a further *enhancement of the role and importance of the Communist Party* as the leading and guiding force of Soviet society" (Reading 63). Aside from these Orwellian features, there are still unanswered the questions as to how the utopia will be achieved. The methods are undefined. Private dreams, needs, and desires are permitted to fill in the details. For to specify the means might be the end of private hope; to describe might be to alienate. Perhaps, also, Feodor Dostoevski was right when he intimated in the "Legend of the Grand Inquisitor" that the heart of an ideological tyranny must remain a mystery.[2]

---

[1] Senate Committee on Foreign Relations, *U.S.S.R. and Eastern Europe,* 86th Cong., 2nd sess., 1960 (Washington, D.C.: Government Printing Office, 1960), p. 40.

[2] Alexander V. Riasanovsky and Alvin Z. Rubinstein, "Russian Utopia and Soviet Communism," *Social Science,* XXXVIII, No. 3 (June, 1963), 167.

For insight into the psychological bases of contemporary totalitarianism, see the brilliant essay in the chapter on "The Grand Inquisitor" in Feodor Dostoevski's *The Brothers Karamazov.*

60 PROSPECTS FOR EASTERN EUROPE

Senate Committee on Foreign Relations, *U.S.S.R. and Eastern Europe,* 86th Cong., 2nd sess., 1960 (Washington, D.C.: Government Printing Office, 1960), excerpted from pp. 50–52.

The following passages were taken from a study on the U.S.S.R. and Eastern Europe, *which was prepared by a Columbia-Harvard Research Group for the Senate Committee on Foreign Relations.*

. . . [W]hat may we anticipate with respect to the future of Eastern Europe? Little is to be gained by attempting a prediction, as our inability to foretell such events as Tito's break with Stalin in 1948 or the Hungarian revolution of 1956 demonstrates. Nevertheless, we may extrapolate, from the present configuration of forces, one possible line of development for the next 5 or 10 years.

The events of 1956 and their catastrophic denouement in Hungary may have marked the end of one phase of Eastern European history, in that they provided the definition of several limits: the limit of the ability of the people to free themselves; the Soviet Union's limit of tolerance; the limit of permissible deviation within the framework of communism; the limit of the West's will and capacity to intervene. This demonstration ended in a double failure: the failure of the people to achieve liberty by main force, or of the West to liberate; and the failure of communism to gain even the appearance of real acceptance. Brute power turned out to be the answer to both failures.

This being so, it may be that the peoples of Eastern Europe will, in varying degrees from country to country, be more inclined to take their Communist regimes as a fact of life—like inclement weather—with little expectation of a change of system or effective assistance from outside, but with, perhaps, increased ability, acquired through hard experience, to reach a tolerable accommodation with their rulers, to blunt the edge of governmental pressures, and even to make limited gains in material conditions and private, if not public, freedom. Such a climate might have the following characteristics:

1. The effectiveness of elements of opposition, or of moderation, is likely to be proportional to the degree to which they have been included within, rather than excluded from, the new social order which the Communist regimes have created. A Catholic church which has, as in Poland, achieved an uneasy modus vivendi with the regime may be more influential

378

than one suffering harassment and martyrdom as a declared enemy of the people. A national spirit which finds common cause on certain specific issues with a section of the party leadership is more likely to be felt than an underground operating outside the system, with little hope of reinforcement, in the absence of a general catastrophe. These prospects are increased by the fact that the personnel of the party will increasingly be made up of men whose training, experience, and orientation are centered in local problems and affairs, in contrast to many of the older party members with their background of exile and activity in Moscow or in the West. It is obvious, of course, that such forms of partial accommodation and identification may strengthen the regimes and increase their stability. It is also obvious that the Communist leadership is exceptionally sensitive to the potential danger of such elements within their system. But however we may judge the outcome of such a mixture of accommodation and resistance, it may well be the chief arena for political change.

2. A byproduct of this local play of forces would be a tendency toward increased diversity within the bloc as a whole, a modest diversity not exceeding the limits of Communist tolerance, but still a significant departure from the mechanical uniformity of the Stalin era. And despite the Communists' own impulse toward conformity, some of their own policies, such as the development of economic specialization within the orbit, may contribute to these differences. From the evidence available it is unlikely that the economic relations of the orbit will be those of predatory exploitation which characterized the earlier years of Communist rule. While we may expect the economies of Eastern Europe to be closely integrated with that of the Soviet Union, the form of their dependence may be substantially different. Both slavery and division of labor imply dependence, but the latter is more productive of diversity and change.

It is not easy to say whether this will "weaken" or "strengthen" the Communist orbit. As a more rational form of economic organization, increased integration and specialization are of positive advantage; at the same time they could promote a troublesome degree of diversity and increased play of divergent interests.

3. The course of such developments in Eastern Europe is likely to be decisively affected by the presence or absence of reinforcing developments within the Soviet Union itself and by what we might call a continuing if muted dialogue being carried on between the Communist parties of the orbit (including the Chinese Communists). We may suggest the proposition that the future evolution of Eastern Europe, if it is not to be stifled, cannot greatly outpace change in the Soviet Union. If it does it will probably produce the same type of counteraction as that of 1956–57. Contrary to the thesis that major alterations in the Soviet orbit can be brought about by changes on the periphery working their way to the center through a process of erosion, it seems more likely that in such a system

changes at the periphery cannot get very far unless they are reinforced by changes in the center. There can, of course, be a reciprocal interplay of influences. Poland, since 1956, has obviously had a considerable impact on the rest of the orbit and to some extent has also served as a transmission belt for Western influences, especially in the cultural and literary sphere. At the same time the basic political impulses, whether for change or for stabilization, continue to emanate from Moscow.

If this be the case, then it would follow that constructive and lasting changes in the orbit—whether in the direction of a greater degree of personal freedom and welfare or in the direction of national autonomy and diversity—must be in consonance or at least not incompatible with corresponding developments in the Soviet Union itself.

It should be stressed that this particular course of development in Eastern Europe is not offered as a prediction of what will happen. It is a possibility, the odds for which are not calculable. Indeed as an avenue for a modest degree of nonviolent and beneficial change one can have no assurance that it is even likely. Anyone knowing the history of Eastern Europe can hardly count on peaceful evolution in this tormented area. We can certainly not exclude the possibility of an Eastern Europe frozen in the grip of post-Stalinist Communist orthodoxy for an indefinite period; nor can we dismiss the chances of future convulsions or a spasmodic alternation between repression and relaxation.

Allen Kassof

61 THE ADMINISTERED SOCIETY: TOTALITARIANISM WITHOUT TERROR

Allen Kassof, "The Administered Society: Totalitarianism without Terror," *World Politics,* XVI, No. 4 (July, 1964), excerpted from pp. 558–62, 571–75.

Allen Kassof is Assistant Professor of Sociology at Princeton University.

As an orchestra conductor sees to it that all the instruments sound harmonious and in proportion, so in social and political life does the Party direct the efforts of all people toward the achievement of a single goal.

Each person must, like a bee in the hive, make his own contribution to increasing the material and spiritual wealth of society. People may be found who say that they do not agree with this, that it is coercion of the individual, a return to the past. To this my answer is: We are living in an organized socialist society where the interests of the individual conform to the interests of society and are not at variance with them.[1]

More than a decade after Stalin's death, the time is ripe for a fresh view of Soviet society. Many of the conventional patterns of analysis, developed largely during the period of Stalinist absolutism, seem to be no longer adequate for this purpose. This article proposes that a new concept, the "administered society," may be useful in summarizing and evaluating recent changes in the Soviet system and in identifying current trends.

Like other ideal-typical concepts, that of the administered society by no means pretends to account for all of the concrete detail of a social order. Instead, it draws attention (through emphasis, and hence a certain exaggeration) to very general features which constitute a society's ethos or prevailing themes—in the Soviet case, centering around the drive of the regime to establish a highly organized and totally coordinated society, and the consequences of that drive.

The administered society can be defined as one in which an entrenched and extraordinarily powerful ruling group lays claim to ultimate and exclusive scientific knowledge of social and historical laws and is impelled by a belief not only in the practical desirability, but the moral necessity, of planning, direction, and coordination from above in the name of human welfare and progress.

Convinced that there should be complete order and predictability in human affairs, the elite is concerned not merely with the "commanding heights," but also to an overwhelming degree with the detailed regulation of the entire range of social life, including those institutions which, in the West, typically have been regarded as lying beyond the legitimate scope of public authority and political intervention. The rulers of the administered society refuse to grant the possibility of unguided coordination and integration; they believe, on the contrary, that not only the masses but responsible subgroups (for example, the professions) are incapable of maintaining a viable social order on their own, without the precise and detailed supervision of an omniscient political directorate. The elite believes, and through a far-reaching program of education and propaganda tries to teach its subjects, that the only possible good society is one that is *administered*.

The administered society is thus a variant of modern totalitarianism, with the important difference that it operates by and large without resort to those elements of gross irrationality (in particular, the large-scale and often self-defeating use of psychological terror and physical coercion as

---

[1] Nikita Khrushchev, March 8, 1963.

basic means of social control) that we have come to associate with totalitarian systems in recent decades.

The administered society, however, should be distinguished from the conventional welfare state in that it is not involved simply or principally in creating minimal conditions of social welfare within an otherwise pluralistic political framework, but instead treats welfare as an incidental—and instrumental—element in the larger scheme of social planning and reform. While an administered society may display more or fewer welfare features of a material or service nature, they are neither final goals nor the most important determinants of overall policy. To put it another way, the elite regards the promotion of total coordination as itself the ultimate form of welfare under modern conditions.

Plainly enough, the administered society is not the authentic good society of faithful Marxists, for it is characterized by the growing size and importance of an elite party and state bureaucracy, in contrast to the withering-away of governmental apparatus which Marxism predicts and upon which it insists.

Nor, finally, should the administered society be confused with a rational technocracy, even though here there are some superficial parallels. The leadership of the administered society, to be sure, is forced to rely on scientific and technical cadres as sources of essential information and in the execution of highly complex economic and social planning. But the political elite is not bound solely or principally by considerations of technical rationality; the technicians and experts operate only under license of the political elite and in terms of the latter's self-proclaimed ultimate knowledge about the proper uses of science and technology in the larger sociohistorical setting. The experts, in short, are servants rather than masters or even independent practitioners. They lack the power of veto on grounds of technical rationality over political decisions (though in the end the limits of technology itself, if not the will of the technocrats, of course impose certain restraints). And their potential for independent influence in the society is decisively cut short by the elite's consistent practice of defining *all* decision-making as political and therefore beyond the competence of any group other than itself. Similar considerations are applied—if anything, with more vigor—to the producers of the more "esoteric" goods and services—the artists and writers, professors and critics and journalists. Like technicians in the more literal sense, they are construed by the elite as turning out "commodities" whose creation, distribution, and consumption demand coordination from above in the pursuit of order and planned progress.

Let us see how this preliminary definition of the administered society can be applied to an understanding of Soviet developments, and with what advantages.

By now it must be clear even to the most reluctant analyst that the cumulative change in Soviet society since Stalin's death is too great to dismiss as merely superficial. The transformation of Soviet society during this period, though by no means a wholesale departure from earlier patterns, nevertheless has been extensive. The conventional label for this change has been "liberalization." The reference point is to the state of Soviet totalitarianism under Stalin and to the degree of departure from that condition.

To be sure, the totalitarian model could only approximate the underlying reality. Even at the zenith of Stalinism, we know, there were major and numerous exceptions to the effective realization of absolute despotism. Piecemeal information such as the testimony of refugee informants showed that many individuals were able to preserve for themselves or to create tiny islands of privacy and to maintain attitudes of doubt and skepticism about the system in the face of the relentless propaganda that penetrated every corner of the society. We know, too, that in the midst of what was surely the most thoroughgoing system of political and social controls ever devised, there were widespread and patterned evasions of official demands in places high and low. The factory manager engaged in self-defensive falsification of production statistics; the peasant stealing time from the collectivized sector to work on his private plot; clandestine listeners to forbidden foreign radio broadcasts—these and other types are amply familiar to students of Stalinist Russia. For those who were caught (as well as for many of the totally innocent) the costs were horrendous, often final. But even at its most extreme the system of surveillance and punishments did not stamp out pockets of resentment, awareness, inner resistance.

Nevertheless, if Soviet totalitarianism under Stalin was not exactly an Orwellian 1984 and if, in important respects, it departed from the analysts' model of the totalitarian society, it came very close indeed (perhaps as close as is possible in a modern complex society) to approximating that model. Extraordinary was the near-completeness, if not actual totality, of the invasion of society by Party and State. . . .

It is also clear that substantial liberalization has taken place since the dictator's death. But this measure, useful in many ways, creates very serious problems in analysis and evaluation. For although liberalization tells something about where the Soviet system has come from, it does not say very much about where it is *going*. To say that the system is being liberalized is like walking away backwards from a receding reference point, a procedure that gives too little information about what lies on the road ahead. After all, if the society has become less totalitarian, then what is it? To conclude, in effect, that it is still more of the same but somehow less so than it used to be may be essentially correct, but it is not a very satisfactory answer. And the understandable fascination with the political drama of on-and-off-again de-Stalinization has led to a partial neglect of its *social* consequences—in some quarters, too, to an imprecise assumption that political liberalization (the moderation of one-man despotism and the probably genuine efforts to avoid extreme abuses of absolute power) also spells some kind of broad social liberalization (even leading, perhaps, to a form of society more familiar—and less antagonistic?—to the Western experience).

Indeed, it may be that the use of liberalization as the key criterion for measuring changes in Soviet society is responsible for some of the confusion and disagreement among analysts of various persuasions. Thus, those of a conservative or pessimistic disposition have been inclined to deny that the changes are so significant (or that some of them have really taken place) because of the implication that liberalization also means *liberation,* a prospect they reject as too unlikely; while their more optimistic colleagues (especially those who see in Khrushchevism the harbinger of a welfare state) have attached far more significance to the same developments.

The core of the difficulty lies in the fact that, under Stalin, there was an amalgamation of totalism with terror and coercion, and that we may have overlearned a lesson about the necessary association between the two on the basis of that highly convincing record. The concept of the administered society is proposed as a way of saying that there can be totalism *without* terror; it recognizes that the changes in the Soviet Union have been real and vast (after all, totalism without terror is something new); but it insists that, far from developing alternatives to totalism, Soviet society is being subjected to new and more subtle forms of it, and that the Stalinist past is being streamlined rather than rejected. . . .

The case for the administered society is not subject to proof of an absolute kind, for not only is such a concept more or less useful rather than right or wrong, but its application to the affairs of a live society cannot possibly cover all contingencies. It does, however, provide a general framework for depicting the Soviet system under Khrushchev (and probably his successors as well), sensitizing us to interpretations that otherwise might go unnoticed and enabling us to see patterns in apparently unconnected trends . . . for example, the growing emphasis on "public" participation in social control through voluntary assistance to the militia, the Komsomol street patrols' enforcing of dress, decorum, and taste, the quasi-judicial comrades' courts, and so forth. . . .

The passion for organization, for perfect coordination and integration of social life—a kind of compulsive's dream of beehive order projected upon an entire society—has partly replaced the original impetus of Bolshevik ideology. The denial that there can be any real conflict in the good society, the belief that all legitimate human needs can be satisfied simultaneously, that interest groups are subversive, that only uninformed selfishness or disregard of organizational principles stands between the present and the utopia of the future—these are some of the ingredients of the new ideology. If it lacks some of the romantic appeal of barricade-storming, it is perhaps no less revolutionary in its consequences, for its purveyors insist that they will not rest until all societies have undergone the transformation to superorganization. Its potential impact on an audience, say, of hard-pressed political leaders and court philosophers of developing nations may be considerable, for the idea of total coordination must tempt many of them as the answer to problems and frustrations of economic backwardness and the awkward necessities of coping with competing political interests. And for mentalities especially sensitive to the real and apparent disarray of human affairs or philosophically intolerant of ambiguity in social structure, there is, after all, a great utopian charm in such an image: much like the classical Marxist formula of salvation, it seems to promise a final answer to the centuries-old dislocations generated by modernism and science and a return to a latter-day version of a medieval world where everything—and everyone—apparently had a proper place in the universe.

Assuming this assessment of the basic aspirations of the Soviet regime to be correct, there is the quite different question of how far they are likely to be realized in practice. Naturally it would be unrealistic to expect complete and literal fulfillment of the dream, any more than one could have expected perfect totalitarianism to exist under Stalin. The issue, then, is how closely it will or can be approximated. Without going into the kind of detailed discussion that is far beyond the scope of these early notes, the best that can be done is to suggest some of the factors in a balance sheet of probabilities.

In the background is the ancient dilemma of how to combine personal with public interest in such ways as to put an end to politics. If the record of other complex societies (not to mention the history of the Soviet Union itself) is a guide, we may be excused for having serious doubts about such a grandiose conception. To deny that there is social conflict, as the Soviet leadership essentially does, is not to be rid of it. Even the most superficial reading of the Soviet press daily provides an endless catalogue of the stresses and strains arising from the pursuit of private or group interests against the demands for conformity emanating from the center. Some of the examples are petty, more of them are serious, all of them reflect the underlying tensions of an imperfectly coordinated society; they usually fall short of posing immediate threats to the political directorate but often have cumulative consequences of an unplanned and unintended nature. Moreover, broad areas of deviant behavior and subversive attitudes which once were suppressed by the application of prophylactic terror now have to be handled by more patient and indirect means. It is too early to say whether the new machinery of social control will be as adequate to the task as was pure Stalinism.

Then there is the paradoxical discovery, finally dawning on the regime, that the gradual alleviation of extreme material want that has been behind so many traditional problems may produce new and more subtle issues of control over a long-deprived population experiencing relative affluence for the first time. Failures to satisfy these wants are the obvious danger; success breeds more subtle risks, however, for a rising standard of living (as we have seen in the case of other industrial nations) often results in new forms of emotional investment that are to a great extent antithetical to the high level of public commitment obviously essential in realizing the administered society. We already have some evidence of this in the form of a troublesome youth problem in the Soviet Union: one of the greatest headaches of the post-Stalin regime has been how to prevent the drive for individual advancement and the intoxication with consumption from becoming the basis for a privatism that could easily wreck long-term intentions. So far the problem has been most visible among youth, but there is reason to believe that it is widespread. . . .

Most important is the fact that, during almost half a century of Communist rule, the possibilities for alternative institutional forms have been largely wiped out. Even were the will to democratic or pluralistic institutions substantially present—and it is not—it is highly doubtful that the resources currently available by way of formal structures, source philosophies, or practical experience would go very far. The Bolshevization of a society, if it goes on long enough, is an irreversible process, because it is so intense and so total that it indelibly alters not only earlier institutional forms but the entire pattern of a population's expectations of reasonable and workable alternative possibilities for social order. This is not to say that the Soviet leaders have mastered history, for even a process that is irreversible can move forward in unintended and undesired directions. But the prospects of developing viable substitutes for a social system that has so long been based upon extreme and centralized organization are very poor. Ironically, the regime is probably correct—at least in the case of Soviet society—when it insists that any form of pluralism is impossible. The best that can be expected is a more or less benign totalism within the limits of the administered society, with a very slow erosion of the Boshevik heritage; the worst, a surrender of good intentions to manage the society without terror and a return in some form to the excesses and cruelties of classical Stalinism.

How one evaluates this situation depends on his general political outlook and his preferences about the good society. Surely no one will deny that the Soviet citizen is, in the most elementary sense, better off today than he was under Stalin. And certainly no one will claim that the Soviet citizen prefers to be brutalized as he was then. Still, the thoroughgoing bureaucratization, the superorganization, of social life contains a special nightmare quality of its own even when shorn (as probably it must be if it is to operate efficiently) of raw psychic brutality and terror. And the easing of the terror, while an obviously welcome development, also has the consequence of diminishing the awareness of living in an essentially closed society and of reducing the capacity to act from moral indignation towards a freer life.

Perhaps the concept of the administered society, in this preliminary form, errs on the side of pessimism by making too much of the dream and not enough of the sheer confusion of reality. Daily life in the Soviet Union is far richer, far more problematical to its rulers, far less certain than an abstraction can depict; no doubt the framework of this modest idea will have to be considerably filled in before it can be of much use in practical analysis. But it does call attention to the inadequacy of the liberalization formula in understanding contemporary Soviet developments and the new ideology driving the regime.

Benjamin Schwartz

62 MODERNIZATION AND THE MAOIST VISION: SOME REFLECTIONS ON CHINESE COMMUNIST GOALS

Benjamin Schwartz, "Modernization and the Maoist Vision: Some Reflections on Chinese Communist Goals," *The China Quarterly*, No. 21 (January–March, 1965), excerpted from pp. 3, 9–19. Footnote references have been deleted.

Benjamin Schwartz is Professor of History and Government in the area of East Asian studies at Harvard University.

What can be said at this point about the broad goals and motivations of the present Chinese Communist leadership? The question is, of course, distressingly imprecise and begs further definition. Is the leadership a monolithic group? Have its goals remained constant and unchanging? Is there a rigid Chinese Communist "goal structure," etc.? . . .

The [Maoist] vision involves not only a conception of the good society of the future but also a sanctified image of the methods by which this vision is to be achieved. Certainly Marxist-Leninist-Stalinist ideology is one of the main sources of this vision, but this does not preclude the possibility that in some of its aspects it coincides with certain traditional Chinese habits of thought and behavior. It draws above all on the actual experience of the

Communist movement during the thirties and forties, and the interpretation of this experience enshrined in the Yenan writings of Mao Tse-tung and Liu Shao-ch'i. As has often been pointed out, the "Yenan syndrome" seems to occupy a central, hallowed place in the vision of Mao Tse-tung and most of the elements which form part of the Maoist vision first appear, at least in their embryonic form, during this period. . . .

What are some of the essential elements of the Maoist vision? There is first of all the overriding commitment to a society united by something approaching a total consensus and a society marked by radical collectivism. It may seem superfluous to speak of the collectivist goal of a Communist society, and yet the image of collectivity which has emerged in China, particularly since 1958, seems somewhat different in kind from that projected in the Soviet Union. The emphasis on the individual's total self-abnegation and total immersion in the collectivity as ultimate goods; the frequent reference to the model of military life with its nostalgic allusions to the heroic and idyllic guerrilla bands of the past are particular characteristics of the Maoist projection of the future. Lenin's own projection of Utopia in *State and Revolution* still draws heavily on Marx's own meagre and vague descriptions which, as we know, speak in terms of the total liberation and self-fulfilment of the individual. Whether this language makes Marx a sort of ultimate liberal as some of his interpreters would have us believe, may be open to serious doubt, yet there is the fact that the individual and his situation does play a central role in Marx's Utopia. While the Soviet official ideology has been as deeply suspicious of the whole notion of alienation in the young Marx as the Chinese, a somewhat crasser form of the concern with the interests of the individual can nevertheless be discerned in its projection of Communism. The Maoist version on the other hand projects a kind of collectivist mysticism. Commenting on the European and Soviet discussions of Marxism, Chou Yang states:

> . . . [I]n advocating the return of Man to himself they are actually advocating absolute individual freedom and asking the people who live under Socialism to return to the human nature of bourgeois individualism and to restore the capitalism by which it is fostered.

Even more characteristic has been the enormous emphasis on the power of spiritual transformation (indoctrination seems to be far too weak a term) to bring about this society of collective man. The hope is that of a kind of internalised total consensus achieved mainly by spiritual methods. The ultimate roots of this emphasis may be sought in Lenin's own emphasis on the conscious factor (further extended by Stalin) perhaps fed to some extent by the Confucian faith in the power of moral influence. Its more immediate background is to be sought in the circumstances of the Yenan period when the methods of "remoulding" were first applied to members and prospective members of the Communist Party. The notion was later vastly extended to include the whole "people" including the "national bourgeoisie" however defined. The doctrine that all can be saved—even some "counter-revolutionary elements"—has, of course, always been heavily qualified by the retention of the class notion. People of the wrong classes are not easily transformed, and continue to generate poisons of wrong thought. Yet they *can* be transformed while those of good class background *can* be led astray. In the end the main criterion for assigning persons to the "people" or "non-people" is to be sought in their spiritual attitudes rather than in the facts of their class origin. The doctrine of salvation stresses simultaneously that almost all men may be saved; that salvation is enormously difficult for all men, and that backsliding is an ever present possibility. Paradoxically the emphasis on spiritual transformation may lend itself to quite disparate policies. The "Hundred Flowers" campaign may have been predicated on the genuine belief that the intelligentsia had been basically transformed during the 1949–55 period, while the "anti-rightist" campaign of 1957 was based on precisely the opposite assumption. The "great leap forward" may have been based on the assumption that the "masses" (unlike the intelligentsia) had been basically transformed and that their "subjective forces" were at the disposal of the leadership while the present campaign of "Socialist education" seems to be predicated on the assumption that there is still much work to be done.

Populism

The emphasis on spiritual transformation is closely linked to the "populist" theme—because the whole people (defined as a union of four classes) can be transformed, the whole Chinese people can participate in the building of Socialism and Communism. This doctrine finds its formal institutional expression in the coalition structure of government, and can, of course, be harnessed to the nationalist goals of the régime as well as to project the Chinese model to the "emerging world" where there is such an obvious political need to "unite with whom one can unite." The obverse side of the formula—the notion that the "people" is not homogeneous but composed of different classes which still engender "non-antagonistic" (and even antagonistic) contradictions, has, however, been of equal importance. It has justified the need for constant vigilance and unremitting indoctrination, but was also used to justify the vaguely defined legitimate area of "blooming and contending" of the "Hundred Flowers" period. On this side, it is particularly closely linked to another element of the Maoist vision, namely, the enormous stress on struggle, conflict and high tension as positive values. Mao Tse-tung's commitment to these values probably preceded his conversion to Marxism-Leninism and has, as we know, even coloured his vision of the utopian future which he seems reluctant to think of in terms of stasis and total harmony. When directed against those defined as the outer enemy, struggle makes for solidarity "within the people." On another level, however, the enemy must be conceived of as ever present in the minds of the people itself in the form of "bourgeois thought." The struggle against this bourgeois thought is not only a negative factor. "Fighting against wrong ideas is like being vaccinated—a man develops greater immunity from disease after the vaccine takes effect. Plants raised in hot-houses are not likely to be robust." At the time when it was uttered, this doctrine was linked to the lenient policies of the "Hundred Flowers" period. One can easily see how the same doctrine can be given a much more draconic interpretation.

Another element of the vision which is closely linked to the emphasis on spiritual transformation and collectivity is the stress on man rather than weapons or tools as the "decisive force in history." By transforming men's minds and consolidating their collective energies one can achieve enormous results in spheres where others have relied on material power. Here again the Yenan experience provides the shining example. Where one has mobilised the collective energies of men, motivated by the Maoist vision, economic advancement, national power and social transformation are no longer purely dependent on "material prerequisites."

Another theme which has been stressed, with varying degrees of intensity, is the necessity of contact with the masses, and "participation in physical labour" on the part of intellectuals, students, professionals and lower bureaucrats. This may reflect the genuine belief that "participation in labour" is a form of thought reform which will induce respect for physical labour and keep these elements from over-weening pretensions. At the same time it is made crystal clear that one is not free to find among the masses any view of reality which contradicts the Maoist vision.

The Role of the Communist Party

Finally there is the enormous pivotal role of the Communist Party as the "proletarian" vanguard of society. Again, we seem to be dealing here with standard Marxist-Leninist doctrine, but as has been pointed out by many, the Party has probably played a more crucial and concrete role in China than in the Soviet Union at least during the lifetime of Stalin. The transformation of the Chinese people must be carried out by the Party. Ideally speaking, the Party maintains its supremacy not simply by dint of its organisational machinery but by its ability to internalise its "proletarian nature" into every party member. The "proletarian nature" of the Party no longer resides, of course, primarily in the industrial workers but has become a kind of spiritual essence embodied in the Party and yet still endowed with all those transcendental and universal qualities which Marx attributes to the working class. It is this idea of the "proletarian nature" of the Party which sets strict limits to the whole populist drift of the Chinese vision. In fact since the beginning of the Sino-Soviet conflict, the Party has stressed its proletarian nature more than ever. The Party does not derive its transcendent moral status and historic role in China or in the world at large from the fact that it merely represents the Chinese people, but from a higher source. The Party may serve the interests of Chinese nationalism but it does so from a supra-national stance. . . .

Mao's Vision and Modernisation

These it seems to me are some of the more salient elements of the Maoist vision. What have been the relations of this vision to the goal of modernisation?

The official view of the present leadership is that the vision—no matter how its interpretation may fluctuate—not only provides the most effective means for achieving modernisation, but is also an end in itself. The only desirable modernisation is a modernisation which can be incorporated into the Maoist vision. At the other extreme, we have the view that the vision runs completely athwart the prerequisites of modernisation or that it is a sort of rationalisation of the failures and difficulties of modernisation in China. One makes a virtue of necessity according to this view because the necessity is intractable. Where weapons and capital are scarce what is to be lost in stressing the organisation of human energies? Where material incentives are not available, why not stress the "Communist ethic"? Oddly enough, the official ideology also seems to stress the relation of necessity to virtue. It was, after all, the peculiarities of Chinese conditions which made possible the stress on guerrilla warfare. It is the "poverty and blankness" of China, Mao insists in 1958, which makes possible the achievement of Communism long before the insidious corruptions of capitalism and revisionism have set in. The fact that "virtue" is associated with necessity by no means implies that the belief in virtue may not be genuine and fervent particularly since the belief is also linked to the power interests of the leadership.

Surveying the history of the People's Republic since 1949, we find that various elements of the vision play an enormous role in the enormous effort of the first few years to bring about political and ideological consolidation. "Study," "thought reform," "confession," etc., were applied on various levels not only to prospective party members but to the "people" as a whole. The "small group" technique and the technique of mass organisation were universally applied. The Party seemed to be proving that totalitarian consolidation of a people could be carried out effectively by relying on "man" rather than technology. Except for those defined as counter-revolutionaries and reactionaries, there was considerable reason for belief that the spiritual transformation was succeeding. Some parts of the vision seemed, and seem, to be quite compatible with certain aspects of modernisation. Many tasks of public health, police work, social control and even economic undertakings, which depend primarily on labour intensivity, lend themselves to Maoist methods.

The Relevance of the Soviet Model

However, while the vision did permeate large sectors of political and social activity, in the areas most crucial to the modernisation effort—particularly as related to state power goals—it was the Soviet model which was followed. This involved some retreat in the concept of Party omnicompetence, considerable emphasis on a "rational" division of labour and professionalisation and some emphasis on the need for a professional state bureaucracy. This does not mean that one should see an absolute antagonism between the Soviet model of modernisation and the Maoist vision. Obviously the gravitation toward the total nationalisation of industry and the collectivisation of agriculture was entirely in line with both. In fact, it may well have been high confidence and exuberance (as well as a desperate sense of haste) induced by the success of his vision in the political and social spheres which led Mao and those closest to him in 1955 to feel that collectivisation could be speedily consummated in China without the dire effects it had produced in the Soviet Union. The fact remains, however, that on the whole Mao modestly deferred to the "superior experience" of the Soviet Union in these areas.

With the beginning of the "Hundred Flowers" experiment, the picture becomes more complex. On the one hand the experiment seems to mark a further concession to the requirements of modernisation. This can be discerned in the effort to give professionals and specialists a greater sense of security and freedom, in the rectification campaign directed against the Party with the implied admission that in some areas the specialists knew more than the Party and even in the new concern with legal codification. The campaign also seems to have coincided, however, with some dawning doubts about the complete applicability of the Soviet model of modernisation to Chinese conditions. These doubts were certainly encouraged by the death of Stalin and the new winds blowing in the Communist bloc itself. This new emphasis on the requirements of modernisation as well as the doubts about the Soviet model did not, however, necessarily diminish the role of the Maoist vision. On the contrary, the "Hundred Flowers" formula was presented as a precious new contribution of Mao Tse-tung (the first since 1949) to the storehouse of Marxism-Leninism and it is, of course, quite easy to see how many ambivalent elements of the vision lent themselves to the "soft" interpretation of this period. In fact, Mao may have genuinely believed that in the course of thought reform "the political outlook of the Chinese intellectuals has undergone a fundamental change." The growing doubts about the complete applicability of the Soviet model of modernisation may have even encouraged the view that the Maoist vision was applicable in areas where "Soviet experience" had hitherto reigned supreme.

In fact the Great Leap Forward and commune movement of 1957–59 mark the high tide of the application of the Maoist vision to the very tasks of modernisation. If the intelligentsia had shown its fundamental untrustworthiness, the subjective forces of the masses were still available for heaven-storming feats. The emphasis on man as the decisive factor, on the negligible role of "material prerequisites," on the superior efficacy of collective subjective forces and on the omnicompetence of the Party all enter into this experiment, and give it its utopian, apocalyptic flavour.

Contraction and Revival

The retreat from the Great Leap in 1960–62 again seems to mark a return to a sober estimate of the requirements of modernisation but no longer on an exclusively Soviet model. It also seems to mark a contraction in the influence of the Maoist vision even though the new economic model with its emphasis on "agriculture as the base" was quite distinctly Chinese. One may, in fact, argue as has been suggested that the modernisation policies of this period are much more "rational" in terms of Chinese realities than the policies of the Soviet period. They have led, it would appear, to a substantial economic recovery. Yet, as we know, ever since the end of 1962 there has again been a rising crescendo of emphasis on "socialist education." At this very moment the Maoist vision, in one of its most extreme formulations, again occupies the centre of the stage. The beginnings of this new revival are perhaps to be discerned in the crisis surrounding the army in the 1959–62 period. As we know, P'eng Teh-huai, who seems to have become the spokesman of military professionalism and perhaps of professionalism in general, had also become an "anti-party" element, that is a menace in the realm of power, while the crisis of morale in the army revealed in the *Bulletin of Activities* (*Kung-tso T'ung-hsun*) documents suggested that the threat to the vision, at least in this sphere, was also regarded as a threat to power. Thus the campaign of "Socialist education" was begun very early in the army, and having been judged a success, we find the army projected as a model for society as a whole. Here again we note what Stuart Schram has called Mao's "military deviation"— his tendency to think of a well-indoctrinated army as providing a paradigm of Communist life. . . .

Above all, however, there is the fact that the ageing Mao and those closest to him are genuinely concerned with the survival of the vision. The whole current fervid campaign of "Socialist education" is permeated more by a kind of pervasive anxiety than by a mood of high confidence. The leadership may be quite optimistic about China's present economic situation and posture in the world at large, but it is precisely in the ideological sphere that one detects a mood of concern. . . .

While the "Socialist education" campaign has, however, fallen with an enormous weight on the literary, artistic and cultural spheres and perhaps on all non-vocational areas of social life, while the cult of Mao has been raised to unprecedented heights, it is still not clear whether it has again been allowed to affect the strategy of modernisation, particularly in the economic sphere. In fact, one may speculate that in the areas of highest priority—such as nuclear development—the Maoist vision has never been allowed to interfere with the requirements of technology. As far as one can judge at the present, experts are now expected to be diffused with redness even while devoting a maximum of attention to expertise and the system of higher education is more oriented than ever to the production of experts. Yet all this may change. It would certainly be the gravest of errors to assume that because the 1960 economic strategy has proven fairly successful, economic considerations will necessarily override the concern with the "succession to the revolutionary heritage."

The leadership's concern is probably justified. It is difficult to believe that the vision will survive at least in its present extreme form. It is difficult to believe not only, or even primarily, because in some of its aspects it runs counter to the requirements of modernisation. Even more immediately, it involves such a constricted and terribly simplified view of human life that one is inclined to doubt whether it is humanly viable. In terms of modernisation, however, it is difficult to believe that the vision will be allowed in the long run to interfere particularly with those aspects of modernisation most relevant to the achievement of national power. While the vision may retreat, however, we are in no position to foresee the extent of the retreat or to predict what will remain. Modernisation may not be fully compatible with the Maoist vision but neither has it been fully compatible with Jeffersonian democracy. China may depart from the Maoist vision yet still move into a future uniquely its own. As long as Mao and those close to him remain at the helm, we may expect them to be as much concerned with the vision as with any of the other goals of the régime.

63 BUILDING COMMUNISM IN THE SOVIET UNION

Excerpted from *Program of the Communist Party of the Soviet Union* (Moscow: Foreign Languages Publishing House, 1961).

At its Twenty-second Congress in October 1961, the C.P.S.U. adopted a new program which laid out the blueprint for the building of a communist society by the 1980's.

The building of a communist society has become an immediate practical task for the Soviet people. The gradual development of socialism into communism is an objective law; it has been prepared by the development of Soviet socialist society throughout the preceding period.

What is communism?

Communism is a classless social system with one form of public ownership of the means of production and full social equality of all members of society; under it, the all-round development of people will be accompanied by the growth of the productive forces through continuous progress in science and technology; all the springs of co-operative wealth will flow more abundantly, and the great principle "From each according to his ability, to each according to his needs" will be implemented. Communism is a highly organised society of free, socially conscious working people in which public self-government will be established, a society in which labour for the good of society will become the prime vital requirement of everyone, a necessity recognised by one and all, and the ability of each person will be employed to the greatest benefit of the people.

A high degree of communist consciousness, industry, discipline, and devotion to the public interest are qualities typifying the man of communist society.

Communism ensures the continuous development of social production and rising labour productivity through rapid scientific and technological progress; it equips man with the best and most powerful machines, greatly increases his power over nature and enables him to control its elemental forces to an ever greater extent. The social economy reaches the highest stage of planned organisation, and the most effective and rational use is made of the material wealth and labour reserves to meet the growing requirements of the members of society.

Under communism there will be no classes, and the socio-economic and cultural distinctions, and differences in living conditions, between town and countryside will disappear; the countryside will rise to the level of the town in the development of the productive forces and the nature of work, the forms of production relations, living conditions and the well-being of the population. With the victory of communism mental and physical labour will merge organically in the production activity of people. The intelligentsia will no longer be a distinct social stratum. Workers by hand will have risen in cultural and technological standards to the level of workers by brain.

Thus, communism will put an end to the division of society into classes and social strata, whereas the whole history of mankind, with the exception of its primitive period, was one of class society. Division into opposing classes led to the exploitation of man by man, class struggle, and antagonisms between nations and states.

Under communism all people will have equal status in society, will stand in the same relation to the means of production, will enjoy equal conditions of work and distribution, and will actively participate in the management of public affairs. Harmonious relations will be established between the individual and society on the basis of the unity of public and personal interests. For all their diversity, the requirements of people will express the sound, reasonable requirements of the fully developed person.

The purpose of communist production is to ensure uninterrupted progress of society and to provide all its members with material and cultural benefits according to their growing needs, their individual requirements and tastes. People's requirements will be satisfied from public sources. Articles of personal use will be in the full ownership of each member of society and will be at his disposal.

Communist society, which is based on highly organised production and advanced technology, alters the character of work, but it does not release the members of society from work. It will by no means be a society of anarchy, idleness and inactivity. Every able-bodied person will participate in social labour and thereby ensure the steady growth of the material and spiritual wealth of society. Thanks to the changed character of labour, its better technical equipment and the high degree of consciousness of all members of society, the latter will work willingly for the public benefit according to their own inclinations.

Communist production demands high standards of organisation, precision and discipline, which are ensured, not by compulsion, but through an understanding of public duty, and are determined by the whole pattern of life in communist society. Labour and discipline will not be a burden to people; labour will no longer be a mere source of livelihood—it will be a genuinely creative process and a source of joy.

Communism represents the highest form of organisation of public life.

All production units and self-governing associations will be harmoniously united in a common planned economy and a uniform rhythm of social labour.

Under communism the nations will draw closer and closer together in all spheres on the basis of a complete identity of economic, political and spiritual interests, of fraternal friendship and co-operation.

Communism is the system under which the abilities and talents of free man, his best moral qualities, blossom forth and reveal themselves in full. Family relations will be freed once and for all from material considerations and will be based solely on mutual love and friendship.

In defining the basic tasks to be accomplished in building a communist society, the Party is guided by Lenin's great formula: *"Communism is Soviet power plus the electrification of the whole country."* . . .

In the current decade (1961–70) the Soviet Union, in creating the material and technical basis of communism, will surpass the strongest and richest capitalist country, the U.S.A., in production per head of population; the people's standard of living and their cultural and technical standards will improve substantially; everyone will live in easy circumstances; all collective and state farms will become highly productive and profitable enterprises; the demand of Soviet people for well-appointed housing will, in the main, be satisfied; hard physical work will disappear; the U.S.S.R. will have the shortest working day.

The material and technical basis of communism will be built up by the *end of the second decade* (1971–80), ensuring an abundance of material and cultural values for the whole population; Soviet society will come close to a stage where it can introduce the principle of distribution according to needs, and there will be a gradual transition to one form of ownership— public ownership. Thus, *a communist society will in the main be built in the U.S.S.R.* The construction of communist society will be fully completed in the subsequent period. . . .

As a result of the victory of socialism in the U.S.S.R. and the consolidation of the unity of Soviet society, the Communist Party of the working class has become the vanguard of the Soviet people, a Party of the entire people, and extended its guiding influence to all spheres of social life. The Party is the brain, the honour and the conscience of our epoch, of the Soviet people, the people effecting great revolutionary transformations. It looks keenly into the future and shows the people scientifically-motivated roads along which to advance, arouses titanic energy in the masses and leads them to the accomplishment of great tasks.

The period of full-scale communist construction is characterised by a further *enhancement of the role and importance of the Communist Party as* the leading and guiding force of Soviet society.

.   .   .

The enhancement of the role of the Party in the life of Soviet society in the new stage of its development derives from:

the growing scope and complexity of the tasks of communist construction, which call for a higher level of political and organisational leadership;

the growth of the creative activity of the masses and the participation of fresh millions of working people in the administration of state affairs and of production;

the further development of socialist democracy, the enhancement of the role of social organisations, the extension of the rights of the Union republics and local organisations;

the growing importance of the theory of scientific communism, of its creative development and propaganda, the necessity for improving the communist education of the working people and struggling to overcome the survivals of the past in the minds of people.

There must be a new, higher stage in the development of the Party itself and of its political, ideological, and organisational work that is in conformity with the full-scale building of communism. The Party will continuously improve the forms and methods of its work, so that its leadership of the masses, of the building of the material and technical basis of communism, of the development of society's spiritual life will keep pace with the growing requirements of the epoch of communist construction.

Being the vanguard of the people building a Communist society, the Party must also be in the van in the organisation of Internal Party life and serve as an example and model in developing the most advanced forms of public communist self-government.

. . .

In the period of full-scale communist construction the role and responsibility of every Party member will steadily increase. It is the duty of a Communist, in production, in social and personal life, to be a model in the struggle for the development and consolidation of communist relations, and to observe the principles and norms of communist morality. The C.P.S.U. will reinforce its ranks with the most politically conscious and active working people, and keep pure and hold high the name of Communist.

The development of inner-Party democracy must ensure greater activity among Communists and enhance their responsibility for the realisation of the noble ideals of communism. It will promote the cultivation in them of an inner, organic need to act always and in all matters in full accordance with the principles of the Party and its lofty aims. . . .

. . . It is not through war with other countries, but by the example of a more perfect organisation of society, by rapid progress in developing the productive forces, the creation of all conditions for the happiness and well-being of man, that the ideas of communism win the minds and hearts of the masses.

The forces of social progress will inevitably grow in all countries, and this will assist the builders of Communism in the Soviet Union.

The Party proceeds from the Marxist-Leninist proposition: history is made by the people, and communism is a creation of the people, of its energy and intelligence. The victory of communism depends on people, and communism is built for people. Every Soviet man brings the triumph of communism nearer by his labour. The successes of communist construction spell abundance and a happy life to all, and enhance the might, prestige and glory of the Soviet Union. . . .

Under the tried and tested leadership of the Communist Party, under the banner of Marxism-Leninism, the Soviet people have built socialism.

Under the leadership of the Party, under the banner of Marxism-Leninism, the Soviet people will build communist society.

The Party solemnly proclaims: The present generation of Soviet people shall live in communism!

Bibliography

Braverman, H., *The Future of Russia*. New York: The Macmillan Company, 1963.

Denno, T., *The Communist Milennium*. The Hague: Nijhoff, 1964.

Elegant, R. S., *The Center of the World: Communism and the Mind of China*. New York: Doubleday & Company, Inc., 1964.

Greene, F., *Awakened China*. New York: Doubleday & Company, Inc., 1961.

Laqueur, W. Z., and L. Labedz, eds., *The Future of Communist Society*. New York: Frederick A. Praeger, Inc., 1962.

Lattimore, O., *Nomads and Commissars: Mongolia Revisited*. New York: Oxford University Press, Inc., 1962.

Novak, J., *The Future Is Ours, Comrade*. New York: Doubleday & Company, Inc., 1960.

Schapiro, L., ed., *The U.S.S.R. and the Future*. New York: Frederick A. Praeger, Inc., 1963.

Skilling, H. G., *Communism National and International: Eastern Europe after Stalin*. Toronto: University of Toronto Press, 1964.